Grand Old Unraveling

Grand Old Unraveling

THE REPUBLICAN PARTY, DONALD TRUMP, AND THE RISE OF AUTHORITARIANISM

John Kenneth White

© 2024 by the University Press of Kansas
All rights reserved
Second printing

Published by the University Press of Kansas (Lawrence, Kansas 66045), which was organized by the Kansas Board of Regents and is operated and funded by Emporia State University, Fort Hays State University, Kansas State University, Pittsburg State University, the University of Kansas, and Wichita State University

Library of Congress Cataloging-in-Publication Data
Names: White, John Kenneth, 1952– author.
Title: Grand Old Unraveling : the Republican party, Donald Trump, and the rise of authoritarianism / John Kenneth White.
Description: Lawrence, Kansas : University Press of Kansas, [2024] | Includes bibliographical references.
Identifiers: LCCN 2023037202 (print) | LCCN 2023037203 (ebook)
    ISBN 9780700636532 (cloth)
    ISBN 9780700637089 (paperback)
    ISBN 9780700636549 (ebook)
Subjects: LCSH: Republican Party (U.S. 1854–)—History. | Conspiracy theories—United States—History. | Contested elections—United States—History. | United States—Politics and government—1901–1953. | BISAC: POLITICAL SCIENCE / Political Process / Political Parties | POLITICAL SCIENCE / American Government / Executive Branch
Classification: LCC JK2356 .W469 2024 (print) | LCC JK2356 (ebook) | DDC 324.6/50973—dc23/eng/20240118
LC record available at https://lccn.loc.gov/2023037202.
LC ebook record available at https://lccn.loc.gov/2023037203.

For Samuel Sprunk
A cui sono profondamente grato

What's past is prologue
William Shakespeare, *The Tempest*

Contents

Preface: The Gathering Storm, ix

Introduction: Passions and Interests—Republicans Shatter a Delicate Balance, 1

1 Democracy on Trial—Again, 16

2 A Broken Party, 1932–1952, 33

3 The Price of Victory: Dwight Eisenhower's 1952 Campaign and the Cult of Personality, 51

4 Of Conspiracy Theories, Lies, and Stolen Elections, 77

5 A Party Transformed, 110

6 A Clear and Present Danger, 135

Afterword 2023: A Reflection and a Reckoning, 172

Acknowledgments, 183

Notes, 185

Index, 255

Preface: The Gathering Storm

> There are some things that you just can't imagine happening in your life. This is one of them.
> —Mitt Romney accepting Donald Trump's endorsement, February 2, 2012

On February 2, 2012, Mitt Romney and his wife, Ann, mounted the stage at an opulent, gold-plated Las Vegas hotel to accept a political endorsement. Unlike other routine testimonials, this one was different. The person making the endorsement was a controversial celebrity who had never held political office and had been, until recently, a member of the opposite party. Donald J. Trump calculated that the former Massachusetts governor was the likely 2012 Republican nominee, although as late as the day prior many speculated that Trump would endorse Romney's erstwhile opponent, former House Speaker Newt Gingrich. After all, Gingrich and Trump had much in common: both had reputations for being rhetorical bomb throwers, were subjects of messy divorces, and shared a mutual contempt for their Democratic opponents. But Trump coldly calculated that Romney was a winner, calling him "tough, sharp, and smart."[1]

The event took place in a circus-like atmosphere at the Trump-owned hotel, something that would become commonplace for Donald Trump's future rallies. The Romneys, both devout Mormons who adhered to that religion's strict moral codes, were decidedly uncomfortable in Trump's presence, as Mitt Romney candidly admitted to reporters covering the event: "There are some things that you just can't imagine happening in your life. This is one of them."[2] Ann Romney was even more discomfited, and she hurried off the stage at the earliest possible moment. Then *New York Times* reporter Mark Leibovich described how the candidate's wife's cheeks "grew increasingly red through Mr. Trump's remarks, and she appeared on the verge of either laughter or terror during the whole show."[3] Democrats mocked the Trump endorsement, and the Democratic National Committee issued a statement claiming both Romney and Trump enjoyed dismissing employees, citing Trump's signature line on the hit television show *The Apprentice*: "You're fired!" Jon Lovett, a speechwriter for Barack Obama, tweeted, "I guess I'll take my lead from one of America's more garish and despicable figures."[4]

For many close observers of politics, the event became a subject of late-night laughs. David Letterman joked that Romney's decline in the polls was the inevitable aftereffect of Trump's endorsement.[5] But *New York Times* reporter Maggie Haberman recalled that Trump was energized by the event and wanted more appearances with Romney, a request the campaign rejected.[6] Months earlier Trump had regretfully announced that he would not seek the presidency, even as he boasted, "My potential candidacy continues to be validated by [my] ranking at the top of the Republican contenders in polls across the country."[7] Days after Romney's loss to Barack Obama, Trump trademarked what would become his campaign slogan, "Make America Great Again," and his 2016 campaign for the Republican nomination began to unfold.[8]

A decade after Romney received this endorsement—after the tumultuous events of the Trump presidency, two impeachments, and an attempted coup—no one is laughing. Mitt Romney's discomfiture turned into scorn when he delivered a stinging rebuke of Trump in 2016, calling him "a con man, a fake," and dismissively concluded, "Dishonesty is Donald Trump's hallmark."[9] Democrats were in disbelief when Trump astonished the political world by beating Hillary Clinton. And few were amused when Trump cast aside accepted presidential norms of behavior, or when he was twice impeached, or when the US Capitol was invaded by an angry mob on January 6, 2021. Even now, the threats to our democracy, which many believed would subside after Trump's 2020 defeat, remain. In 2022, nearly three hundred Republican nominees for offices with the power to certify future elections either questioned the results of the 2020 election or believed the election was stolen.[10] While many lost, Donald Trump continues to exercise unparalleled power within his own party—even as he is subjected to numerous criminal investigations and indictments. As this is written, Donald J. Trump is the leading contender to win the Republican nod in 2024, something only the defeated Richard M. Nixon achieved in the last fifty-five years. And Nixon's narrow victory in 1968 was due to the extraordinary circumstances of an unpopular war abroad and racial unrest at home.

How did we get here? Some believe that an exhausted conservative agenda that was once revived by Ronald Reagan in 1980 had reached its natural death. Much of what Reagan did as president—enacting tax cuts, slowing the growth rate of federal spending, eliminating government regulations, and positioning the United States to defeat the Soviet Union (a country Reagan derisively referred to as the "evil empire")—now occupied dog-eared pages in dusty history books.[11] The shopworn question asked by admirers of the late president, "What would Reagan do?," was no longer relevant. By 2020, the paucity of conservative ideas was such that the Grand Old Party, for the first time in its history, did not write a platform. The emerging issues of climate change, growing economic inequality, and post–Cold War overseas challenges have substantially altered the domestic political agenda. While Americans still distrust government, and younger citizens hardly know a time when government worked effectively, when faced with a pandemic most people wanted government to do more. Joe Biden ascended to the presidency determined to make government work again. At the same time, the Reagan coalition—evangelical, white, married, middle class, and suburban—was eroding thanks to a multiracial, less religiously affiliated country, whose younger voters cast ballots in ever-larger numbers for Democratic candidates. The white, middle-class, suburban Republican majority that gave Dwight D. Eisenhower, Richard M. Nixon, and Ronald Reagan historic landslide victories could no longer deliver. Just as Democrats celebrated Franklin D. Roosevelt and the New Deal long after their expiration dates, in 2016 Republicans were still honoring a deceased president and a tiresome agenda. Donald Trump saw the vacuum and filled it.

In 1844, Ralph Waldo Emerson wrote that in the United States

> the conservative party, composed of the most moderate, able, and cultivated part of the population, is timid, and merely defensive of property. It vindicates no right, it aspires to no real good, it brands no crime, it proposes no generous policy, it does not build, nor write, nor cherish the arts, nor foster religion, nor establish schools, nor encourage science, nor emancipate the slave, nor befriend the poor, or the Indian, or the immigrant.[12]

For Emerson, conservatives were a party of memory, enamored with a romanticism of the past and determined to preserve it. Liberals, said Emerson, had no such devotion but instead were a party of hope. Freed from the constrictions of memory, they could inspire their followers to pursue new horizons and revolutionary beginnings.[13] Emerson believed that while the *best men* were often found in a conservative movement, the *best causes* were those espoused by unshackled liberals.[14]

Political parties thrive when they embody both memory and hope. For Republicans, Ronald Reagan is the preeminent example of a successful politician who did both. Reagan summoned the happy memories of a prosperous and contented post–World War II era—a country bursting with energy, and an economic colossus whose city dwellers were boarding station wagons and moving into spanking new suburban homes. There was a boundless optimism that the twentieth century would be, as Henry Luce predicted prior to the United States' entry into World War II, "an American Century."[15] James Q. Wilson wrote the following description of "Reagan Country": "Each family had a house; there it was for all to see and inspect. With a practiced glance, one could tell how much it cost, how well it was cared for, how good a lawn had been coaxed into uncertain life, and how tastefully plants and shrubs had been set out."[16] These Sunday drive picture postcards became centerpieces for Reagan's consistent recitation of the homespun values embodied in family, work, neighborhood, peace, and freedom.[17] But Reagan's appeal to a pleasantly remembered past was also accompanied by a firm belief that the future remained hopeful. Even after having been diagnosed with the Alzheimer's disease that would claim his life, Reagan issued a final farewell, ending with these words, "I know that for America there will always be a bright dawn ahead."[18]

But Emerson saw danger when parties become subject to the bidding of unprincipled leaders who "reap the rewards of the docility and zeal of the masses, which they direct."[19] Inevitably, Emerson believed, parties of principle "degenerate into personalities," which become a source of danger.[20] By 2020, both major parties were animated by neither memory nor hope, but by fear. Most Republicans believe the memories they cherish can no longer be preserved. Emerson himself forecast that, with fading memories, conservatives had an instinctive proclivity to see society as sick, taking "as low a view of every part of human action and passion."[21] Today, it is this sickness, as Emerson predicted, that "has got into the ballot-box" that Donald Trump and his progenitors so skillfully exploit.[22] John Daniel Davidson writes that the animating values of "individual rights, family values, [and] religious freedom" have been lost to an "ascendent left" that has transformed America into a "woke dystopia."[23] This includes a redefinition of marriage, the First Amendment, any semblance of control over our borders, the fundamental distinction between men and women, and, "especially of late, the basic rule of law."[24] For Davidson, only two paths remain: "Awake from decades of slumber to reclaim and re-found what has been lost [or] watch our civilization die."[25]

It is this fear that all is lost, and that Republicans must use whatever means necessary to avoid being relegated to permanent minority status (or even political oblivion), that has prompted party-led efforts to suppress the vote and contest elections they did not win. In 1980, conservative Paul Weyrich told a gathering of evangelicals, "Our leverage in the elections goes up as the voting populace goes down."[26] Six years later a "ballot integrity initiative" underwritten by the Republican National Committee tried to expunge an estimated sixty to eighty thousand names from the voting rolls. An internal party memo stated that, if successful, the program would keep "the black vote down considerably."[27] In 1994, California Republican Michael Huffington refused to concede his US Senate loss to Democrat Diane Feinstein, citing "overwhelming" evidence of illegal ballots cast by undocumented immigrants. A Feinstein spokesperson denounced Huffington as "a spoiled rich kid and a sour grapes loser."[28] Only months later did Huffington issue a concession statement. In 1996, House Speaker Newt Gingrich charged "we now have proof" that a close congressional contest won by a Democrat was stolen thanks to "a sufficient number of non-citizens voting." That same year, the Senate Rules Committee voted unanimously to accept the results of the Louisiana state senate election that gave Democrat Mary Landrieu another six-year term. Landrieu's opponent, Woody Jenkins, marketed brightly colored socks reading: "Don't Get Cold Feet. Sock It to Voter Fraud." But Jenkins's case collapsed when witnesses were allegedly schooled as to how they could invent stories of voter fraud. Eventually, four of Jenkins's six witnesses recanted their testimony.[29] In 2000, Florida Republicans spurred an effort to purge thousands from the state's voter rolls, nearly all Democrats and half of them African American. David Bositis, a senior research associate at the Joint Center for Political and Economic Studies, concluded that the effort led by Republican governor Jeb Bush and Secretary of State Katherine Harris was "a patently obvious technique to discriminate against black voters."[30] The program proved vitally important in securing the presidency for Bush's brother George when Harris certified his wafer-thin 537 vote victory over Al Gore in a state that decided the election. Twenty-two years later, Florida Republican governor Ron DeSantis created the Office of Election Crimes and Security and ordered the arrests of those with prior felony convictions who were issued voting cards. Making the announcement, DeSantis said, "They're going to pay the price."[31] Those arrested faced up to five years in jail and a $5,000 fine. The arresting officers confessed that they had never encountered similar warrants.[32]

When did the Republican Party begin its transformation into a Trump-dominated party that many of its former members hardly recognize? Some believe it began in 1964 with the rise of Barry Goldwater and his rejection of "me-too" New Dealism and his tacit embrace of the John Birch Society. Others cite Richard Nixon's embrace of the "Southern Strategy" in 1968 whose coded language transformed the party's historic commitment to civil rights into a largely white-dominated party that would find a home in the once-Democratic South. Others believe it began with the ascent of Newt Gingrich to the House Speakership. Gingrich's rise coincided with his use of loaded speech and the frustration of his fellow Republicans at the party's "go along, get along" approach to Democratic congressional leaders. In a 1990 memo titled "Language, a Key Mechanism of Control," Gingrich advised Republicans to use words such as "destructive," "liberal," "welfare," "traitors," "radical," "anti-child," and "corruption" when describing their opponents, saying: "You're fighting a war. It is a war for power."[33] Former Democratic congressman Barney Frank recalled that Gingrich "transformed American politics from one in which people presume the good will of their opponents even as they disagreed, into one in which people treated the people with whom they disagreed as bad and immoral. He was a kind of McCarthyite who succeeded."[34]

Thanks to a combination of "Newt Speak" and the party's frustration with continually losing control of the House, Gingrich was Republicans' inevitable choice to assume the Speakership in 1995. Gingrich once told his staff that his primary purpose in politics was not to legislate or win reelection but to "save Western civilization."[35] In his book *The Deconstructionists: The Twenty-Five-Year Crack-Up of the Republican Party*, Dana Milbank describes how the Republican Party, under Gingrich's leadership, morphed into its present-day form. Attacking political opponents and government bureaucrats during his presidency, Donald Trump employed his own version of "Newt Speak," labeling them as "bad," "dirty," "horrible," "evil," "sick," "corrupt," "lowlifes," and "the crookedest, most dishonest, dirtiest people I've ever seen."[36]

But a longer view shows that for several decades the Republican Party contained the strands of Trump-like antidemocratic thinking that are now fully manifest. Those origins began with the five successive defeats of Republican presidential candidates, starting with Herbert Hoover's landslide loss in 1932, and ending with Thomas E. Dewey's surprising defeat in 1948. A close look at these contests reveals a frustrated party that latched onto conspiracy theories of foreign involvement that covertly assisted the Democrats, to nefarious actions by Democratic officials, to questioning whether ballots were properly counted, to blaming voters who were dependent on federal government programs for their losses. Even when Republicans won the presidency, the party establishment became so obsessed with winning that little was done to strengthen the party organization. Beginning with Dwight Eisenhower, Republican presidents treated the party as a kind of Hertz Rent a Car, used only for the purpose of gaining universal ballot access while building their own personal apparatuses whose loyalties were to a single individual. For many Republicans, the joys of winning meant embracing a personal presidency whose occupants would float above the party yet dominate it—a phenomenon that would quickly envelop the Democrats. As one House Republican remarked after signing a petition challenging the 2020 election results, "The things we do for the orange Jesus."[37]

Some readers may wonder whether I have overlooked abuses of power employed by past Democratic presidents, including Woodrow Wilson's 1920 Red Scare campaign, Franklin D. Roosevelt's 1942 internment order imprisoning Japanese US citizens, Internal Revenue Service audits of prominent Republicans conducted by Democratic administrations, the electronic surveillance and harassment of Martin Luther King under the auspices of the Kennedy administration, and Lyndon B. Johnson's bugging of Barry Goldwater's 1964 presidential campaign, to name but a few. These abuses have been well cataloged.

But there is a qualitative difference between these abuses of power and a Republican Party under the domination of a single, flawed individual who poses a threat to our democracy. That threat became crystal clear on January 6, 2021, when a mob incited by Donald Trump invaded the US

Capitol, waved a Confederate flag, and sought to overturn a presidential election. Their aim was to stop the peaceful transfer of power, an extra-constitutional right established with Thomas Jefferson's peaceful transition into the presidency in 1801. Not even during the Civil War had the Capitol been invaded and political violence ensued, including the deaths of five police officers and hundreds of others with life-changing injuries. The delirious, angry rioters were convinced that the 2020 election had been stolen and saw Donald Trump's impending defeat as a political Armageddon, one that must be averted at all costs. Ashli Babbitt, an insurrectionist cloaked in a Trump campaign flag, posted these final words the day before she was killed by a Capitol Police officer as she attempted to enter the House of Representatives whose members had donned gas masks, cowered under seats, and barricaded the doors: "The storm is here, and it is descending on D.C. in twenty-four hours."[38] Babbitt was an air force veteran who had voted for Barack Obama but became a QAnon believer and died in the service of Donald Trump.

In 1861, faced with another insurrection, Abraham Lincoln told Congress that the Civil War was "a war upon the first principle of popular government—the rights of the people." Any abridgment of the existing right of suffrage, Lincoln said, "is the source of all political evil," concluding, "In my present position I could scarcely be justified were I to omit raising a warning voice against this approach of returning despotism."[39] Lincoln's admonition is, once again, especially pertinent. In the aftermath of the Capitol insurrection, two-thirds of Americans believed the divisions within the country had worsened, and three in five anticipated an increase in political violence in the coming years. An astonishing 43 percent predicted another civil war was either "very likely" or "somewhat likely," with 53 percent of Trump voters sharing this view.[40] After the FBI conducted a search warrant on Trump's Mar-a-Lago property, the former president posted online that the 2020 election was "irreparably compromised," and a "minimal solution" would be to have "a new Election, immediately!"[41] Far from tamping down the emotions of his followers, Donald Trump continues to incite their anger and anxieties. Memory and hope have given way to fear and rage.

For decades, I have studied and written about the Republican Party, beginning with *The Fractured Electorate*, a look at the GOP in three southern New England states—Massachusetts, Rhode Island, and Connecticut;[42] to

The New Politics of Old Values, which traced the rise of Ronald Reagan and how his emphasis on the values of family, work, neighborhood, peace, and freedom resonated with voters;[43] to *The Values Divide*, which saw the beginnings of a partisan chasm where an emphasis on values spurred by pleasant memories of the past was giving way to a culture war that Republicans feared losing;[44] to *Still Seeing Red*, which examined the creation of a Cold War party system that propelled the Republican Party into the presidency;[45] to *What Happened to the Republican Party?*, which traced the challenges the party faced after failing to win the popular vote in every election from 1992 to 2012, with the sole exception of George W. Bush's victory in 2004.[46] These works, as well as the history of the Republican Party since the 1930s, read differently today in light of Donald Trump's presidency and its tumultuous aftermath. As historian Matthew Dallek notes, the radicalization of the Republican Party was "contingent, halting, and gradual, not foreordained and inevitable."[47] Yet, from rereading that history, the antidemocratic strains within today's Republican Party trace their antecedents to events that occurred decades earlier.

In his aptly titled memoir *The Gathering Storm*, which chronicles the events leading up to and including World War II, Winston Churchill wrote that it was his purpose to demonstrate that the war was enabled by "the malice of the wicked [and] was reinforced by the weakness of the virtuous."[48] Churchill concluded that "the structure and habits of democratic states, unless they are welded into larger organisms, lack those elements of persistence and conviction which can alone give security to humble masses."[49] It is this fight between malice and virtue, between hope and fear, between memory and rage, that threatens the underpinnings of our democracy. Summoning the ghost of Abraham Lincoln, Representative Jamie Raskin noted that our "constitutional democracy is the silver frame upon which the golden apple of freedom rests."[50] That frame still holds, but its foundations are weakened. Unless democracy is vigorously and continuously defended, historian Timothy Snyder warns, "We're looking almost certainly at an attempt [by the Republicans] in 2024 to take power without winning the election."[51] Unless we heed the lessons taught by Winston Churchill and the wisdom of Abraham Lincoln, democracy will continue to hang in the balance.

Introduction: Passions and Interests—Republicans Shatter a Delicate Balance

No democracy without parties.
    —Clinton Rossiter, *Parties and Politics in America*

On January 7, 2005, an unusual event took place at a joint session of Congress called to certify the results of the previous presidential election. For the first time in 128 years, the normally placid proceeding was interrupted when the certified electoral votes from Ohio were officially challenged. Objecting were Democratic congresswoman Stefanie Tubb Jones and Democratic senator Barbara Boxer. The state's official count gave George W. Bush a 118,601 plurality over John F. Kerry—a clear victory. But Democrats charged that voter irregularities provided Bush with the win. In Lake County, Ohio, a handful of voters reported receiving flyers claiming they were ineligible to vote. As the charges of fraud intensified, the county's elections commissioner said: "I have had an election year I'd never thought I'd experience in my twenty-one years. I've had to do so much damage control."[1] After Bush declared victory the morning after Election Day, conspiracy theories abounded that Ohio's voting machines had inexplicably switched votes from Kerry to Bush. Rising from her seat in the House chamber, Boxer argued that Congress had a responsibility to "cast the light of truth on a flawed system which must be fixed now."[2] Republicans howled in protest. House majority whip Tom DeLay lamented the Democratic "quadrennial crying [of] wolf," asserting that any fraud charges were "Hollywood inspired."[3] The supposedly wronged Democrat, John Kerry, was not even present as he was abroad visiting US troops. After a two-hour debate, Democrats conceded defeat, and the drama ended. But Republicans remained aggrieved, with Senator Rick Santorum calling time spent on the issue a "travesty" and declaring that Democrats were "not over the 2000 election, let alone the 2004 election."[4] Santorum had a point. Reflecting on her objection, Boxer admitted she had made a "mistake" in not objecting to the outcome of the Bush versus Gore race four years earlier.[5]

The hard feelings many Democrats had about the George W. Bush presidency stemmed from accumulated resentments after the contentious Bush versus Gore contest. The controversial Florida vote, officially certified by the Republican secretary of state as giving Bush a 537-vote win and the presidency, was upheld by a five-to-four decision of the Supreme Court.[6] Conceding defeat after thirty-six days of recounts and court battles, Al Gore declared, "We will stand together behind our new President."[7] Gore cited Stephen Douglas, who, after losing the presidency to Abraham Lincoln in 1860, proclaimed that "partisan feeling must yield to patriotism," adding that the "strength of American democracy is shown most clearly through the difficulties it can overcome."[8] Gore promised to do everything possible to "bring Americans together in fulfillment of the great vision that our Declaration of Independence defines and that our Constitution affirms and demands."[9] His gracious concession gave Bush the needed legitimacy to begin his administration. Democracy had endured.

But during the thirty-six days before the Supreme Court decision ended the 2000 election, Democrats and Republicans accused each other of subverting democracy. Given that Florida's electoral votes would determine the next president, partisan feelings swelled as Democrats and Republicans swarmed county clerk offices and battled one another in the courts. Democrats argued that votes should be accurately counted, while Republicans contended for the rule of law. Gore's campaign chief William Daley declared, "If the will of the people is to prevail, Al Gore should be awarded a victory in Florida and be our next President."[10] But the *Wall Street Journal* countered that if nefarious Democrats engineered a Gore victory thanks to a friendly judge, the United States would be transformed into a "banana republic," with Gore seizing power thanks to a "coup d'état."[11] The *Weekly Standard*, an influential journal of conservative Republican thinking, claimed that the "central processes of our democracy" were being "upended by the fanatic ambition of a single demagogue."[12]

When the time came for Congress to officially certify the results, several House Democrats rose to challenge the Florida count. Eddie Bernice Johnson claimed to have "overwhelming evidence that George W. Bush did not win this election either by the national popular vote or the Florida popular vote."[13] With her outraged Democratic colleagues shouting "fraud" and "disenfranchisement,"[14] Johnson said that if Bush was declared the winner, he should be "on notice that without justice there will be no peace."[15] But each time a House Democrat rose to object, senators remained seated. Without a senator joining the House Democrats' objections, the presiding officer, Vice President Al Gore, ruled the challenges out of order. After the contentious ceremony ended, Gore stood and declared, "May God bless our new President and our new Vice President, and may God bless the United States of America."[16] The defeated Democrat then left the Capitol to cheers and applause. Once more, democracy had endured another stress test.

A third disputed election also reaffirmed the strength of American democracy and the vital role political parties have historically played in preserving it. In 1876, Democrat Samuel J. Tilden won the popular vote but lost the Electoral College after a congressional commission ruled that Rutherford B. Hayes won the controversial electoral votes cast in Florida, South Carolina, and Louisiana, thus keeping the presidency in Republican hands. Democrats were outraged. One Democrat decried the "imbeciles who allowed the consummation of this wicked scheme."[17] Another wanted Tilden to "call upon your party to immediately inaugurate you," promising his fellow Democrats "will swarm from every section of the country to carry out your wishes."[18] A third promised that his fellow partisans would "resist to the last extremity and until eternal justice prevails."[19] Others advised Tilden to take his case to the Supreme Court. Right up to Inauguration Day, it was uncertain whether Hayes or Tilden would take the presidential oath. Barring any final challenge, it was Hayes who said the magic words mandated by the Constitution to become president, doing so privately on March 4, 1877, since it was a Sunday. (A public ceremony followed the next day.) In his inaugural address, Hayes cited the extraordinary circumstances surrounding the election, noting that for the first time an "enlightened" tribunal appointed by Congress had certified the outcome.[20] Hayes conceded that "opinion will widely vary as to the wisdom of the several conclusions announced by that tribunal" but added, "The fact that two great political parties have in this way settled a dispute in regard to which good men differ as to the facts and the law no less than as to the proper course to be pursued in solving the question in controversy is an occasion for general rejoicing."[21] Hayes noted that in having settled their differences, both parties gave "to the world the first example in history of a great nation . . . hushing party tumults to yield the issue of the contest to adjustment according to the forms of law."²² Months later, Tilden officially conceded, saying, "If my voice could reach throughout our country and be heard in its remotest hamlet I would say, 'Be of good cheer. The Republic will live. The institutions of our fathers are not to expire in shame. The sovereignty of the people shall be rescued from this peril and be re-established.'"²³

POLITICAL PARTIES: THE ESSENTIAL INSTRUMENTS OF DEMOCRACY

Political scientist Harvey Mansfield captured the essence of the partisan disagreements surrounding these three disputed contests, writing: "The Republicans stand for the rule of law, and the Democrats for the rule of the people. And the Democrats, because they stand for the rule of the people, believe that rule should be paramount, and the technicalities are subordinate to that will. Whereas Republicans believe in doing things properly or legally."²⁴ The contested elections of 1876, 2000, and 2004 were struggles involving these essential principles. Although sometimes conflicting, adherence to both the popular will and the rule of law is necessary to make democracy work. It is the essential role of parties to uphold both principles, even as they disagree as to which should be given the greater weight. Political scientists, therefore, have placed great value on the vitality of political parties, making them necessary concomitants to ensure democratic government.

Since the founding of political science as a separate academic discipline at the turn of the twentieth century, scholars have extolled the value of parties. At various moments, their praise has reached a crescendo with the advent of wars and the fall of authoritarian regimes. Both during and after World War II, political scientists loudly proclaimed the vital role parties play in ensuring free, democratic governance. Writing in 1942, E. E. Schattschneider declared, "It should be flatly stated that the political parties created democracy and that modern democracy is unthinkable save in terms of parties."²⁵ In 1960, Clinton Rossiter employed his own tautology that elegantly summarized the parties' essential role: "No America without democracy, no democracy without politics, no politics without political parties."²⁶ Rossiter likened the Democratic and Republican Parties to "vast, gaudy, friendly umbrellas under which all are invited for the sake of being counted in the next election."[27] In 1964, V. O. Key Jr. wrote:

> Political parties constitute a basic element of democratic institutional apparatus. They perform an essential function in the management of succession to power, as well as in the process of obtaining popular consent to the course of public policy. They amass sufficient support to buttress the authority of governments; or, on the contrary, they attract or organize discontent and dissatisfaction sufficient to oust the government. In either ease they perform the function of the articulation of the interests and aspirations of a substantial segment of the citizenry, usually in ways contended to be promotive of the national weal.[28]

Another influential political scientist, Maurice Duverger, agreed with Key, stating, "On the whole the development of parties seems bound up with that of democracy, that is to say with the extension of popular suffrage and parliamentary prerogatives."[29] Decades later, Gerald Pomper succinctly made his case for vibrant political parties: "We must either acknowledge the mutual reliance of our parties and democracy—or lose both."[30] The fall of the Soviet Union only strengthened the academy's belief that, according to Pomper, "freedom requires political parties seeking power in fair and open elections."[31] For Pomper and his colleagues, establishing flourishing democracies in the former Soviet Union and Eastern Europe depended on whether the contending parties could popularly contest elections and accept those outcomes.

Political scientists understood that parties provided more than structure and form to contest elections. Ideological commitments made political parties into something more than the dispassionate, rational entities envisioned by Anthony Downs whose only purpose is to garner enough votes to obtain power.[32] Notably, it was a political scientist, Woodrow Wilson, who saw his election to the presidency in 1912 as more than a personal victory, asserting that voters had commandeered the Democratic Party to make changes in governance. In his 1913 inaugural address, Wilson declared:

> The success of a party means little except when the Nation is using that party for a large and definite purpose. No one can mistake the purpose for which the Nation now seeks to use the Democratic Party. It seeks to use it to interpret

a change in its own plans and point of view. . . . Our duty is to cleanse, to reconsider, to restore, to correct the evil without impairing the good, to purify and humanize every aspect of our common life without weakening or sentimentalizing it.[33]

Another president, Martin Van Buren, held a similar view:

> It has always struck me as more honorable and manly and more in harmony with the character of our People and our Institutions to deal with the subject of Political Parties in a sincerer and wiser spirit—to recognize their necessity, to give them the credit they deserve, and to devote ourselves to improve and to elevate the principles and objects of our own and to support it ingenuously and faithfully.[34]

Gerald Pomper writes that a party without an ideology is akin to a party without a soul: "Contemporary parties require an ideological purpose if they are to gain support, they must save their souls if they would win the world of power. At the same time, the search for salvation by an ideological community can distort the parties as instruments of electoral politics. There is no moral profit for parties that save their souls but corrupt the world of democracy."[35]

BALANCING PASSIONS AND INTERESTS

Pomper's warning that ideological fervor could corrupt democracies captures the fears of the nation's founders, who deplored "factions" as threats to liberty. In his famous Federalist 10 essay, James Madison defined factions as "a number of citizens whether amounting to a majority or minority of the whole, who are united and activated by some common impulse of passion, or of interest, adverse to the rights of other citizens, or to the permanent and aggregate interests of the community."[36] Madison conceded that citizens inevitably organized themselves into many contending groups. Thus, controlling the "violence of faction"[37] meant corralling factions into the republican form of government that the Constitution envisioned. Eventually, however, Madison, together with Thomas Jefferson, formed what became the Democratic Party even as Jefferson proclaimed,

"If I could not go to heaven but with a party, I would not go there at all."[38] In his own way, Madison agreed with Edmund Burke's definition of a political party as "a body of men united for promoting by their joint endeavors the national interest upon some particular principle in which they are all agreed."[39]

Madison's warning about the "dangerous vice" of factions was foreshadowed by his antecedents.[40] The French philosopher Voltaire wrote that a "faction" is "a seditious party when it is still feeble, when it does not rejoin the entire State."[41] But when factions and states are joined, they become despotic. Giovanni Sartori believed the word "faction" conveys "an idea of hubris, of excessive, ruthless, and thereby harmful behavior."[42] The English philosopher David Hume agreed, writing, "Factions subvert government, render laws impotent, and beget the fiercest animosities among men of the same nation."[43] Sartori noted that when the heads of competing parties become intertwined with governing, the result is that parties both *divide and share*[44]—their divisions centering around what Gerald Pomper called "passions and interests,"[45] even while sharing the larger purpose of creating a central government given to compromise and obedience to the rule of law. For Hume, establishing interparty harmony is "the most agreeable prospect for future happiness."[46]

It was, however, this dissension and lack of happiness within his cabinet that prompted George Washington to issue his famous warning about the dangers posed by political parties in his Farewell Address. His speech, still read aloud on the floor of Congress, warned of the tendency of political parties to "render alien to each other those who ought to be bound together by fraternal affection."[47] Parties, he wrote, "serve to organize faction; to give it an artificial and extraordinary force; to put in the place of the delegated will of the nation the will of a party, often a small but artful and enterprising minority of the community."[48] Washington believed that, over time, parties would become "potent engines by which cunning, ambitious, and unprincipled men will be enabled to subvert the power of the people and to usurp for themselves the reins of government, destroying afterwards the very engines which have lifted them to unjust dominion."[49] Governed by "ill-founded jealousies and false alarms," these animosities "perpetrated the most horrid enormities," even the occasional "riot and insurrection" that causes "the minds of men to seek security and repose in the absolute power of an individual."⁵⁰ Thus, Washington concluded, the "common and continual mischiefs of the spirit of party" were responsible for "the ruins of public liberty."⁵¹

Despite Washington's admonitions, parties are the inevitable result of a combination of voters' passions and interests. The French constitutional thinker Benjamin Constant wrote in 1815: "One cannot hope to exclude factions from a political organization, where the advantages of liberty are wont to be preserved."⁵² For Constant, the inevitability of parties required continuous labor to render them "as harmless as possible."⁵³ In his masterpiece, *The American Commonwealth*, James Bryce wrote: "Parties are inevitable. No large country has been without them. No one has shown how representative government could be worked without them."⁵⁴ Giovanni Sartori agreed, noting, "Parties came to be accepted—subconsciously and even so with formidable reluctance—with the realization that diversity and dissent are not necessarily incompatible with, or disruptive of, political order."⁵⁵ By establishing rules and order, parties inherently confine conflict within certain bounds, with outcomes adhered to by all sides once either the voters or the courts have settled the matter. This truism held until 2021, when an outgoing president instigated an insurrection against both the rule of law and popular sovereignty itself.

UPSETTING THE BALANCE: THE TRUMP MOVEMENT AND THE HOLLOWING OUT OF THE REPUBLICAN PARTY

Speaking before the Conservative Political Action Committee (CPAC) Conference in March 2023, Donald Trump declared that his followers belong to a "movement like has never been seen, I think we could probably say, never been seen anywhere in the world."⁵⁶ Historically, parties have been buffeted by movements like the Know-Nothings of the early nineteenth century, or the antislavery movement at that same century's midpoint, or the populists at its conclusion that transformed American politics yet subsumed their most passionate supporters into one of the major parties whose disparate elements served to temper their demands. The pluralistic nature of American society has meant that shifting coalitions inevitably occurred both within the major parties and between them. As Sidney Tarrow notes in his book *Movements and Parties*, "These noisy participants... have often been transformed by their encounters with parties, sometimes becoming what sociologists call 'institutionalized' and sometimes becoming parties themselves."[57] Historically, political scientists have cited two distinct functions to each phenomenon: movements *articulate* interests; parties *aggregate* them.[58] As Samuel Huntington has written, "The function of the party is to organize participation, to aggregate interests, *to serve as the link* between social forces and the government."[59]

Movement success, says Tarrow, means combining both insider and outsider tactics—infusing new blood into a party while responding to others who want their demands translated into laws.[60] At key moments, the intersections of movements and parties fulfilled Martin Luther King's aphorism that "the arc of the moral universe is long, but it bends toward justice."[61] Organized labor, the women's movement, and the civil rights movement garnered influence, particularly, but not exclusively, within the Democratic Party. Yet as they competed with other intraparty factions, their demands were tempered by the party's response. According to Tarrow, "People who enter public life through movements veer into parties, and parties shift their ground to embrace new issues and attack the cleavages exposed by the conflict."[62] For today's Democrats, movement politics involves demands based on race, gender, the environment, and sexual preference that have resulted in necessary compromises underwritten by the Democratic Party. Joe Biden's 2020 nomination illustrates this point. While Biden won overwhelming support from older Black voters, especially women and centrist Democrats, Bernie Sanders, a self-proclaimed socialist and movement leader, was the overwhelming choice of young voters, liberals, gays, and environmentalists. Biden prudently joined forces with Sanders, and together they wrote the 2020 Democratic platform.

What made the Trump movement possible and gave it such power was a long hollowing out of the Republican Party's establishment wing. As Tarrow notes, Republicans absorbed several ideologically driven right-wing movements, while a paucity of conservative thought gave the Trump movement an opportunity for a hostile takeover. The conditions that gave rise to Donald Trump were long in the making. Political scientist Wilson Carey McWilliams once compared parties to "institutions of higher learning," claiming they were indispensable instruments in "the school of citizenship."[63] But, over the years, the delicate balance between passions and interests became tilted in favor of passion. As McWilliams notes, fans of a particular political party "have no serious bond of interest" and are "rooted in a feeling of being *with* certain people more than being *for* certain programs or policies."[64] McWilliams carried the analogy further, noting that sports fans are eager to buy tickets, but their allegiance survives even repeated defeats."[65] Political parties are now dominated by their passionate, sometimes insufferable, supporters.

This imbalance between passions and interests has turned the academy's decades-long defense of political parties on its head. As passion overrules interest and partisans find a sense of belonging in being with fellow travelers—even sometimes to the exclusion of an articulation of interests or, worse, the creation of a false sense of reality based on "alternative facts"—there arises a heretofore unthinkable situation that George Washington in his Farewell Address once envisioned but contemporary defenders of American political parties could hardly imagine. The Democratic Party has its passionate fans, but the party retains enough diversity to articulate a series of competing interests. While Democrats are passionate about winning elections, they are equally passionate about governing. The late Mario Cuomo put it this way: "You campaign in poetry [but] you govern in prose."[66] President Joe Biden is no poet, but he is basing his reelection campaign on the prose found in the texts of legislation he has signed during his first two years in office.

But the Republican Party has become driven by the passions and contradictory issue positions espoused by its undisputed leader, Donald J. Trump. On January 6, 2021, Donald Trump Jr. told a gathering of armed protesters in front of the White House who were preparing to storm the US Capitol, "This is Donald Trump's Republican Party."[67] His boast was not one of mere braggadocio but a statement of fact. Virtually without precedent, no movement—save perhaps for the Populists of the 1890s—has been given carte blanche by a political party. As Donald Trump's followers became overwhelmed by their sense of disenfranchisement and grievance, many gathered in Washington, DC. Responding to Trump's call to arms, they attempted an insurrection. Addressing his loyal followers, Trump declared, "You'll never take back our country with weakness. You have to show strength and you have to be strong."[68] David Corn writes that Trump "had engineered a distorted reality—as had all those Republicans who did not refute Trump's baseless claims about the election."⁶⁹ Historian Ruth Ben-Ghiat maintains that Donald Trump transformed the Republican Party into "an authoritarian party culture [where] not only do you go after external enemies, but you go after internal enemies. You're not allowed any dissent."⁷⁰ Ben-Ghiat believes that Trump, unlike the Democrats with their panoply of diverse interests, succeeded in imposing an authoritarian culture within the Republican Party thanks to his messaging that was almost uniformly echoed by other Republican politicians and conservative news media outlets.⁷¹

As a movement leader, Jessica Mercieca has identified five rhetorical devices that Trump employed to cement the loyalties of his cultlike following:

- *Ad hominem arguments*, like his attacks on former president Barack Obama with the false claim that Obama was not born in the United States;
- *Ad populum* devices, appealing to the wisdom of the crowd, as when he praised his followers for being wiser than the "corrupt political elites";
- *Misogyny*, for example, attacking Fox News broadcaster Megyn Kelly, who asked him in a debate about his demeaning comments about women;
- *Reification*, as when he attacked Hillary Clinton for what he called "playing the women's card"; and
- *Xenophobia*, as when, in his first campaign appearance, he attacked Mexico for sending us bad people.⁷²

Donald Trump's ascension to the presidency allowed a demagogue to assume power in an era in which long-standing trends going back to Franklin Roosevelt's New Deal diminished the power of the party apparatus at the expense of an expanding presidency. Desmond King and Sidney Milkis write that today's partisanship "is no longer a struggle over the size of the State. It is an executive-centered struggle for the services of national administrative power."⁷³ The enlargement of the presidency, together with a hollowing out of the Republican establishment, led to a bastardization of the Republican Party that, according to Tarrow, is led by "lieutenants and drill sergeants at its base [who] are connected to the archipelago of white nationalists, evangelical Christians, and anti-black and anti-Semitic groups."[74] The rage of Trump's supporters on January 6, 2021, upended the traditional Republican commitment to the rule of law, not to mention the Democrats' faith in popular sovereignty. Giovanni Sartori wrote, "Conflict over fundamentals is not a possible basis for democracy, nor indeed for any polity: Such conflict—i.e., real conflict—calls for internal war and for succession as its only solution."[75] Republican congresswoman Marjorie Taylor Greene has called for just that: a "national divorce" between the red states and blue states.[76] Addressing a CPAC audience in 2023, Trump all but declared war on his opponents: "In 2016, I declared I am your voice. Today, I add, I am your warrior. I am your justice. And, for those who have been wronged and betrayed, I am your retribution."[77]

In his book *Totalitarian and Authoritarian Regimes*, Juan J. Linz defines authoritarian regimes as "political systems with limited, not responsible, political pluralism, without elaborate and guiding ideology, but with distinctive mentalities, without extensive nor [sic] intensive political mobilization, except at some points in their development, and in which a leader or occasionally a small group exercises power within formally ill-defined limits but actually quite predictable ones."[78] In some regimes, Linz notes, when mass mobilization occurs it is often within the context of a single party led by a strong individual or group of individuals that is the driving engine behind it.[79] For more than a century, political scientists have extolled the American two-party system as the ultimate guardian against authoritarian rulers and necessary aggregators of diverse interests that, balanced between competing passions and interests and guided by principles of law and the practicalities of compromise, made our form of constitutional government work. In 1986, political scientist Leon Epstein wrote:

> In a century when American parties appear to have lost public support and to have become less effective, it is striking that there should have developed a preponderant scholarly commitment to the desirability, if not the absolute necessity, of parties in a democratic system. The commitment is mostly clearly discernible among political scientists who study parties as a specialized subject. Treating parties as a large and important segment of politics generally, several of these specialists have been influential members of their academic discipline. . . . Remarkably few political scientists dissent. Almost none contemplate happily the possibility of doing without parties altogether.[80]

So committed are political scientists to the idea of vibrant parties that any ills that beset governance are often blamed on any deficiencies associated with them. The Committee for Party Renewal, an organization of leading party scholars, declared in 1976: "Without parties there can be no organized and coherent politics. When politics lacks coherence, there can be no accountable democracy. Parties are indispensable to the realization of democracy. The stakes are no less than that."[81] In his book *Why Parties?*(1995), John Aldrich elaborated how a weakened party system translated into do-nothing government:

> Members of Congress are too concerned with their own reelection . . . to be able or willing to think of the public good. The president worries about his personal popularity, spends too little time leading the nation, and when he does turn to Congress, finds it impossible to forge majorities—heretofore primarily partisan majorities—to pass his own initiatives or to form workable compromises with Congress. Divided partisan control of the government seems to be the rule . . . , with unified control the exception. Elections are candidate-centered, turning on personality and image. Party platforms are little more than the first order of business at national conventions, only to be passed quickly and, party leaders hope, without controversy or media attention, so that the convention can turn to more important business. . . . Lamenters of party decline argue the major historical vehicle for aggregating the interests of this diverse republic, articulating them into coherent plans of action, and providing a means of holding elected officials accountable for success or failure of their programs is all too often lost.[82]

For the vast majority of political scientists, the weaker parties became, the more vigorously they defended them. This book is the story of how one political party—the Republicans, long before the advent of Donald Trump—contained the seeds of its own demise that not only challenged the fundamentals of American democracy but threatened its continued existence. The story does not begin with Donald Trump, however, but is one that has been decades in the making. It is a tale that weaves several strands into a dangerous tapestry: an attempt to overthrow a popularly elected president, casting blame on a corrupt "deep state," and allowing conspiracy theories to assume that victories denied meant those elections were inherently corrupt. The challenge today's Republican Party poses to democracy undermines the beneficial qualities the academy once associated with the political parties.

This book is a deeply personal journey, one whose findings challenge what we think we know about the essential nature of our political parties and their history but actually do not. For decades, I have vigorously advocated for stronger political parties, sharing the consensus view that strong parties made both the government and the Constitution work. Weak parties, I believed, resulted in a series of disappointing presidencies—from the depths of Richard Nixon's Watergate to the malaise of Jimmy Carter, to the scandals that beset the Bill Clinton administration. But the warning in a famous 1950 dissent authored by Julius Turner to the academic consensus that stronger parties meant nationalizing them bears particular resonance to the present. Turner foretold that uniformly united parties "would give weapons to the dominant groups in each party by means of which (1) the number of one-party areas in the United States would be increased, and (2) the self-destructive tendencies of the minority party would be accentuated."[83] In many ways, Turner's prediction has become our unhappy present.

Historically, American political parties exercised power within a diverse constellation of various state and local party organizations. Their diversity meant that there were, as an old maxim states, fifty different Democratic and Republican Parties scattered across the wide expanse of the United States. As Turner pointed out: "You cannot give Hubert Humphrey a banjo and expect him to carry Kansas. Only a Democrat who rejects at least a part of the Fair Deal can carry Kansas, and only a Republican who moderates the Republican platform can carry Massachusetts."[84] But the centralization of power in the presidency, combined with the nationalization of the parties and a paucity of conservative thought, made Donald Trump's transformation of the Republican Party possible. It is that transformation, one long in the making, that forms the heart of this book.

Chapter 1 outlines the crisis facing our democracy and the distance we have traveled from the end of Ronald Reagan's presidency to the present. Chapter 2 examines the history of the Republican Party from 1932 to 1952 and finds strands of today's GOP deeply rooted in its past. Chapter 3 describes how Dwight D. Eisenhower outmaneuvered Robert Taft to win in 1952 but notes that his personal victory produced a weakened

Republican Party whose remaining conservatives were dismayed at Eisenhower's embrace of "Modern Republicanism" and how little he had done to strengthen the party's organization and appeal. Chapter 4 chronicles how the Republican Party came to embrace lies and conspiracy theories, a phenomenon that began long before Donald Trump. Chapter 5 illustrates how Republicans abandoned their historic commitment to civil rights and voting rights, and instead promoted legislation designed to undermine both. Chapter 6 depicts how the Republican Party discarded the traditional role of the loyal opposition to become an insurgent party, consumed with obtaining power and slavishly devoted to one man. The afterword describes how the Republican Party remains under Donald Trump's influence and is busily attempting to rewrite the history of January 6, 2021.

Throughout this book, one may ask whether the Republican Party is irredeemably damaged or whether it can be saved. This is an open question, one whose answer is unlikely to be given in the next presidential contest, or even the one after that. That is a story yet to be told. To survive, the Republican Party will need to jettison Donald Trump, by either continued electoral losses or the workings of the judicial system. But more will be required, including embracing converts with different points of view, a rearticulation of conservative thought, and a rebalancing of passions and interests. Whatever its ending, the history of today's Republican Party will form several chapters of a tale that, once again, will answer the question asked of Benjamin Franklin at the conclusion of the Constitutional Convention: "Well, Doctor, what have we got a republic or a monarchy?" Franklin's memorable response was, "A republic, if you can keep it."[85]

1. Democracy on Trial—Again

Too much of what's happening in our country today is not normal.
—Joe Biden, Philadelphia, September 1, 2022

TWO PRESIDENTS, TWO SPEECHES

On the evening of January 11, 1989, Ronald Reagan strode into the Oval Office to address the nation for one final time as president. Reflecting on his eight years in office, Reagan rekindled John Winthrop's image of the United States as a "shining city on a hill."[1] Embellishing the analogy, Reagan described his brilliant city as one "built on rocks stronger than oceans, wind-swept, God-blessed, and teeming with people of all kinds living in harmony and peace—a city with free ports that hummed with commerce and creativity, and if there had to be city walls, the walls had doors and the doors were open to anyone with the will and the heart to get here."[2] Reagan's speech represented the zenith of American exceptionalism—the idea that the United States is set apart from other nations and united by its devotion to the values of freedom, individual rights, and equality of opportunity. Reagan advised his listeners to never forget the ideas enunciated in the country's founding documents: "As long as we remember our first principles and believe in ourselves, the future will always be ours."[3]

On that January night, the future looked bright. The problems Reagan was leaving behind—especially the gargantuan federal budget deficits and widening economic inequality—could wait. Unlike the disappointing presidencies of Lyndon B. Johnson, Richard M. Nixon, Gerald R. Ford, and Jimmy Carter, Ronald Reagan was departing the White House as a beloved figure—revered by Republicans and setting the gold standard for their future leaders. Then House minority whip Dick Cheney echoed the sentiments of most Americans: "Discount if you wish for the fact that I'm a Republican and a Reagan supporter, but you have to believe the office is in better shape now than when he came to town."[4] Reagan himself was satisfied, saying his shining city was "more secure and happier" than it was eight years earlier and remained "a beacon for all the pilgrims from all the lost places who are hurtling through the darkness toward home."[5]

In a memo sent to the president prior to delivering his Farewell Address, Reagan's chief pollster, Richard Wirthlin, outlined three conditions that underpin the "can do spirit" required for presidential success:

- There must be strong public confidence and pride in America—belief in the great experiment.
- There must be trust in the government and a confidence that elected officials can deal effectively with problems.
- The public view of the future must be hopeful and optimistic.[6]

Thirty-three years later, another president delivered a very different prime-time speech. From the steps of Independence Hall in Philadelphia, Joe Biden spoke words once considered unthinkable for any chief executive to utter. Claiming that democracy is "under assault," Biden declared, "Donald Trump and the MAGA [shorthand for Make America Great Again] Republicans represent an extremism that threatens the very foundations of our republic."[7] He described how Trump's Republican Party fanned the flames of violence by refusing to accept a peaceful transition of power and were living "not in the light of truth but in the shadow of lies."[8] Remembering the violence of January 6, 2021, Biden saw inherent contradictions that Trump and his followers refused to acknowledge: "You can't be pro–law enforcement and pro-insurrection. You can't be a party of law and order and call the people who attacked the police on January 6th 'patriots.'"[9] "For God's sake," he concluded, "whose side are you on?"[10] In response, Trump called Biden "an enemy of the state."[11] As that remark demonstrated, in today's Trump-dominated Republican Party, the role once played by the loyal opposition has been cast aside.

During the Trump presidency, the national motto changed from "E Pluribus Unum" ("out of many, one") to "E Pluribus Duo"—out of many, two distinct and vastly different Americas. The conditions Richard Wirthlin stipulated for presidential success have given way to self-doubt in the American experiment; a belief that our constitutional form of government no longer works; a nation whose trust in public officials is a matter of tribal loyalties; and a fading American Dream that has been replaced by visions of a dark and dismal future. This is a far cry from the hope Joe Biden expressed in his inaugural address when he solemnly declared, "At this hour, democracy has prevailed."[12] Little more than a year later, Biden reached a very different conclusion.

In his book titled *On Tyranny*, Timothy Snyder defined what patriotism is *not*:

> It is not patriotic to dodge the draft and to mock war heroes and their families.... It is not patriotic to avoid paying taxes, especially when American working families do pay.... It is not patriotic to admire foreign dictators.... It is not patriotic to call upon foreign leaders to intervene in American presidential elections.... It is not patriotic to try to sabotage an American election, nor to claim victory after defeat. It is not patriotic to try to end democracy.[13]

Snyder's indictment of Donald Trump makes an important distinction between nationalism and patriotism, one that few nations have embraced. A nationalist defines patriotism as rooted in a common ethnicity whose citizens occupy a particular landmass. Historically, Americans have embraced a very different form of patriotism in which informed citizens from different backgrounds respect differences of opinion while still adhering to the principles enunciated in the Declaration of Independence and the US Constitution. In her book *Twilight of Democracy*, Anne Applebaum writes that Donald Trump was a nationalist, but not one in the American sense of the word. Rather than describing an exceptional nation, Trump's American nationalism saw the United States as a place whose citizens were bound together by white skin, a certain idea of Christianity, and an attachment to a landmass surrounded by a wall.[14] In Trump's view, Ronald Reagan's American exceptionalism, which envisioned a "shining city on a hill," had been replaced by a country whose "mothers and children [are] trapped in poverty in our inner cities, rusted-out factories [are] scattered like tombstones across the landscape of our nation . . . and the crime, and the gangs, and the drugs that have stolen too many lives and robbed our country of so much unrealized potential."[15] Hearing Trump utter these words, George W. Bush—who fashioned himself as a Reagan-style Republican and espoused his own enlarged view of American exceptionalism after the attacks of 9/11—reportedly said, "That was some weird shit."[16]

In his homespun farewell, Ronald Reagan recounted the story of a sailor on the USS *Midway* who spotted a leaky boat crammed with Vietnamese refugees. As the ship set forth to bring the boat people to safety, one refugee, spying a sailor on deck, called out, "Hello American sailor—hello freedom man."[17] For Reagan, that moment defined what it meant to be an American, living in a contented place where "we, the people" are free.[18] Today, Reagan's quaint anecdote and hopeful farewell are distant memories for some, while others have no direct recollection of it. For those born after Reagan left office, there are embedded in the chords of their memories vivid pictures of political division and turmoil with a government unable to cope. Concluding his Philadelphia address, Joe Biden warned, "Too much of what's happening in our country is not normal."[19] For older Americans, like Biden, that statement rings true. But for those who have not yet reached elderly status, there is a new normal that has, once more, placed our democracy on trial.

DEMOCRACY ON TRIAL

During World War II, E. B. White was asked by Franklin Roosevelt's Writers' War Board to compose an answer to a simple question, "What is democracy?" In response, White wrote:

> Surely the Board knows what democracy is. It is the line that forms on the right. It is the "don't" in don't shove. It is the hole in the stuffed shirt through which the sawdust slowly trickles; it is the dent in the high hat. Democracy is the recurrent suspicion that more than half of the people are right more than half of the time. It is the feeling of privacy in the voting booths, the feeling of communion in the libraries, the feeling of vitality everywhere. Democracy is a letter to the editor. Democracy is the score at the beginning of the ninth. It is an idea which hasn't been disproved yet, a song the words of which have not gone bad. It's the mustard on the hot dog and the cream in the rationed coffee. Democracy is a request from a War Board, in the middle of a morning, in the middle of a war, wanting to know what democracy is.[20]

White's answer paints an idyllic portrait of how Americans saw themselves near the middle of the twentieth century. Even as democracy was under assault elsewhere, most Americans sought reassurance that their government was impenetrable to authoritarian impulses whether from home or abroad. This view persisted long after World War II ended, and it was reinforced after Richard Nixon's resignation in 1974. Taking the oath of office the day Nixon resigned, Gerald R. Ford reiterated what most Americans believed were unshakable truisms: "Our Constitution works; our great Republic is a government of laws and not of men. Here the people rule."[21] But despite Ford's reassurances, there has always been an undercurrent of doubt as to whether our institutions were up to the challenges they faced. Less than a decade after E. B. White described democracy in glowing terms, Arthur M. Schlesinger Jr. saw an emerging age of anxiety: "The grounds of our civilization, of our certitude, are breaking up under our feet, and familiar ideas and institutions vanish as we reach for them, like shadows in the falling dusk."[22] The Cold War and worries about the spread of communism at home and abroad spurred a sense of a country under siege. Harry Truman tried to quell those growing concerns, saying, "Confident people do not become communists."[23] But doubts remained, and they were amplified by the appearance of new demagogues, especially those within the Republican Party led by Wisconsin senator Joseph R. McCarthy, who used fear to win power and prominence.

By the twentieth century's end, doubts about our democracy had multiplied—not because of any foreign threats (the Soviet Union had fallen, and 9/11 had yet to occur) but by internal forces tearing at its fabric. In 1995, Jean Bethke Elshtain, a leading political theorist, penned an important book titled *Democracy on Trial*. In it, she argued that the extant anger split the country into "little islands of bristling difference where we comport with those just like ourselves: no outsiders welcome."[24] Rather than achieving peaceful compromise, which Elshtain viewed as "the *only* way to do democratic politics,"[25] she saw a growing "civic zaniness" where different islands were issuing a "cascading series of manifestos that tell us we cannot live together; we cannot work together; we are not in this together; we are not Americans who have something in common."[26] In this new world, Elshtain argued, one was either "a victim or victimized, oppressed or oppressor, abject or triumphant."[27] Politics had become a zero-sum game.

In Elshtain's view, these culturally conforming enclaves forbade entry by others with different lifestyles and opposing political views. The American emphasis on individualism, once celebrated by Alexis de Tocqueville, had morphed into a cultural libertarianism where, in some islands, lifestyle choices were the sole province of individual decisions, while in other enclaves most believed in eternal truths that persisted from one generation to the next. These new divisions had religious overtones, as those who attended church often liked their "morality writ large," to borrow a phrase from Alan Wolfe, while those who were either infrequent attendees or never entered church doors preferred their "morality writ small."[28] These two cultural perspectives produced a profound generational divide, as older, more devout Americans were juxtaposed with younger citizens, many of whom labeled their religious preference as "none."[29] Historically, Americans have tolerated diverse viewpoints, a characteristic, Elshtain argued, that allowed the American Revolution to succeed, whereas the French emphasis on conformity inevitably led to the Reign of Terror following that country's revolution.[30] For Elshtain, diversity and a common belief in the founding principles of the United States defined what it meant to be an American: "It means sharing the possibility of a brotherhood and sisterhood that is perhaps fractious—as all brotherhoods and sisterhoods are—and yet united in a spirit that's a spirit of more good than ill will."[31]

But over time the lack of a common understanding of what it meant to be an American, coupled with a culture war based on very different value judgments, led to a decline of "social capital"—that is, a lack of civic engagement where individuals were bound to one another in a common enterprise. In 1995, Robert Putnam coined the term "social capital" in a famous article titled "Bowling Alone."[32] Americans, he discovered, were not joining bowling leagues, which had been popular in the 1950s and 1960s and created a sense of camaraderie, but instead were individually indulging in the sport whenever they pleased. This lack of social capital, Putnam maintained, eroded the communal ties and common bonds once found in the American story. Many agreed with Putnam and cited a significant decline in voter turnout as evidence that his conclusions were accurate. In 1996, those who trekked to the polls in the Bill Clinton–Bob Dole contest were the fewest since the uninspiring Calvin Coolidge–John W. Davis race of 1924.[33] Thanks to the isolating effects of the internet and the lack of friendship, Elshtain saw more Americans moving toward "the edge of quiet desperation."[34] In this new world of loneliness, fear, and anxiety, conditions were ripe for authoritarian leaders and antidemocratic solutions.

The Clinton presidency added fuel to the raging cultural fire. Bill Clinton's scandalous affair with Monica Lewinsky, and his lying under oath about it, galvanized sanctimonious House Republicans to vote for his impeachment, even while their leader, Newt Gingrich, was engaged in his own extramarital affair. Although Clinton was later acquitted, the baby boomer president forced voters to make a choice they desperately wanted to avoid—whether to keep a president whose policies they liked or remove that chief executive because his personal morality was so deplorable.[35] George W. Bush offered some temporary relief, but the unity the nation experienced after 9/11 crumbled in the face of two failed wars and the Great Recession. Barack Obama's promise to relegate the politics of race to the ash heap of history gave way to a depiction of him as the "other." Fears of an emerging nonwhite majority, combined with ever-greater economic inequalities, reminded many of Aristotle's maxim that inequality inevitably breeds instability.[36] Donald Trump understood this new age of anxiety and, unlike George W. Bush and Barack Obama, never sought to bridge the growing racial and cultural divides. Instead, Trump exacerbated division, even boasting of his ability to do so: "I bring out the rage in people."[37] The divisions are now so severe that Joe Biden acknowledged that in a post-Trump world, unifying the country had become an increasingly elusive goal, conceding, "Things have changed a whole bunch."[38]

Donald Trump's presidency caused alarm bells over the state of our democracy to ring even more loudly. In 2018, Steven Levitsky and Daniel Ziblatt published *How Democracies Die*. They set forth three conditions that made their dire prognosis likely to happen here: (1) a rejection of (or weak commitment to) democratic rules of the game, (2) denying the legitimacy of one's political opponents, and (3) a readiness to curtail civil liberties and attack independent thought.[39] In the United States, these conditions manifested themselves in critical ways. Nearly three-quarters of Republicans refused to accept the results of the 2020 election.[40] Donald Trump's demagoguery, including branding his opponents with nicknames that stuck like "Crooked Hillary" and "Sleepy Joe," helped delegitimize the opposition for his eighty-one million Twitter followers. A rising corps of militia groups, whose violent rhetoric became even more extreme after Trump left office, posed a direct threat to our democratic institutions and civil liberties. On January 6, 2021, members of the Oath Keepers and Proud Boys helped coordinate an attack on the US Capitol.

Donald Trump's depiction of an "American carnage," which he espoused long before the events of January 6, 2021, exacerbated the calls for political violence and the desire of his followers to establish their own version of "law and order," a Republican rallying cry that dated back to Richard Nixon's 1968 presidential campaign.[41] In 2014, Trump declared: "You know what solves [the problems we face]? When the economy crashes, when the country goes to total hell, and everything is a disaster. Then you'll have . . . riots to go back to where we used to be when we were great."[42] Ending chaos and promoting order are promises made by authoritarian leaders. Summoning the spirit of another authoritarian leader, Trump told his chief of staff, John Kelly, a retired Marine Corps general, "Why can't you be like the German generals in World War Two?"[43] Trump's call for loyalty and order, coupled with his embrace of political violence, was especially evident in his rallies, where on more than one occasion he incited attendees to use fisticuffs against protesters.

Once in power, Trump used the instruments of government to punish his political enemies. In a 2019 phone call to Volodymyr Zelensky, he conditioned US military aid to Ukraine upon Zelensky's willingness to find dirt on Trump's leading rival, Joe Biden.[44] Appalled by Trump's conduct, Mitt Romney became the first person belonging to a president's party to support his impeachment and removal from power. As Romney stated: "Corrupting an election to keep oneself in office is perhaps the most abusive and destructive violation of one's oath of office that I can imagine."[45] Trump's willingness to use the instruments of government against his perceived enemies was evident even before he took office. At a rally in Fort Worth, Texas, in 2016, Trump promised that if he became president, Jeff Bezos, owner of the *Washington Post*, was "going to have such problems."[46] When he was president, the Justice Department became Trump's preferred weapon of choice either to reward his allies or extract retribution from his enemies. Revelations by former US attorney Geoffrey Berman describe the pressure he faced to prosecute former secretary of state John Kerry on a scurrilous charge that Kerry violated the Logan Act by privately communicating with the Iranian government about the status of US-Iranian nuclear negotiations. When Berman declined to

24   Chapter One

issue an indictment, the Justice Department turned to the US attorney in Maryland, who likewise did not pursue a case.[47] Trump also loved using his pardon power to exempt allies from criminal prosecutions regardless of what crimes they may have committed. Trump knew those pardoned would remain forever in his debt, and any potentially embarrassing revelations would never see the light of day in a court of law.

ALTERNATIVE FACTS BECOME ALTERNATIVE REALITIES

Joe Biden's warning about an imperiled democracy stems from the notion that the constant repetition of untruths creates an aura of simplicity whose adherents are unwilling to cast aside—despite whatever facts contradict their perceived realities. During the sentencing of Paul Manafort, who was Donald Trump's 2016 campaign manager, his lawyers continued to misrepresent the facts of the case. A frustrated Judge Amy Berman Jackson interrupted the proceedings to exclaim, "If people don't have the facts, democracy can't work."[48] As the late Daniel Patrick Moynihan famously observed, "Everyone is entitled to his own opinion but not his own facts."[49] But in Donald Trump's world, facts became "alternative facts."[50] This was evident on Inauguration Day when press secretary Sean Spicer went before the television cameras to falsely declare that Trump's crowd was "the largest audience ever to witness an inauguration, period, both in person and around the globe."[51] This contradicted the clear photographic evidence showing Barack Obama's 2009 inaugural gathering was vastly larger. But that reality hardly mattered to Spicer's boss, who insisted he make an unscheduled appearance claiming it was Trump who had the bigger crowd. Spicer's surprise announcement set the tone for the next four years. In Trump's first few weeks in office, his chief of staff, Reince Priebus, issued this directive: "Back up whatever the President said or tweeted, regardless of its accuracy."[52] This became a maxim of the Trump presidency. Defending Trump's claim of a stolen election in 2020, Rudy Giuliani declared, "Truth isn't truth."[53] Trump's final chief of staff, Mark Meadows, maintained, "Everybody has their impression of what truth is."[54]

The late David Foster Wallace once wrote that television promotes what Americans want to see as "normal," adding, "Television, from the surface on down, is about desire."[55] Even as he repeatedly denounced most cable network news programs as promulgating "fake news," Trump's successful television shows, *The Apprentice* and *Celebrity Apprentice*, gave audiences what they desired—that is, creating a mythical Horatio Alger-like Trump and marketing that image to the public. In 2016, *New York Times* reporter Maggie Haberman asked an Iowa Republican why he was attending a Trump rally. Thinking the man was there to view the spectacle before Trump's candidacy inevitably ended, Haberman was surprised to hear him say he was committed to Trump because "I watched him run his business."[56] Creating such artificially based realities is hardly a new phenomenon. In 2004, an adviser to George W. Bush told journalist Ron Suskind that the media was part of a "reality-based community," claiming that reporting based on observable facts had become passé: "We are an empire now, and when we act, we create our own reality."[57] While such braggadocio fell victim to the harsh realities of the wars in Afghanistan and Iraq, the technique of promoting "alternate facts" into artificially created realities became a political phenomenon that Donald Trump raised to a new art form.

Living in alternative realities appeals to those who eschew complexity in their personal lives and political preferences. Jonathan Askonas describes how a new "alternate reality game" draws its adherents into a singular collaborative enterprise. According to Askonas, players "neatly slot vast reams of information into intelligible characters and plots, like 'Everything that has gone wrong is the product of evil actors or systems, but there are powerful heroes coming to the rescue, and they need your help.'"[58] For Anne Applebaum, these alternative realities promote an "authoritarian predisposition" where order is valued and diversity is unwelcome.[59] This authoritarian predisposition creates a mindset in which joy is found in achieving a high degree of certainty. Askonas describes how this "confirmation bias"—namely, the notion that people are more likely to believe things that confirm what they already believe—creates an "emotional relish," a sheer delight when our perceptions comport with our deepest feelings about the state of the world.[60] According to Askonas, those "narrative-enhancing reports will spread widest and fastest, regardless of whether they are overturned by later reporting."[61] The widespread use of social media platforms whose purpose is often to ratify what the viewer already believes illustrates Askonas's point. A study done by the *Washington Post* found seventy-seven individuals saw vast increases in their online followers once they posted claims that the 2020 election was stolen. When Kyle Becker, a former Fox News producer, began tweeting feverishly about election fraud, his modest 15,000 followers grew by 5,000 in just four hours. By January 6, 2021, Becker had 177,000 Twitter followers, and he left his Fox News job to become an influential right-wing pundit—commenting on everything from the war in Ukraine to the FBI's search of Donald Trump's Mar-a-Lago residence.[62]

The comfort of such confirmation biases fulfills a deeply held human desire for symmetry. Barack Obama recalls how the military bases in Hawaii appealed to him as a young boy, "with their tidy streets and well-oiled machinery, the crisp uniforms, and crisper salutes." Obama says he still finds pleasure "from a well-played baseball game," while his wife enjoys watching reruns from the familiar *Dick Van Dyke Show*.[63] But in the information age, these orderly confirmation biases create differing narratives that often do not converge. And the more the storylines differ, the more anger rises in equal proportion to the level of disagreement. These resentments are based not only on perceived intrusions of unwelcome realities but also on what each side *imagines* those contrasting realities to be.[64] Desiring approval, political leaders not only reinforce their followers' confirmation biases but create a nostalgia for a perceived past where unpleasant realities are glossed over by the romantic portraits they re-create.

Ronald Reagan was a master at romanticizing a bygone era and creating his own alternate realities. While campaigning for the presidency in 1980, Reagan told the tale of a B-17 pilot whose plane was badly shot up during a World War II bombing mission. According to Reagan, one crew member was severely wounded and could not be extricated from the damaged ball turret. As the aircraft began to lose altitude, the commander ordered the remaining crew to bail out and then lay down beside the injured man. Reagan described how the doomed officer took the young man's hand and said, "Never mind, son. We'll ride it down together." Reagan concluded, "Congressional Medal of Honor, posthumously awarded." Reagan often repeated the story, even as observant journalists wondered how the event he described was possible since everyone on board the doomed aircraft died. Investigations found no record of a congressional medal. Further inquiry revealed the tale bore a strong resemblance to the plot of a 1944 film, *A Wing and a Prayer*—a movie well known to the former Hollywood star.[65]

Ronald Reagan's acting background helped him perfect his talent for allowing audiences to suspend their disbelief, drawing them into whatever reality he created. His emergence as a Hollywood star came in the film *Knute Rockne, All American* (1940), in which he portrayed famed Notre Dame football star George Gipp. In a famous deathbed scene, Gipp supposedly said to Coach Rockne, "Sometime, Rock, when the team's up against it and the breaks are beating the boys—tell them to go in there with all they've got and win just one more for the Gipper. I don't know where I'll be then, Rock. But I'll know about it, and I'll be happy."[66] Thereafter, Reagan happily embraced the moniker "The Gipper" and used it to great effect. But the reality of George Gipp's short life was very different from the scenes portrayed in the movie: no one ever called George Gipp "The Gipper"; Coach Rockne never visited Gipp in the hospital; and that famous deathbed dialogue was never spoken. The unpleasant reality was that Gipp was a ne'er-do-well student who skipped classes and examinations, was disliked by his teammates, drank too much, and bet large sums of money on Notre Dame football games. But the myth of "The Gipper" became a dream fulfilled in the minds of Reagan's audiences. For years, freshmen entering Notre Dame were required to sit and watch the film. At its premiere on October 9, 1940, movie stars Bob Hope and Rudy Vallee made appearances along with Reagan, who was accompanied by Franklin D. Roosevelt Jr.[67] Anne Applebaum describes how "restorative nostalgics," like Reagan, become "mythmakers and architects, builders of monuments and founders of nationalist political projects."[68] The ability of the best actors to get their audiences to willingly suspend their disbelief and draw them into the plot became a prerequisite for the successful politician.

But too much restorative nostalgia can devolve into an embrace of conspiracy theories that create their own distorted realities. Conspiracy theorists find these explanations compelling because they believe the nation is being stripped of its greatness. To them, as Applebaum notes, "someone has attacked us, undermined us, sapped our strength."[69] Often the objects of their wrath are establishment politicians, academicians, and so-called experts whom they view as espousing a form of "political correctness" that rejects any alternative views they may have or political standing they seek to acquire. Florida Republican governor Ron DeSantis is the latest practitioner of the technique—whether it be denouncing critical race theory (which is not taught in Florida schools), or removing "offensive" books from library shelves, or denouncing "woke CEOs" who seek to impose "an ideological agenda on the American people" by championing the values of "diversity, inclusion, and equity."[70] DeSantis depicts himself as a fighter, telling his supporters, "We stand for the values of places like Destin, Dunedin, and Deland—not Davos"—the latter a political shorthand for the "other."[71] Bill Clinton rightly observes that Republicans always "find some new way to scare the living daylights out of swing voters about something."[72]

These scare tactics often create their own mass movements. During the Cold War, California longshoreman Eric Hoffer described how "fanaticism, enthusiasm, fervent hope, hatred, and intolerance" release "a powerful flow of activity in certain departments of life; all of them demand blind faith and singlehearted allegiance."[73] Hannah Arendt claimed that followers of mass movements "believe everything and nothing [and] think that everything was possible and that nothing was true."[74] For Arendt, such followers "take refuge in cynicism," believing they had been lied to all along, and they admire mass movement leaders "for their superior tactical cleverness." In turn, the leaders embrace the lies because they give them power over their followers for whom belief is essential.[75]

The Trump movement feeds on alternative realities and creates a hyperpartisanship that upends formerly valued customs and norms—a place where uncommitted thinkers are nearly impossible to find. In a polarized country with fewer uncommitted voters occupying what was once quaintly called the center, any perceived fulfillment of one side's most fervent wishes angers the opposition and leads to a series of never-ending battles. The result is that parties no longer offer voters a panacea of what life will be like under their rule but instead a dystopian vision of what will happen if they lose. Isaiah Berlin once wrote that there is a human desire for a "final solution," but he warned that "the notion of total human fulfilment is a formal contradiction, a metaphysical chimera."[76] For Berlin, "the best that one can do is to try to promote some kind of equilibrium, necessarily unstable, between the different operations of different groups of human beings—at the very least to prevent them from attempting to exterminate one another and, so far as possible, to prevent them from hurting each other."[77]

THE NEED FOR VIRTUE

Baron de Montesquieu once observed that not much probity is needed for maintaining or sustaining a monarchial government or a despotic government, adding, "But in a popular state, one more recourse is necessary, which is virtue."[78] For Montesquieu, virtue meant a love of one's country *and* equality, labeling political virtue as "the spring which sets the republican government in motion."[79] Those possessing virtue, Montesquieu maintained, were honest individuals who were faithful to the laws of their country. In a 2022 address, Attorney General Merrick Garland summoned the spirit of Montesquieu, telling a gathering of immigrants who had just sworn an oath to become American citizens: "The responsibility to ensure the Rule of Law is and has been the duty of every generation in our country's history. It is now your duty as well. And it is especially urgent today at a time of intense polarization in America."[80] Garland warned that adherence to the law "demands that we tolerate peaceful disagreement with one another on issues of politics and policy. It demands that we listen to each other, even when we disagree. And it demands that we reject violence and threats of violence that endanger our democracy."[81]

Montesquieu believed that when virtue dissipates, laws are undone, and the once glorious republic becomes a cesspool of intrigue and corruption. In this environment, ambition becomes paramount and "avarice possesses the whole community."[82] Montesquieu warned that political virtue was a historical rarity: "Ambition in idleness; meanness mixed with pride; a desire of riches without industry; aversion to truth; flattery, perfidy, violation of engagements, contempt of civil duties, fear of the prince's virtue; hope from his weakness, but above all, a perpetual ridicule cast upon virtue; are, I think, the characteristics by which most courtiers in all ages and countries have been constantly distinguished."[83]

Virtue is often equated with honesty and truth. But truth was something with which Donald Trump was entirely unfamiliar, and his daily lying became a feature of his presidency. The *Washington Post* uncovered more than thirty thousand lies Trump told during his four years in office, an average of twenty-one per day.[84] As Jonathan Lemire reminds us, Trump lied about many things: his sex life; his wealth; how many times he was on the cover of *Time* magazine; his television ratings; Barack Obama's place of birth; his claim to having witnessed Muslims rejoicing after the collapse of the World Trade Center on 9/11; and that Vladimir Putin once called him a "genius."[85] Steve Bannon, who for a time acted as Trump's chief political strategist, told White House aides, "Trump would say anything, he would lie about anything to win that moment."[86] Trump's lies were not meant merely to glorify himself but served to undermine the legitimacy of our institutions. Refusing to see himself as a loser, Trump declared that any defeat was automatically illegitimate, thereby making the democratic process itself suspect. For example, in 2016, he told attendees at a rally in Columbus, Ohio: "I'm afraid the election is going to be rigged. I have to be honest."[87] Trump declared he would "totally accept the results of this great election," but paused dramatically to add, "If I win."[88] Trump ally Roger Stone threatened to lead an effort to shut down the government if Trump lost, angrily proclaiming, "We will not stand for it."[89] For Trump, even winning the Electoral College wasn't enough; he falsely claimed in 2016, "I won the popular vote if you deduct the millions of people who voted illegally."[90] In a speech at the Hinckley Institute of Politics in Utah, Mitt Romney summoned John Winthrop's imagery to declare that a Trump presidency "would mean that America would cease to be a shining city on a hill."[91] In 2020, House impeachment manager Adam Schiff said of Trump: "He has betrayed our national security, and he will do so again. He has compromised our elections, and he will do so again. You will not change him. You cannot constrain him. He is who he is. Truth matters little to him. What's right matters even less, and decency matters not at all."[92] Virtue was hardly a quality associated with Donald Trump, and his lack of decency and the alternative realities he created led Joe Biden to accuse Trump and his fellow Republicans of engaging in a form of "semi-fascism."[93] In 1938, Yale professor Halford E. Luccock warned that if fascism came to America it would be wrapped in a flag and carrying a cross: "The high-sounding phrase 'the American way' will be used by interested groups, intent on profit, to cover a multitude of sins against the American and Christian tradition, such sins as lawless violence, tear gas and shotguns, denial of civil liberties."[94]

THE UNRAVELING

On the eve of the 1940 election, Franklin D. Roosevelt took to the airwaves to address his fellow countrymen. World War II had already struck

Europe and was threatening to advance onto American shores. Roosevelt acknowledged that while the nation remained at peace, bombs were falling on not-too-distant lands. Casting politics aside for the moment, Roosevelt offered this prayer:

> Almighty God, who hast given us this good land for our heritage; we humbly beseech Thee that we may always prove ourselves a people mindful of Thy favor and glad to do Thy will. Bless our land with honorable industry, sound learning, and pure manners. Save us from violence, discord, and confusion; from pride and arrogancy, and from every evil way. Defend our liberties, and fashion into one united people the multitudes brought hither out of many kindreds and tongues. Endue with the spirit of wisdom those to whom in Thy Name we entrust the authority of government, that there may be justice and peace at home, and that, through obedience to Thy law, we may show forth Thy praise among the nations of the earth. In the time of prosperity, fill our hearts with thankfulness, and in the day of trouble, suffer not our trust in Thee to fail.[95]

Roosevelt would win that election, just as he had beaten the Republicans in two previous contests. But as the next chapter describes, Republican presidential campaigns of the 1930s and 1940s contained signs of a desperate party that was increasingly willing to blame its losses on devious Democrats and had begun to create its own alternative realities that eventually threatened our democracy's continued existence. Roosevelt's political successes began an unraveling of our nation's democratic strands whose unspooling would undermine the delicate instruments of governance that the Constitution's framers had so carefully constructed. Levitsky and Ziblatt warn that such assaults often begin slowly, even imperceptibly, and "each individual step seems minor—none appears to truly threaten democracy."[96] At first, Republicans were hardly perceived to be a threat. After all, voters in the 1930s and 1940s rejected Republican candidates despite the party's claims that those elections lacked legitimacy. And each time, those losing candidates accepted defeat, despite claims made by some Republican partisans that Democratic policies and behind-the-scenes maneuvering rigged those contests in the Democrats' favor. In 1944, Thomas E. Dewey graciously conceded to Franklin D. Roosevelt, telling his ardent followers that "every good American will wholeheartedly accept the will of the American people."[97]

But with each assault on our institutions, combined with a desperation to win, the Republican Party tolerated conspiracy theories that had taken hold among its key constituencies. And when Republicans finally won the presidency, they helped create an enlarged executive office free of the constraints that a party might impose—a project begun by Franklin D. Roosevelt. In so doing, Republicans ignored Dwight Eisenhower's warning that any political party "deserves the approbation of America only as it represents the ideals, the aspirations, and the hopes of Americans. If it is anything less, it is merely a conspiracy to seize power."[98] Today, the Republican Party is a cult of personality whose leader is determined to seize power at whatever cost. Former House Speaker John Boehner concedes the obvious: "There is no Republican Party. There is a Trump Party.... The Republican Party is taking a nap somewhere."[99] Patrick J. Buchanan happily concluded that the Republican establishment "bends the knee to Caesar."[100] Such bending has already placed the judiciary under assault. Judge Amy Berman Jackson observes that Trump's lies about the 2020 election have become a litmus test for high-ranking Republican members of Congress and state officials who are "so afraid of losing their power."[101] The threats of violence perpetrated on elected officials and members of the judiciary are such that Jackson believes the judiciary "has to make it clear: It is not patriotism, it is not standing up for America to stand up for one man—who knows full well that he lost—instead of the Constitution he was trying to subvert."[102] Yascha Mounk, a political scientist at Johns Hopkins University, believes the crisis has metastasized to a point that, come 2024, for the first time in US history, a legitimately elected president will not assume office.[103] Eisenhower's prophetic warning that the Republican Party must never become a conspiracy to seize power has come to pass.

While many saw Donald Trump's 2020 defeat as ending the dangers posed to our democracy, the dangers persist. During his first meeting with foreign leaders as president, Joe Biden declared, "America is back," only to hear President Emmanuel Macron of France exclaim, "For how long?"[104]

2. A Broken Party, 1932–1952

My Dutch is up.

—Franklin D. Roosevelt, 1932

During the opening years of the twentieth century, the Republican Party became accustomed to wielding power. With the sole exception of the Woodrow Wilson presidency, Republicans routinely controlled the White House and virtually all other levers of power. William McKinley began the new century as president, having engineered a political realignment that turned the Republican Party into an electoral powerhouse. Rather than winning by close margins, which had so often been the case after the Civil War, Republicans swamped their vastly outnumbered Democratic opponents. When the McKinley realignment began in 1896, he received 51 percent of the popular vote (the highest percentage since Ulysses S. Grant won reelection in 1872), carried every swing state, and flipped ten states won by Democrat Grover Cleveland just four years earlier.[1] Wielding power became natural for a party accustomed to having it. George W. Bush strategist Karl Rove noted that by 1896 the Republican Party was no longer a "shrinking and beleaguered organization" but instead had become a "frothy, diverse coalition of owners and workers, longtime Americans and new citizens, lifetime Republicans and fresh converts drawn together by common beliefs and allegiances."[2] The GOP became so powerful that between 1896 and 1932 it held the White House for twenty-eight of those thirty-six years, the Senate for thirty, and the House for twenty-six.[3] Only when former president Theodore Roosevelt bolted the party in 1912 did the Republicans temporarily relinquish their hold on the presidency.

Herbert Hoover's victory over Al Smith in 1928 followed what had become the familiar pattern. In the national popular vote, Hoover bested Smith by a two-to-one margin and won forty states to Smith's eight. Smith, a Roman Catholic, even lost part of the so-called Solid South to Hoover. The aftermath of the Hoover landslide saw Republicans holding three hundred seats in the House and fifty-nine in the Senate, comfortable majorities by any measure.[4] In many ways, 1928 was the zenith of the Republican Party's grasp on power. Accepting his party's accolades at the

1928 Republican National Convention, Hoover declared, "We shall soon with the help of God be in sight of the day when poverty will be banished from this nation."[5] Standing triumphantly on the inaugural platform a few months later, Hoover proclaimed that "in no nation are the fruits of accomplishment more secure."[6]

A PARTY IN CRISIS

The Great Depression upended this natural Republican majority. Four months into the crisis, Hoover maintained that "all evidence indicates that the worst effect of the crash will have been passed within the next sixty days."[7] Such happy talk flew in the face of a devastating economic reality. Even in the earliest days of the Great Depression, some Republicans embraced the idea that there was a subterranean plot to remove them from power. In 1930, Simeon D. Fess, chair of the Republican National Committee, claimed that "persons high in Republican circles are beginning to believe that there is some concerted effort on foot to utilize the stock market as a method of discrediting the Administration. . . . Every time an Administration official gives out an optimistic statement about business conditions, the market immediately drops."[8]

When Democrats gathered in 1932, anticipation of victory was rampant even as pundits declared their nominee, Franklin D. Roosevelt, to be an affable, but weak, standard-bearer. Journalist H. L. Mencken said, "Here was a great convention nominating the weakest candidate before it,"[9] concluding that the Democrats remained hell-bent "to carry on their quadrennial suicide pact."[10] Columnist Walter Lippmann was equally critical: "Franklin D. Roosevelt is no crusader. He is no tribune of the people. He is no enemy of entrenched privilege. He is a pleasant man who, without any important qualifications for the office, would very much like to be President."[11] FDR was determined to prove the critics wrong, breaking with precedent to personally accept his party's nomination. But aside from hearing his promises of a "new deal for the American people,"[12] no one knew how Roosevelt would translate his hyperbole into reality.

But Roosevelt's platitudes hardly mattered. By 1932, industrial production had fallen by 53 percent, and one-third of the electorate was without either work or regular income.[13] In New York City, one million people were unemployed; in Akron, Ohio, 60 percent of the workforce could not find jobs; and in Donora, Pennsylvania, near Pittsburgh, just 277 out of 14,000 workers received regular paychecks.[14] New York City public schools closed because the city could not afford to pay its teachers, and in Chicago public libraries could not purchase a single book.[15] African Americans, whose loyalties to the Republican Party had been cemented by the Civil War, began to question their partisan roots. Robert L. Vann, editor of the influential *Pittsburgh Courier*, encouraged his largely African American readership to vote for Roosevelt, saying, "I see millions of Negroes turning the picture of Lincoln to the wall."[16] But for one last time, the old tribal loyalties still prevailed. One study showed Roosevelt receiving 23 percent of the Black vote in Chicago while another had FDR getting 29 percent of the Black vote in Cincinnati.[17] While accurate data are hard to ascertain in an era before polling, this would be the last time Republicans would win the Black vote in a presidential election. The Republican Party that once championed African American suffrage would no longer claim the loyalties of its most faithful supporters.

Accepting his renomination, Hoover told Republican delegates that the country had experienced "a great and unparalleled shock."[18] That "shock" would be enough to sink any incumbent president. Hoover realized this, privately admitting, "I'll tell you what our trouble is—we are opposed by six million unemployed, ten thousand bonus marchers, and ten cent corn."[19] Trying to make himself oblivious to the economic blight, Hoover was even quoted as saying, "Many people have left their jobs for the more profitable one of selling apples."[20] Back then, the best public opinion polls were taken on the streets or in the voting booths. And on the streets Hoover's unpopularity was such that it was unsafe for him to campaign in person. In Detroit, for example, mounted police were required to ensure his safety.[21]

Smart politicos advised Roosevelt to lie back and wait, telling him the election was in the bag. Long before James Carville coined the maxim "It's the economy, stupid!," the Great Depression sealed Hoover's fate and began a two-decade GOP expulsion from the White House. Three years of economic pain—in some parts of the country even longer than that—caused the hapless Hoover to complain that he, too, wanted to turn the corner to economic prosperity. Roosevelt charged that Hoover "refused to recognize and correct the evils at home...delayed relief...[and]

forgot reform."[22] Hoover dismissed Roosevelt's accusations and vividly described him as "a chameleon on plaid."[23] A Roosevelt victory, Hoover warned, would "enslave" taxpayers with a "soak the rich program" that would "crack the timbers of the Constitution."[24]

A RESURGENT DEMOCRATIC PARTY

A feisty Hoover aroused Roosevelt's anger. Ignoring the advice of his advisers to relax and enjoy the inevitable victory, FDR told Democratic national chair James Farley, "My Dutch is up."[25] It was an angry sentiment that Roosevelt, like clockwork, would employ again and again and again as if on cue every four years. Whether it was to decry the despondent Hoover, or employ class warfare against Alf Landon, or correct the falsehoods uttered by Wendell Willkie and Thomas Dewey, Roosevelt's ire not only aroused the Democratic faithful but provoked Republicans to the point of despair. The only president to win four straight victories, all by comfortable margins each time, earned him the nickname "the Champ." Roosevelt's quadruple wins were followed by one more: the surprisingly victorious Harry Truman in 1948.

The power of the New Deal coalition fashioned by FDR is shown in table 2.1. Over five presidential elections, Democrats won 56 percent of the popular vote and 83 percent of the electoral votes cast. Republicans captured 44 percent of the popular votes and only 17 percent of the Electoral College ballots—consistent routs by any measure.

The sheer size and scope of the Democratic Party's dominance was evident in the 1932 election results. Not only did Franklin Roosevelt win forty-two states and 472 electoral votes, but Democrats also captured overwhelming congressional majorities. In the House of Representatives, there were just 117 Republicans ready to oppose 313 Democrats. The Senate seated just 36 Republicans while 59 Democrats took their places. Four years later, Roosevelt enjoyed an even larger victory, winning every state save for Maine and Vermont and amassing 523 electoral votes, an Electoral College sweep that would be unmatched until Ronald Reagan's reelection romp in 1984. By 1936, the Democratic margins in Congress grew to unprecedented levels. In the House, Democrats captured 333 seats to the Republicans' 89. In the Senate, there were 75 Democrats arrayed against

Table 2.1 A Broken Republican Party, 1932–1948

Election	Democratic Vote Popular	Democratic Vote Electoral	Republican Vote Popular	Republican Vote Electoral
1932	22,821,857	477	15,761,841	59
1936	27,751,597	523	16,679,583	8
1940	27,243,466	449	22,304,755	82
1944	25,602,504	432	22,006,285	99
1948	24,105,812	303	21,970,065	189
Total	127,525,236	2,179	98,722,529	437
Percentage	56	83	44	17

17 Republicans. Democrats so flooded the floors of Congress that there wasn't enough room for them to sit on their traditional sides of the aisles.

Seeking an unprecedented third term in 1940, Roosevelt again dominated both the popular and the electoral vote counts, leading Democrats to joyfully use a baseball metaphor and declare FDR "safe on third."[26] A final fourth term saw Roosevelt again dominate, although Republicans posted a somewhat better showing. Each time, Roosevelt got "his Dutch up," denouncing his last Republican opponent, Thomas E. Dewey, as a "son of a bitch."[27]

1936 SETS THE TERMS OF DEBATE

For twenty years, the White House doors were locked to the Republican Party. The GOP tried everything to pick the electoral lock, literally swerving from one failed strategy to another. After Hoover was soundly beaten by Franklin Roosevelt, Republicans nominated Kansas governor Alf Landon for president. Even though the Depression continued to ravage the country, Republicans were apoplectic, seeing the New Deal and its vast government programs as an existential threat to American democracy and constitutional government. Addressing the 1936 Republican National Convention former president Herbert Hoover challenged the delegates: "Will you, for expediency's sake ... offer will-o'-the-wisps which beguile the people? Or have you determined to enter into a holy crusade for liberty which shall determine the future and the perpetuity of a nation of free men?"[28] To shouts of "NO!" and "YES!," Republicans nominated Landon, who echoed their cries and assailed the "folly" and "boon-doggling" of Roosevelt's New Deal.[29] He derided the new Social Security law as "unjust, unworkable, stupidly drafted, and wastefully financed," later adding that any continuation of the "New Deal policies would lead to the guillotine."[30] The Republican platform was equally apoplectic, declaring that Roosevelt had usurped the constitutional powers given to Congress and threatened the integrity of the Supreme Court. The writers ominously concluded:

> America is in peril. The welfare of the American men and women and the future of our youth are at stake. We dedicate ourselves to the preservation of their political liberty, their individual opportunity, and their character as free citizens, which today for the first time are threatened by government itself.... We pledge ourselves to maintain the American system of Constitutional and local self-government [and] to preserve the American system of free enterprise, private competition, and equality of opportunity, and to seek its constant betterment in the interests of all.[31]

The party faithful agreed. When asked by the Gallup Organization in 1936 whether "the acts and policies of the Roosevelt administration may lead to a dictatorship," 83 percent of Republicans said yes; only 9 percent of Democrats concurred.[32] Repeatedly, Republicans asserted that Roosevelt was in league with the dictatorial communists. A 1936 headline in the conservative *Chicago Tribune* read, "Moscow Orders Reds in the U.S. to Back Roosevelt."[33] Roosevelt countered that it was Republicans who were promoting communism thanks to their disastrous economic policies.[34] This would not be the first time that one party would charge that victory by the other would end American democracy. But, as in 2020, when the Republicans actively sought to overturn a legitimate election, this particular accusation had little merit. Roosevelt was not in league with domestic communists and viewed the Republicans' overwrought rhetoric as a ruse designed to scare voters.

When he assumed the presidency, Roosevelt noted, "All our great Presidents were leaders of thought at times when certain historic ideas in the life of the nation had to be clarified."[35] For Roosevelt, that meant a much more active role for the federal government in the lives of ordinary, poor Americans, with the presidency as the center of action. Launching his New Deal programs, Roosevelt declared his intention to act: "I shall ask the Congress for the one remaining instrument to meet the crisis—broad Executive power to wage a war against the emergency, as great as the power that would be given to me if we were in fact invaded by a foreign foe."[36] These inaugural words were met with thunderous applause, and throughout his remaining presidential campaigns Roosevelt cast himself as the defender of the little guy. In his 1936 campaign against Landon, Roosevelt liked to tell of New York City subway riders who wore FDR buttons when they entered the subway but substituted them for Landon pins once they approached Wall Street.[37] That year, Roosevelt happily enlisted his fellow Democrats in a crusade against the rich and powerful, giving a memorable speech at Madison Square Garden in which he stated:

> For twelve years our Nation was afflicted with hear nothing, see nothing, do-nothing Government. The Nation looked to that Government, but that Government looked away. Nine mocking years with the golden calf and three long years of the scourge. Nine crazy years at the ticker and three long years in the breadlines. Nine mad years of mirage and three long years of despair. And, my friends, powerful influences strive today to restore that kind of government with its doctrine that that Government is best which is most indifferent to mankind.
>
> Never before in all our history have these forces been so united against one candidate as they stand today. They are unanimous in their *hate* for *me—and I welcome their hatred.*
>
> I should like to have it said of my first Administration that in it the forces of selfishness and of lust for power met their *match*. I should like to have it said of my second Administration that *in it these forces met their master.*[38]

The historian James MacGregor Burns wrote that when Roosevelt uttered these words "a raucous, almost animal-like roar burst from the crowd, died away, and then rose again in wave after wave."[39]

When the votes were counted, FDR won approximately five million more ballots than he received the first time around and accumulated the largest electoral majority given to any presidential candidate since 1820.[40] Big cities were key to FDR's victory: from 1928 to 1936, the Democratic vote in New York increased from 60 percent to 75 percent; in Chicago, 48 percent to 65 percent; in Philadelphia, 39 percent to 60 percent; and in Los Angeles, 28 percent to 67 percent.[41] Landon was lambasted as a hapless loser, but Republicans blamed the voters, saying they had been "bought" by the programs of the New Deal.⁴² Surveying the electoral wipeout, Landon likened it to a Kansas cyclone that left a farmer and his wife standing on bare ground. When the farmer started laughing and his wife asked why, he replied, "The completeness of it."⁴³ The *Albany Times Union* put it this way: "It is very difficult to analyze a tornado. Particularly so, when the ground is covered by debris, left in the wrack of the storm."⁴⁴ But what is often overlooked is that Landon actually *won* approximately one million more votes than Hoover did four years earlier. However, like Barack Obama in 2008, Franklin D. Roosevelt was a polarizing figure who, in 1936, galvanized more than seven million new voters to come to the polls.⁴⁵ Among those whom Roosevelt won over were African Americans who benefited from his New Deal programs and turned out for him large numbers. In 1936, 71 percent of African Americans cast a ballot for FDR, even though just 44 percent called themselves Democrats.⁴⁶ This would, of course, change over the decades, as African Americans aligned their party identifications with their presidential votes. After Lyndon B. Johnson signed the Civil Rights Act of 1964 and the Voting Rights Act of 1965, the Republican voting percentage among African Americans dwindled into the low double digits. While the political conversion of African Americans did not pose an immediate threat to Republicans, nearly a century later, as the country approached majority-minority status, Republicans remained a mostly all-white party. Absent a greater appeal to minority voters, this posed an existential threat to the party's future electoral prospects.

A DESPERATE PARTY TRIES SOMETHING NEW

Following Landon's overwhelming defeat, Republican senator William Borah called on Republicans to try something new, saying, "I don't think there is room in this country for an old conservative party," and adding, "People can't eat the Constitution."⁴⁷ Enough Republicans agreed, and by 1940 the GOP embarked on a new course by taking the unusual step of nominating a former Democrat and FDR supporter, Wendell Willkie, for the presidency. Willkie had been a delegate to the contentious 1924 Democratic National Convention, voted for FDR in 1932,⁴⁸ and called himself a Democrat until 1938.⁴⁹ Saying he was anxious to meet "the Champ,"⁵⁰

Willkie cultivated a cultish following that bypassed the Republican establishment and was powerful enough in an already weakened party to capture the nomination. Richard Nixon and Gerald Ford became Willkie fans, and Nixon campaigned extensively for him in 1940.[51] Despite his newfound party affiliation, Willkie remained estranged from longtime Republicans, once beginning a campaign address with the words "You Republicans."[52] In many ways, the Willkie phenomenon was replicated in 2016, this time with Donald Trump.

Attempting to accommodate the party to Roosevelt's revolution, Willkie promised to maintain (and even improve) the New Deal programs instituted by Roosevelt. The 1940 platform pledged to expand old-age benefits on a "pay-as-you-go" basis, supported extending unemployment compensation under the Social Security Act, and even pledged to support organized labor's right to organize and engage in collective bargaining.[53] Willkie echoed these pledges: "There is no issue between the third term candidate and myself on the questions of old age pensions, unemployment insurance, collective bargaining, laws which guarantee minimum wages and prohibit men working more than so many hours per week, or the elimination of child labor and the retention of federal relief. I am not alone for all these laws, but I will advocate their improvement and reinforcement."[54]

Roosevelt mocked the Republican Party's conversion to progressive thinking. Speaking before a Democratic rally in Philadelphia, he declared: "These same Republican leaders are all for the new progressive measures now; they believe in them so much that they will never be happy until they can clasp them to their own chests and put their own brand upon them. If they could only get control of them, they plead, they would take so much better care of them, honest-to-goodness they would."[55]

A CAMPAIGN OF LIES AND CONSPIRACY THEORIES

Willkie got Roosevelt's "Dutch up" by insinuating that the president was plotting the United States' entry into World War II. He charged that Roosevelt's promise "to keep our boys out of foreign wars is no better than his promise to balance the budget, they're already almost on the transports."[56] Willkie recklessly maintained that Roosevelt had precipitated the war by telephoning "Hitler and Mussolini and urged them to sell Czechoslovakia down the river," charging that in so doing FDR "courted a war for which the country is hopelessly unprepared" and "emphatically does not want."[57] Willkie added that if Roosevelt was reelected, "You will be serving under an American totalitarian government before the long third term is finished."[58]

This prompted a tart response from Roosevelt that has echoes in today's unhappy present. Saying he was "fighting mad,"[59] Roosevelt told a rally of Philadelphia Democrats: "Truthful campaign discussion of public issues is essential to the American form of Government," but, he added, "Willful misrepresentation of fact has no place either during election time or at any other time."[60] Besides his reputed phone calls to Hitler and Mussolini, Roosevelt's list of "willful" Republican misrepresentations pointed out that "the unfortunate unemployed of the nation are going to be driven into concentration camps"; "the Social Security funds of the Government of the United States will not be in existence when the workers of today become old enough to apply for them"; and "the election of the present Government means the end of American democracy within four years."[61] Roosevelt added a prescient warning about an increasingly desperate Republican Party:

> Certain techniques of propaganda, created and developed in dictator countries, have been imported into this campaign. It is the very simple technique of repeating and repeating and repeating falsehoods, with the idea that by constant repetition and reiteration, with no contradiction, the misstatements will finally come to be believed.
>
> Dictators have had great success in using this technique; but only because they were able to control the press and the radio, and to stifle all opposition. This is why I cannot bring myself to believe that in a democracy like ours, where the radio and a party of the press . . . remain open to both sides, repetition of deliberate misstatements will ever prevail.
>
> I make the charge now that those falsifications are being spread for the purpose of filling the minds and the hearts of the American people with fear. They are used to create fear by instilling in the minds of our people doubt of each other, doubt of their Government, and doubt of the purposes of their democracy.[62]

Roosevelt's anger and sarcasm produced the desired result. Despite having traveled some nineteen thousand miles and giving approximately five hundred speeches in thirty-one states, Wilkie decisively lost.⁶³ Roosevelt outpaced Willkie by nearly five million votes and captured 449 electors to Willkie's 82. Thirty-eight states fell into the Roosevelt column compared with just ten for Willkie. Speaking to dejected supporters on Election Night, Willkie told them, "Don't be afraid and never quit."⁶⁴ But the Republican experiment with nominating a "me-too" candidate failed, leaving what historian Louis Gould described as a "permanent grievance" within the party's conservative base.⁶⁵ Willkie was never at home in the Republican Party, and by 1944 he even considered leaving it. In secret discussions with Roosevelt's advisers, Willkie supported forming a liberal alliance that would drive conservative southerners out of the Democratic Party and liberal Republicans from the GOP. Together with Roosevelt he hoped to construct a two-party system that would be purely divided along liberal and conservative lines, thereby creating a party government without the usual internal bickering. Roosevelt said he "100 percent" agreed with Willkie that the United States should have "two real parties."⁶⁶ But Willkie died suddenly before these talks could progress further, and the United States' entry into World War II made any such prospects of a party reorganization remote.

1944: ONCE MORE, WITH FEELING

By 1944, Roosevelt had transformed himself from Dr. New Deal into Dr. Win the War. That year, Roosevelt told Democratic delegates: "The people of the United States will decide this Fall whether they wish to turn over this 1944 job—this worldwide job—to inexperienced and immature hands . . . or whether they wish to leave it to those who saw the danger from abroad, who met it head on, and who now have seized the offensive and carried the war to its present stages of success."⁶⁷ Republicans countered that Roosevelt was a tired old man who believed he was "indispensable."⁶⁸ Journalist Anne O'Hare McCormick wrote that Republican convention attendees thought that "the old, tired, bureaucratic, and divided minds of the Democrats" would be replaced with "the fresh, eager, resourceful, and harmonious direction of the Republicans."⁶⁹ To make this a reality, Republicans selected the popular governor of New York, Thomas E. Dewey. Dewey was something of a political phenomenon who came close to defeating Democrat Herbert Lehman for governor in 1938.[70] Four years later he won a resounding victory, besting his hapless Democratic opponent by nearly 650,000 votes.[71] *Time* magazine described him as a "dragon slayer";[72] the Democratic National Committee labeled him "one of the best [politicians] in the country."[73]

With the imprimatur of the political pros, Dewey led a unified Republican Party against "the Champ." But behind the scenes Republicans emerged from their 1944 convention in a sour, defeatist mood. Hard-core conservatives who detested FDR still dominated the party machinery, and they were bitter that their choice, Robert Taft, nicknamed "Mr. Conservative," did not seek the nomination, conceding that Roosevelt skillfully cut "the ground from under our feet."[74] Dewey, however, did not share the defeatist mood, telling a friend, "Don't you realize that Franklin Roosevelt is the easiest man in the world for me to beat?"[75] To prove his point, Dewey accused Roosevelt of having "failed for eight straight years to restore our domestic economy . . . [leading] the most wasteful, extravagant, and incompetent administration in the history of the nation," and claimed Roosevelt had "lost faith in the American people."[76]

A campaign memo cowritten by Prescott Bush, father of George H. W. Bush, reached a similar conclusion and advised Dewey never to "get involved in the opposition's campaign or ever be put on the defensive."[77] The Republican National Committee echoed Bush's advice, publishing a sixty-three-page booklet titled *What to Talk About*, advising Republicans that "every speech should be an *attack* speech."[78] But rather than attacking Roosevelt's New Deal, Dewey avoided the subject and instead declared that "government must be the means by which our people, working together, seek to meet the problems that are too big for any one of us or any group to solve individually."[79] Conservatives, including Taft, were not pleased—an indication of future fights to come within the Republican Party. As early as 1944, one can trace the development of an intraparty split that would divide the Republicans in 1952 and crest with the rise of Barry Goldwater in 1964.

Like FDR's previous opponents, Dewey aroused Roosevelt's ire. As FDR confidentially told his son James, "I'm going right after Dewey and make this a real campaign."[80] Roosevelt likened himself to a cat, saying, "I make a quick stroke and then I relax."[81] In 1944, that quick stroke came before an address to the Teamsters Union. Resorting to his old standby that Republicans were progressives in name only once every four years, Roosevelt charged that Dewey's new tune when it came to the New Deal could be summarized in a single sentence: "What the Republican leaders are now saying in effect is this: 'Oh just forget what we used to say, we have changed our minds now; we have been reading the public opinion polls about these things and now we know what the American people want.'"[82] With words that echo in the present, Roosevelt launched an assault on the Republican Party, charging that it was, once more, repeating falsehoods whose mere repetitions would be accepted as truisms by a gullible public:

> The opposition in this year has already imported into this campaign a very interesting thing, because it is foreign. They have imported the propaganda technique invented by dictators abroad. Remember, a number of years ago, there was a book, *Mein Kampf*, written by Hitler himself. The technique was all set out in Hitler's book, and it was copied by the aggressors of Italy and Japan. According to that technique, you should never use a small falsehood; always a big one, for its very fantastic nature would make it more credible, if only you keep repeating it over and over and over again. Well, let us take some simple illustrations that come to mind. For example, although I rubbed my eyes when I read it, we have been told that it was not a Republican depression, but a Democratic depression from which this nation was saved in 1933; that this administration—this one today—is responsible for all the suffering and misery that the history books and the American people have always thought had been brought about during the twelve ill-fated years when the Republican Party was in power.[83]

Speaking before a national radio audience, Roosevelt then delivered the coup de grace:

> These Republican leaders have not been content with attacks on me, or my wife, or on my sons. No, not content with that, they now include my little dog, Fala. Well, of course, I don't resent attacks, and my family doesn't resent attacks, but Fala does resent them. You know, Fala is Scotch, and being a Scottie, as soon as he learned that the Republican fiction writers, in Congress and out, had concocted a story that I had left him behind on the Aleutian Islands and had sent a destroyer back to find him—at a cost to the taxpayers of two, or three, or eight, or twenty million dollars—his Scotch soul was furious. He has not been the same dog since.[84]

James MacGregor Burns wrote that the Fala speech was "a dagger thrust ... the blade lovingly fashioned and honed."[85] Presidential assistant Bill Hassett heard these words and remarked that, once again, Roosevelt "got his Dutch up."[86]

As he had done three times previously, FDR emerged triumphant, winning thirty-six of the forty-eight states and 432 electoral votes to Dewey's 99. George H. W. Bush's prediction that the "southern boys will support Roosevelt" came true; as Bush also commented, "The ones I've talked with seem to think he's some sort of a god."[87] Roosevelt carried every state of the Old Confederacy with ease. Even the hotly contested 47 electoral votes of New York were, once more, won by Roosevelt. *Time* magazine said of the result: "It was Franklin Roosevelt in a walkover. His popular percentage was a shade lower than 1940, his electoral college vote a smashing victory. Once the returns began pouring in, there was no doubt."[88] Dewey, meanwhile, took some solace in knowing that Roosevelt's popular vote margin was cut to 54 percent, and that Dewey won the hometowns of the Roosevelt-Truman ticket: Hyde Park, New York, and Independence, Missouri.[89] Dewey emerged from defeat as the odds-on favorite in 1948 and, many believed, would finally unlock the White House doors for the GOP.

1948: THE GOP CRISIS DEEPENS

Nineteen forty-eight started out as a surefire Republican year. Two years before, Republicans had seized control of Congress, a startling comeback after the devastating defeats the party suffered during the 1930s. Republicans emerged from the 1946 midterm elections with a six-seat majority in the Senate and a fifty-five-seat plurality in the House. Suburban America, which would eventually become a bedrock of GOP strength, swung mightily toward the Republicans, including the outlying areas of Philadelphia, Detroit, New York City, and Chicago.[90] Moreover, Harry Truman was president, and he was no FDR. Republicans excoriated Truman as the product of a corrupt Democratic machine in Kansas City. Although Truman received accolades following the defeats of Germany and Japan, soaring to an astronomical 87 percent approval rating in the Gallup poll,[91] he fell victim to labor strikes, meat shortages, and the difficult transition from a wartime to a peacetime economy. A popular euphemism was "To err is Truman." By November 1946, Truman's job approval had fallen to 34 percent.[92] Two years later, Claire Booth Luce declared he was "a gone goose" whose "time is short; his situation is hopeless."[93] The 1948 Republican platform summarized the party's case: "We shall waste few words on the tragic lack of foresight and general inadequacy of those now in charge of the Executive Branch of the National Government; they have lost the confidence of citizens of all parties."[94]

Democrats were so despondent that nineteen leaders sought to dump Truman in favor of Dwight D. Eisenhower, including Franklin Roosevelt's sons, James, Elliot, and Franklin Jr., with James Roosevelt urging the Democratic delegates to nominate the "ablest, strongest man available."[95] Jersey City Democratic boss Frank Hague endorsed Eisenhower, saying: "The public will not get world leadership in either Truman or the Republican candidate. General Eisenhower led us to victory through the greatest war in history, and we want him back to complete the job."[96] Unlike its coverage of past Democratic conventions, the *New York Times* reported that the delegates entered into "an atmosphere of gloom and despondency and encountered a spirit of defeatism among party leaders already here that amounted to a confession that President Truman seemed to have little chance of election."[97] Truman adviser Clark Clifford ruefully observed, "We've got our backs on the one-yard line with a minute to play."[98]

Once more, Republicans nominated Thomas E. Dewey. Although Dewey lost to Roosevelt four years before, Republicans believed he had run a gallant campaign in the face of insuperable odds. Dewey himself was optimistic, proclaiming that the Republican Party had moved beyond its defeatist attitude: "Sixteen years in the wilderness transforms a party . . . great things happen to its soul as well as to its membership and its ideals."[99] Seeking to quell any dissent, Dewey took a shot at the conservatives, including Robert Taft, his erstwhile rival for the nomination: "There remain, of course, those who would like to restore the dim, departed, almost forgotten and surely never to be recovered past."[100] Dewey's confidence was echoed by the opinion polls, journalists, and politicos alike. *Time* magazine wrote that the Dewey-Warren ticket was "so photogenic, so confident, so politically winning . . . that [it] could not fail to sweep the Republican Party back into power."[101] The final Gallup poll conducted in October showed Dewey at 50 percent and Truman at 45 percent.[102] The publishers of *Who's Who in America* were so certain of a Dewey win that they sent the Republican candidate its 1949 edition listing his address as 1600 Pennsylvania Avenue, Washington, DC.[103] Dewey himself remained supremely confident: "I will be president. It is written in the stars."[104]

But there were signs that all was not well. Herbert Brownell, who Dewey installed as Republican national chair, recalled that he found the party's national organization "in a shambles."[105] The previous chair, Harold Spangler of Iowa, was a man in his seventies, and he, like many of his colleagues, was wedded to the policies of the Harding, Coolidge, and Hoover years. Another sign of trouble came from a survey commissioned by Dewey that showed the Republican Party remained in a weakened state. Pollster Claude Robinson concluded the Republicans "must find fresh, vigorous righteous appeals to recruit youth or their long-term outlook is bearish."[106]

Charging ahead, Truman hit the stump, campaigning against Republicans who, he blamed, had fostered the Great Depression. Calling labor and farmers "the most ungrateful people in the world" if they did not vote for the Democratic ticket, Truman appealed to their self-interest.[107] In a speech to Iowa farmers, Truman crystallized his argument:

> You remember that in 1932 the position of the farmer had become so desperate that there was actual violence in farming communities. You remember that insurance companies and banks took over much of the land of small independent farmers—223,000 farmers lost their farms. . . . I wonder how many times you have to be hit on the head before you find out what is hitting you? The Democratic Party represents the people. . . . These Republican gluttons of privilege are cold men. They are cunning men. . . . They want a return of Wall Street economic dictatorship.[108]

By the end of the campaign, Truman was confident of the outcome: "Victory has become a habit of our party. It has been elected four times in succession, and I am convinced it will be elected a fifth time."[109] On Election Day, Truman was proved right, despite the universal belief that Dewey was a shoo-in. The *Wall Street Journal*'s lede that day began: "Government will remain big, active, and expensive under President Thomas E. Dewey."[110] But by early dawn the next morning it was clear that Truman was the victor. He captured twenty-eight states and 303 electoral votes, to Dewey's sixteen states and 189 electoral votes, and Strom Thurmond's

39. Adding to the stunning outcome was the Democratic Party's winning back control of Congress—adding 75 House seats, bringing the party's total to 263, and counting 11 new senators (including Lyndon B. Johnson and Hubert H. Humphrey), giving Democrats a comfortable majority of 54. Drawing some 40,000 fewer votes than he had won in 1944,[111] a shaken Dewey emerged from his hotel room and exclaimed: "What do you know? The son of a bitch won."[112] Walter Lippmann wrote that "with much justice, and without detracting from Mr. Truman's remarkable personal performance, that of all Roosevelt's electoral triumphs, this one in 1948 is the most impressive."[113]

Dewey's loss embittered Republicans. One Republican wrote to a convention delegate, "Outside of Pearl Harbor itself I do not know of another single great event that has quite so much disturbed my mental equilibrium."[114] Another wrote Dewey, "I am beginning to think we are a nation of morons, incapable of intelligent thinking."[115] An internal party study blamed the candidate, criticizing Dewey's "aloofness" and accusing him of "swallowing uncritically the Democratic propaganda."[116] Alice Roosevelt Longworth, referring to Dewey's two losing presidential campaigns, was characteristically cutting: "A souffle never rises twice."[117] Robert Taft made the case that Dewey should have argued for conservative principles; had he done so, stated Taft, "I am confident he would have won."[118] Senator Henry Cabot Lodge of Massachusetts advocated abolishing the Electoral College to give Republicans a better chance of victory, even though the party continued to lose the popular vote by sizable margins.[119] Behind Lodge's proposed reform was a realization that at no time in American history had a major party lost five straight presidential elections and survived. Although Lodge's proposal did not gain much traction, this would not be the last time Republicans would attempt to rejigger the electoral system to work to their benefit.

Either blaming the candidate or wanting to change the rules is a long-time refuge for losing parties, but hardly a remedy for what ails them. For his part, Dewey offered this prescient analysis:

> The Republican Party is split wide open. It has been split wide open for years, but we have tried to gloss over it. . . . We have in our party some fine, high-minded patriotic people who honestly oppose farm price supports, unemployment insurance, old age benefits, slum clearance, and other social

programs. These people consider these programs horrendous departures into paternalism. . . . These people believe in a laissez faire society and look back wistfully to the miscalled "good old days" of the 19th century.[120]

In a series of lectures at Princeton University in 1950, Dewey defended his pragmatic approach, saying he refused to be "against sound government action supporting such basic modern concepts as collective bargaining, minimum wages, unemployment insurance, regulation of markets for capital, old age insurance, or equal rights for all regardless of race, color, creed, or national origin."[121] He excoriated party conservatives who chastised him for supporting these programs: "They ought to go out and try to get elected in a typical American community and see what happens to them. But they ought not to do it as Republicans."[122] Unless it embarked on a different course, Dewey said, "you can bury the Republican Party as the deadest pigeon in the country," arguing it would be "a catastrophe if the party should falter now and listen to the croaking voices of reaction or isolation."[123]

Robert Taft and his fellow conservatives resented Dewey's commitment to what Dewey vaguely called "forward-looking principles," and they castigated him as a Democrat in New Deal clothing.[124] The crisis the Republican Party faced would come to the forefront at its 1952 convention. Following a tectonic battle with the conservative Taft, who most establishment Republicans and many Democrats believed could never win a national election, even as he won the hearts of the Republican faithful, Dwight D. Eisenhower would rebrand a "modern" GOP. But when Eisenhower unlocked the White House doors in 1953, he also unlocked a cult of personality, as Republican voters, accustomed to defeat, celebrated a string of presidential victories that led them to lionize their chief executives. Twenty years of defeat, discouragement, and anguish had created a culture of despair that would transform a grateful party into a subservient one. The signposts of today's Republican Party that promotes lies about "stolen elections" and defers to its presidents were already there long before Donald Trump entered the political arena.

3. The Price of Victory: Dwight Eisenhower's 1952 Campaign and the Cult of Personality

It really does feel as though we have been let out of jail, doesn't it?
—Thomas E. Dewey, 1952

The 1952 election was a pivotal one for the Republican Party. Republicans entered the year with a unique opportunity to win the presidency for the first time since 1928. Harry Truman's job approval had fallen to 22 percent, down from the stratospheric highs when he assumed office, and still remains the lowest score for any president in the history of the Gallup poll.[1] The Korean War was at a stalemate, General Douglas MacArthur had been fired by Truman to considerable outrage, and a series of minor corruption scandals beset the Truman administration. After twenty years of Democratic rule, voters wanted change. But the Republican Party was torn between its heart and its head. The heart of the party remained wedded to the conservatism of the Harding, Coolidge, and Hoover years, which exercised a powerful influence among the GOP rank and file. The head of the Republican Party was singularly focused on a golden chance to seize the presidency after twenty years in exile. The year 1952 saw a culminating battle between conservatives and pragmatists in their desire to regain power. This titanic battle culminated at that year's Republican National Convention and set the party's course for decades to come.

Ohio senator Robert A. Taft, son of former president William Howard Taft and a perennial presidential candidate, launched his candidacy as the representative of the powerful Harding/Coolidge/Hoover wing of the Republican Party. Taft was an ardent admirer of Herbert Hoover, having served on the former president's staff.[2] He and his followers were particularly aggrieved at the prior nominations of Wendell Willkie and Thomas Dewey, whom they denounced as "me-too" losers. Taft deeply resented those who wanted to "reform" the party, remembering that another reformer, Theodore Roosevelt, had denied his father a second term in 1912, and he had a devoted following that was determined not to nominate another "me-too" New Deal candidate.[3] Taft's animus toward the New Deal was long-standing. In July 1942, he wrote: "There is only one way to beat the New Deal, and that is head on. You can't outdeal them."[4] Conservative resentment about repeated GOP losses boiled over at the party's 1952 convention. Taft's campaign manager, David S. Ingalls, angrily declared that "all semblance of morality has been discarded by the Dewey-Eisenhower forces who are now engaged in a brutal pressure drive to force a Dewey candidate and a Dewey campaign down our throats."[5]

The Republican establishment was singularly focused on winning, and it had only one candidate in mind: Dwight D. Eisenhower. Eisenhower, the supreme commander of the Allied invasion of Europe during World War II, had been summoned by Harry Truman in 1951 to serve as the first supreme Allied commander in a postwar Europe. From his perch in Paris, Eisenhower watched the popular groundswell for his candidacy grow, culminating in a massive rally at Madison Square Garden that was captured on film and sent to the general. Eisenhower, who described the movie as "a real emotional experience for Mamie and me," believed the crowd reflected America's longing "for some kind of reasonable solution for her nagging, persistent, and almost terrifying problems."[6] Eisenhower had always been particularly coy about his politics, previously disavowing any presidential ambitions. Many Democrats, including Truman, had unsuccessfully courted Eisenhower to be their party's nominee in 1948.[7] Four years later, a growing coterie of Republican leaders saw Eisenhower as the only candidate who could woo disenchanted Democrats and independents, and an intense courtship of the reticent general began.

Yet Eisenhower remained elusive, writing to a friend: "The seeker is never so popular as the sought. People want what they cannot get."[8] The C. F. Moore, the town clerk in Eisenhower's boyhood town of Abilene, Kansas, told New Hampshire's attorney general, "I don't think he has any politics."[9] But the more Ike demurred, the more anxious establishment Republicans became. Henry Cabot Lodge pleaded with him to announce his candidacy. As Eisenhower recalled, Lodge offered a candid assessment of the Republican Party's past losses:

> Cabot believed that although the Republicans, during the past two decades had nominated men with a variety of political opinions and beliefs such as Governor Alfred M. Landon and Mr. Wendell Willkie, none of their candidates had been able to generate an appeal strong enough to unify the party

and at the same time attract the independent and Democratic support necessary for election. Moreover, the party was still blamed in many minds for the depression beginning in 1929.[10]

Lodge concluded that "the regular Republican leadership, cast in an opposition role for twenty long years, inescapably gave the country a negative impression."[11] When Eisenhower asked Lodge why he didn't run, his answer was succinct: "You are the only one who can be elected by the Republicans to the presidency."[12] Lodge's argument was especially persuasive to Eisenhower, who recalled: "Unless the one-sided partisan dominance could be promptly reversed, the record presaged the virtual elimination of the two-party system, which we agreed was vital to the ultimate preservation of our national institutions."[13] Thomas E. Dewey was another strong advocate for Eisenhower's candidacy. According to Eisenhower's diary, Dewey told the reluctant candidate, "The country was in danger of becoming a victim of paternalism, socialism, and dictatorship," adding, "What the GOP needed was someone of great popularity and who had not frittered away his political assets by taking positive stands against national planning etc., etc."[14]

HEAD VERSUS HEART: THE EISENHOWER-TAFT BATTLE FOR THE REPUBLICAN NOMINATION

Adroitly, and with impeccable timing, Eisenhower announced in January 1952 that he was a Republican and would accept his party's nomination, if tendered. As one reporter wrote, the general "put aside his five stars and tried for forty-eight."[15] When the first-in-the-nation New Hampshire primary occurred, Eisenhower was well on his way to doing just that with 46,661 write-in votes to Taft's 35,838. Notably, the number of New Hampshire voters requesting a Republican ballot was *triple* that of four years earlier. But Eisenhower's nomination was not preordained and would not happen without a fight. The opposition, led by Taft, who embraced the moniker "Mr. Republican," believed the party must adhere to the conservative principles that had brought it repeated successes in the 1920s. Taft's supporters resented the vagaries of Eisenhower's statements, with one saying they were "analogous to President Coolidge's comment that everybody is against sin."[16] Taft's overriding mission was to roll back the federal government to its pre–New Deal era; he believed the central debate was "between people who want more federal power and action and the people who want less."[17] Not surprisingly, Taft wanted less.

Despite the growing threat posed by the Soviet Union and the need for more military spending to counter it, Richard Nixon recalled that when Taft was asked to name the most important problem facing the country either at home or abroad, his answer "was not communism, but socialism."[18] This was hardly a new position. Reflecting on the Roosevelt years, Taft said: "The measures undertaken by the Democratic administration are alarming. Whatever may be said for them as emergency measures, their permanent incorporation into our system would practically abandon the whole theory of American government and inaugurate in fact socialism."[19] Speaking to his fellow Democrats before the 1952 Jefferson-Jackson Day dinner, Harry Truman excoriated Taft (while secretly rooting he would be named the Republican nominee), saying Taft would "try to make people believe that everything the government has done for the country is Socialism."[20]

The break between Eisenhower and Taft came when Eisenhower privately queried him on whether he agreed that "collective security is necessary for us in Western Europe—and will you support this idea as a bi-partisan policy?"[21] If Taft agreed, Eisenhower promised to publicly take himself out of the running. Taft refused, saying he could not give Eisenhower such a commitment, an answer that alarmed Eisenhower and led him to conclude that "isolationism was stronger in Congress than I had previously suspected."[22]

Taft's isolationism was nothing new. In 1941, he told a friend that it "would be fatal to the future of the Party if [Wendell] Willkie and [Henry] Luce . . . together with the wealthy crowd in the East, succeed in their [internationalist] aim."[23] By 1947, with his isolationism firmly intact, Taft voted against the Marshall Plan.[24] Two years later he led the opposition to the NATO treaty, decrying it as threatening to transform the United States into a "garrison state."[25] Taft especially objected to Article 5, which stated that an "armed attack against one or more (members) shall be considered an armed attack against them all."[26] Addressing the press corps in June 1952, Eisenhower confessed: "All right, I'll tell you why I'm running for the presidency. I'm running because Taft is an isolationist. His election would be a disaster."²⁷ In private, he was even more caustic, calling Taft "a very stupid man [with] no intellectual ability, nor any comprehension of the world."²⁸

Taft's strength among the dedicated rank-and-file Republicans was supplemented by those who worked for the party at the state and local levels and who, by custom, controlled the selection of delegates to the party convention. A June 1952 survey of state Republican Party chairs found 61 percent backing Taft; just 31 percent liked Ike.²⁹ Taft's appeal was strongest in the more conservative and isolationist Midwest, where he beat Eisenhower in the Nebraska, Wisconsin, Illinois, and South Dakota primaries. Taft's pre–New Deal conservatism was especially popular among those partisans who detested Franklin Roosevelt and Harry Truman. One ardent pro-Taft Texas delegate denounced the New Deal and the Fair Deal, labor, internationalists, the Congress of Industrial Organizations, "and left-wingers so far left that the Texas Democrats don't want them."³⁰ Other conservatives resented Eisenhower's favorable media coverage, with Taft's 1948 campaign manager proposing that conservatives back a "propaganda" media outlet to combat the liberal *New York Times*.³¹ Everett Dirksen, an avowed Taft supporter, publicly excoriated Thomas E. Dewey from the convention rostrum, saying, "We followed you before and you took us down the road to defeat."³² Taft's strength was reflected in the initial delegate count, with him having 527 committed votes to just 427 for Eisenhower, both short of the 604 votes needed for the nomination.³³

The battle between Taft and Eisenhower—a contest between the heart and head of the Republican Party—was colossal. The Taft forces believed the country must be kept safe from the New Dealers, "whatever their party label."³⁴ Minnesota congressman Walter Judd, a close friend of Taft's, neatly summarized the intraparty dilemma, "You're the King, Bob, but Ike's the ace as far as getting votes is concerned."³⁵ In a letter to the convention delegates, Henry Cabot Lodge made the case for Eisenhower solely on the premise of electability: "We of the Eisenhower Campaign Committee are convinced, regardless of the merits of the other candidates, that in Dwight D. Eisenhower we are supporting a candidate who can return the Republican Party to victory."³⁶

Behind the scenes, Eisenhower's forces saw the conflict as involving a small cadre of Republicans who would "rather wreck the party than lose control."³⁷ The battle became so intense that the job of uniting the party would become a major challenge. Actor John Wayne, an ardent Taft supporter, jumped out of his cab at the 1952 Republican National Convention in Chicago to confront Eisenhower's mess sergeant, who was broadcasting from an Eisenhower sound truck, and yelled, "Why don't you get a red flag?"[38] When Richard Nixon asked Ohio senator John Bricker, the 1940 Republican vice presidential candidate, to nominate him for the vice presidency, Bricker refused, citing his own bitterness over the outcome.[39] Shortly after the Republicans nominated Eisenhower, only 44 percent of voters thought he could unite the party; 37 percent believed "lots of disagreement and dissatisfaction" remained.[40] Democratic nominee Adlai Stevenson described the Republican party as having a "split personality" whose candidate "has been called upon to minister to a hopeless case of political schizophrenia."[41]

Democrats kept hoping that Taft would emerge from the brutal battle with Eisenhower as the Republican nominee. Polls showed Taft in a weak position with general election voters. A Gallup survey found him barely edging the unpopular Truman, 45 percent to 42 percent, while Eisenhower handily beat Truman, 64 percent to 28 percent.[42] On the eve of the Republican National Convention, Truman confided to an aide, "I'm afraid my favorite candidate is going to be beaten."[43] Later, Truman lamented: "It looks very much like my candidate for the Republican nomination has beaten himself. Of all the dumb bunnies, he is the worst."[44] As a candidate, Taft was beset by political and personal weaknesses, as he grudgingly admitted: "I don't know how to do any of the eloquence business which makes for applause."[45] Richard Nixon remembers that when a little girl approached Taft asking for an autograph, with the television cameras running, he "explained to her with devastating reasonableness that handshaking took less time than signing autographs, and since he had a very busy schedule, he could not interrupt it to sign anything for her."[46] Television audiences did not like what they saw. Only 8 percent thought Taft made an impressive showing on the new medium, compared with the 29 percent who had a favorable impression of Eisenhower's appearances.[47]

Harry Truman understood the power of the Eisenhower candidacy. When voters were asked who they would like to see the Republicans nominate, 52 percent chose Eisenhower; only 21 percent supported Taft.[48] After Eisenhower succumbed to Republican entreaties and threw his hat into the ring, Truman wrote him a typically acerbic note reading, "I hope you will be happy in your new role."⁴⁹ Eisenhower realized that there was no turning back from the pre–New Deal days, and that any successful Republican candidate must embrace the newfound power of the federal government to promote progressive domestic policies to win support from disenchanted Democrats and independents.⁵⁰ For Eisenhower, that task proved to be an easy one. The real battle was winning the nomination. Entering the Republican National Convention just seventy-four delegates shy of victory, the Eisenhower forces contested the pro-Taft delegations in Texas, Georgia, and Louisiana, among others, whose members were appointed by local party leaders.⁵¹ The Eisenhower team successfully barred them from voting, brilliantly citing the need for "Fair Play" until the matter was settled.⁵² When the convention voted to seat the pro-Eisenhower delegates from these states, his nomination was assured. One disappointed Taft supporter, exasperated at yet another loss, exclaimed, "This means eight more years of socialism."⁵³

Even after losing, conservatives continued to beat the drum that Eisenhower adopt Taft-approved policies. Yale law student Brent Bozell, who would later become a promoter of Barry Goldwater and Ronald Reagan, believed "a 'me-too' on ignorance won't do."⁵⁴ *Human Events* founder Frank Chodorov claimed that if he were governor of a state, he would secede from the union to resist the centralization of the federal bureaucracy, regardless of who won. Although the Eisenhower-Taft contest was settled, the forces that spurred both men into combat continued to lurk behind the seemingly unified Republican ranks. They would reemerge to divide the party in the decades ahead, and, unlike Taft, conservatives would triumph.

A REPUBLICAN VICTORY, BUT AT A PRICE

Following the party conventions, John Foster Dulles, serving as a foreign policy adviser to candidate Eisenhower, cabled Adlai Stevenson, "Tough luck that you have to try to beat the unbeatable."⁵⁵ Entering the general election, Eisenhower was in a strong position. Saying, "If elected, I shall go to Korea," he assured voters that he would bring that war to a prompt end.⁵⁶ (An armistice was signed in 1953.) Eisenhower cast the Democrats as naive when it came to communism, saying their tolerance created "a government by men whose very brains were confused by the opiate of this deceit."[57] To create a semblance of party unity, Eisenhower embraced Joe McCarthy, saying the two differed only in methods, not strategy, and campaigned side by side with him in Green Bay, Wisconsin, despite McCarthy's questioning the patriotism of Eisenhower's mentor, George C. Marshall. Eisenhower was hardly the only Republican to embrace McCarthy. Robert Taft praised him, saying, "I think he has done the country a real service."[58] All this infuriated Truman, who confided to aides: "[Eisenhower] knew—and he knows today—that General Marshall's patriotism is above question.... He ought to despise McCarthy, just as I do.... I had never thought the man who is now the Republican candidate would stoop so low."[59] Truman and Eisenhower remained embittered for years, reconciling only after the assassination of John F. Kennedy.

For their part, Democrats resorted to the tactics that brought them success under the Roosevelt-Truman regimes. Addressing the Democratic National Convention in 1952, Adlai Stevenson told the assembled delegates: "It was here, my friends, in Chicago just twenty years ago this month that you nominated Franklin Roosevelt; twenty years during which we have fought total depression to victory and have never been more prosperous; twenty years during which we have fought total war to victory, both East and West, and have launched the United Nations, history's most ambitious experiment in international security."[60] But Stevenson's reprise of the glorious New Deal–Fair Deal days fell on deaf ears. When the votes were counted, Eisenhower won 55 percent of the popular vote and thirty-nine states, accumulating 442 electoral votes; Stevenson won 44 percent and nine states, giving him a mere 89 electoral votes.[61] Voter turnout rose 26 percent from 1948, but the greater numbers did not help Stevenson, even though he received three million more votes than Truman won in 1948. Eighteen states that consistently voted Democratic in every contest since the Roosevelt-Hoover matchup swung into the Eisenhower column, including Texas, Virginia, Oklahoma, Tennessee, and Florida, formerly bastions of the Democratic Party's Solid South.[62] In 670 counties spread throughout the northern states that had voted for Roosevelt and Truman, Eisenhower won majorities in one-quarter. Moreover, in Illinois, Indiana, Maryland, and New Mexico, Eisenhower carried counties that had *never* voted Republican. Even Cook County, Illinois—that bastion of the Chicago Democratic machine—voted for Eisenhower.[63] Journalist Samuel

Lubell wrote: "From the Eisenhower electoral maps, the proverbial visitor from Mars would never know that Franklin D. Roosevelt had lived."[64]

Watching the election returns with a group of young Democrats, Secretary of State Dean Acheson and Supreme Court justice Felix Frankfurter saw them overcome by "a feeling of despair, almost of panic." Acheson offered this reassurance: "Most of you are so used to a Democratic Administration and recollect so little of anything else that you think this state of affairs as normal. But it was not normal."[65] Once Eisenhower's victory was assured, Thomas E. Dewey confided to a colleague, "It really does feels as though we've been let out of jail, doesn't it?"[66] Sizing up Eisenhower's victory following the traditional victory and concession speeches, CBS News commentator Edward R. Murrow offered this perceptive analysis:

> This was the end of an era in American politics. A great exclamation point in our national history. Because tonight after twenty long years, the traditional concessions of defeat came not from Republicans but from Democrats. And for those millions of Americans who voted, who voted and worked and hoped for a change, tonight they have got it. They have assured a return to the White House of a Republican president. There is a great moment of triumph for them, of vindication. The tangible proof that now, after two decades through the use of the ballot box, the American people have finally agreed with them that it was time for a change. Millions of people in their homes, in their living rooms, perhaps living rooms that they bought and paid for during a Democratic administration, you have heard a gallant winner and a gallant loser. It was universally said in Chicago [site of the party conventions] that both parties had chosen men who were worthy of the nation. One has been chosen, the other has not. To me, the most impressive thing about tonight is again a demonstration that the people of this country are sovereign, that they are unpredictable, and somehow in a fashion that is as mysterious to pollsters as it is to reporters, the great normal majority in this country made up its mind as to the man it wanted to lead it.[67]

Unlike for Franklin D. Roosevelt, however, the Eisenhower landslide was not a tidal wave but a ripple. For the first time since the brief interlude after the 1946 midterm election, Republicans won both the House and the Senate, albeit barely.[68] In the House, Republicans added twenty-two seats, giving them an eight-seat majority, while the party held a one-seat margin in the Senate, forty-eight to forty-seven.[69] Notably, not one Republican serving in that Congress had ever done so alongside a Republican president.[70] Despite the Eisenhower landslide, Democrats continued to retain their broad appeal.[71] A Gallup poll found 50 percent of respondents choosing the Democratic Party as "best for people like yourself"; Republicans were preferred by only 30 percent.[72] The Democrats' continued strength when it came to handling the economy and domestic affairs gave rise to the ticket splitting that dominated American politics from the 1950s through the 1980s. In Florida, for example, Eisenhower won 54.6 percent of the vote, but the Republican gubernatorial candidate received a paltry 27 percent. In Massachusetts, Henry Cabot Lodge was defeated by Democrat John F. Kennedy, who bucked the Eisenhower tide. Other Democratic senatorial candidates also won and went on to serve long careers, including Stuart Symington, Mike Mansfield, and Henry Jackson. In total, Eisenhower received six million more votes than his ticket mates—a *10 percent* differential. House Speaker Joseph Martin conceded the obvious, "I don't think we would have won if Eisenhower had not headed the ticket."[73]

A MAN APART FROM PARTY

Throughout 1952, Eisenhower recognized the lingering unpopularity of the Republican Party and sought to distance himself from it. To help do that, he created Citizens for Eisenhower and invited Democrats and independents to join. Headed by Walter Williams, a mortgage banker, Citizens for Eisenhower included in its leadership positions Paul Hoffman, president of the Ford Foundation; General Lucius Clay, a former World War II commander; Stanley M. Rumbough Jr., a member of the Colgate-Palmolive Company; Charles F. Willis Jr., a former fighter pilot; Sidney Weinberg, a Democrat who served as the group's treasurer; Oveta Culp Hobby, a powerful Texas Democrat; Cliff Roberts, Augusta National Golf Club cofounder; and Mary Pillsbury Lord, whose grandfather founded the Pillsbury Company. Lord and Williams argued that Citizens for Eisenhower could reach up to ten million more voters than the Republican National Committee because "the Regular Republican [sic] organization has little appeal."[74] Local Eisenhower clubs supplemented the work of Citizens for Eisenhower by working from a handbook based on the *General Foods Sales Manual*.⁷⁵ At the end of the campaign, there were more than eight hundred Eisenhower clubs in forty-two states, some even in the once-solid Democratic South.⁷⁶ Citizens for Eisenhower gave its candidate the luxury of presenting him to voters as a "nonpartisan" who was conveniently renting the top of the Republican ticket while voters, in turn, could like Ike without making any partisan commitment just as Eisenhower had intended. Theodore J. Lowi wrote, "If such an outside strategy were to be adopted, the Republicans would be the party to adopt it."⁷⁷

It was truly a marriage of convenience, one where the traditional machinery of the Republican Party assumed a subservient role. In 1956, Citizens for Eisenhower once more emerged as a powerful force. On the eve of that election, Eisenhower stopped at the Republican National Committee headquarters and expressed his desire to "keep the Citizens groups alive under the name of Citizens for Good Government, or whatever you want to call it."⁷⁸ He even tried to reassure Republicans this would be a welcome development, since "the focus of your interests [would be] represented in each county, each village of America. If that could be done, I think it would mark the real turning point in American politics."⁷⁹ Eisenhower's vision did not materialize in the way he hoped, but he was right that the separation of president from party would mark a "real turning point." This tactic would long outlive Eisenhower and eventually be adopted by every Republican and Democratic president since.

EISENHOWER'S "MODERN REPUBLICANISM"

By 1954, the power centers within the Republican Party that once challenged Eisenhower had become enfeebled. Robert Taft died in 1953; Joseph McCarthy was censured by the US Senate the following year and would die of alcoholism in 1957. Herbert Brownell, formerly the Republican National chairman and now the attorney general under Eisenhower, wrote, "It would take the force of Eisenhower's personality, and the death of Taft in 1953, for the Republicans to achieve the kind of political unity that was needed to make them a viable alternative to the Democrats."⁸⁰ Eisenhower proceeded to put his own stamp on the GOP by espousing his version of Republicanism, which he dubbed "Modern Republicanism." For Eisenhower, Modern Republicanism meant having not only a strong national defense, which the party later sloganized as "Peace through Strength," but also an expanded role for both the federal government and the president. In 1953, Eisenhower supported the creation of a new cabinet-level department, Health, Education, and Welfare, one that remained intact until Jimmy Carter proposed a separate Department of Education. In 1954, Eisenhower opposed the Bricker Amendment, which would have limited the president's authority to enter into executive agreements. After intensive lobbying from the White House, the amendment failed by one vote.[81] That same year, Congress approved construction of the Saint Lawrence Seaway, the largest federal construction project to that point in history, while also approving a housing bill that authorized construction of 144,000 homes.[82] Eisenhower supported an expansion of the Social Security Act, with ten million new enrollees and increased payments to future retirees.[83] Two years later the Eisenhower-approved Federal Highway Act created the modern interstate highway system now named in his honor. In 1956, Eisenhower also endorsed an increase in the minimum wage from seventy-five cents per hour to one dollar.[84] Describing his approach, Eisenhower declared that his purpose was to ensure that the federal government would "take the lead in making certain that the productivity of our great economic machine is distributed so that no one will suffer disaster, privation, through no fault of his own."[85] As one of Eisenhower's supporters wrote, "If a job has to be done to meet the needs of the people, and no one else can do it, then it is the proper function of the federal government."[86]

Taking note of Eisenhower's embrace of big government, Adlai Stevenson told delegates at the 1956 Democratic National Convention: "I shall have to confess, that the Republican administration has performed a minor miracle—after twenty years of incessant damnation of the New Deal they not only haven't repealed it, but they have swallowed it, or at least most of it, and it looks as though they might be able to keep it down until at least after [the] election."[87] Later, after having been comfortably reelected, Eisenhower approved the National Defense Education Act, which appropriated $1 billion to advance education in the fields of science and math. That bill contained language that sounded like words from a reincarnated Franklin D. Roosevelt: "We must increase our efforts to identify and educate more of the talent of our Nation. This requires programs that will give assurances that no student of ability will be denied an opportunity for higher education because of financial need."[88] Addressing critics of his education policy, Eisenhower defended his position:

> There is a vast difference between Federal domination and Federal performance of a job that needs to be done ... inadequate education of our youth could, and would unless greater facilities were provided, become a *national calamity*. Consequently, the Federal government, without trying to take any control of education to assume any dominant position with respect to it, still has to view with the deepest concern the failure of the states to move promptly and adequately in this regard.[89]

Accepting renomination in 1956, Eisenhower placed his stamp firmly on the Republican Party and heralded the advent of Modern Republicanism:

> The Republican Party is again the rallying point of Americans of all callings, ages, races, and incomes. They see in its broad, forward-moving, straight-down-the-road, fighting program the best promise for their own steady progress toward a bright future. Some opponents have tried to call this a "one-interest party." Indeed, it is a one-interest party; and that one interest is the interest of every man, woman, and child in America! And most surely, as long as the Republican Party continues to be this kind of one-interest party—a one-universal-interest-party—it will continue to be the Party of the Future.[90]

Arthur Larson, a former Rhodes scholar and dean at the University of Pittsburgh who joined the Eisenhower administration as undersecretary of labor, wrote a book titled *A Republican Looks at His Party*. In it, he described the emergence of an "Authentic American Center" united in the common defense to stop Soviet advancement abroad and the need for the federal government to adopt a moderate progressivism at home. Larson argued that, by occupying the "Authentic American Center," the Republican Party had been transformed from a bunch of naysayers into a party that could consistently win the presidency and become a majority.[91] Richard Nixon wrote that Eisenhower "recognized that he had the almost superhuman job of getting Republicans to think positively after having been in the opposition for twenty years ... [and that] it was his responsibility to broaden the base of the party so that it would be as strong as its leader, but he never felt at ease with most of the things he had to do to achieve that end."[92] Eisenhower himself believed that unless Republicans followed a middle course, "only the promises of the extreme right and the extreme left would be heard in public places."[93]

But conservative Republicans were unhappy at this turn of events. *National Review* noted that "the greatest difference between the two parties lies in the fact that they back different people, not different ideas, for office."[94] The critiques that Robert Taft had of Dwight Eisenhower were later revised and expanded upon by Arizona senator Barry Goldwater. Like Taft, Goldwater had little use for Roosevelt's and Truman's use of big government, and he denounced Eisenhower's domestic policy as amounting to nothing more than a "dime-store New Deal." Critiquing the "tax and tax, spend and spend" policies of the New Deal and the Fair Deal, Goldwater tartly noted: "In the Republican Party, there are also vociferous exponents of this incredible philosophy. It may be, in fact, that they are the 'Modern Republicans' about whom there has been so much discussion in recent months. Certainly, the faulty premises of 'Modern Republicanism' do not refute this budget concept."[95]

Echoing Taft's criticisms of government spending, Republican congressman Noah Mason condemned Modern Republicanism as "a form of bribery to buy votes with the voters' own money."[96] Robert T. Mount, a Republican National Committee member from Oregon, agreed: "If we don't get back to fundamental Republicanism, we are not men of distinction, but men of extinction."[97] Eisenhower denounced these "mossbacks," an antiquated term coined during the Civil War that referred to those who avoided service in the Confederate army and was later used as a pejorative to refer to a conservative, old-fashioned way of thinking. Writing an impassioned letter to his brother Edgar, who prided himself on being the only "real Republican" in the family,[98] Dwight Eisenhower defended Modern Republicanism as the only means to ensure Republican victories: "Should any political party attempt to abolish Social Security, unemployment insurance, and eliminate labor laws and farm programs, you would not hear of that party again in our political history."[99] Deriding the party's conservatives as "a tiny splinter group," Eisenhower said their numbers are "negligible and they are stupid."[100]

1956: ONE MAN'S TRIUMPH

Having described himself as a "responsible progressive," Eisenhower fulminated against the conservative old guard once led by Robert Taft, saying they were "the most ignorant people now living in the United States."[101] Eisenhower's pique led him to ruminate about abandoning the Republican Party and forming his own, or letting conservatives do the same. During his first term, Eisenhower kept himself above the partisan fray, preferring that any attacks be carried out by his loyal vice president, Richard M. Nixon. Even Henry Cabot Lodge advised Eisenhower not to "go too far" in campaigning for Republican candidates in the 1954 midterm elections, saying that if Ike did so, he would be blamed for the party's losses.[102] After the Republican rout that year, Eisenhower wrote of his conservative critics: "If the right wing wants a fight, they're going to get it. If they want to leave the Republican Party and form a third party, that's their business, but before I end up, either this Republican Party will reflect progressivism, or I won't be with them anymore."[103]

Furious that more Republicans were not following his lead, Eisenhower continued to espouse Modern Republicanism in his 1956 reelection effort. The result was another Eisenhower triumph, in which he won 57 percent of the popular vote and forty-one states to Adlai Stevenson's 42 percent and seven states. The Electoral College showed another Eisenhower landslide, with Eisenhower receiving 457 votes to Stevenson's 73. As in 1952, the South proved hospitable to Eisenhower's message. Louisiana voted Republican for the first time since the disputed election of 1876. Kentucky and West Virginia defected from Stevenson in 1952 to back Ike. Maryland cast its largest Republican vote ever, giving Eisenhower a 138,111-vote margin. Every northern state landed in the Eisenhower column, including Stevenson's home state of Illinois. Eisenhower's wins in Connecticut and New Jersey were the largest in those states' histories, and his 1.5-million-vote plurality in New York exceeded Warren Harding's in 1920. Even Chicago voted Republican, the first time that had happened since 1928, with other big cities—Baltimore, Los Angeles, Milwaukee, San Francisco, Jersey City, and New Haven—joining them. The day after the balloting, *New York Times* correspondent James Reston wrote, "Dwight David Eisenhower won yesterday the most spectacular presidential election victory since Franklin D. Roosevelt submerged Alfred M. Landon in 1936."[104] Samuel Lubell declared the result was "1936 in reverse."[105]

But these analyses missed the mark. Unlike Roosevelt's, Eisenhower's victory was marred by continued Democratic control of Congress. Eisenhower won the dubious distinction of becoming the first president since Zachary Taylor not to win at least one house of Congress for his party. Embittered, Eisenhower told Richard Nixon on election night: "You know why this is happening, Dick? It's all those damned mossbacks and hard-shell conservatives we've got in the party. I think that what we need is a new party."[106] Vowing to go out and declare victory, Eisenhower told Nixon he would preach Modern Republicanism to the waiting crowd, much to the annoyance of the conservative hard-liners. Eisenhower did exactly that, saying: "I think that modern Republicanism has now proved itself. And America has approved of modern Republicanism."[107] More accurately, voters approved of Eisenhower, not the Republican Party. Harold Stassen, the former governor of Minnesota and longtime Republican presidential aspirant, wrote: "It is clear that a significant and decisive portion of the American voters do not believe that the Republican Party represents the same policies as those of the President. Under these circumstances it seems to me to be very important that the President carry out an active Party leadership."[108] But former vice presidential candidate and senator John Bricker denounced Eisenhower's Modern Republicanism, saying, "Much that sails under the banner of Republicanism today is certainly not Republicanism as we know it in Ohio."[109] Eisenhower resented the attacks and reminded his former White House chief of staff that he had been "forced down the throats" of conservatives in 1952, and "some will never forget it."[110]

Reflecting on the Eisenhower years, Richard Norton Smith captured Thomas E. Dewey's frustration that Republicans could not build on Eisenhower's successes: "His own disappointment with Eisenhower's presidency stemmed from the feeling that a great political opportunity had been missed. Republicans were no closer to being America's majority party in 1960 than in 1952, and Dewey and Nixon alike blamed much of the drift on a president for whom politics was always a distasteful adjunct to national leadership."[111] Sidney Milkis noted that the Eisenhower years were "enervated by an undue emphasis on presidential politics and governance," and that Eisenhower "slouched towards providing such opposition to the New Deal."¹¹² In his exhaustive book on the 1952 election, John Robert Greene concluded that "the Eisenhower administration was more loyal to its president than it was to the party, and it essentially ignored its party duties."¹¹³

AN EMERGING CULT OF PERSONALITY

What the Eisenhower years proved was that marketing a candidate mattered more than the selling of a party. Accepting the Democratic nomination in 1956, Adlai Stevenson declared, "This idea that you can merchandise candidates for high office like breakfast cereal, that you can gather votes like box tops is, I think, the ultimate indignity to the democratic process," adding, "What this country needs is not propaganda and a personality cult."¹¹⁴ Leonard Hall, chair of the Republican National Committee, acknowledged the new reality: "You sell your candidate and your programs the way a business sells its products."¹¹⁵ But what Hall failed to realize is that the Republican product was not as appealing as its candidate. The result was a cult of personality built around the presidency, a legacy Eisenhower would be loath to claim but remains a fact. And grateful Republicans realized that their presidents who followed Eisenhower would have to rely on their salesmanship abilities to win—something that the ultimate salesman in Donald Trump completely understood. Reflecting on this change, Theodore J. Lowi wrote in *The Personal President*: "A candidate for president must be above party. In the language of the theater, be a single."¹¹⁶ The outcome, said Lowi, was "a virtual cult of personality revolving around the White House."¹¹⁷

This reverence for the presidency captivated voters of both parties. Advising Richard Nixon in 1967, speechwriter Raymond Price wrote, "Potential presidents are measured against an ideal that's a combination of leading man, God, father, hero, pope, king, with maybe a touch of the avenging furies thrown in."¹¹⁸ Price added that the 1968 Nixon campaign

> should be concentrating on building a *received* image of RN as the kind of man proud parents would ideally want their sons to be: a man who embodies the national ideal, its aspirations, its dreams, a man whose *image* the people want in their homes as a source of inspiration and whose voice they want as

their representative of their nation in the councils of the world, and of their generation in the pages of history. . . . That's what being a "winner" means, in Presidential terms.[119]

An ensuing mythology enveloped the presidency. In 1962, historian Daniel Boorstin wrote: "We have become so accustomed to our illusions that we mistake them for reality. We demand them. And we demand that there always be more of them, bigger and better and more vivid. . . . The presidency seems the ultimate extension of our error."[120]

Error or not, Republicans remained grateful to their presidents for providing them with solitary victories. Richard Nixon once confided to an aide that the American people "are like helpless children yearning for leadership, someone to tell them what to do."[121] Nixon could have said much the same of Republican loyalists who elevated their presidents to heroic status. Today, the presidents Republicans most admire are Ronald Reagan and Donald Trump, the latter despite Trump's two impeachments, a losing 2020 campaign, and criminal indictments.[122] The often-lonely Republican presidential wins produced what Theodore J. Lowi called a "presidency by plebiscite," a harsh terminology, he admitted, that evoked "the powerful imagery of Roman emperors and French authoritarians who governed on the basis of popular adoration, with the masses giving their noisy consent to every course of action."[123] As early as 1950, the American Political Science Association issued a prescient warning:

> *When the President's program actually is the sole program . . . either his party becomes a flock of sheep or the party falls apart. In effect this concept of the president disposes of the party system by making the President reach directly for the support of a majority of the voters.* It favors a President who exploits skillfully the arts of demagoguery, who uses the whole country as his political backyard, and who does not mind turning it into the embodiment of personal government.[124]

The plebiscitary presidency coincided with the development of what Lowi termed the "administrative state," having its roots in the Roosevelt presidency with the creation in 1939 of the Executive Office of the President and passage of the Hatch Act, both of which helped cement the separation of president from party. Lowi noted "the development of a large professional bureaucracy and the enlargement of the presidency, based upon a new political theory that democracy could be maintained and even enhanced as long as the capacity to govern was lodged in the White House."[125] That capacity to govern would depend on the will of the people. The Brownlow Commission, formed by Franklin Roosevelt to study the operations of the executive branch, proclaimed, "There is but one grand purpose namely, to make our democracy work today in the National Government; that is, to make our Government an up-to-date, efficient, and effective instrument for carrying out the will of the nation."[126] The commission concluded that the presidency required "thoroughly modern tools of management." But with the passage of time those managers became the president's personal courtiers, often separated from the party and the public.[127]

This separation of presidents from party created an even greater urgency among Republicans to make sure their candidates inhabited the Oval Office. Over time, Republican administrations became staffed by people whose party credentials were less than sterling but who acquired strong administrative skills and were personally loyal to their presidents. Many had never held elective office; rather, their expertise lay in managing bureaucracies and their accumulated technical expertise in doing so. Henry Kissinger, George Shultz, Caspar Weinberger, and James Baker are prominent examples. And within the Executive Office of the President, the personnel appointees often came directly from the campaign itself. James MacGregor Burns wrote that during the George W. Bush presidency, "The task of his White House staff was to enforce loyalty and discipline, to ensure that the president's will reached into the departments and agencies."[128] During the Trump years, the White House was populated by acolytes whose sole requirement was to demonstrate their fealty to the president or be fired. Trump even went so far as to install his daughter and son-in-law in prominent roles, despite their previous affiliations with the Democratic Party, with them having registered as Republicans only in 2020. Staff turnover during the Trump presidency became commonplace, as anyone who Trump perceived as crossing him would instantaneously be fired, often by tweet.

As the separation between president and party achieved its completion, Republican presidents followed Eisenhower's lead by establishing their own personal campaign apparatuses. The preeminent example was Richard Nixon's Committee to Reelect the President, which had the unfortunate acronym of CREEP, that became a partner in Nixon's downfall and resignation in 1974. By now, the pattern was clear. Republicans liked the idea of "running alone," as Burns once called it. Burns cites Nixon as a preeminent example, calling him a "supreme opportunist... consistent mainly in his inconsistency."[129] In 1972, Nixon himself expressed his disdain for the Republican Party, saying what it "most lacked was the ability to *think* like a majority party, to take risks, to exhibit the kind of confidence the Democrats had because of their sheer numbers."[130] Rather than embrace the GOP, Nixon touted his "New American Majority" that included conservative Democrats and independents. Like Eisenhower, Nixon flirted with creating his own party. Accepting renomination in 1972, Nixon told the assembled Republican delegates: "I ask everyone listening to me tonight—Democrats, Republicans, independents, to join our new majority—not on the basis of the party label you wear in your lapel, but on the basis of what you believe in your hearts."[131] Four years later Gerald Ford was advised that he must be a stealth candidate, avoiding any references to the Republican Party or publicly campaigning on its behalf: "The President must not campaign for GOP candidates. This will seriously erode his support among independents and ticket-splitters. The President should not attend any party functions. Any *support* given to a GOP candidate must be done in a manner to *avoid* national attention."[132] What Arthur Schlesinger once called "the imperial presidency" became a political fact of life, a phenomenon that would forever transform the Republican Party.[133]

CONCLUSION: A DIRECT LINE TO TRUMP

The presidential reverence that enveloped the Republican Party eventually came to include the Democrats. Lyndon Johnson's press secretary, George Reedy, spoke of the "twilight of the presidency," writing, "The life of the White House is the life of a court."[134] But Democrats remained a diverse bunch, always interested in governing and factionalized in ways that sometimes gave their presidents fits. In June 1993, *Time* magazine published a cover story titled "The Incredible Shrinking President." The story detailed Bill Clinton's uphill struggles to pass a $16 billion stimulus package and health care reform, both of which failed thanks to resistance from moderate Democrats. Conservative Democrats wanted caps on entitlement spending, which immediately prompted a liberal revolt, a struggle that was finally settled in the wee hours of the morning. Lani Guinier, Clinton's nominee for assistant attorney general, had her nomination pulled in the face of stiff Democratic opposition.[135] Joe Biden's first two years in office were likewise characterized by intraparty struggles, as liberals and conservatives battled over his Build Back Better plans, with Biden having to scale back his FDR-like policy objectives and West Virginia's Joe Manchin exercising a one-man veto power in the US Senate.

But the president-as-king concept swallowed the Republican Party whole, in ways heretofore unthinkable. While William McKinley engineered a party realignment that took the GOP to new heights, political power remained concentrated at the state and local levels, where Republicans were just as adept as the Democrats in empowering their party machines. But as state and local party apparatuses eroded, and the cabinet declined in importance, the White House assumed the aura of a king's court. Senior Nixon White House staffer John Ehrlichman captured the tone: "There shouldn't be a lot of leeway in following the president's policies. It should be like a corporation, where the executive vice presidents (the cabinet officers) are tied closely to the chief executive, or to put it in extreme terms, when he says jump, they only ask how high."[136] As the executive-centered presidency took hold, the idea that the president is the party became standard fare. As the late Thomas P. "Tip" O'Neill said of Ronald Reagan, he was a poor chief executive but "a hell of a king."[137]

The disappointing presidency of George W. Bush and the failed candidacies of John McCain and Mitt Romney eviscerated the Republican establishment and paved the way for Donald Trump. Trump understood the frustrations of Republican voters and, like the businessman he is, undertook a hostile takeover of the party and transformed it into a cult of personality. At first, many elected Republicans rolled their eyes at Trump's behavior, even while publicly agreeing with the policies he pursued. Given time, many thought, Trump would inhabit the office and become, as Trump himself once put it, "presidential."[138] That never happened. Despite two impeachments, a losing reelection campaign, and an insurrection, Trump became even more powerful. Immediately after the January 6 riot at the US Capitol, South Carolina senator and close Trump ally Lindsey Graham took to the Senate floor and said, "All I can say is count me out. Enough is enough."[139] Seven days later, House minority leader Kevin McCarthy denounced Trump's actions: "The President bears responsibility for Wednesday's attack on Congress by mob rioters. He should have immediately denounced the mob when he saw what was unfolding. These facts require immediate action by President Trump, accept his share of responsibility, quell the brewing unrest and ensure President-elect Biden is able to successfully begin his term."[140] Following the failure of the Senate to convict Trump after his second impeachment trial, minority leader Mitch McConnell denounced the former president in the strongest possible terms:

> January 6th was a disgrace. American citizens attacked their own government. They used terrorism to try to stop a specific piece of domestic business they did not like. Fellow Americans beat and bloodied our own police. They stormed the Senate floor. They tried to hunt down the Speaker of the House. They built a gallows and chatted about murdering the vice president. They did this because they'd been fed wild falsehoods by the most powerful man on earth because he was angry. . . . There is no question, none, that President Trump is practically and morally responsible for provoking the events of the day.[141]

But in the days that followed, Trump convinced an overwhelming majority of rank-and-file Republicans that the 2020 election was stolen, and he used his power not just in national races but in once-overlooked state and local contests—including secretaries of state and school boards. Never before has any president exercised such influence. Even in his heyday, Franklin D. Roosevelt failed to pack the Supreme Court and purge recalcitrant Democrats. In February 2021, Kevin McCarthy, who just weeks before called for Trump's censure, visited him at Mar-a-Lago in Florida and paid homage to the former president. By springtime, Lindsey Graham denounced Congresswoman Liz Cheney's criticisms of Trump and endorsed her expulsion from the House leadership, telling the *Washington Post*: "There is no way this party is going to stay together without President Trump and his supporters. There is no construct where the party can be successful without him."[142] When Republican senator Rick Scott tried to counter the narrative that the GOP belonged to the people, not Trump, Trump responded, "But the people like me the best, by far."[143] Democratic congresswoman Kathleen Rice says of today's GOP, "It's a wholly owned subsidiary of Trump Inc."[144]

After meeting with John F. Kennedy in the Oval Office following the 1960 election, presidential chronicler Theodore H. White described the "hush, an entirely personal hush, surrounds this kind of power, and the hush is deepest in the Oval Office of the West Wing of the White House, where the President, however many his advisers, must sit alone."[145] White's reverence for the presidency was typical of the exaltation of the office that surrounded it from its very inception. Unlike our other institutions of government, the presidency is entirely personal, and the conduct of that office lies entirely within the person occupying it. Presidential character, not policies per se, are not only keys to continued survival not only of the office but also of the many myths that have enveloped it. Schoolchildren still learn of George Washington's mythical cherry tree, Abraham Lincoln's real log cabin, the heroism of Franklin Roosevelt's rising from the ravages of polio, John F. Kennedy's heroics during World War II, the decency of Gerald R. Ford, the piety of Jimmy Carter, the admiration for Ronald Reagan's conduct after he was shot, George W. Bush's memorable speech after the terrorist attacks of September 11, and Joe Biden's fortitude in the wake of personal tragedy. Presidents such as Richard Nixon and Bill Clinton, both of whom disgraced the office, are far less admired. In 2018, when asked to name the best presidents since World War II, only 10 percent of respondents cited Clinton and just 1 percent named Nixon. Ronald Reagan and Barack Obama were overwhelming favorites with 28 percent and 24 percent, respectively.[146]

Donald Trump understood the personal nature of the presidency. In one sense, it suited him. In every business venture undertaken by Trump, the one thing he always sought to achieve was dominance. He carried that characteristic into his political endeavors. In 2016, Trump asserted his physical dominance during a debate with Hillary Clinton, standing inches behind her as she answered a question. The presidency was, in its own way, well suited to a man accustomed to the sole exercise of power who would boast, "I alone can fix it."[147] What Trump also brought to the presidency was a willingness to bend the rules to suit his ends. This, too, was a feature of his business career. That willingness to flout established norms of behavior led Trump to the brink: his attempt to overturn a free and fair election in 2020, and the insurrection of the Capitol that followed his provocative January 6 address on the White House Ellipse.

But Trump's personal behavior not only was unsuited to the presidency but also weakened it. From the beginning, George Washington placed great emphasis on how a president should behave and the importance of the chief executive's deportment in uniting the country. As one woman said of Washington, "He is polite with dignity, affable without familiarity, distant without haughtiness, grave without austerity, modest, wise, and good."[148] James Monroe agreed, saying Washington had "a deportment so firm, so dignified, but yet so modest and composed, I have never seen in any other person."[149] Washington's primacy on presidential character was such that, as he once said, it could either unite the country or destroy it: "We are either a United people, or we are not. If the former, let us, in all matters of general concern act as a nation, which have national objects to promote, and a national character to support. If we are not, let us no longer act a farce by pretending to it."[150] Defending Washington's endorsement of the Jay Treaty, Alexander Hamilton wrote in July 1795:

> It is only to consult the history of nations to perceive, that every country, at all times, is cursed by the existence of men who, actuated by an irregular ambition, scruple nothing which they imagine will contribute to their own advancement and importance. In monarchies, supple courtiers; in republics, fawning or turbulent demagogues, worshiping still the idol power wherever placed, whether in the hands of a prince, or of the people, and trafficking in the weaknesses, vices, frailties, or prejudices of the one or of the other.[151]

Thomas Jefferson took issue with Washington and Hamilton, giving primacy to the political party and the people's voices within it. Jefferson wanted the executive branch to be imbued with officeholders who, as Abraham Lincoln later put it, regularly took a "public opinion bath": "We think in America it is necessary to introduce the people into every department of government as far as they are capable of exercising it."[152] Jefferson described his contested victory in the 1800 presidential election as being "as real a revolution in the principles of our government as that of 1776 was in its form."[153] That revolution, Jefferson believed, gave white, male property holders ownership over the executive branch. In his second inaugural address, Jefferson extolled his forthcoming term as "reflecting

[the] character of our citizens at large, who, by the weight of public opinion, influence and strengthen the public measures," and he complimented "the zeal and wisdom" of those elected to public office "who lay the foundations of public happiness."[154] Jefferson's conception of the presidency was echoed by those supporting ratification of the US Constitution. Writing under the pen name "An American Citizen," Tench Coxe, a member of the Continental Congress, editorialized that the president "is originally one of the people," and "he is created by their breath."[155] The president could, he maintained, act with "vigor and impartiality when his office depends on the popular voice."[156] As Stephen Knott notes, Jefferson's faith in the public's ability to "distinguish 'between truth and falsehood ... and to form a correct judgment between them' became a central tenet of Jeffersonianism."[157]

Analyzing the American presidency, political scientist Clinton Rossiter added one more important role for its modern-day officeholders: voice of the people. Rossiter believed that the president must be "the leading formulator and expounder of public opinion in the United States."[158] For him, this extended beyond the president speaking for his or her political party; rather, the president must serve "as moral spokesman for all."[159] Noting how radio and television had transformed the presidency, Rossiter warned that any president "must be especially on his guard not to pervert these mighty media that are his to command," adding:

> It is one thing for a huckster to appeal to the people to buy a mouthwash; it would be quite another for a President to appeal to them to stampede the Senate. I like to think that our sales resistance would be as dogged in the second case as in the first, but there is no denying that, even in defeat, a President could do a great deal of damage to our scheme of representative government.[160]

And then came the huckster-in-chief, Donald Trump, the attack on the Capitol, and the damage Trump inflicted on the carefully constructed constitutional framework. Trump's flawed personality, his self-aggrandizement, the enlargement of the presidency in both reality and myth, the weakening of the party establishment, and the desperation of Republican voters to find a winner and pay that person homage created the conditions whereby the Republican Party was transformed from one of conservative principles into a party dominated by one man who was willing to bend the Constitution and long-established rules of behavior. And the party's willingness not only to countenance Trump but to accept his lies reveals a mindset that did not suddenly appear with Trump. Rather, the strain within the Republican Party that often bowed to conspiratorial thinking has been a long-standing one and is the subject of the next chapter.

4. Of Conspiracy Theories, Lies, and Stolen Elections

> It is the use of the big lie and the unfounded accusation against any citizen in the name of Americanism and security.
> —Harry S. Truman defining McCarthyism, November 17, 1953

Campaigning for the US Senate in 1964, George H. W. Bush was accused by the John Birch Society of being a "One World Tool of the Communist-Wall Street international conspiracy."[1] Pamphlets distributed by a Texas chapter of the organization charged Bush's father-in-law, then president of the McCall's publishing company, with distributing a communist manifesto called *Redbook* magazine. Barbara Bush, whom the Birchers described as an "heiress who spent all of her time on [Cape Cod]," tartly wrote her father asking if she had inherited a fortune and, as her husband recounted years later, "was disappointed in the answer."[2] Reflecting on his 1964 loss, the elder Bush wrote:

> The Birchers are bad news, and I don't like them a bit. They gave me fits here in Houston and in other places in Texas, and I think in retrospect I should have cracked down on them more. This mean, humorless philosophy which says everybody should agree on absolutely everything is not good for the Republican Party or for our state. When the word moderation becomes a dirty word, we have some soul searching to do.[3]

Thirty-five years later, when Bush's son Jeb was a gubernatorial candidate in Florida, conspiracy theories likewise dogged his campaign. At a campaign rally in St. Petersburg, a female weapons factory worker queried the younger Bush about his family's supposed involvement in a nefarious conspiracy "to take control of the United States":

> Woman: "You're familiar with the Skull and Crossbones society? . . . I mean, Skull and Bones."
> Bush: "Yeah, I've heard about it."
> Woman: "And you're familiar with the Trilateral Commission and the Council on Foreign Relations?"

Bush: "Yeah."

Woman: "Well, can you tell the people here what your family membership in that is? Isn't your aim to take control of the United States?"

Bush: "There are very few people who have served this country with the honor and distinction of my Dad."[4]

REPUBLICANS AND THE ROOSEVELT CONSPIRACIES

Long before the arrival of Donald Trump, the Republican Party was riddled with intrigues and conspiracy theories about stolen elections that became ever more prevalent as the frequency of the party's losses escalated. During the 1930s and 1940s, Republicans charged that Franklin D. Roosevelt had secretly conspired with the Soviet Union and welcomed the participation of the US Communist Party in domestic politics for the purpose of manipulating election outcomes in Roosevelt's favor. The GOP claimed the New Deal was a front for the US Communist Party, which was colluding with Roosevelt to move the country down a path toward socialism. In 1932, Herbert Hoover began his reelection campaign charging that Roosevelt would take the country down the road of socialism, which, in turn, would endanger the rights guaranteed by the US Constitution: "Every expansion of government and business means that government in order to protect itself from the political consequences of its errors and wrongs is driven irresistibly and without peace to greater and greater control of the nation's press and platforms. Free speech does not live many hours after free industry and free commerce die."[5] Two years later, the *Los Angeles Times*, then a mouthpiece for the Republican Party, ran an editorial under the banner headline "IS THIS STILL AMERICA?" The editorial charged that the New Deal was a Soviet-inspired plot with communists hidden in every nook and cranny throughout the country: "The foe is camouflaged. The Reds are not lined up in solid ranks. Their menace is secret and subtle. Their agent may be your cook or your trusted friend or the movie star whom you admire on the screen."[6] One Republican document claimed: "The banner year for the Marxists in America was 1933—the arrival of the New Deal. The Marxists twins [socialism and communism] swarmed into Washington with their sleeves rolled up to make America over," adding that "the most susceptible party [i.e., the Democrats] had finally been penetrated."⁷ As evidence, Republicans cited Roosevelt's 1933 resumption of diplomatic relations with the Soviet Union, characterizing his order as "a formal step which three preceding Republican Presidents had refused to take because it would give the Soviet Union the enormous advantage of being able to create listening posts and subversive centers in America with complete diplomatic immunity."⁸ Republicans derided the New Deal's "reckless atmosphere" in which "any radical who could talk Marxian dialectics fluently was regarded as a genius far beyond the average American."⁹

Campaigning for reelection in 1936, Roosevelt denounced the GOP conspiracy-tinged attacks. Addressing the Democratic state convention in Syracuse, New York, Roosevelt charged: "Partisans, not willing to face realities, will drag out red herrings—as they have always done—to divert attention from the trail of their own weaknesses."¹⁰ He proceeded to recall the miseries of the Great Depression, including starving children, homeless boys seeking work, farmers facing foreclosure, and business leaders pleading for help.¹¹ Roosevelt characterized the Republican Party as "desperate in mood, angry at failure, and cunning in purpose," and he firmly rejected communism "or any other alien 'ism' which would by fair means or foul change our American democracy."¹² Instead, Roosevelt touted the New Deal as a patriotic program meant to ensure "the safeguarding of democracy," and he skillfully turned the issue on its head, charging it was *the Republicans* who had promoted the spread of domestic communism during the ruinous Hoover years, citing "the injustices, the inequalities, the downright suffering" that left the nation unprepared.¹³ After his landslide victory, *The Phoenix Republic* editorialized that Franklin Roosevelt's "present position is comparable only with that of Joseph Stalin."¹⁴

Despite their landslide losses in 1936, Republicans clung to dark conspiracies involving Roosevelt and the communists whose sole aim was to keep the Republican Party out of power. In 1944, the Republican vice presidential nominee, John W. Bricker, alleged that the Soviet Union had infiltrated the Roosevelt administration with the goal of stealing the election:

> Today, as never before, a foreign influence of the most subversive kind is trying to take over our American government by boring from within. . . . A for-

eign fifth column . . . is trying to swing a Presidential election. The all-out Communist support for the fourth term admits of no other interpretation. There has never been anything like this before because no American party or group has been willing to live as the obedient instrument of the policies of a foreign power."[15]

Bricker's running mate, Thomas E. Dewey, chimed in, charging that Roosevelt had placed the Democratic Party on the auction block for sale to the highest bidder. He concluded, "In America, a Communist is a man who supports the Fourth Term so our form of government may more easily be changed."[16] The Republican National Committee accused the Roosevelt administration, the Democratic Party, organized labor, and the nation's colleges and universities with housing a communist infestation whose purpose was to keep FDR in office by whatever means necessary. In a radio advertisement sponsored by the committee, a narrator ominously intoned: "During Roosevelt's administration we have seen Communism, like a snake crawl into control of many labor unions and many once-respected educational organizations. We find fellow-travelers in high posts in government bureaus. Notorious fellow-travelers have been guests in the White House! . . . Why are the Communists and fellow-travelers so anxious to keep Roosevelt in the White House? Vote for Dewey on November 7."[17]

The Japanese assault on Pearl Harbor escalated the conspiratorial rhetoric. Republicans charged that Roosevelt had participated in a plot designed to keep the public in the dark about the facts surrounding the Japanese attack. Robert Taft darkly suggested that the commander in chief had advance knowledge of the offensive and let it happen to ensure US involvement in World War II.[18] Claire Booth Luce publicly stated that FDR had taken part in a cover-up and was "the only American President who ever lied us into a war because he did not have the courage to lead us into it."[19] John Bricker accused FDR of withholding the facts about "the disgraceful Pearl Harbor episode" because of the harm it would inflict on Roosevelt's bid for a fourth term. Bricker's sentiments were echoed by Thomas E. Dewey, who accused Roosevelt of knowing "what was happening before Pearl Harbor, and instead of being reelected he ought to be impeached."[20] Democratic vice presidential nominee Harry Truman responded by labeling Dewey and Bricker "a couple of fakirs who just want to get into power."²¹ Long after Roosevelt's death, Republicans continued to believe he had participated in a secret cover-up about what happened at Pearl Harbor. The John Birch Society accused Roosevelt and General George Marshall of committing "unadulterated treason" by hiding "the real facts," which, had they been exposed, would have been "absolutely fatal" to Roosevelt's reelection prospects and surely would have resulted in his "impeachment despite the war."²² Robert Welch, the organization's founder, wrote that Roosevelt "contrived to have perjury, postponements, decisions against the evidence, and every necessary means used, before or in connection with one hearing after another, to keep the truth from getting into the record."²³

After Roosevelt's death, the Republican attacks intensified, this time focusing on Roosevelt's supposed "sellout" at the Yalta Conference of 1945. These charges stemmed from the presupposition that Roosevelt was either sympathetic to, or naively conspiring to advance, the interests of Josef Stalin's Soviet Union. Republican senator William E. Jenner spoke for many in his party when he declared, "At Yalta, under the influence of Alger Hiss, a dying American President sold Asia down the river."²⁴ Seeking reelection to the US Senate in 1946, John Bricker challenged his Democratic rival to "bring on your New Deal, Communistic, and subversive groups. If we can't lick them in Ohio, America is lost anyway."²⁵ His colleague Hugh Butler of Nebraska put it even more starkly: "If the New Deal is still in control of the Congress after the election it will owe that control to the Communist Party."²⁶ Even progressive Republicans joined in the attacks. California governor Earl Warren criticized former vice president Henry Wallace, saying he was leading the charge of "leftist organizations that are attuned to the Communist movement."²⁷ The Republican national chairman described the 1946 midterms as "a fight basically between communism and Republicanism," and the Republican National Committee distributed 683,000 brochures accusing the Democrats of a "Communist penetration of government" that culminated in the "appeasement" and "cynical betrayal" at Yalta. Wisconsin representative Alvin O'Konski beseeched his supporters to vote the Republican ticket, charging that Roosevelt had returned from the Yalta Conference peddling "typical Communist apologies" for the seizure of Poland, Yugoslavia, Finland, Latvia, Estonia, and Lithuania. Soon, O'Konski warned, America will be divided by the communists, and he implored his supporters: "Don't vote Red—vote red, white, and blue on Election Day! Vote Republican!"[28] Eventually, references to Yalta became such a frequent staple of Republican speeches that one Texas Democrat was heard to moan, "Oh God, Yalta this and Yalta that."[29]

In California, Richard M. Nixon echoed the Republican charge that Roosevelt was "soft as taffy" on communism.[30] Running against incumbent Democratic congressman Jerry Voorhis, Nixon won a comfortable 57 percent to 43 percent victory thanks to his repeated accusations that communists had infiltrated the highest levels of the US government. Describing Voorhis's voting record as "more socialistic and communistic than it is Democratic,"[31] Nixon told a group of American Legionnaires that communists and their fellow travelers were conspiring to obtain "positions of importance in virtually every federal department and bureau ... calculated to gradually give the American people a Communist form of government."[32] Nixon biographer Roger Morris writes that Republican boiler rooms bustled with calls to voters with this message: "This is a friend of yours but I can't tell you my name. I just wanted you to know that Jerry Voorhis is a communist."[33] With that, the caller would abruptly hang up. The day prior to the election, the *Los Angeles Times* was emblazoned with banner-sized boxes that read: "VOTE AGAINST NEW DEAL COMMUNISM! VOTE REPUBLICAN! VOTE AMERICAN!"[34]

Nixon's success was replicated across the country. Ten years after the Roosevelt landslide of 1936, Republicans seized control of Congress, gaining 55 House seats for a total of 246 representatives to the Democrats' 188, the largest Republican gain in a midterm election since 1894—and one not equaled until 1994. Thirteen Republicans were added in the US Senate—including a newly minted senator from Wisconsin, Joseph R. McCarthy—for a majority of fifty-one. For the first time since 1930, there was divided partisan control of the federal government. Republicans took full advantage of the fears and conspiracies that swept the country. Through outright innuendo, lies, and accusations of dark intrigues, they scared the hell out of voters, and in so doing found a means to energize their base while appealing to worried Democrats and independents. In Chicago, for example, Democratic candidates lost an average of ten percentage points among Catholic Polish Americans from their 1944 totals, many of whom had relatives locked behind the Iron Curtain.[35]

Despite their success, Republicans continued to promulgate fears that future elections would be stolen from them thanks to Moscow's interference and help from communist sympathizers and Democrats. A year before the 1948 election, a Republican operative wrote a memo that landed on the desk of Thomas E. Dewey. In it, the consultant maintained: "The Kremlin will make no serious move in the direction of establishing peace in Europe and elsewhere before the 1948 election in the United States has been decided. In the meantime, it will try to influence the result of the 1948 election by every means conceivable."[36] The memo warned that a dirty campaign lay ahead, led by those who profited from the New Deal:

> When one considers, for instance, that including their families there are millions of people who directly and indirectly have spent almost half of their adult lives in drawing support from the payrolls of the Federal government; [and] when one further realizes the degree of sheer desperation that will surely envelop these millions when faced with the threat of losing their regular income from this source, one need not wonder how vituperative and reckless will be the language and actions of this formidable contingent of Democrats.[37]

Thus, the writer argued, the Kremlin was sure to prefer Democratic control of the White House: "Not that these men love the Democrats; they only hate Republicans more or, what is more to the point, the men in the Kremlin are afraid of the Republicans more than they are of the tested Democrats."[38] The operative concluded, "The United States of America is fair game for Moscow and has been for years. And, as far as anyone is willing to see, the year 1948 will be the year in which Soviet Russia will do everything in its power to influence the election here."[39]

JOE MCCARTHY AND "TWENTY YEARS OF TREASON"

In 1947, Wisconsin senator Joseph R. McCarthy was a Republican backbencher with no significant national following or legislative accomplishments. Determined to elevate his status, McCarthy found an issue that resonated with a public frightened by the emergence of an ambitious Soviet Union abroad and fearful of communists at home. In February 1950, McCarthy delivered an infamous Lincoln Day address in Wheeling, West

Virginia, accusing the Truman administration of "traitorous actions" centered in the State Department. He stated: "I have in my hand a list of two-hundred-five who were known to the Secretary of State as being members of the Communist Party and who nevertheless are still working and shaping the policy of the State Department."[40] McCarthy read into the *Congressional Record* the case files of eighty-one officials whose loyalties he thought were compromised.[41] In his speech, McCarthy not only described communists inside the US government as a threat aided and abetted by Democratic presidents but skillfully presented the Democratic Party as aligned with a class of citizens whose values were alien to key components of the working-class New Deal coalition assembled by Franklin D. Roosevelt: "It is not the less fortunate, or members of minority groups who have been selling this nation out, but rather those who have had all the benefits the wealthiest nation on earth has had to offer—the finest homes, the finest college educations, and the finest jobs in the government that we can give."[42] Feasting on the attendant publicity, McCarthy addressed a Richard Nixon for Senate rally one month later, claiming Harry Truman headed the "Administration Commicrat Party of Betrayal."[43] Gratified by McCarthy's appearance, Richard Nixon applauded and said, "God give him courage to carry on."[44] The National Republican Congressional Campaign Committee followed with a radio commercial that exacerbated voter fears. Over the roar of machinery, an ominous male voice exclaimed: "These are the printing presses of the Communist Party. Listen to them!"[45]

By June 1951, McCarthy was wildly swinging at the Truman administration, claiming Secretary of Defense George Marshall had been party to "a conspiracy so immense and an infamy so black as to dwarf any previous such adventure in the history of man."[46] McCarthy's charges gathered support from Republicans, Democrats, and independents alike. His 1952 reelection campaign even secured a $5,000 contribution from Joseph P. Kennedy, father to John F. Kennedy, who, in his senatorial bid in heavily Catholic Massachusetts, tiptoed around McCarthy, a fellow Catholic with enormous popularity in the state.[47] Some Democrats even sought to out-McCarthy McCarthy. In 1954, Senator Hubert H. Humphrey sponsored an amendment outlawing the US Communist Party and stripping communist-controlled unions of their right to operate under the National Labor Relations Act. Professing to be tired of "this talk of twenty years of treason" by Republican "blowhards," Humphrey said, "The Communist Party isn't really a political party, it's an international political conspiracy."[48] Humphrey's amendment was approved 85 to 0. Columnists Joseph and Stewart Alsop wrote that Humphrey's ploy was "cleverly conceived, ruthlessly executed, and politically adroit."[49] But Hubert Humphrey was not the only Democrat given to excessive McCarthy-like rhetoric. Texas governor Allen Shivers proposed making membership in the US Communist Party a capital offense.[50] Political scientist Seymour Martin Lipset observed that McCarthy's greatest source of support came from "nineteenth century liberals"—those opposed to big trade unions and large corporations—in short, those who resembled Alexis de Tocqueville's America.[51]

That support correlated closely with powerful elements of the Republican coalition of the early twentieth century. And Republicans, long shut out of the White House, were grateful to have it. Ohio senator John Bricker gave McCarthy his due: "Joe, you're a real SOB, but sometimes it's useful to have SOBs to do the dirty work."[52] In Arizona, Senate candidate Barry Goldwater held a rally with McCarthy and said, "Now is the time to throw out the intellectual radicals and the parlor pinks and the confused and the bumbling."[53] Robert Taft spoke darkly of a "procommunist group in the State Department" and encouraged McCarthy to "keep talking and if one case doesn't work, he should proceed with another."[54] Voters were spooked: 81 percent believed there were "communists or disloyal people" working in the State Department, and 58 percent thought these individuals had done "serious harm" to national security.[55]

In 1952, McCarthy mounted the rostrum at the Republican National Convention and won hearty applause with these lines: "I say, one communist in a defense plant is one communist too many. One communist on the faculty of one university is one communist too many. One communist among the American advisers at Yalta was one communist too many. And even if there were only one communist in the State Department, there would be one communist too many."[56] The party platform echoed McCarthy's views, accusing Truman of appeasing "communism at home and abroad" and permitting "communists and their fellow travelers to serve in many key agencies and to infiltrate our American life," while sanctimoniously concluding, "There are no communists in the Republican Party."[57] Recalling McCarthy's appeal, Susan Eisenhower, the granddaughter of Dwight D. Eisenhower, wrote that McCarthy had an instinct for innuendo and "what is now called 'fake news' [which] strengthened the senator's power and influence."⁵⁸ At the time, however, it was McCarthy's support that Dwight D. Eisenhower was grateful to have. While privately calling the 1952 Republican platform "a bit savage,"⁵⁹ Eisenhower embraced McCarthy on the campaign trail. Appearing with him in Wisconsin, Eisenhower presented prepared remarks, distributed to the press in advance of their joint appearance, containing paragraphs in which he praised his World War II patron, General George Marshall, as "a man and as a soldier . . . dedicated with singular selflessness and the profoundest patriotism to the service of America," adding that McCarthy's indictment of Marshall was a "sobering lesson in the way freedom must *not* defend itself."⁶⁰ But when the time came to deliver his speech, Eisenhower omitted the offending paragraph, prompting considerable criticism. The *New York Times* opined that Eisenhower's omission "could not have been a happy day for General Eisenhower . . . nor was it a happy day for many supporters."⁶¹ Publisher Arthur Hays Sulzberger cabled Ike, saying, "Do I need to tell you that I am sick at heart?"⁶² But Sulzberger's unhappiness was overridden by advice Eisenhower received from the powerful GOP newspaper publisher Eugene Pulliam, who advised that it would be "a tragic mistake" to rebuke McCarthy, noting he "has the confidence of literally millions of people who think he is being directed by God in his campaign."⁶³

During the first years of Eisenhower's presidency, McCarthy's influence grew even stronger. He opposed Eisenhower's nomination of Chip Bohlen to be ambassador to the Soviet Union in 1953, bringing eleven other Senate Republicans along with him.⁶⁴ Eisenhower was incensed and even contemplated forming a third party while hoping to persuade his fellow Republicans to adopt a mantra of "teamwork and party responsibility."⁶⁵ Arthur Larson, a key Eisenhower adviser, later observed that Ike "had a sense of loathing and contempt [for McCarthy] that had to be seen to be believed."⁶⁶ Privately, Eisenhower's frustration at his growing predicament intensified. He conceded that McCarthy "is, of course, so anxious for headlines that he is prepared to go to any extreme in order to secure some mention of his name in the public press."⁶⁷ Writing to his boyhood friend Everett Hazlett, Eisenhower elaborated: "I think that the average honorable individual cannot understand to what lengths certain politicians would go for publicity. They have learned a simple truth of American life. This is that the most vicious kind of attack from one element always creates a very great popularity, amounting to almost hero worship, in an opposite fringe of society."[68]

But publicly, the Eisenhower administration ignored McCarthy. In 1953, Eisenhower confided to his brother Milton: "Only a shortsighted or completely inexperienced individual would urge the use of the office to the Presidency to give an opponent the publicity he so avidly desires.... I have no intention whatsoever of helping promote the publicity value of anyone who disagrees with me—demagogue or not!"[69] Susan Eisenhower described her grandfather's strategy of dealing with McCarthy as "containment without confrontation"[70]—an approach eerily similar to the one many Republicans undertook to unsuccessfully cope with a publicity-seeking Donald Trump decades later. In a diary entry for April 1953, Eisenhower wrote: "The best treatment for McCarthy is to ignore him. That is one thing he cannot stand and if we continue this sort of silent treatment, he will blow his top and still sink lower in political importance."[71] By 1955, following McCarthy's censure in the US Senate, Eisenhower's silent treatment became official White House policy. Press secretary James Hagerty said of McCarthy:

> All of us on the staff, including the President, will make it a point not to have a comment whatsoever on anything McCarthy says or does. We have him relegated to the back pages of the papers and he knows he is not news anymore. Consequently, he is desperately trying to get back on the front pages and is trying to stir up anything he can to cause him to become once again a controversial subject, particularly between himself and the White House.[72]

But between the start of the Eisenhower presidency and McCarthy's censure, Joseph McCarthy, like Donald Trump, could be neither contained nor ignored. In the fall of 1953, Harry Truman was incensed that Eisenhower's attorney general, Herbert Brownell, accused Truman of appointing a known communist as assistant Treasury secretary and later naming him to a position at the International Monetary Fund.[73] In a national address broadcast over radio and television, the former president heaped scorn on the Republican criticisms leveled at him, including those by McCarthy, saying:

> The attack is without parallel, I believe, in the history of our country. I have been accused, in effect, of knowingly betraying the security of the United

States. This charge is a falsehood and the man who made it has every reason to know it is a falsehood. . . .

It is now evident that the present Administration has fully embraced, for political advantage, McCarthyism. I'm not referring to the Senator from Wisconsin—he's only important in that his name has taken on a dictionary meaning in the world. And that meaning is the corruption of our historical devotion to fair play.

It is the abandonment of "due process" of law. It is the use of the big lie and the unfounded accusation against any citizen in the name of Americanism and security. It is the rise to power of the demagogue who lives on untruth; it is the spread of fear and the destruction of faith in every level of society.

My friends, this is not a partisan matter. This horrible cancer is eating at the vitals of America, and it can destroy the great edifice of freedom.[74]

Adlai Stevenson echoed Truman, saying the Republican Party was "hopelessly, dismally, fatally, torn and rent . . . divided against itself, half McCarthy, and half Eisenhower."[75] Reflecting on the episode, Eisenhower wrote that "the long, heated argument left many scars."[76]

Refusing to be ignored and still seeking maximum publicity, McCarthy escalated his rhetoric, in 1954 accusing the US Army of harboring communists—a charge that caused millions to turn on their newfangled television sets to watch the army-McCarthy hearings. Vigorously defending McCarthy was his chief adviser, New York attorney Roy Cohn, whose penchant for defending the indefensible was such that he later became a mentor to Donald Trump.[77] The proceedings against McCarthy culminated when army special counsel Joseph Welch leveled a stinging rejoinder to McCarthy's sensational charge that the army protected communist sympathizers: "Have you left no sense of decency, sir, at long last? Have you no sense of decency?"[78] With that, the Senate voted 67 to 22 to censure McCarthy, despite an armored Brink's truck arriving at the Capitol on that very day with 1,000,816 pro-McCarthy signatures.[79] Barry Goldwater opposed McCarthy's censure, claiming that the liberal Americans for Democratic Action had spied on and "double crossed" McCarthy.[80] But Eisenhower's policy of containment had finally worked. Party chair Leonard Hall declared that he could no longer "go along" with McCarthy's sniping at "persons who are fighting communists just as conscientiously as he is."[81] Republican senator Ralph Flanders accused McCarthy of "doing his best to shatter the party label he wears."[82] Privately, Eisenhower told White House staffers, "I've made up my mind that you can't do business with Joe, and to hell with any attempt to compromise."[83] He promised to end McCarthy's political career, including any presidential ambitions McCarthy may have harbored, vowing, "He's the last guy in the world who'll ever get [to the White House] if I have anything to say."[84] Speaking at a 1954 dinner at Columbia University, Eisenhower indirectly criticized McCarthy and warned: "Whenever, and for whatever reason, people attempt to crush ideas, to mask their convictions, to view every neighbor as a possible enemy, to seek some kind of divining rod by which to test for conformity, a free society is in danger."[85] Decades later, Eisenhower's sentiments were echoed by Wyoming congresswoman Liz Cheney, who said of Donald Trump: "I will do everything I can to ensure that the former president never again gets anywhere near the Oval Office."[86] In Eisenhower's case, his worries were relieved by McCarthy's censure and his death from alcoholism in 1957 at the age of forty-eight.

But although McCarthy was gone, McCarthyism was not. In 1954, Richard Nixon claimed that upon taking office the Eisenhower administration discovered "in the files a blueprint for socializing America" and fired "thousands" of subversives.[87] But when asked to produce the file, Nixon claimed he had been speaking metaphorically, and the head of the civil service denied his assertion that "thousands" of government employees had been fired.[88] Utah Republican governor J. Bracken Lee warned that the federal government was akin to a "dictatorship," one no different from the Russian government.[89] McCarthyism continued to find a home within a Republican Party that espoused various conspiracy theories and issued false charges of subversion. Years after McCarthy's death, former ambassador Chip Bohlen reflected on the reasons McCarthy had gained such a powerful grip within the GOP:

> McCarthy was a product of sixteen years of being out of office. Eisenhower had not been alone in thinking that McCarthy's crusade against Communists in the government was a tactic he used for getting the attention he craved after ten years of serving in obscurity in a Democrat-controlled Congress. The Senator, in fact, apparently had help in crafting his first speech on the subject

in Wheeling, West Virginia in 1950. His charges were resonant with the times, though not everyone saw the Communist threat as a force that [was likely] to distort our own institutions.⁹⁰

REPUBLICANS TURN THE FIRE ON THEMSELVES: THE EMERGENCE OF THE JOHN BIRCH SOCIETY

The demise of Joe McCarthy did not end McCarthyism, or the belief that continued to percolate within the Republican rank and file that McCarthy was on to something when he charged that a vast communist conspiracy lurked within the federal government. On December 8, 1958, Robert H. Welch Jr., inheritor of a vast candy fortune, gathered eleven of his fellow business leaders for a two-day conference in Indianapolis and founded the John Birch Society, named after an army intelligence officer who was killed in a confrontation with Chinese communist soldiers the week after World War II ended.⁹¹ The Birchers were ardent admirers of Joseph McCarthy and believed, as did Welch, that communists constituted a "fifth column" that penetrated all levels of government.⁹² Welch dubbed the assembled group "God's Angry Men!" and commended them for "devoting all or a major part" of their lives "to anti-collectivist activities."⁹³

In the organization's founding document, titled *The Blue Book of the John Birch Society*, Robert Welch claimed the communist conspiracy became even more insidious during the Eisenhower years. Welch insisted its purpose was to successfully take down Joseph McCarthy, and that in that endeavor it had been aided and abetted by Eisenhower himself:

> To anybody who had watched the way the administration moved heaven and earth to keep McCarthy from getting at the Army Loyalty Board, or from getting at the protectors within the Pentagon of the whole nest of traitors at Fort Monmouth, it was clear that treason—and a willingness to close one's eyes to treason, which is itself treasonous—were widespread and rampant in our high army circles. . . . Now the real significance of what I have just said lies in the fact that this door of betrayal is known to be wide open, and nobody—in Congress, in the executive branch, in the Pentagon itself—nobody even dares to try to close it.⁹⁴

Eisenhower was reportedly "hopping mad" at the accusation, while former president Truman called the Birchers "the sick among us."⁹⁵

The installation of a Republican president in 1953, one to whom most Republican voters were grateful for ending their twenty-year exile from the White House, did not signal an end to the conspiracy culture that took hold within the GOP during the Roosevelt and Truman years. Instead, Soviet advances in Eastern Europe and the communist takeover of China, coupled with continued Republican congressional losses after 1952, enhanced the underlying belief of the Birchers that a pro-communist deep state remained in control. Welch himself described Eisenhower as a "dedicated, conscious agent of the communist conspiracy" whose "betrayal" of Robert A. Taft at the 1952 Republican National Convention was "the dirtiest deal in American political history," and argued that had it not been for Eisenhower's machinations, Taft would have been nominated and elected and, according to Welch, "McCarthy would be alive today."[96] Welch's contempt for Eisenhower even caused him to believe the president had deliberately ceded the 1954 and 1956 congressional elections to the Democrats: "The communists wanted Eisenhower as president, standing out in single glory above a repudiated Republican Party. They wanted, to work with him, a Democratic Congress—the more 'left wing' the better. And the final blocking of Joe McCarthy by that Democratic Congress was just one of the many objectives they had in mind, to be achieved by the combination."[97] Vice President Richard Nixon, who had built his political career on his strident anticommunism, likewise did not escape Welch's scorn, with the tycoon accusing him of "quietly knifing McCarthy" and mocking Nixon as a "rider of waves" and "one of the ablest, shrewdest, most disingenuous, and slipperiest politicians that ever showed up on the American scene."[98]

The John Birch Society quickly grew to a membership of thirty thousand people, including two Republican House members, a staff of 240 employees, and more than four hundred bookstores scattered across the United States, with an annual income of $1.3 million from dues collected from its members.[99] Each John Birch Society chapter was limited to twenty members, a design that Welch believed would preserve secrecy and attract "top-flight men . . . who think the same way you and I do."[100] In a 1961 report authored by the state attorney general of California, home to three hundred John Birch Society chapters, members of the organization were described as "wealthy businessmen, retired military leaders, and little old ladies in tennis shoes."[101] H. L. Hunt, a prominent Texas oilman, praised the group on his radio program *Life Line*, saying Welch "knows a good deal about the communist conspiracy."[102] *Life Line*—heard five to seven times a week on 311 radio stations and twice daily on 40 others, reaching forty-six states—proclaimed, "Extreme patriotism is the constructive answer to the mistaken plot to kill freedom everywhere."[103] The Reverend W. A. Criswell, head of a large Southern Baptist congregation, commended the John Birch Society and railed against "the leftists, the liberals, the pinks, and the welfare statists who are soft on communism and easy towards Russia."[104] Major General Edwin Walker, commander of ten thousand troops in post–World War II Europe and recipient of the Silver Star, distributed Bircher material to those under his command with instructions to read it—an act that led to an internal investigation, censure, and subsequent resignation at the request of the Kennedy administration.[105] During a news conference after Walker's departure, President Kennedy said, "I am not sure that the John Birch Society is wrestling with the real problems which are created by the communists' advance around the world," later telling a Democratic party fundraiser, "There have always been those on the fringes of our society who have sought to escape their own responsibility by finding a simple solution, an appealing slogan or a convenient scapegoat."[106]

In the aftermath of Walker's resignation, Attorney General Robert F. Kennedy labeled the John Birch Society "a tremendous danger" and excoriated "those, who, in the name of fighting communism, sow the seeds of suspicion ... against the foundations of our government—Congress, the Supreme Court, and even the presidency itself."[107] Myer Feldman, a deputy special counsel to the president, warned, "The radical right-wing constitutes a formidable force in American life today."[108] Kennedy was advised to base his 1964 reelection campaign on the dangers posed by extremists such as the John Birch Society, with one Democratic senator writing the White House, "There is a popular revulsion against the extremists of the right wing [and the administration should] keep the villain alive and kicking for a year from now."[109]

Many Republicans embraced the support they received from the John Birch Society even as they refrained from explicitly criticizing Robert Welch. Barry Goldwater praised the Birchers, saying "they believe in God, they believe in the Constitution, they believe in freedom," and called them "the finest people in my community [and] the kind [of people] we need in politics."[110] Goldwater claimed that the John Birch Society was not "extremist," telling a University of Nevada audience in 1964: "If you could read the purposes of the John Birch Society, it would be very difficult for any American to disagree with them. It's sort of like free beer and mother love. You got to go along with them."[111] Goldwater also praised the organization's followers: "Every other person in Phoenix is a member of the John Birch Society. I'm not talking about commie-haunted apple pickers or cactus drunks. I'm talking about the highest cast of men of affairs."[112] Running for governor of California in 1966, Ronald Reagan said it was unfair to label all Birchers "crazies." He welcomed their support, stating, "Any member of the society who supports me will be buying my philosophy. I won't be buying theirs."[113]

Fueling the Birchers' appeal was their unshakable conviction that the United States was on the verge of a communist takeover. Welch stated that the "Communists are much further advanced and more deeply entrenched than is realized by even most of the serious students of the danger among the anti-Communists."[114] This, he believed, was the result of the implementation of a strategy that was "so gradual and insidious that Soviet rule is slipped over so far on the American people, before they even realize it is happening, that they can no longer resist the Communist conspiracy as free citizens but can resist the Communist tyranny only by themselves becoming conspirators against established government."[115] According to Welch, the evidence was in plain sight:

> (1) Greatly expanded government spending, for missiles, for so-called defense generally, for foreign aid, for every conceivable means of getting rid of ever larger sums of American money—as wastefully as possible. (2) Higher and then much higher taxes. (3) An increasingly unbalanced budget, despite the higher taxes.... (4) Wild inflation of our currency, leading rapidly towards its ultimate repudiation. (5) Government controls of prices, wages, and materials supposedly to combat inflation. (6) Greatly increased socialistic controls over every operation of our economy and our daily lives. This is to be accompanied, naturally and automatically, by a correspondingly huge increase in the size of our bureaucracy, and in both the cost and reach of our domestic government. (7) Far more centralization of power in Washington, and the practical elimination of our state lines.[116]

The Birchers created an apocalyptic vision in which politics was no longer an ordinary battle between two parties but a conflict "between light and darkness; between freedom and slavery; between the spirit of Christianity and the spirit of anti-Christ for the souls and bodies of men."[117] Welch cast this conflict in the familiar terms that characterize today's culture wars: "All faith has been replaced, or is rapidly being replaced, by a pragmatic opportunism with hedonistic aims."[118]

This infusion of values associated with individual rights, along with an evangelical-like Christianity, made any loss akin to a political Armageddon, which gave the John Birch Society its raison d'être and energized its supporters. Welch defined the terms of the struggle: a communist believes "that a collectivist society should swallow up all individuals, make their lives and their energies completely subservient to the needs and the purposes of the collectivist state; and that any means are permissible to achieve this end."[119] The *"true Americanist,"* on the other hand, "believes the individual should retain the freedom to make his own bargain with life, and the responsibility for the results of that bargain; and that means are as important as ends in the civilized social order which he desires."[120] For Welch, the struggle was already at a tipping point: "We have no chance unless the specific battles are fought *as part of a larger and more lasting movement to restore once again an upward reach to the heart of man.*"[121]

Welch was no fan of either Franklin Roosevelt's New Deal or Dwight Eisenhower's Modern Republicanism, seeing both as furthering the aims of the communists and moving the country down a socialist path. His opposition to big government was not rooted merely in a philosophical difference and a longing for an earlier, simpler time but in a conviction that the enlargement of government had been led *"by a determined minority"* of presumed communists and Democrats who subverted elections and thwarted the will of the majority.[122] For Welch and his followers, the acquisition of political power was obtained by closed-door conspiracies unseen and unknown by a vast majority of the public. Thus, hidden enemies lay everywhere, both inside the federal government and among foreign adversaries. These included the United Nations, "the instrument of Communist global conquest,"[123] which would be used to obtain "the gradual surrender of American sovereignty,"[124] and the civil rights movement whose goal was to tear the country asunder and establish an "independent Negro-Soviet Republic."[125] After watching a filmed meeting of the John Birch Society, Arthur Larson, architect of Dwight Eisenhower's Modern Republicanism, said: "I have never had the privilege of seeing a

John Birch Society meeting at first hand before, and if someone had told me I never could have believed it. I feel as though I've come out of a totally different planet. I see things being stated as fact that bear no relation to the facts at all."[126]

Welch saw the Republican Party as incapable of stopping the advance of socialism and the loss of the country, believing the Eisenhower administration was engaged in the same backroom conspiracies that kept the Democratic Party in power. It was this firm conviction that prompted Welch to speak of his supporters as "one mighty weapon" whose purpose should be to create "a phalanx of tens of thousands of spears which can be hurled simultaneously as one mighty weapon against any vulnerable spot in the Communist line."[127] This led Welch to advocate a militaristic-style takeover of the Republican Party: "We are at a stage, Gentlemen, where the only sure political victories are achieved by non-political organization; by organization which has a surer, more positive, and more permanent purpose than the immediate political goals that are only means to an end; by the organization which has a backbone, and cohesiveness and strength, and definiteness of direction, which are impossible for the old-style political party organization."[128] To that end, Welch proposed gathering "a million men and the resources consistent with the dedication of these men" that could "move in on the elections thereafter with both more manpower and more resources."[129] That meant ruthlessly taking over the Republican Party from the outside with, presumably, Welch in charge, and establishing an American version of authoritarianism. As Welch stated: "The John Birch Society will operate under completely authoritative control at all levels.... As I have said before, no collection of debating societies is ever going to stop the Communist conspiracy from taking over, and I have no intention of adding another frustrated group to their number. We mean business every step of the way."[130]

DONALD TRUMP AND THE "PARANOID STYLE" REDUX

In 1960, Richard M. Nixon ended his long apprenticeship as vice president to seek the Republican presidential nomination. But Nixon's ascendance to the top of the Republican ticket was threatened by the rise of Nelson

A. Rockefeller, who, in 1958, was elected governor of New York in a landslide. Rockefeller, scion of the famous Rockefeller dynasty, was the first undersecretary in the newly created Department of Health, Education, and Welfare and was emerging as a favorite among liberal Republicans who saw Nixon's election as hardly assured and thought a ticket headed by the popular governor was the better bet. Rockefeller fully subscribed to Eisenhower's Modern Republican philosophy, once boasting, "You could plop me down in a town of two hundred people, and the first thing I'd do is try to start solving their problems." One conservative voter, less than enthralled with Rockefeller's approach, wrote the governor, saying, "Thank God our town is too small for your plopping."[131] Throughout 1960, Rockefeller hinted he would submit to a draft at the Republican National Convention—a threat made even more potent by Eisenhower's tepid endorsement of Nixon's renomination as vice president in 1956. Seeking to avert any potential challenger, the two men met secretly in New York City and worked out a compromise on the 1960 platform, with Nixon acceding to Rockefeller's demands on defense, health care, and civil rights policy.

The Compact of Fifth Avenue, as the deal was derisively termed by outraged conservatives, angered Barry Goldwater, who called it "a surrender," the "Munich of the Republican Party," and a guarantee of "Republican defeat in November."[132] In his best-selling manifesto, *Conscience of a Conservative*, Goldwater strongly criticized those Republicans, including Nixon and Eisenhower, who believed the party's candidates "should be economic conservatives, but conservatives with a heart."[133] Addressing the 1960 convention, Goldwater extolled the principles of freedom and limited government, telling the delegates: "The true Republican philosophy is a dynamic, compelling doctrine dealing with the full nature of man and not with his material needs alone.... The touchstone is freedom. The goal: the improvement of man and his society.... And the perpetuation of that concept of limited central government which provides a climate for maximum social and individual progress."[134] Robert Welch got on the Goldwater bandwagon and believed that Nelson Rockefeller wanted "a one world international socialist government.[135] The John Birch Society sent postcards to Republican delegates that read, "Nominate anybody you please, I'm voting for Goldwater."[136] But after the Nixon-Rockefeller compact was announced, Goldwater issued this rallying cry: "Let's grow up, conservatives! If we want to take this Party back, and I think we can someday, let's get to work."[137]

Nixon's loss to Kennedy both angered and empowered the conservative movement, and four years later it was Goldwater who was the Republican nominee for president. Goldwater had the enthusiastic endorsement of Robert Welch. But, more important, his nomination energized conservatives, who were long accustomed to defeat at the hands of the party establishment. Despite a last-ditch attempt to thwart Goldwater's nomination, the establishment could not agree on a replacement. Richard Nixon was out of the picture, having lost his 1962 gubernatorial race in California; Nelson Rockefeller also was out, having lost to Goldwater in the primaries after his quick divorce, remarriage, and birth of his son doomed his campaign.[138] At the last minute, Pennsylvania governor William Scranton threw his hat into the ring, but it was too little, too late.

Still, the party establishment did not give up without a fight. In a letter to the convention delegates, the Scranton forces denounced Goldwaterism as "a whole crazy-quilt collection of absurd and dangerous positions that would be soundly repudiated by the American people in November."[139] As if to emphasize Scranton's censure, Goldwater delegates vetoed a resolution condemning the John Birch Society and other extremist groups. Addressing the convention, Nelson Rockefeller fumed over "these people who have nothing in common with Americanism."[140] At this, one Goldwater delegate shouted, "You goddamned Socialist!—get that fink."[141] Theodore H. White presciently observed that neither Rockefeller nor Scranton could prevent the arrival of "a new thing in American conventions—not a meeting, not a clash, but a *coup d'etat.*"[142] Conservatives departed the convention hall, thrilled they had finally won a presidential nomination for one of their own. More recruits were added to their ranks as new players took center stage. In California, Ronald Reagan made his political debut with a television endorsement of Goldwater—a performance that catapulted him into the California governorship two years later.

Accepting the nomination, Goldwater issued his famous declaration: "I would remind you that extremism in the defense of liberty is no vice! And let me remind you also that moderation in the pursuit of justice is no virtue."[143] One college student, inspired by Goldwater, said, "You walk around with your Goldwater button, and you feel that thrill of treason."[144] Democrats were giddy at the prospect of labeling Goldwater an extremist, with one member in the press gallery exclaiming, "My God, he's going to run as Barry Goldwater."[145] But Republicans applauded Goldwater's take-no-prisoners attitude. As one delegate put it, "I would rather be one against 20,000 and believe I was right. That's what I admire about Goldwater. He's like that."[146] Others praised Goldwater with comments such as "He is straightforward"; "He does not compromise"; "He doesn't pander to the public; he's against expediency"; "He is frank"; "He has courage"; "He stands up for what he believes"; "He won't play footsie with the people"; "He votes his convictions when he knows he's right"; "He doesn't go along with the crowd"; "He meets issues head-on"; "Goldwater speaks about things others avoid. Most politicians like to avoid issues"; "He keeps his promises"; "He doesn't change his mind"; and "He is not confused."[147]

Addressing the convention, Dwight Eisenhower seized on the populist revolt, adding these lines to his prepared speech: "Let us particularly scorn the divisive efforts of those outside our family, including sensation-seeking columnists and commentators, because, my friends, I assure you that these are people who couldn't care less about our party."[148] Forecasting the importance of cultural issues in politics, Eisenhower added: "Let us not be guilty of maudlin sympathy for the criminal, who roaming the streets with switchblade knife and illegal firearms seeking a helpless prey, suddenly becomes upon apprehension a poor, underprivileged person who counts upon the compassion of our society and the laxness or weaknesses of too many courts to forgive his offence."[149] At this, the Goldwater delegates roared their approval.

Goldwater's nomination represented more than a comeback for conservatives who had long been frustrated in their futile attempts to win back control of their party. For them, Goldwater's triumph represented what historian Richard Hofstadter termed the "paranoid style" of conspiratorial thinking that had long been evident on the Republican right:

> As a member of the avant-garde who is capable of perceiving the conspiracy before it is fully obvious to an as yet unaroused public, the paranoid is a militant leader. He does not see social conflict as something to be mediated and compromised, in the manner of the working politician. Since what is at stake is always a conflict between absolute good and absolute evil, what is necessary is not compromise but the will to fight things out to a finish. Since the enemy is thought of as being totally evil and totally unappeasable, he must be totally eliminated—if not from the world, at least from the theatre of operations to which the paranoid directs his attention. This demand for total triumph leads to the formulation of hopelessly unrealistic goals, and since these goals are

not even remotely attainable, failure constantly heightens the paranoid's sense of frustration. Even partial success leaves him with the same feeling of powerlessness with which he began, and this in turn only strengthens his awareness of the vast and terrifying quality of the enemy he opposes.[150]

Hofstadter's depiction of the paranoid style had long been part of Republican politics—a by-product, as he aptly put it, of "angry minds" who see themselves as "manning the barricades of civilization" against those determined to create an apocalypse that would destroy the world as they know it.[151] Goldwater's landslide defeat, the largest GOP loss since Alf Landon's in 1936, served to temporarily quell the conspiracy thinking within the Republican Party. Congressional Republican leaders Everett Dirksen and Gerald Ford urged every Republican to "reject membership in any radical or extremist organization, including any which attempts to use the Republican Party for its own ends or which seeks to undermine the basic principles of American freedom and constitutional government."[152]

But the tendency of the Republican Party to be home to extreme right-wing organizations and conspiracy thinkers remained. During the 1970s, many Republicans, including Nixon himself, believed there was a conspiracy to remove Richard Nixon from office. Prior to Watergate, Nixon ordered break-ins into the office of Daniel Ellsberg's psychiatrist's after Ellsberg made the *Pentagon Papers* public; Nixon also endorsed a burglary of the Brookings Institution looking for material that could damage his presidency. Even though Nixon had denounced the John Birch Society long before, he believed, like that organization, that a deep state composed of angry Democrats and government bureaucrats was conspiring to embarrass him and take down his presidency.[153] In a taped Oval Office conversation, Nixon told his national security adviser, Henry Kissinger: "The press is the enemy. The establishment is the enemy. The professors are the enemy."[154] Nixon even went so far as to compose an "enemies list" that included the names of political opponents and prominent journalists.

Like those in the John Birch Society, many Republicans believed they were victims of a "deep state" that was willing to subvert the will of the majority, resulting in what Irving Kristol perceptively forecast in 1966 was an emerging New Right—appealing to self-reliant voters who saw themselves losing control over their destiny and that of their children, who saw that "whatever is happening, it is happening *to* them, that they are the objects, not the subjects, of contemporary history."[155] With the passage of time, there grew within the Republican Party a deep-seated alienation and fear of the future. In 1985, John Dolan, head of the National Conservative Political Action Committee, wrote that although Ronald Reagan had twice been elected to the presidency by landslide margins, "his—our—agenda is stymied by people who simply disregard the will of the American public and continue to proceed with their own liberal programs."[156] Conservatives rallied around the slogan "Let Reagan Be Reagan," but the reality was that Reagan was always an adroit politician who knew the limits of what he could accomplish. Even so, New York senator Daniel Patrick Moynihan presciently saw an emerging mutation of conservative thought that would pose problems in the years ahead. According to Moynihan, "there have been few voices heard from the political ranks" to quash what he called an emerging "paranoid style on the Right." "Frankly," Moynihan wrote, the reason for this emerging paranoid style was clear: "I smell fear."[157]

The rise of Donald Trump gave the paranoid style a new lease on life. As Hofstadter noted, the modern right wing "feels dispossessed," believing that "America has been largely taken away from them and their kind, though they are determined to try to repossess it and to prevent the final destructive act of subversion."[158] For them that final, destructive act is the by-product of a powerful clique, often located deep inside the federal government, that is determined to thwart the majority. Those who subscribe to this paranoid style see themselves as victims of dark, sinister forces, and the resultant battle is its own Armageddon of good versus evil. In 2016, Richard Anton likened the Donald Trump–Hillary Clinton contest to the doomed Flight 93 that crashed in Pennsylvania on September 11, 2001. Anton envisioned a Clinton presidency as ensuring a political Armageddon, whereas with Trump voters should take their chances: "2016 is the Flight 93 election: charge the cockpit or you die. You may die anyway. You—or the leader of your party—may make it into the cockpit and not know how to fly or land the plane. There are no guarantees. Except one: if you don't try, death is certain."[159]

Donald Trump capitalized on this view, telling his followers they were victims of powerful forces that had taken away their jobs and were conspiring to change the country's contours by giving open access to minority groups who would soon become the new American majority. Only

Trump, as he later put it, could "Save America." In his inaugural address in 2017, Trump described how powerful elites victimized those with little influence:

> For too long, a small group in our Nation's Capital has reaped the rewards of Government while the people have borne the cost. Washington flourished, but the people did not share its wealth. Politicians prospered, but the jobs left, and the factories closed. The establishment protected itself, but not the citizens of our country. Their victories have not been your victories; their triumphs have not been your triumphs; and while they celebrated in our Nation's Capital, there was little to celebrate for struggling families all across our land.[160]

Notwithstanding Trump's denunciation of the establishment, 55 percent of Trump voters in 2020 continued to believe that "regardless of who is officially in charge of the government and other organizations, there is a single group of people who secretly control events and rule the world together."[161]

Despite his riches, Trump aligned himself with his working-class supporters and, like them, cast himself as a victim of the deep state. Trump's sense of victimhood, and his belief that within the labyrinths of the bureaucracy were those determined to stop him, had long been evident in his persona. In 2016, Trump claimed there were "millions of people registered to vote that shouldn't be registered to vote."[162] Even as he was on the verge of winning, Trump asserted that the election was about to be stolen. In a final debate with Hillary Clinton, Trump alleged there were illegal votes about to be cast. Clinton's response and Trump's angry rejoinder were especially prescient of what was to come:

> Clinton: You know, every time Donald thinks things are not going in his direction, he claims whatever it is, is rigged against him. The FBI conducted a year-long investigation into my emails. They concluded there was no case; he said the FBI was rigged. He lost the Iowa caucus. He lost the Wisconsin primary. He said the Republican primary was rigged against him. Then Trump University gets sued for fraud and racketeering; he claims the court system and the federal judge is rigged against him. There was even a time when he didn't get an Emmy for his TV program three years in a row and he started tweeting that the Emmys were rigged against him.
>
> Trump: Should have gotten it.[163]

Trump reiterated his sense of victimhood once he began to comprehend that he lost the 2020 election, telling his supporters in the early morning hours after the polls closed: "This is a fraud on the American public. This is an embarrassment to our country. We were getting ready to win this election. Frankly, we did win this election."[164]

Donald Trump's claims gave rise to conspiracy theories and groups that espoused them. Addressing the Proud Boys from the 2020 debate stage, Trump refused to disown them, instead advising that they "stand back and stand by."[165] These words signaled that if he should lose, it was the result of political shenanigans and stolen votes engineered by a powerful cohort that was determined to oust him from the White House. This thinking gained momentum among previously serious conservative thinkers. Claes Ryn, a political theorist and influential voice on the American right, wrote in the *American Conservative* that fraudulent ballots were cast in Pennsylvania; that election workers in Georgia "pulled out suitcases with ballots from under a covered table" and "fed them into the voting machines"; that "dead people, non-citizens, and non-residents" voted. This, Ryn charged, was "organized manipulation on a large scale," adding: "Over the last few years, we have lived through deep, protracted, intense hostility to Donald Trump. Attempts to cripple or get rid of him have evinced considerable ruthlessness, and they have obviously involved much elaborate collusion."[166]

Such thinking emphasizes the sense of victimhood that characterized Trump and his followers. In 2018, David Frum noted, "The desire to wipe the smirk off the condescending face of some resented critics—to expose them, diminish them, *hurt* them—is that not the mainspring for so much of the pro-Trump political movement?"[167] Indeed it was, and springing forth from such resentments came the desire for payback. In text messages to White House chief of staff Mark Meadows after the 2020 ballots had been cast and counted, Ginni Thomas, wife of Supreme Court justice Clarence Thomas, wrote, "The majority knows Biden and the Left is attempting the greatest Heist of our history."[168] Seeing the struggle in biblical terms, Meadows responded: "This is a fight of good versus evil. Evil always looks like the victor until the King of Kings triumphs. Do not grow weary in well doing. The fight continues. I have staked my career on it."[169] Thomas then advised Meadows to "release the Kraken and save us from the left taking America down"—the Kraken being a name mentioned earlier by discredited Trump attorney Sidney Powell.[170] During the insurrection at the US Capitol on January 6, 2021, the so-called QAnon Shaman, with his painted face and horned cap, sat on the Senate dais and offered a prayer thanking God "for allowing us to get rid of the Communists, the globalists, and the traitors within our government."[171] Such thinking is akin to that of the John Birch Society, and the insurrection itself was in the spirit of Robert Welch, who once said that a great nation should not be ruled by "the sudden whims of the electorate."[172]

In the 1960s, serious conservatives agreed with William F. Buckley that groups like the John Birch Society were a "menace" to the conservative movement.[173] Buckley wondered how the organization's members could tolerate "such paranoid and unpatriotic drivel."[174] Denouncing the Birchers in *National Review*, Buckley wrote, "The underlying problem is whether conservatives can continue to acquiesce quietly in a rendition of the causes of the decline of the Republic and the entire Western world which is false."[175] Barry Goldwater and Ronald Reagan welcomed the support of the Birchers but kept a strategic distance from them and refused to espouse their conspiracy theories. Richard Nixon's election to the presidency in 1968, followed by Republican presidents Gerald Ford, Ronald Reagan, and the two Bushes, helped keep the conspiracists at bay. But the rise of Barack Obama gave rise to conspiracy theories that would haunt Democratic campaigns for years to come. Daniel Allott reports that Kathy Vinehout, a Democratic state senator from western Wisconsin, described how her constituents often repeated various conspiracy theories: "I heard over and over again from the election judges that if Hillary [Clinton] won, people would not be able to fill their freezer. This is really important in a rural area because people do hunt for food, and they have for generations."[176] Others consistently repeated that Clinton would "take away all the guns and abolish the Second Amendment."[177]

But Trump gave the conspiracists an amplified voice. One of the most potent conspiracy theories to take root during the Trump years was a belief that an anonymous military intelligence officer, operating inside the government under the pseudonym Q, revealed secret knowledge of a coming world event his followers dubbed "the storm."[178] Anonymous social media users were encouraged to distribute and interpret these cryptic messages on their internet accounts.[179] This movement began with an offhand comment Trump made on the evening of October 5, 2017. Standing with a group of military leaders and their families, Trump told the assembled reporters: "You know what this represents? Maybe it's the calm before the storm," implying something big was about to happen.[180] Nearly a year later at a Trump rally in Tampa, Florida, hundreds of people were wearing Q shirts and holding aloft signs with Q slogans.[181] Between 2018 and 2020, nearly one hundred Republican candidates professed their belief in the mysterious Q.[182] Michael Flynn, Trump's former national security adviser, took the "digital soldier oath" over the July 4, 2020, weekend, which made him a true QAnon enlistee.[183] For his part, Donald Trump retweeted fantasies and wild memes posted by Q supporters. Followers of Q believed Democrats were secretly trafficking children and forcing them to engage in illegal sex acts, that Hillary Clinton was already under arrest, that the infamous Steele dossier linking Donald Trump to Vladimir Putin was a forgery, and that an imposter was playing the role of Joe Biden as president.[184] When asked about QAnon, Trump replied evasively, "I don't know much about the movement other than I understand they like me very much, which I appreciate."[185] By January 6, 2021, many QAnon followers were active participants in the Capitol insurrection. And with Trump out of office, their numbers grew, and Trump rallies became filled with QAnon believers and paraphernalia. At one 2022 Trump gathering, many in the audience raised their index fingers, mimicking the QAnon salute, "Where We Go One, We Go All."[186]

As with the John Birch Society of the 1950s, conspiracists are making their influence felt within the Republican ranks. In a 2022 article in *The Bulwark*, Robert Tracinski compares today's conspiracy groups to the John Birch Society, writing: "The Birchers are back. And they're winning." According to Tracinski, the similarities between the two movements are striking:

> We have a conspiracy theory that explains everything conservatives think has gone wrong in the world by positing the machinations of a secret cabal that controls everything from the intelligence agencies to the schools.
> We have the rapid spread of these crackpot theories to otherwise normal and respectable people in the rank and file of the movement.
> We have an attempt to make the conspiracists into the ultimate representatives of opposition to totalitarian communism, and a corresponding attempt

to dismiss any conservative critics of the conspiracists as weak-kneed appeasers handing over the country to its enemies.

We have the uneasy balancing act of conservatives in the media and in politics who don't want to denounce the crackpots for fear of angering their party's base.[187]

Back in the 1950s, Richard Nixon, echoing Machiavelli, said: "People react to fear, not love. They don't teach you that in Sunday School—but it's true."[188] Despite his penchant for braggadocio, the core of Donald Trump's appeal did not rest on his Horatio Alger–like story of accumulating wealth upon more wealth but on fear: fear of racial minorities; Muslims; foreign powers, especially China; feminists; powerful media conglomerates; college professors; the deep state; Democrats; and—most important—the future.[189] Barack Obama's ascendance to the presidency gave Trump a platform on which to raise questions about Obama's legitimacy and label him as the "other"—someone who was deeply un-American and a threat to the nation. At an Iowa candidate forum, Trump said of Obama, "I don't know if he loves America."[190] For years, Trump claimed that Obama was an illegitimate president who was born in Kenya. In numerous personal and media appearances, Trump sowed doubts about Obama, posting on Twitter on August 6, 2012, that "an 'extremely credible source' has called my office and told me that @BarackObama's birth certificate is a fraud."[191] Trump later claimed that he had people researching Obama's birth, saying, "They cannot believe what they're finding."[192] An annoyed Obama denounced what he called "carnival barkers."[193] He told reporters, "We do not have time for this kind of silliness."[194] Obama sent a representative to Hawaii to produce a long-form birth certificate proving once and for all that he was born in the state.[195]

But Donald Trump's innuendo found a ready-made audience among Republicans who believed their party's losses were the by-products of a conspiracy designed to hide the truth and keep Obama in power—similar, in fact, to the conspiracy theories that claimed a secret cabal thwarted a Republican majority and elected Franklin D. Roosevelt and Harry Truman. Republicans bought the lies. In 2016, 72 percent of registered Republican voters doubted Obama's citizenship, with 41 percent saying he was *not* born in the United States.[196] When Trump finally conceded the obvious, he immediately regretted it, telling a source he would have done better in the polls if he had continued to promote the lie.[197] Trump acolyte Roger Stone called Trump's charge "brilliant" in its singular appeal to his right-wing base.[198] But Trump didn't stop there, snidely implying that Obama was a Muslim and suggesting there was something on Obama's birth certificate, "maybe religion, maybe it says he is a Muslim."[199] Once more, Trump sowed doubt: according to a 2015 survey, only 28 percent of Republicans correctly answered that Obama was a Christian while 43 percent said he was a Muslim.[200] These charges had one important aim: to present Obama as a symbol of the "other," an illegitimate occupier of the White House whose race and perceived religious and cultural identities portended an ominous future. One Trump rally attendee in 2016 captured his appeal: "We have a problem in this country. It's called Muslims. You know our current president is one. You know he's not even an American."[201] Indeed, much had changed since John McCain took away the microphone after a supporter called Obama "an Arab." Back then, McCain chastised the woman, saying: "No ma'am. He's a decent family man, [a] citizen that I just happen to have disagreements with on fundamental issues."[202]

It wasn't only these falsehoods that Trump promoted. Before, during, and after his presidency, Trump spouted a variety of conspiracies, each designed to cast himself and his supporters as victims. The list is a particularly long one: that Obama wiretapped Trump Tower; that Muslim Americans celebrated the 9/11 attack; that global warming is a Chinese hoax; that vaccines cause autism and wind turbines cause cancer; that Ted Cruz's father helped assassinate John F. Kennedy; that Supreme Court justice Antonin Scalia died by mysterious means; and, of course, that the 2020 election was "stolen." With each preposterous claim, Trump's dominance grew, and the power of the presidency gave Trump the means to act. Thus, the "guardrails" and institutional restraints incorporated into the Constitution came under a severe test. And Trump's continued dominance of the Republican Party after his 2020 defeat transformed it from a party of opposition into an insurgent party that sees itself as victimized and is bent on exacting revenge. Eschewing serious policy proposals, Republicans came to believe that an array of powerful forces stood at the ready to disenfranchise them. Donald Trump's rise to the presidency gave permission slips to those both inside and outside of government to adopt

Hofstadter's paranoid style, and—most important—to act on it. Announcing his 2024 candidacy, Trump derided the "weaponization" of the Justice Department, telling his ardent supporters, "I am a victim."[203] Roderick P. Hart concluded, "Once in office, the paranoid style became Trump's master more than he its."[204] Hart added, "Typically, he would maintain his reserve as long as possible and then—boom—another explosion."[205]

While conspiracy theories have long been part of American history dating back to the Anti-Mason Party of the 1830s, the Know-Nothing Party of the 1850s, and the Populist Party of the 1890s, these third-party movements flamed out as the two major parties reasserted their dominance. What makes today's crisis different is that the conspiracy culture that germinated for decades within the Republican Party, but was always thwarted by an establishment determined to win support from independents and Democrats, is, for now, a dominant strain that encourages magical thinking and has transformed the GOP into an entity that threatens the future of democracy. Hart writes that a "nation that becomes addicted to the paranoid style is surely in trouble."[206]

A PARTY WHERE CONSPIRACY THEORIES THRIVE

Social media has increased the additive power of conspiracy theories among Republicans. To cite but one example, in a poll taken in March 2022, 53 percent of Trump voters said it was either "definitely true" or "probably true" that "top Democrats are involved in elite child sex-trafficking rings."[207] The issue has taken on a life of its own. A spokesman for Florida Republican governor Ron DeSantis characterizes anyone opposed to the state's "Don't Say Gay Bill" as "probably a groomer, or at least you don't denounce the grooming of four-to-eight-year-old children."[208] Republican congresswoman Marjorie Taylor Greene went even further, describing Democrats as "the party of princess predators from Disney."[209] Elise Stefanik, chair of the House GOP Conference, tweeted that the Democrats and the "usual pedo[phile] grifters" are "out of touch" with ordinary Americans.[210] These comments speak to Republican base voters, and that is where the energy of the party resides, not in a shattered GOP establishment.

In a major study conducted by the Associated Press and the National

Opinion Research Center, about one-third of Republicans were classified as "high conspiratorial thinkers," compared with 24 percent of Democrats and 25 percent of independents. Looking at white "high conspiracy thinkers," 59 percent identified as Republicans, and 51 percent cast ballots for Donald Trump in 2020. The views of these "high conspiratorial thinkers" continue a strain of conspiratorial thinking in American history—attitudes that mirror the views once held by Robert Welch and the John Birch Society:

- 96 percent agree, "Even though we live in a democracy, a few people will always run things anyway."
- 94 percent believe, "The people who really 'run' the country are not known to voters."
- 89 percent say, "Big events, like wars, recessions, and the outcomes of elections are controlled by small groups of people who are working in secret against the rest of us."
- 85 percent believe, "Much of our lives are being controlled by plots hatched in secret places."[211]

In a speech he gave at Stanford University in 2002, Barack Obama noted the dangers posed by unregulated content posted on social media. Citing the ubiquitous "personal information bubbles," Obama declared that "our prejudices aren't challenged, they're reinforced."[212] Polling confirms Obama's thesis: a post-2020 election survey found 71 percent of Republican respondents believed that Joe Biden was "probably not" or "definitely not" a legitimate president.[213] Taking note of such extraordinary numbers, Obama concluded, "That's a lot of people."[214] According to Obama, the danger posed by today's Republican Party is not just a paucity of information and ideas but a corrosion of the democratic process itself: "People like [Vladimir] Putin and Steve Bannon, for that matter, understand that it's not necessary for people to believe this information in order to weaken democratic institutions. You just have to flood a country's public square with enough raw sewage. You just have to raise enough questions, spread enough dirt, plant enough conspiracy theorizing that citizens no longer know what to believe."[215] Or, as Bannon himself put it, the best way to deal with the media is "to flood the zone with shit."[216] In today's social media environment, facts are not welcome, but doubt is.

REPUBLICANS ABANDON THE IDEA OF RESPONSIBLE GOVERNMENT

The diminishment of moderate Republicans and traditional conservatives, who were once attracted to the Republican Party by a commitment to ideas and principles, means that the politics of conspiracy, victimhood, and grievance makes the political scientists' long-held vision of a "responsible party government," in which parties articulated policies and elections were based on voters choosing between differing ideas and programs, now passé.[217] Advocates of a return to accepted norms of political conflict are calling on Republicans to articulate ideas that can restore the party to greatness. Even Democrats, who long for the days of a contest based on ideas, seek a revived Republican Party centered around a reiteration of conservative principles. Former House Speaker Nancy Pelosi recently offered this advice to Republicans: "Take back your party. The country needs a strong Republican Party, not one that has been hijacked as a cult."[218] But for the moment, a revitalized Republican Party is not on the horizon. As Jonathan Haidt perceptively noted, Trump understood that "outrage is the key to virality, stage performance crushes competence."[219] That lesson has not been lost on other would-be Trump Republicans.

Absent serious ideas, a culture of conspiracy has become embedded within the Republican Party, and as it has grown, trust has given way to doubt and denial. As Barack Obama noted in his warning about the corrosive effects of disinformation and the Republican Party's willingness to promote it, "Once [people] lose trust in their leaders, in mainstream media, in political institutions, in each other, in the possibility of truth, the game's won. And as [Vladimir] Putin discovered leading up to the 2016 election, our own social media platforms are well-designed to support such a mission, such a project."[220] Or, as Edward H. Miller wrote in his biography of John Birch Society founder Robert Welch, "We live in an age of Robert Welch," an age where doubt and conspiracy theories abound in the twenty-first century.[221]

Thus, the question that lies before us is this: Is the game over? Republicans may be well on their way to a final victory by creating so much fear, distrust, and doubt that the rules of the game are permanently altered, as the next chapter explores.

5. A Party Transformed

> The man who has come to regard the ballot box as a juggler's hat has renounced his allegiance.
> —Benjamin Harrison, inaugural address, March 4, 1889

In 1860, Georgia Democratic congressman James Jackson stood before a town hall gathering and denounced the Republican Party as an organization "banded together by . . . one common tie—*hostility to you and to your property*" whose mission was to destroy "*the equal rights of every citizen of every state.*" Jackson warned that if Republicans were not stopped, "your peace is at an end—your property destroyed—your land now blooming like a garden [would be] left desolate as a desert." Failure would create a political cloud that is "black and ominous and threatens to discharge its flood of fury—its storm of hail and lightening [sic] upon you at any moment."[1]

Abraham Lincoln's Republican Party would not be thwarted despite the dark cloud of fury that became the Civil War. Once that cloud dissipated, the Republican Party resumed its mission to, in the words of historian Heather Cox Richardson, "make men free."[2] In 1865, a Republican-controlled Congress ratified the Thirteenth Amendment abolishing slavery, with enough states concurring. Two years later, another Republican-controlled Congress approved the Military Reconstruction Act allowing Blacks to choose delegates and rewrite the state constitutions of the Old Confederacy.[3] But while more than 90 percent of Blacks resided in the South, southern white supremacists were determined to prevent them from casting a ballot.[4] Some even dressed in white sheets to imitate dead Confederate soldiers and terrorized the former slaves to prevent their entrance into the voting booths.[5] For decades, southerners maintained the new state constitutions were, in the words of Mississippi's Democratic senator Theodore G. Bilbo, "the products of fraud and coercion."[6] But despite the intimidation, many Blacks voted, and the rewritten constitutions were ratified.

In 1868, the Fourteenth Amendment granted African Americans full citizenship with a guarantee of due process of law. Its ratification was the death knell for the infamous *Dred Scott v. Sandford* case of 1857, in which the Supreme Court ruled that African Americans "are not included, and were not intended to be included, under the word 'citizens' in the Constitution."[7] Charles Evans Hughes, the 1916 Republican presidential nominee who later became chief justice, cited *Dred Scott* as imposing "self-inflicted wounds" from which it took a generation to recover.[8] By 1870, Republicans had completed their constitutional rewrite by approving the Fifteenth Amendment giving male African Americans the right to cast free and fair ballots.

After the accidental presidency of Andrew Johnson—whose opposition to the Fourteenth Amendment caused Republicans to accuse him of acting "treacherously to the people who elected him and the cause he was pledged to support"[9]—the GOP used its grip on the White House and Congress to ensure its work would be implemented.[10] In 1870, Congress passed the Enforcement Act, which imposed criminal penalties on anyone denying the franchise to Blacks. Congress ordered the Justice Department to enforce the Fourteenth Amendment, and it prosecuted more than one thousand cases against the Ku Klux Klan, which was formed in December 1865 under the leadership of former Confederate general Nathan Bedford Forrest.[11] The Klan was a paramilitary force that promoted its version of "Americanism,"[12] wherein whites waged war against Blacks and immigrants who, they believed, would use their newfound votes to upend the existing white power structure. President Ulysses S. Grant called on the military to suppress the Klan, and in 1871 nine counties in South Carolina were placed under martial law.[13] Grant also signed the Enforcement Act, which transferred power to oversee elections from the states to the federal government, thereby giving Republicans the power to guarantee equal voting rights and representative governments across the Old Confederacy.[14]

The resistance was immediate. Southern Democrats denounced "power-crazed" Republicans "whose racial madness knew no bounds."[15] In Tippah County, Mississippi, the Ku Klux Klan rounded up seventy African Americans and threatened to whip them if they voted for the Republican ticket.[16] Historian Eric Foner writes that the Klan set out to "destroy the Republican infrastructure, undermine the Reconstruction state, reestablish control of the black labor force, and restore racial subordination in every aspect of Southern life."[17] One reason for the white supremacists' resistance was their fear that Blacks would vote for politicians who promised more and better hospitals and schools—measures they claimed would raise taxes and create a new kind of enslavement they called "socialism."[18] By 1876, these so-called Redeemers controlled the southern states, and Reconstruction came to an abrupt halt. Georgia instituted a poll tax in 1877, and by the following year just 10,000 of the state's 369,511 eligible Black voters were registered.[19] Florida, Alabama, Tennessee, Arkansas, Louisiana, and Mississippi quickly followed suit.[20] As one Black man said of life in the South, "We are a majority here, but you may vote till your eyes drop out or your tongue drops out, and you can't count your colored man in one of them boxes, there's a hole gets in the bottom of them boxes some way and lets out our votes."[21] Black disenfranchisement became a hallmark of southern life after 1876 when Congress created a commission that awarded the disputed electoral votes of Louisiana, South Carolina, and Florida to Republican Rutherford B. Hayes, despite his losing the popular vote to Democrat Samuel J. Tilden. Although cries of "Tilden or Blood" filled the air, southern Democrats supported Hayes in return for the removal of Federal troops from the South.[22]

As more African Americans departed the South to find refuge elsewhere, they found little comfort. In Indiana, white Democrats vowed to "cleanout all the g-d d-n n-ggers."[23] At a Rockport rally to cheer the 1880 Democratic nominee, Winfield Scott Hancock, Blacks were attacked as the crowd shouted, "Kill them, kill them."[24] After one African American bystander was shot and killed, the white gunman stood over the body and exclaimed, "One vote less."[25] Indiana Republican governor Oliver P. Morton depicted the Democratic Party using graphic imagery: "Every wolf in sheep's clothing . . . everyone who shoots down Negroes in the streets, burns Negro school-houses and meeting-houses, and murders women and children by the light of their flaming dwellings, calls himself a Democrat."[26]

Despite the deal to put Hayes into the presidential seat, Republicans renewed their cause of establishing African American voting rights, arguing their disenfranchisement amounted to the Democrats "stealing" elections.[27] In the parlance of Donald Trump, Republicans were determined to "stop the steal." The 1888 platform reaffirmed the party's "unswerving devotion . . . to the supreme and sovereign right of every lawful citizen, rich or poor, native or foreign-born, white or black, to cast one free ballot in public elections and to have that ballot duly counted."[28] If elected, Republicans promised to enact "legislation to secure the integrity and purity of elections, which are the fountains of public authority."[29] Maintaining that Grover Cleveland's presidency was illegitimate, Republicans charged, "The present Administration and the Democratic majority in Congress owe their existence to the suppression of the ballot by a criminal nullification of the Constitution and laws of the United States."[30]

Accepting his party's nomination, Benjamin Harrison promised to act. As he stated: "The disfranchisement of a single legal elector by fraud or intimidation is a crime too grave to be regarded lightly. The right of every qualified elector to cast one free ballot and to have it honestly counted must not be questioned. Every constitutional power should be used to make this right secure and to punish frauds upon the ballot."[31]

After a close election, Harrison took the presidential oath on March 4, 1889. In his inaugural address, he declared that denying voters the right to vote was un-American: "The man who has come to regard the ballot box as a juggler's hat has renounced his allegiance."[32] In his first annual message to Congress, Harrison demanded action: "In many parts of our country where the colored population is large, the people of that race are by various devices deprived of any effective exercise of their political rights and of many of their civil rights. The wrong does not expend itself upon those whose votes are suppressed. Every constituency in the Union is wronged."[33] Claiming that the federal government was well within "its well-defined constitutional powers [to] secure to all our people a free exercise of the right of suffrage," Harrison went further, saying, "The colored man should be protected in all of his relations to the Federal Government, whether as litigant, juror, or witness in our courts, as an elector for members of Congress, or as a peaceful traveler upon our interstate railways."[34] One year later, in a second message, Harrison accused Democrats of using "cunningly contrived" election laws "to secure minority control, while violence completes the shortcomings of fraud."[35] Once more, he demanded "Federal supervision of congressional elections" and noted that any objection based on racial hatred "cannot be given any weight in the discussion without dishonor."[36]

Harrison proposed placing federal supervisors in any district where voters petitioned the courts to oversee voter registration. Republicans knew that if Congress acted as Harrison wished, it would dramatically increase their numbers in the House and mitigate any chances for future Democratic majorities. But for many this was a step too far. Even the pro-Republican *New York Times* editorialized against the bill, calling Harrison's men "desperate" to win.[37] Although it passed the House, Senate Democrats blocked the measure when a more pressing priority, the McKinley Tariff bill, awaited enactment.[38] The McKinley bill's sponsors—Republicans Matthew Quay and Donald Cameron of Pennsylvania—were accused of subordinating "the plight of the Negro" to enact protective trade measures.[39] Federal action would have to wait another seventy-five years until the presidency of Lyndon B. Johnson.

Congress's failure to act prompted Republicans to engage in other tactics designed to counter Democratic shenanigans in the South. After the GOP sweep of 1888, Congress approved the admission of Montana and Washington State into the union, and it cut the Dakota Territory in two, creating North Dakota and South Dakota. This gave Republicans three new states—Washington, North Dakota, and South Dakota (with Montana going to the Democrats)—and six new votes in the US Senate.[40] The following year, Republicans added Idaho and Wyoming—rushing to bring them into the union ahead of the midterm elections—an addition of six states in just two years.[41] *Harper's Weekly* noted that the one hundred thousand people residing in Wyoming and Idaho in 1890 would have four senators and two representatives, whereas the two hundred thousand people living in New York's First Congressional District had just two senators and one representative.[42] Benjamin Harrison's son, Russell, believed these new states, together with New York, would keep the Republicans in power.[43] The result was a further inflammation of partisan tensions. Republican senator George F. Hoar caricatured the Democrats as the party of "the old slave-owner and slave-driver, the saloon-keeper, the ballot-box stuffer, the Kuklux [a reference to the Ku Klux Klan], the criminal class of the great cities, [and] the men who cannot read or write."[44]

THE PARTIES REVERSE POSITIONS

The struggle over voting rights intensified after Benjamin Harrison's short time in office. In 1896, William Jennings Bryan, the presidential nominee of both the Democratic Party and the Populist Party, straddled differences between the two on the issue of voting rights. The Populists set themselves apart from the Democrats, pledging: "Believing that the elective franchise and an untrammeled ballot are essential to a government of, for, and by the people, the People's Party condemns the wholesale system of disfranchisement adopted in some States as unrepublican and undemocratic, and we declare it to be the duty of the several state legislatures to take such action as will secure a full, free, and fair ballot and an honest count."[45] However, Bryan ignored the Populist Party's plea for universal ballot access, knowing it would destroy any chance he had of prompting southern Democrats to instinctively pull the party lever. In the years ahead, the populists would exploit the racial resentments of poor southern whites and blame African Americans for their financial difficulties, many of whom would have agreed with the sentiments expressed by an Alabama farmer depicted in a novel when he said, "Them black bastards is takin' the food out 'n mouths. . . . They're down there sharin' the good things with the rich while good white folks in the hills have to starve."[46]

Central to Bryan's appeal (and later critical to Donald Trump's success) was the notion that "the people," whom the populists purport to represent, were the *producers* (i.e., those who personify the American Dream), while their enemies were the *takers* (i.e., Wall Street bankers, immigrants, those who reject conventional social mores and values, and especially Blacks and other racial minorities whom they saw as posing an existential threat to their understanding of "Americanism"). Any attempt to extend equal opportunities to "inferior" groups, they believed, was rooted in a racism that mistakenly assumed any reform would disempower whites. The German political scientist Jan-Werner Müller writes that populism "is always *a form of identity politics*" and "tends to pose a danger to democracy. For democracy requires pluralism and the recognition that we need to find fair terms of living together as free, equal, but also irreducibly diverse citizens."[47]

The "us versus them" politics of the late nineteenth century inevitably spawned racial resentments that Democrats exploited well into the twentieth century. As president, Woodrow Wilson fired African Americans from their federal posts, with one administration appointee saying, "A Negro's place is in the cornfield."[48] Wilson, a son of the South, hosted a White House screening of D. W. Griffith's film *The Birth of a Nation*, which glorified the Ku Klux Klan.[49] By the mid-twentieth century, southern Democrats' views on racial matters remained unchanged from those of the late 1880s. In 1947, Mississippi senator Theodore G. Bilbo authored a book titled *Separation or Mongrelization* in which he argued:

> Surely, every decent white man and woman in America should have cause to be alarmed over the mongrelization of their white race and loss of their white civilization when Dr. Ralph S. Linton, a leading Professor of Anthropology at Columbia University, New York City, said just recently that at the present rate of intermarrying, interbreeding, and intermixing within nine generations, which is only 300 years, that there would be no white or Black race in America—that we would all be yellow.[50]

Echoing the Democrats of yore, Bilbo declared, "The clock has struck, when something must be done by every white man to escape the certain and tragic fate that awaits the future of our children's children of generations yet to be born."[51] Bilbo advocated that "every red-blooded white man [should] use any means to keep the [Black people] away from the polls," adding, "And if you don't know what that means, you are just plain dumb."[52] For Bilbo, enfranchising Blacks meant "Negroes would have to be given business, industrial, political, social, and matrimonial equality with the whites."[53] In other words, Blacks would be the "takers" who would deprive the "makers"—that is, southern whites—from the social and cultural status they enjoyed. As evidence, Bilbo noted that Black employees constituted 19 percent of the federal workforce, a higher percentage than the total African American population, which, he claimed, caused "thousands of white girls" to leave their jobs "because they have refused to work as clerks and stenographers under Negro executives holding high salaried jobs."[54] Senator Robert Taft called Bilbo a "disgrace,"[55] and when Republicans took control of the Senate in 1947, they argued that Bilbo had rigged the polls to exclude Blacks and debated whether he should be seated. But they were spared from making a final decision when Bilbo died of oral cancer later that year.

The partisan shift in Black voter enfranchisement took decades to complete. As late as 1940, only 5 percent of African Americans of voting age were registered in the South, even as the Black population there doubled between 1920 and 1940.[56] But just one year after Bilbo's death, the Democratic Party signaled an important change by accepting a minority civil rights plank at its 1948 convention.⁵⁷ Minneapolis mayor Hubert H. Humphrey led the charge, saying, "The time has arrived in America for the Democratic Party to get out of the shadow of states' rights and to walk forthrightly into the bright sunshine of human rights."⁵⁸ Humphrey's speech catapulted him onto the national stage and ensured his election to the US Senate. But the speech caused southern Democrats, led by South Carolina's Strom Thurmond, to storm out of the convention hall and form the Dixiecrat Party, which ardently opposed any civil rights legislation, including the extension of voting rights. Thurmond carried four states in 1948, all in the Deep South.⁵⁹ Other southern Democrats echoed Thurmond's opposition to civil rights. Seeking a seat in the US Senate in 1948, Lyndon Johnson attacked Truman's civil rights program, stating: "This civil rights program, about which you have heard so much, is a farce and a sham—an effort to set up a police state in the guise of liberty."⁶⁰ By 1964, when Johnson, now president, led the effort to pass civil rights legislation, Humphrey said of the remaining southern Dixiecrats: "They're old and they haven't any recruits. They know it—one of them said to me, 'You simply have to overwhelm us.' And so, we have to beat them to a pulp."⁶¹ It was that beating that led white southerners to migrate to the Republican Party beginning with Barry Goldwater's nomination in 1964—led by so-called Movement Conservatives who, a century earlier, called themselves Confederates.⁶²

Contributing to the partisan shift was the Supreme Court's desegregation order in *Brown v. Board of Education* (1954) based on its enforcement of the Fourteenth Amendment that fostered a series of crises during the Eisenhower and Kennedy administrations. Within the Republican Party a division emerged. Robert Welch, founder of the John Birch Society, said of *Brown*, "The storm over integration has been brought on by the Communists."⁶³ Billboards sponsored by the Birchers appeared advocating the impeachment of Chief Justice Earl Warren. Barry Goldwater opposed the Supreme Court's decision by appealing to God and nature: "Where government presumes to control equality, forgetting that in its essential areas it lies within God's province and laws of nature, there can be only conformity. Government must consider and trust all men as equal in the areas of law and civic order. Otherwise, and in no other area, can it make men equal."⁶⁴

In 1957, for the first time since Reconstruction, Dwight Eisenhower sent federal troops to Little Rock, Arkansas, when protests erupted over nine Black students entering Little Rock Central High School. Senator Richard Russell, a Georgia Democrat, sent Eisenhower a telegram condemning the "highhanded and illegal methods" used to carry out "on your orders to mix the races," comparing the use of federal troops to Adolf Hitler's storm troopers.[65] Eisenhower defended his action, stating that in Hitler's case "military power was used to further the ambitions and purposes of a ruthless dictator," whereas he sought "to preserve the institutions of free government."[66] Five years later, John F. Kennedy enforced a court desegregation order at the University of Mississippi that left two people dead and three hundred injured. Capitalizing on the overt racism and opposing Kennedy's actions, the John Birch Society raised more than $1 million.[67] In 1963, when another court ordered the desegregation of the University of Alabama, Governor George Wallace stood in the doorway and denounced both the court order and the federal troops summoned by Kennedy to enforce it. In a televised address, Kennedy embraced the civil rights cause, stating: "One hundred years of delay have passed since President Lincoln freed the slaves, yet their heirs, their grandsons, are not fully free. They are not yet freed from the bonds of injustice. They are not yet freed from social and economic oppression. And this Nation, for all its hopes and all its boasts, will not be fully free until all its citizens are free."[68]

After Kennedy's assassination five months later, Lyndon Johnson portrayed him as a martyr to the civil rights movement and cajoled Congress into passing the Civil Rights Act of 1964 and, more important, the Voting Rights Act of 1965. Speaking before a joint session of Congress following an attack on voting rights supporters in Selma, Alabama, that left John Lewis battered and bleeding, Johnson invoked the anthem of the civil rights movement, saying, "We shall overcome."[69] Benjamin Harrison's long-forgotten pleas for enforceable federal voting rights legislation were being fulfilled. The bill passed the Senate by a vote of 77 to 19, with only two Republicans—Strom Thurmond of South Carolina, and John Tower of Texas—voting no.[70] At a signing ceremony, Johnson declared that the law was "a triumph for freedom as huge as any victory that has ever been won on any battlefield."[71]

But southern resistance remained strong. Thurmond argued that the Voting Rights Act made Congress "the final resting place of the Constitution and the rule of law. For it is here that they will have been buried with shovels of emotion under piles of expediency in the year of our Lord, 1965."[72] Alabama's Lister Hill, another no vote, condemned the legislation as a "head-on rush to the destruction of the basic rights of the individual states and the liberties of the American people to satisfy the demands, the clamor, and the expediency of the day."[73]

As a growing number of Republicans opposed granting equal opportunities to Blacks and other racial minorities, they attracted support from alienated, resentful whites. Barry Goldwater's opposition to the Civil Rights Act of 1964 won him five states in the Deep South: Alabama, Mississippi, Georgia, Louisiana, and South Carolina. His Republican nemesis, New York governor Nelson Rockefeller, called his party's embrace of states' rights an "act of political immorality rarely equaled in human history."[74] Historian Richard Rovere writes that in 1964 Goldwater spoke in "a kind of code that few in his audience had any trouble deciphering": bullies and marauders meant African Americans, states' rights meant opposition to civil rights, and the federal judiciary meant integrationist judges.[75] Four years later, Richard Nixon forged a compact with South Carolina's Democrat-turned-Republican senator Strom Thurmond by promising to "go-slow" on civil rights, while Thurmond, in turn, backed Nixon at the 1968 Republican National Convention. Baseball great Jackie Robinson, who had endorsed Nixon in 1960, but withheld his support in 1968, wrote: "How can you expect to support a man who appeals to the old south and to backlash? America is already in terrible shape in terms of race relations. Nixon's deals with Strom Thurmond points [sic] to future dangers."[76]

But Nixon's southern strategy paid off, with only Georgia, Louisiana, Arkansas, Mississippi, and Alabama voting for the third-party presidential candidate, George Wallace. Four years later the Old Confederacy swept Nixon back into office by landslide proportions.[77] Other Republicans followed Nixon's example. In 1980, Ronald Reagan opened his presidential campaign in Philadelphia, Mississippi, a few miles from where three civil rights workers were murdered in 1964 by the Ku Klux Klan. Speaking before a largely white audience, Reagan declared, "I believe in states' rights."[78] Eight years later, Reagan's vice president, George H. W. Bush, featured Willie Horton in his television advertisements after Horton, a convicted African American felon on a weekend furlough, raped and assaulted a woman in Maryland. By 2008, the partisan shift was so complete that every state that supported Abraham Lincoln in 1860 voted for Barack Obama.[79]

The shifting racial composition hastened the Republican Party's abdication from its Civil War mission to make men free. With more voters of minority and mixed racial heritage, Republicans became dependent on whites to win elections. The shift was profound. In 1980, 88 percent of those who voted in that year's presidential election were white; just 10 percent were African American.[80] That year, 56 percent of white voters supported Ronald Reagan, making them the driving engine behind his landslide victory.[81] In 2020, however, the number of white voters fell to 67 percent and minority voters rose to 34 percent. Donald Trump won 57 percent of the white vote, one point *ahead* of Reagan. But Joe Biden won overwhelming majorities from Blacks, Hispanics, and Asians, making him victorious.[82] A "birth dearth" among whites, combined with ever greater numbers of nonwhites, led the US Census Bureau to forecast that by the mid-2040s the United States will be a majority-minority nation—as it is already among those aged eighteen and younger.[83] For years, smart Republican strategists—including Ken Mehlman and Ed Gillespie, both former chairs of the Republican National Committee—argued that the party must prioritize its appeal to racial minorities.[84] After Mitt Romney's loss to Barack Obama in 2012, Republican National Committee chair Reince Priebus commissioned a report that insisted Republicans must "work harder" to win minority voters, especially Hispanics: "If Hispanic Americans hear that the GOP doesn't want them in the United States, they won't pay attention to our next sentence. It doesn't matter what we say about education, jobs, or the economy."[85]

But after Barack Obama's 2008 victory, resentful whites found a home in the Republican Party. Tea Party Republicans were filled with anger over the "loss" of a country they once knew. Christopher S. Parker and Matt A. Barreto write that the Tea Partiers saw Obama as "the face of *their* country, as the commander in chief of *their* armed forces."[86] Rachel M. Blum concluded that as an insurgent faction the Tea Party adopted "ruthless strategies for remaking its host party."[87] Noting the Tea Partiers' anger, Parker and Barreto drew parallels between the Tea Party, the Ku Klux Klan, and the John Birch Society.[88] Like their antecedents, the Tea Partiers thought of themselves as the "real Americans."[89] And like the Klan and the John Birch Society, the Tea Party gained followers because, like them, it operated in an era of profound change. Parker and Barreto write that while the Klan was concerned with ethnocultural change and the John Birch Society was preoccupied with ideological change, Tea Partiers saw Barack Obama's victory as a harbinger of a dismal future where a once dominant white, Christian country was quickly becoming a foregone memory of a romanticized past.[90] Another similarity between the Klan, Birchers, and Tea Partiers was their ability to easily fall prey to wild conspiracy theories and numerous falsehoods. Theda Skocpol and Vanessa Williamson noted that those who attended Tea Party gatherings believed Obamacare established "death panels" that would arbitrarily end their lives and abolish Medicare in the process.[91] Some also thought their 401K plans were about to be seized by the Obama administration in order to eliminate the national debt.[92] A weak Republican establishment allowed the Tea Party to firmly embed itself within its host party, a triumph that made Donald Trump's ascendance possible.

Donald Trump embodied the outrage of non-college-educated whites, especially men, who were alarmed by the racial transformation of the nation's population and loss of jobs that once seemed secure. Trump argued that immigration was a Democratic plot to win voting majorities by admitting as many illegal immigrants as possible and giving them a ballot. In 2016, he declared: "I think this will be the last election that the Republicans have a chance of winning because you're going to have people flowing across the border . . . and they're going to be legalized, and they're going to be able to vote, and once that all happens you can forget it. You're not going to have one Republican vote."[93] This, too, represented a departure from the founding principles of the Republican Party. In their 1860 platform, Republicans opposed any changes in which the rights of immigrants "shall be abridged or impaired," and they promised to protect "the rights of all classes of citizens, whether native or naturalized, both at home and abroad."[94]

One year after Trump's 2016 win, white supremacists marched in Charlottesville, Virginia, shouting: "The Jews will not replace us! The blacks will not replace us! Immigrants will not replace us!"[95] Writing in *The Atlantic*, Joe Biden accused white supremacists of engaging in "domestic terrorism" and graphically depicted their "crazed, angry faces illuminated by torches."[96] Biden pinpointed the source of their animus: "A hate that through the media and politics, the Internet, has radicalized angry, alienated, lost, and isolated individuals into falsely believing that they will be replaced—that's the word, 'replaced'—by the 'other'—by people who don't look like them and who are therefore, in a perverse ideology that they possess and being fed, lesser beings."[97] After ten people were murdered by a white supremacist in Buffalo, New York, in 2022, Biden described the American experiment as being in grave danger: "Hate and fear are being given too much oxygen by those who pretend to love America but who don't understand America."[98] White supremacy, he concluded, was a "poison" that has been "allowed to fester and grow right in front of our eyes."[99]

After a pro–civil rights protester was killed in Charlottesville, Donald Trump said of the riot, "You had very fine people on both sides."[100] The alt-right leader Richard Spencer said he was "really proud" of Trump's response while the former Ku Klux Klan Grand Wizard, David Duke, who was also in Charlottesville, tweeted, "Thank you President Trump for your honesty & courage to tell the truth about #Charlottesville & condemn the leftist terrorists in BLM/Antifa."[101] Biden was furious at Trump's clumsy attempt to equate white supremacists with civil rights advocates: "Today, we have an American president who has publicly proclaimed a moral equivalency between neo-Nazis and Klansmen and those who would oppose their venom and hate."[102] Biden then set forth the terms of his forthcoming engagement with Trump: "We are living through a battle for the soul of this nation."[103] Charlottesville marked a turning point in Biden's decision to forgo retirement and seek the presidency in 2020.

THE GREAT REPLACEMENT THEORY

Michael Kazin writes that the populist tradition represented by Donald Trump includes a definition of "the people" that includes only "citizens of European heritage—'real Americans' whose ethnicity alone afforded them a share in the country's bounty."[104] This version of populism, Kazin writes, "alleges that there is nefarious alliance between evil forces on high and the unworthy, dark-skinned poor below—a cabal that imperils the patriotic (white) majority in the middle."[105] It is this type of populism—now known as Trumpism—that dominates Republican thinking and is fueled by the notion that a combination of changing demographics and Democratic Party shenanigans are working to replace Republican voters with Democratic ones. A survey from February 2019 found that 79 percent of Republicans agreed that "the political system is stacked against more traditionally minded people."[106] One reason these viewpoints have become so dominant is a widespread belief that the power of white voters is being threatened by a rising tide of immigrants and people of color. In a 2022 Facebook advertisement, House Republican Conference chair Elise Stefanik claimed: "Liberal Democrats are planning their most aggressive move yet: a PERMANENT ELECTION INSURRECTION. Their plan to grant amnesty to 11 MILLION illegal immigrants will overthrow our current electorate and create a permanent liberal majority in Washington."[107] Taking note, the *Albany Times Union* editorialized that Stefanik "couches the hate in alarmist anti-immigrant rhetoric that's become standard fare for the party of Donald Trump," adding, "If there is anything that needs replacing in this country—and in the Republican Party—it's the hateful rhetoric that Ms. Stefanik and far too many of her colleagues so shamelessly spew."[108] Donald Trump has praised Stefanik, calling her "one of my killers."[109] Liz Cheney, who lost her House Republican conference chair position to Stefanik, writes that Republican leaders have "enabled white nationalism, white supremacy, and antisemitism."[110]

But Cheney is a lonely, isolated voice in today's Trump-dominated Republican Party. In 2022, the Texas State Republican Party adopted a resolution calling for the 1965 Voting Rights Act to be repealed.[111] In 2022, Marjorie Taylor Greene told a GOP rally in Arizona: "Joe Biden's 5 million illegal aliens are on the verge of replacing you—replacing your jobs and replacing your kids in school and coming from all over the world. They're also replacing your culture, and that's not great for America."[112] Fox News has echoed Greene's sentiments, especially former top-rated host Tucker Carlson, who told his cable audience: "I know that the left and all the little gatekeepers on Twitter become literally hysterical if you use the term 'replacement,' if you suggest that the Democratic Party is trying to replace the current electorate, the voters now casting ballots, with new people, more obedient voters from the Third World. . . . Let's just say it! That's true."[113] The *New York Times* documented that Carlson referred to the "Great Replacement Theory" four hundred times, devoting more than fifty hours of television coverage to this theme.[114] Carlson's Fox News colleague Laura Ingraham says Democrats "want to replace you, the American voters, with newly amnestied citizens and an ever-increasing number of chain migrants," describing these efforts by Democrats as an "insurrection [that] seeks to overthrow everything we love about America by defaming it, silencing it, and even prosecuting it."[115] Most Republican officeholders agree. Ohio senator J. D. Vance says Democrats are trying to "transform the electorate" with an immigrant "invasion."[116] Wisconsin senator Ron Johnson describes the Great Replacement Theory as "the Democrat grand plan."[117] House Freedom Caucus chair Scott Perry maintains, "We're replacing national-born American—native born Americans—to permanently transform the political landscape of this very nation."[118]

This feeling that the American way of life is under assault is widely shared among the Republican rank and file. Sixty-one percent of those who voted for Trump in 2020 believe that "a group of people in this country are trying to replace native-born Americans with immigrants and people of color who share their political views."[119] No wonder 56 percent of Republicans agree with the following statement: "The traditional American way of life is disappearing so fast that we may have to use force to save it."[120] Ronald Ingelhart and Pippa Norris write that Donald Trump's supporters "see themselves as victims of affirmative action and betrayed by 'line cutters'—African Americans, immigrants, refugees, and women—who jump ahead of them in the queue for the American Dream. They resent liberal intellectuals who tell them to feel sorry for the line-cutters, and dismiss them as bigots when they don't. Unlike most politicians, Donald Trump provides emotional support when he openly expresses racist and xenophobic feelings."[121]

The late Wilson Carey McWilliams once observed that the "'populism' of the Right [favors] old hatreds and new resentments, threatening what remains of civic community."[122] In 2016, Michael Lind accurately forecast that Trumpism would come to define the Republican Party:

> In the Republican Party, the inherited program shared by much of the conservative movement and the party's donors, with its emphasis on free trade and large-scale immigration, and cuts in entitlements like Social Security and Medicare, is a relic of the late 20th century, when the country-club wing of the party was much more important than the country-and-western wing. The anger and sense of betrayal of the newly dominant white working class in the Republican Party makes perfect sense.... Mr. Trump has exposed the

gap between what orthodox conservative Republicans offer and what today's dominant Republican voters actually want—middle-class entitlements plus crackdowns on illegal immigrants, Muslims, foreign trade rivals and free-riding allies.[123]

By exposing this gap, Donald Trump implicitly endorsed the animosities held by the white working class. In 2016, Hillary Clinton charged that Trump "has built his campaign on prejudice and paranoia. He is taking hate groups mainstream, and helping a radical fringe take over the Republican Party."[124] While the fate of the former president is unclear, Trumpism, and the hate it inspires, will continue to dominate Republican Party politics.

REPUBLICANS ARE TODAY'S DIXIECRATS

Amarnath Amarasigam, an expert on political violence at Queens University in Kingston, Ontario, argues that the most dangerous dimension of the Great Replacement Theory is the view that "something needs to be done about it and that violence is justified."[125] Amarasigam says that "getting people to the point of what used to be a radicalized idea—that's what has become mainstream. It's on millions of televisions each night."[126] It is this exposure that led a young white supremacist to enter Mother Emanuel Church in Charleston, South Carolina in 2015 and kill nine Blacks, including the pastor. The killer later said, "I would like to make it crystal clear; I do not regret what I did."[127] Prosecutors argued that the assailant sought "to magnify and incite violence in others."[128] In 2019, another white supremacist traveled ten hours from his home and entered a Walmart in Hispanic-dominated El Paso, Texas, where he killed twenty-three people. That killer also subscribed to the Great Replacement Theory, telling police he was targeting "Mexicans."[129] Three years later, an eighteen-year-old white male entered a grocery store in a largely minority community in Buffalo, New York, and assassinated ten people. Social media postings found this killer, too, believed in the Great Replacement Theory and sought to kill as many African Americans as possible, traveling hundreds of miles to do so. In a lengthy post, the assassin wrote that his aim was to "encourage further attacks that will eventually start the war that will save the Western world [and] the White race."[130] Preaching at a funeral for one of the victims, the Reverend Al Sharpton said of the eighteen-year-old killer: "The [Ku Klux] Klan would come and put hoods on. This young man livestreamed himself. They don't even put hoods on no more. They are proud to practice racism."[131]

Most Republicans, including Trump, denounced these killings. But there remains a deeply held insecurity within the Republican Party that stems from a belief in the Great Replacement Theory that affects party elites and the rank-and-file alike. A party that is not confident of its immediate future—or perhaps even its long-term existence—has enacted laws designed to make voting harder; restrict the number of minority voters; give Republican poll watchers more access to the polling places and a greater ability to challenge minority ballots; and, most important, give Republicans the power to count the votes. While Republicans believe that the Constitution gives them automatic advantages in the US Senate and Electoral College, and Republican-controlled state legislatures can gerrymander House districts, they know their party has won the popular vote for president just once since 1992 (in 2004).[132] The likelihood of Democrats winning popular majorities increases as the electorate becomes younger and moves from majority white to majority nonwhite. No wonder 61 percent of Republicans favor retaining the Electoral College in its current form while 71 percent of Democrats would like to scrap it.[133] Thus, Republicans stubbornly cling to a constitutional structure that diminishes popular sentiments and allows them to seize power as a minority party. Conservative political scientist Claes Ryn writes that any contemporary notion of democracy would give the framers fits: "The original American Constitution provides many examples of an effort to counteract such dangers of plebiscitarianism as demagoguery and rabble-rousing, what the Framers scorn as 'democracy.' Not only does the Constitution give no power whatever to a numerical national majority, the American people have standing *only* as members of political subdivisions."[134] But J. Michael Luttig, a conservative judge, disagrees, saying, "America is *both* a republic and a representative democracy, and therefore a sustained attack on our national election is *a fortiori* an attack on our democracy, any political theory otherwise notwithstanding."[135]

The transformation of reliably Republican states like Georgia, Arizona, and North Carolina into more competitive battlegrounds thanks to their rising minority and college-educated populations—with the prospect of more states joining them—gives Republicans heartburn. To mitigate this, Republican governors and state legislatures have approved laws that strip the secretary of state from certifying presidential elections and places that power in the hands of Republican-controlled state legislatures, the only bodies that in Ryn's view have constitutional standing. Joe Biden labels these statutes "election subversion," claiming they represent "the most dangerous threat to voting and the integrity of free and fair elections in our history."[136] This Republican-led effort builds on a last-minute, desperate scheme of the Trump campaign to overturn the results of the 2020 election. On December 14, 2020, with assistance from the Republican National Committee, alternate slates of Trump electors claimed they were the "duly elected and qualified" members of the Electoral College.[137] Using documents created by the Trump campaign, they falsely certified that Trump won the states of Arizona, Georgia, Michigan, Nevada, New Mexico, Pennsylvania, and Wisconsin. These fake documents were transmitted to the National Archives with the goal of presenting Vice President Mike Pence with two sets of electors. On January 6, 2021, Pence could have either counted the false electors or set them aside, either way giving Trump the win.[138]

This plan to invalidate the election was initiated at the highest levels within the Trump White House. The day after the 2020 election, Secretary of Energy Rick Perry texted chief of staff Mark Meadows and proposed an "AGRESSIVE [sic] STRATEGY" to have the state legislatures in question deliver their electoral votes to Trump.[139] Donald Trump Jr. chimed in the next day to propose that Republican legislatures "step in" and put forward separate slates of "Trump electors," adding: "We have multiple paths. We control them all."[140] Arizona Republican congressman Andy Biggs indicated his support for the dual elector scheme, to which Meadows replied, "I love it."[141] Jason Miller, the Trump campaign's lead attorney, emailed Meadows, saying, "We just need to have someone coordinating the electors for states."[142] The plan proceeded under "complete secrecy and discretion."[143] Federal district court judge David O. Carter described the scheme as "fully formed and actionable as early as December 7, 2020," quoting John Eastman, one of Trump's attorneys, as saying implementation of the plan was "critical to the result of this election."[144] Trump's White House counsel objected, warning the arrangement would constitute a "murder-suicide pact" that would "damage everyone who touches it."[145] But the plan went ahead.

At 1:00 a.m. on January 6, Donald Trump tweeted, "If Vice President @Mike_Pence comes through for us, we will win the Presidency."[146] At 8:17 a.m., Trump tweeted: "All Mike Pence has to do is send them back to the States, AND WE WIN. Do it Mike, this is a time for extreme courage."[147] With the insurrection underway, Trump tweeted again: "Mike Pence didn't have the courage to do what should have been done to protect our Country and our Constitution, giving States a chance to certify a corrected set of facts, not the fraudulent or inaccurate ones which they were asked to previously certify. USA demands the truth!"[148] Judge Carter wrote, "President Trump attempted to obstruct an official proceeding by launching a pressure campaign to convince Vice President Pence to disrupt the Joint Session on January 6.[149] He added, "Because President Trump likely knew that the plan to disrupt the electoral count was wrongful, his mindset exceeds the threshold for acting 'corruptly'" under the United States Code. The judge concluded:

> Dr. Eastman and President Trump launched a campaign to overturn a democratic election, an action unprecedented in American history. Their campaign was not confined to the ivory tower—it was a coup in search of a legal theory. The plan spurred violent attacks on the seat of our nation's government, led to the deaths of several law enforcement officers, and deepened public distrust in our political process. . . . If Dr. Eastman's and President Trump's plan had worked, it would have permanently ended the peaceful transition of power, undermining American democracy and the Constitution.[150]

Indeed, the Trump scheme would have made Benjamin Harrison's warning about ballot boxes being turned into jugglers' hats a reality.

But the fact remains that Trump nearly succeeded. The extraconstitutional norm that the losing party accepts the election result was upended. James MacGregor Burns has written that the acceptance of defeat by a losing party and the peaceful transition of power became an extraconstitutional right after the disputed Adams-Jefferson race of 1800. This "second bill of rights," said Burns, was "a notice to future American political leaders that they need not contemplate coups or venture violence in order to succeed."[151] That is, until 2020. Reflecting on the election tumult, Joe Biden said: "In America, if you lose, you accept the results. You follow the Constitution. You try again. You don't call facts 'fake' and then try to bring down the American experiment just because you're unhappy. That's not statesmanship; that's selfishness. That's not democracy; it's the denial of the right to vote. It suppresses; it subjugates."[152] Biden's words could have been easily uttered by leading Republicans during the Harrison and Cleveland eras.

Today's Republican voter suppression efforts build on long-standing techniques, akin to those Democrats employed when they regained control of southern state governments in the late nineteenth century: limiting voter registration, making the casting of ballots harder, and controlling the counting of votes. Following the 2020 election, more than nine out of ten Trump voters believed that "voting shouldn't be easier."[153] Republicans called for "election integrity," and many states enacted draconian laws whose purpose was to give Republicans a better chance of victory. In Georgia, a Republican-controlled state legislature and governor supported legislation designed to purge voters from the rolls, make it a misdemeanor to distribute food and water for those waiting in line, prohibit the unsolicited mailing of absentee ballot applications, and require voters to submit identification for their absentee ballot requests to be approved. The secretary of state was removed from the Elections Board, and the new statute sharply reduced the number of drop boxes.[154] In 2020, Donald Trump lost Georgia by 11,779 votes, and between Election Day and the Biden inauguration, he was repeatedly on the phone charging fraud and urging officials to "find 11,780 votes."[155] Despite Democratic attempts to forestall passage, the bill won overwhelming Republican support, and the state's governor, Brian Kemp, signed it into law under the portrait of a slave plantation, even as an African American state legislator trying to witness the historic act was arrested outside the governor's office.[156]

Florida adopted a similar statute requiring voters to renew their mail-in voting applications every two years and submit an ID to do so. The state also dramatically curtailed the use of drop boxes for voters to submit their ballots.[157] Arizona, another closely contested state in 2020, passed legislation that requires voters who do not vote once every two years to respond to a government notice to remain on the state's popular Permanent Early Voting List. The law stripped the secretary of state, a Democrat and 2022 candidate for governor, from exercising control over recounts.[158] It also denied the secretary the option of defending the state's election law in court should the state attorney general (then a Republican) disagree on a legal strategy, stating, "The authority of the attorney general to defend the law is paramount."[159] Republicans structured the statute to remain in effect through the end of the terms of these state officeholders, giving the Republican attorney general the power to determine the outcome of the 2022 elections.[160]

In July 2021, several Democratic legislators fled Texas in a vain attempt to forestall election "reforms" that would disenfranchise urban and minority voters. By August, enough Democrats had returned to allow Republicans to enact legislation adding criminal penalties for people who break election rules while helping others to vote. The law also gave partisan poll watchers greater access to see and hear the actions of election officials, prohibited the use of unsolicited applications for mail-in voting, and banned drive-through and twenty-four-hour voting.[161] The Republican sponsor claimed the bill was needed, asserting, "Anyone who tells you there's no voter fraud in Texas is telling you a very big lie."[162] Democratic state senator Sarah Eckhardt responded: "To all my colleagues who plan to vote for this bill, know that doing so will further a narrative that is leading us toward authoritarianism, violence, and the kind of insurrectionist actions that we saw in Washington, D.C."[163] But the bill became law and had its desired effect: in the 2022 state primary elections, nearly twenty-three thousand ballots were discarded—an unusually high number—because of questions as to whether those voters had complied with the new statute.[164] In each of the states with new voting restrictions, there was no evidence of election fraud. Taking note, Joe Biden described these Republican efforts as a twenty-first-century Jim Crow "assault" and reprised the famous question once posed to Joe McCarthy, "Have you no shame?"[165]

Meanwhile, attempts by congressional Democrats to strengthen the Voting Rights Act of 1965 have failed. These failures arose from the Supreme Court decision in *Shelby County v. Holder* (2013) that gutted Section 5 of the 1965 law requiring states to submit electoral changes to the Justice Department for review. Eric Holder, the attorney general at the time, notes that after the Supreme Court's decision nearly seventeen hundred polling places were closed, thousands of names were stricken from the voting rolls, and twenty-five states passed laws that have a disproportionate negative impact on communities of color.[166] Attempts to reverse the ruling have been uniformly opposed by Republicans who sound like the Dixiecrats of yore. During a 2021 debate on the John Lewis Voting Rights Act, Illinois Republican Rodney Davis said: "If you vote for this legislation, you are voting for a federal takeover of elections. You are removing the people elected at the state and local level to run elections from making decisions about how elections are run, including voter ID laws, and putting an unaccountable, unelected election czar at the Department of Justice, the attorney general, in charge of all election decisions in this country."[167] Ohio's Jim Jordan agreed, stating, "This bill is not about expanding voting rights; it is about Democrats consolidating their political power . . . and taking it away from the states."[168] Dan Bishop, a North Carolina Republican, echoed his colleagues: "This bill would comprehensively transfer the power to govern elections in this country from the sovereign states to the federal government, permanently and everywhere."[169] Voting Rights Lab vice president Liz Avore contends, "We're seeing two different democracies develop in terms of access to the ballot."[170]

"BE GLAD IT'S 2020 AND NOT 1920"

Following Donald Trump's charge that his presidency had been "stolen"—not by the voters but by nefarious practices of days long gone by—he accused Democrats of having dead people and noncitizens cast ballots; claimed trucks rolling late at night into urban centers were stuffed with Democratic ballots; claimed that suitcases filled with Biden ballots were pulled out from under tables; and even claimed that Italian satellites surreptitiously tapped into voting machines and switched votes from Trump to Biden. Making these wild accusations resulted in a level of intimidation for poll workers that was reminiscent of the Old South, where Blacks were lynched for trying to vote, and every means possible was used to shape election outcomes. Outside the home of Michigan's secretary of state, armed men appeared, shouting obscenities as she was decorating for Christmas with her four-year-old child.[171] In Wisconsin, officials were targeted, and their families threatened with violence. Dane County election official Scott McDonell said the phone calls and emails warning of personal harm to himself and his family were "a coordinated attack . . . on democracy."[172] In Washington State, the election director's home address was posted online along with the message, "Your days are numbered."[173]

Testifying before the House Select Committee investigating the attack on the Capitol, Georgia's Republican secretary of state, Brad Raffensberger, described sexualized text messages his wife received on her cell phone, along with a break-in at the home of his widowed daughter-in-law, after he refused to follow Donald Trump's order to "find 11,780 votes" to make Trump victorious.[174] Arizona's Republican House Speaker, Rusty Bowers, described dreading the weekly Saturday demonstrations outside his home with protesters calling him a "pedophile, pervert, and corrupt politician," while blaring loudspeakers disturbed his daughter as she lay gravely ill.[175] Philadelphia's election commissioner, Al Schmidt, a lifelong Republican, detailed numerous death threats targeting himself and his family after Trump called him a RINO (Republican in name only). Among the threatening messages the Schmidts received was one that read, "You are a traitor. Perhaps 75 cuts and 20 bullets will soon arrive," and another that read, "HEADS ON SPIKES. TREASONOUS SCHMIDTS."[176] Schmidt defended the integrity of the 2020 election but subsequently resigned his post.[177] The Republican Speaker of the Pennsylvania House of Representatives, Bryan Cutler, disconnected his home telephone because "it would ring all hours of the night and would fill up with messages."[178] Nick Fuentes, a white nationalist and talk show host, declared that if Republicans keep losing elections, the solution would be to establish a "dictatorship": "We need to take control of the media or take control of the government and force the people to believe what we believe or force them to play by our rules."[179]

Perhaps the most powerful, and disturbing, testimony before the House Select Committee came from Wandrea "Shaye" Moss, an African American who worked in the Fulton County election headquarters processing absentee ballots and voter registrations and counting votes. On election nights she was assisted by her mother, Ruby Freeman, who also worked for the elections department. Moss loved her job and was inspired to take it by her grandmother, who reminded her that Black Georgians did not always have the right to vote until passage of the Voting Rights Act of 1965. Moss especially enjoyed assisting older voters, even describing making a hospital visit so she could hand deliver an absentee application to an elderly patient.[180] But after former New York City mayor and Trump attorney Rudy Giuliani publicized a security video showing Moss and Freeman counting ballots, and claiming they were "surreptitiously passing around USB ports as if they were vials of heroin or cocaine."[181]

Donald Trump called Freeman "a professional vote scammer and hustler."[182] Fox News repeatedly aired footage of the two women,[183] and both received numerous death threats, with one ominously reading, "Be glad it's 2020 and not 1920."[184]

Their lives were turned upside down. Freeman, who was informed by the FBI that she should vacate her home to ensure her safety, described her two-month out-of-home experience as follows: "I felt homeless. . . . To have to leave my home that I've lived there for twenty-one years. . . . It was hard. It was horrible."[185] Moss described how a group of Trump supporters tried to forcibly enter the home of her elderly grandmother, claiming they were there to make a "citizen's arrest."[186] The harassment didn't stop: pizza deliveries appeared in the dead of night with drivers demanding payment. Crank calls and knocks on the door were commonplace. Describing how the harassment affected her life, Moss said:

> I no longer give out my business card. I don't transfer calls. I—I don't want anyone knowing my name. I don't want to go anywhere with my mom because she might yell my name out over the grocery aisle or something. I don't go to the grocery store at all. I haven't been anywhere at all. I've gained about sixty pounds. I just don't do nothing anymore. I don't want to go anywhere. I second guess everything that I do. It's affected my life in a—in a major way. In every way. All because of lies.[187]

Ruby Freeman put it this way: "Do you know how it feels to have the President of the United States to target you? The President of the United States is supposed to represent every American, not to target one. But he targeted me, Lady Ruby, a small business owner, a mother, a proud American citizen who stood up to help Fulton County run an election in the middle of the pandemic."[188] When Moss was asked how many of her coworkers on the videotape posted by Giuliani remain at their jobs, she replied, "There is no permanent election worker or supervisor in that video that's still there."[189]

A NEW POLITICS BY OTHER MEANS

In 1990, political scientists Benjamin Ginsberg and Martin Shefter authored a book titled *Politics by Other Means*. In it, they concluded, "America seemed to be on the verge of entering a post-electoral era in which elections might be eclipsed in importance by 'other means' of political conflict."[190] That era is here. In a 2022 Yahoo News/You Gov poll, a majority of respondents predicted it is "likely" that America will "cease to be a democracy in the future."[191] Congressman Jamie Raskin, a member of the House Select Committee investigating the January 6, 2021, attack on the Capitol, writes that Republican power brokers "are making sure that our political institutions work at every turn *against* majority rule."[192] Raskin cites gerrymandering, blocking reform, use of the Senate filibuster, restrictive voting laws "designed to suppress voter participation making it harder (or, in the case of baseless voter roll purges, impossible) for some groups to access the ballot," and packing the courts with "right-wing judges to enforce all the exclusion. . . . In short, the leaders of the GOP—not just Trump, mind you—are using every trick in the book to stifle majority rule and to erase popular democracy."[193]

Testifying before the House Select Committee, J. Michael Luttig, a retired federal appeals court judge and a Supreme Court judicial contender during the George W. Bush administration, concluded that a Republican Party controlled by Donald Trump is determined to permanently scrap the norms that govern our constitutional democracy:

> Donald Trump and his allies and supporters are a clear and present danger to American democracy. That's not because of what happened on January 6. It's because to this very day the former president and his allies and supporters pledge that in the presidential election of 2024, if the former president or his anointed successor as the Republican Party presidential candidate were to lose that election, that they would attempt to overturn that 2024 election in the same way that they attempted to overturn the 2020 election but succeed in 2024 where they failed in 2020. I don't speak those words lightly. I would have never spoken those words ever in my life except that that's what the former president and his allies are telling us.[194]

Political theorist Jan-Werner Müller writes that the most important promise of democracy is to give people the ultimate governing authority.[195] But a new politics by other means as practiced by a Trump-dominated Republican Party breaks that promise. The next chapter describes the clear and present danger the Republican Party continues to pose to our constitutional democracy.

6. A Clear and Present Danger

There will come a day when Donald Trump is gone, but your dishonor will remain.
     —Liz Cheney to her fellow Republicans, June 9, 2022

Following Barry Goldwater's landslide loss in 1964, Thomas E. Dewey published a book extolling the virtues of the two-party system. The treatise, based on a series of lectures the New York governor gave at Princeton University in 1950, argued the major parties provide the necessary underpinnings that allow our political system to function: "In spite of passing bitterness and occasional violence at the polls, I think it is safe to say that no great nation makes its political decisions in better temper or with a better will to accept the final verdict."[1] The two-time loser noted the postelection exchanges of pleasantries between victors and vanquished were "a tribute to our national sanity and sense of humor" whose greatest symbols were the appearances of defeated presidents at their successors' inaugurations.[2] Dewey concluded, "If the American two-party system had not existed, we should have invented it."[3]

Despite these paeans of praise, Dewey singled out the Democrats for criticism, claiming they were "more reckless in their charges, more sweeping in their claims, and more lavish in their promises—and much more effective in dramatizing their case."[4] While Dewey believed Republicans worked harder at "the exacting business of government," he criticized their failure to comprehend the "business of campaign management."[5] Nonetheless, he rejected any substantial modifications to the extant party system, specifically discarding Wendell Willkie's proposal that the parties reorganize themselves along ideological lines. Dewey argued that if Democrats ever succeeded in purging the troublesome southerners from their ranks, they would become a "liberal-to-radical" party and, given their electoral strength, the result would be a "one-party system and finally *totalitarian government*."[6]

In a strange about-face, Dewey's warning about totalitarianism is echoed by some contemporary Republicans concerning what remains of the party they once knew. Addressing a conservative audience at the

Ronald Reagan Presidential Library, Liz Cheney warned that the party of her forebears now poses the greatest hazard to our democracy: "We are confronting a domestic threat that we have never faced before. And that is a former president who is threatening to unravel the foundations of our constitutional republic. And he is aided by Republican leaders and elected officials who made themselves willing hostages to this dangerous and irrational man."[7] While Cheney's warning is prescient, her admonitions concerning the perils of totalitarianism within the GOP are hardly new. Coincidentally, a Republican governor of New York, Nelson Rockefeller, warned in 1963 that the party was "in real danger of subversion by a radical, well financed, and highly disciplined minority."[8] Citing the John Birch Society and others who belonged to the "radical right lunatic fringe," Rockefeller argued they had no program to offer "except distrust, disunity, and the ultimate destruction of the confidence of the people in themselves."[9] As evidence, he cited a San Francisco meeting of young Republicans dominated by "extremist groups" who were well versed in the "tactics of totalitarianism" and were "purveyors of hate and distrust."[10] The New York governor declared it was imperative that the Republican Party reclaim the "fundamental principles of our heritage" and "save the nation by first saving itself."[11]

Lyndon Johnson's landslide victory in 1964 made Rockefeller's warning seem both premature and overly dramatic. Although Barry Goldwater won the Republican nomination, voters gave Johnson an overwhelming 61 percent of their ballots. Two years later, Republicans staged an extraordinary comeback, gaining forty-seven seats in the House and three in the Senate. Nelson Rockefeller was easily reelected, and Ronald Reagan began his political rise in California. Gerald Ford led a reinvigorated Republican Party in the House that included moderates and conservatives, while Senate minority leader Everett Dirksen presided over a diverse coalition that included Charles Percy, Edward Brooke, Howard Baker, and Mark Hatfield. Meanwhile, a raucous Democratic Party was torn asunder over civil rights and the Vietnam War. By 1968, Richard Nixon's victory commenced a twenty-year run of nearly uninterrupted Republican control of the White House, save for the brief occupancy of Jimmy Carter. Taking note of the GOP's renewed strength, Lyndon Johnson sarcastically remarked in his 1967 State of the Union address, "I should like to say to the Members of the opposition—whose numbers, if I am not mistaken, seem to have increased somewhat," that Republicans should engage in a "creative debate that offers choices and reasonable alternatives."[12] Echoing Mark Twain's legendary line, reports of the Republican Party's death were greatly exaggerated. The two-party system had, once again, seemingly righted itself.

"THE RULE-OR-RUIN PARTY"

Today, however, there are persistent and ominous signs that the Republican Party presents a clear and present danger to the health of our democracy. Jamie Raskin, a Democratic member of the House Select Committee investigating January 6, writes: "We can now say that the Democratic Party, whatever its faults, *is* the party of democracy and the Republican Party is the party of Trump, authoritarianism, corruption, and insurrection. If they can't control the government, they will do whatever they can to ruin the prospects for the rest of us to make any social progress at all. The Grand Old Party has become the Rule-or-Ruin Party."[13] Disenchanted conservatives have reached similar conclusions. Peter Wehner, vice president and senior fellow at the Ethics and Public Policy Center, believes the January 6 hearings represent a "withering indictment" of his fellow conservatives:

> Every Trump supporter has his story to tell, his defense to offer, his reasons why he did what he did. Massive cognitive dissonance—in this case individuals and a political party that have historically championed law and order, "traditional values," high ethical ideas, moral leadership in political leaders, and a healthy civic and political culture defending at every turn a person who was indecent, cruel, vindictive, demagogic, unstable, and ultimately deranged—can produce some very creative justifications.[14]

For most individuals, cognitive dissonance is a discomforting state of mind. This is particularly true of rank-and-file Republican reactions to the events of January 6, 2021. In June of that year, 33 percent of Republicans described the attack on the Capitol as an "insurrection"; one year later, only 13 percent did so.[15] Similarly, the number of Republicans who saw the Capitol riot as a failed attempt to keep Donald Trump in power fell from 56 percent to 33 percent, while those calling it a "legitimate political protest" rose by twenty points to 67 percent.[16] An overwhelming 78 percent of Republicans paid either little or no attention to the January 6 hearings.[17] Danielle Cobb, a Republican realtor from Tucson, Arizona, called the hearings "nonsense," claiming "the left side" is lying about what happened, and the Capitol Police "let people in."[18] This defied the repeated television images showing gallows built to hang Vice President Mike Pence and calls to shoot House Speaker Nancy Pelosi "in the frickin' brain."[19] The Republican Party's reluctance to acknowledge the seriousness of the insurrection was accentuated by Joe Biden's repeated condemnations of it: "We saw what happened: the Capitol Police, the D.C. Metropolitan Police, other law enforcement agencies were attacked and assaulted before our very eyes. Speared. Sprayed. Stomped on. Brutalized. Lives were lost. . . . Brave law enforcement officers were subject to the medieval hell for three hours, dripping in blood, surrounded by carnage."[20] The tribalism that characterizes both parties does not allow for any nuanced opinions; instead, it is a zero-sum game.

Donald Trump has the dubious distinction of being the first president to disrupt the peaceful transfer of power. But he remains the dominant force within today's Republican Party. In 2022, Trump's triumphs included promoting numerous 2020 election deniers; securing Senate nominations for Hershel Walker, J. D. Vance, and Mehmet Oz; and defeating or forcing into retirement eight of the ten House Republicans who voted for his impeachment in 2021, especially relishing the crushing of his erstwhile nemesis, Liz Cheney.[21] Trump's primary endorsements remain particularly valuable in multicandidate Republican primaries where his imprimatur can deliver votes.[22] As 2024 draws near, Joe Biden argues, "This is not your father's Republican Party."[23] Kamala Harris says the upcoming election represents a choice between democracy and Republican "extremists" who "are willing to subvert the very foundations of our strength."[24]

Liz Cheney has remarked on how many Democrats have told her that they long for the Republican Party of Eisenhower, Nixon, Reagan, and the Bushes. E. E. Schattschneider, the political scientist who vigorously advocated for more "responsible parties," argued that the party that is out of power must be *selective*—meaning that it must choose from a vast array of issues those few on which to base its disagreements with the majority. This was a necessity, Schattschneider maintained, because the opposition party is composed of many factions "held together by compromise and concession ... [and] party managers *need not meet every demand by every interest.*"[25] Schattschneider conceded that while the "language of politics is usually immoderate,"[26] the result has been a "moderate" opposition engaged in lively, yet substantive, debates. When Gerald Ford assumed the post of House minority leader in 1965, he echoed those sentiments, saying it was the Republican Party's responsibility to "oppose those proposals of the President and the majority which for one reason or another are unsound or do not get at the problem in the best way. The minority's task is to offer good alternatives, so the Congress and the people have a real choice."[27]

But moderation does not characterize today's Republican Party led by a man who brooks no hint of opposition. Donald Trump's ego is such that Trumpism without Trump is as unimaginable to him as it is to his most devoted followers. Trumpism isn't so much a philosophy as it is a list of grievances. Conservative scholar Bruce Bartlett writes that "when a political party abandons ideas, demonizes intellectuals, degrades politics, and simply pursues power for the sake of power," the result is an inherent inconsistency.[28] But it is a politics of grievance and contradiction that makes Donald Trump and Trumpism akin to an earlier era in Republican politics—the emergence of what Daniel Bell in 1955 aptly termed the "radical right."

THE RISE OF THE "PSEUDO-CONSERVATIVES"

Arthur Larson, who served as the in-house philosophizer for Dwight D. Eisenhower's vision of Modern Republicanism, distinguished between what he called "good conservatism" and "bad conservatism." Good conservatism, he said, aims to "preserve and foster the great and ultimate values of our country and civilization," whereas bad conservatism ignores "what happens to our traditional ideals and values."[29] Foremost in Larson's mind was the still-fresh battle between Dwight Eisenhower and Robert Taft at the Republican National Convention in 1952. But Daniel Bell saw something sinister lurking on the horizon—a rising "radical right" whose stock-in-trade rested on a tripod consisting of a perceived breakdown in moral fiber, a "control apparatus" that existed within the government that was selling out the country, and a fear that communists were on the verge of taking control of that same government. Bell believed an emerging radical right had the potential to disrupt the "fragile consensus" that formed the underpinnings of the two-party system.[30]

Richard Hofstadter expanded on Bell's thesis, using the term "pseudo-conservatives" to describe the emerging radical right. The term was first coined by philosopher Theodor W. Adorno, who defined it as those "who, in the name of upholding traditional American values and institutions and defending them against more or less fictitious dangers, consciously or unconsciously aims at their abolition."[31] The pseudo-conservatives differed in both class and political outlook from the old guard whose champions were Herbert Hoover, Alf Landon, and Robert Taft. They were decidedly middle class but hardly wealthy. And rather than decry the excesses of the New Deal as did FDR's most militant opponents, pseudo-conservatives had a very different set of grievances in which they believed they were inhabiting a different world where they were "spied upon, plotted against, betrayed, and very likely destined for total ruin."[32] Their certitude rested not on the conviction that government should do less (they liked Social Security, for example), but on their perceived loss of social status in a complex and rapidly changing world. It was this sense of the unfamiliar—accompanied by their fear of domination by powerful political and social elites—that led them to imagine their leaders as "engaged in a more or less continuous conspiracy" designed to downgrade and belittle them.[33] Hofstadter observed that the pseudo-conservatives collectively enjoyed "seeing outstanding generals, distinguished secretaries of state, and prominent scholars browbeaten and humiliated."[34] Writing around the same time, Clinton Rossiter, in his insightful book *Conservatives in America*, noted that the American right had a strong predisposition to scorn and bully "the poet, professor, philosopher, and political theorist."[35] The result, said Rossiter, was a "vicious circle" in which "the more savagely one of them baits, the more savagely he is baited."[36] Given these accumulating hatreds, Hofstadter warned that it was "conceivable that a highly organized, vocal, active, and well-financed minority could create a political climate in which the rational pursuit of our well-being and safety would become impossible."[37]

That threat never materialized because the pseudo-conservatives never found their Donald Trump. Instead, it was Trump who has re-created a modern-day pseudo-conservative movement. Writing in the *Washington Post*, Kevin D. Williamson, editor of *National Review*, noted that for Trump and his followers Trumpism represented "something more like group therapy for conservatives and others who feel alienated from, and hostile toward, the progressive social consensus: political and corporate elites who all seem to have gone to the same schools and belong to the same clubs."[38] At a 2016 rally, Trump exclaimed: "If you see somebody getting ready to throw a tomato, knock the crap of 'em would you? Seriously. OK? Just knock the hell—I promise you. I will pay the legal fees, I promise."[39] Williamson concluded that Trumpism was not a philosophy per se but an "enemies list."[40] Occupying the top spot on the list was Hillary Clinton, who played directly into Trump's hands by deriding his supporters as a "basket of deplorables."[41] They, in turn, repeatedly chanted, "Lock her up!" at every Trump event. The "lock 'em up" catchphrase would eventually be directed at Joe Biden, James Comey, Adam Schiff, and any other Trump critic either real or imagined.

According to Williamson, these chants were a "cathartic confrontation," as Trump perfected the art of exploiting the "bitter divide in our society and culture that will be there long after he has decamped to Mar-a-Largo."[42] The late *Washington Post* columnist Michael Gerson, who, like Williamson, lamented the loss of traditional conservatism, called Trump the "Rembrandt of demagoguery."[43] Former House Speaker Paul Ryan describes Trump as the progenitor of a rising "entertainment wing"—composed of "amoral opportunists who have found they can scale politics much faster than the meritocracy of proving yourself."[44] Donald Trump is this wing's leader, but its ranks also include Ted Cruz, Marjorie Taylor Greene, Lauren Boebert, Paul Gosar, Jim Jordan, Matt Gaetz, and many others. Their sole aim is not to pass legislation but to gain notoriety and campaign contributions from the dispossessed thanks to their constant social media presence.

It was the dispossessed to whom Trump spoke the loudest and who were his most enthusiastic supporters. Many were upset by trade deals and globalization, which, they believed, hurt them economically. Todd Sias of Erie, Pennsylvania, who was unable to find manufacturing work, commented to Daniel Allott, "It doesn't seem like we have any growth in the economy, and it seems like we're literally outsourcing all our economy and commerce out of the country."[45] But Trump's appeal did not simply derive from James Carville's famous aphorism, "It's the economy, stupid!" It also rested on his supporters' perceived lack of social status thanks to what they believed was the flouting of established rules by illegal immigrants and others who were gaming the system. Even some immigrants subscribed to this view. Jasmine, an Iraqi immigrant and Trump supporter, told Allott: "I get annoyed by someone who chose to be here, and they are illegal. They know the law and they break it. . . . Some families, every year, they have a new baby, and you ask them why, and they say they want more benefits. . . . Immigrants are not here to visit. If you left your country, you are not here to visit."[46] Her sentiments were echoed by Pam McKinney, who explained to Allott: "Where I grew up in the San Joaquin Valley, it was a good, solid community, but it fell apart when the government started pandering to all of these immigrants who don't understand our culture and don't want to assimilate. . . . Trump gives us a chance to take things back."[47] These voters like Trump because of his "take no shit" attitude.[48] As one supporter put it, "I definitely feel like he made the rural people feel that they were being listened to and that they were important."[49] In turn, Trump wasted no opportunity to praise his backers as "the forgotten men and women of our country" who "work hard but no longer have a voice." Returning to Washington, DC, for the first time since departing the White House, Trump told his admirers: "Never forget everything this corrupt establishment is doing to me is all about preserving their power and control over the American people. They want to damage you in any form. But they really want to damage me so I can no longer go back to work for you."[50]

Adding to his appeal is Trump's persona as a man of action, even when those actions often lack coherence or contradict his past statements. These inconsistencies long predated Trump's political debut. Over the course of his adult life, Trump changed his New York State party registration five times.[51] His acrobatic policy somersaults were just as mind-boggling. In 1999, he declared, "I am totally pro-choice," but in 2011 he assured the Conservative Action Policy Conference, "I am pro-life."[52] On March 21, 2016, Trump told the *Washington Post*, "I think NATO is a good thing." Six days later he said, "I think NATO is obsolete."[53] In 2000, Trump proclaimed his support for gun control, an assault weapons ban, and a "slightly longer waiting period" before purchasing a weapon.[54] But in 2016, Trump promised Republicans, "I am the strongest person running in favor of the Second Amendment."⁵⁵ Most revealingly, Trump once said, "I'm very capable of changing to anything I want to change to."⁵⁶

These contradictions hardly upset Trump's followers because of their unshakable belief in his action hero persona, convinced he would surely upset the status quo. Daniel Bell perceptively noted that "tough-talking" calls for getting things done are a "dominant aspect of the traditional American character."⁵⁷ It was this American characteristic favoring immediate action that Alexander Hamilton used to urge ratification of the US Constitution. Hamilton touted the new presidential office not only as capable of ending the existing chaos but also as a center of activity, writing, "Energy in the executive is a leading character in the definition of good government."⁵⁸ It is this penchant for action, accompanied by the perception that every battle between the two parties represents a modern-day Armageddon, that has led both Republicans *and* Democrats to upset the delicate balance of power the authors of the US Constitution had so carefully constructed.

THE CONSTITUTION ISN'T WORKING

The US Constitution is the sacred text of American government and civic life. Woodrow Wilson believed that the success of constitutional government depended on three factors:

- To bring the active and planning will of each part of the government into accord with the prevailing popular thought and need, in order that government may be the impartial instrument of a symmetrical national development;
- To give to the law thus formulated under the influence of opinion and adjusted to the general interest both stability and an incorruptible efficacy;
- To put into the hands of every individual, without favor or discrimination, the means of enforcing the understandings of the law alike with regard to himself and with regard to the operations of government, the means of challenging every illegal act that touches him.⁵⁹

For Wilson, bringing these three factors to fruition rested on the formation of a united community with common interests and purposes:

> A people not conscious of any unity, inorganic, unthoughtful, without concert of action, can manifestly neither form nor sustain a constitutional system. ... They can form no common judgment; they can conceive of no common end; they can contrive no common measures. Nothing but a community can have a constitutional form of government, and if a nation has not become a community, it cannot have that sort of polity.[60]

Today, the emergence of a modern-day pseudo-conservative movement led by Donald Trump that has consumed the Republican Party—together with an obdurate Democratic Party opposed to Trump—has frayed the communal bonds that Wilson deemed so essential and has hobbled the effectiveness of our constitutional government. Today, there is an abundance of evidence that the 1787 document isn't working and has created a crisis of confidence in the institutions it created. A 2022 Gallup poll found that just 23 percent of Americans had either a "great deal" or "quite a lot" of confidence in the presidency, down from 48 percent in 2001. Congress, never high in the public's estimation, fell from a low mark of 26 percent in 2001, to a mere 5 percent today. Confidence in the Supreme Court has been cut in half, down from 50 percent to 25 percent. These declining percentages also extend to other civic organizations—including organized religion, public schools, large technology companies, and the media. Only small businesses, the military, and the police remain highly regarded.[61]

This crisis of confidence is more than the personal failings of those who inhabit the governing institutions that the framers so carefully designed. When the Constitution was written, it was assumed that each branch would jealously guard its prerogatives. Presidents were often frustrated by the inability of Congress to find consensus that resulted from disputes within their own party's ranks. John F. Kennedy once remarked that his perception of Congress changed once he entered the Oval Office: "The fact is that the Congress looks more powerful sitting here than it did when I was there in Congress. But that is because when you are in Congress you are one of one hundred in the Senate or one of four-hundred-thirty-five in the House. So, the power is divided. But from here I look at Congress, particularly the bloc action, and it is a substantial power."[62] Southern Democrats frequently reminded Kennedy of their ability to obstruct, particularly on civil rights. But action resulted when the public formed a consensus that the proposed solutions, however inadequate, were needed.

Today, things are different. The battles between the two parties are asymmetrical, lacking a common set of facts and with fights conducted on entirely different battlegrounds. Instead of disagreements based on different interpretations formed by a common set of values, the parties now believe that each election is existential, and reason has given way to fear. This is very different from the unique foundations of the American polity famously described by Louis Hartz during the 1950s that were centered on a "fixed, dogmatic liberalism" based on a common commitment to the values of freedom, equality of opportunity, and individual rights.[63] Beginning in the 1970s, the culture wars emerged and reassembled the parties' coalitions while at the same time making them more internally homogeneous. By the end of the Trump presidency, the "big sort," as journalist Bill Bishop once referred to it, was complete.[64] The Republican faithful became whiter, more rural, blue collar, with little to no college exposure, older, and culturally conservative, while Democratic voters became more upscale, college educated, urban and suburban, multiracial, young, and culturally liberal. Overwhelming majorities akin to those won by Franklin Roosevelt, Dwight Eisenhower, Lyndon Johnson, Richard Nixon, and Ronald Reagan are now impossible to achieve, but landslides within states are commonplace. In 2020, rural counties overwhelmingly voted for Donald Trump, while urban and suburban counties provided Joe Biden with lopsided victories. Voters often imitate their neighbors and like living in areas where their cultural preferences are widely shared. In 2020, 85 percent of counties with a Whole Foods Market sided with Joe Biden, while 74 percent of counties with a Cracker Barrel restaurant voted for Donald Trump.[65] Voters are driven by a belief that a win by the opposite party forever threatens their own well-being and values. Fear is now a dominant motivator, and both parties play to that emotion.

The resulting intraparty harmony has upset the framers' delicate constitutional balance. As historian Herbert Agar concluded: "A federal nation is safe so long as the parties are undogmatic and contain members with many contradictory views. But when the people begin to divide according to reason with all the voters in one party who believe one way, the federal structure is strained."[66] Instead of jealously guarding its constitutional prerogatives, the tripartite system of government has given way to unreasoning partisanship. In 2006, Thomas Mann and Norman Ornstein authored an important book on Congress titled *The Broken Branch*. In it, they derided the abandonment of congressional norms in favor of one party's slavish adherence to whatever its president desires: "We recognized that the American system works best when both the executive and legislative branches are strong and protective of their institutional prerogatives and competitive advantages. But Congress largely abdicated that responsibility as party and ideology trumped institution."[67] The consequence is a lack of adherence to protecting congressional prerogatives. In 2012, Republican senator Susan Collins opined: "What has been lost in recent times is a commitment to Congress as an institution, a sense that we are collectively responsible for addressing the issues that confront our country."[68]

In his classic book titled *Congressional Government*, Woodrow Wilson wrote, "Congress in session is Congress on public exhibition, whilst Congress in its committee-rooms is Congress at work."[69] Implicit in Wilson's observation was that the public exhibitions on the floors of Congress were performative, while the substance of congressional work lay in the "little legislatures" of congressional committees.[70] Today, almost everything in Congress is performative, thanks to what Frances E. Lee calls the "insecure majorities" that define contemporary partisan control of the House and Senate. In 2006, Barbara Sinclair said of Congress: "Each side really does see the other's policy and electoral success as disastrous for the country; and this sometimes generates a feeling that anything goes, anything is justified to avert such a catastrophe."[71] The result is the all-too-often abandonment of policy deliberations in favor of igniting the passions of each party's supporters. In 2011, for example, a contingent of House Republicans persuaded then Speaker John Boehner to cease negotiations with President Obama over fiscal policy, with one member telling the Speaker: "It's no longer policy season. It's message season."[72] Today, the partisan battles waged by each party in Congress are a zero-sum game.

The result is a perversion of once universally accepted congressional norms. In the Senate that has meant the minority party using the filibuster to frustrate the majority, with the majority sometimes bending Senate rules to overcome it. Filibusters were once a rare device that was employed only when either a senator or a group of senators felt so passionately about an issue that floor time would yield to interminable speeches designed to stop legislation from passing. One of the most famous filibusters was a marathon speech by South Carolina's Strom Thurmond, who in 1957 spoke for a record twenty-four hours and eighteen minutes protesting a civil rights bill. Today, the parties use the mere threat of staging a filibuster, meaning that sixty votes are required even to debate an issue without anyone ever having to engage in a Thurmond-like talkathon.

Another change has been the power exercised by party leaders. This began with the speakership of Newt Gingrich, who centralized power and took the unprecedented step of ousting three senior Republicans who were in line to assume committee chairmanships.[73] Nancy Pelosi used her authority in a similar manner. In the Senate, bills are drafted by top leaders, often bypassing the committee process. In one of his last speeches on the Senate floor, John McCain derided the lack of "regular order" and the practice of "mandating legislation from the top down without any support from the other side, with all the parliamentary maneuvers that requires."[74] With Congress frequently stymied, many members believe their job is to continuously elevate passions by using social media as their primary means of communication. Marjorie Taylor Greene has become an internet and fundraising sensation. In one of her most famous encounters, she stalked Parkland High School shooting survivor David Hogg as he lobbied the halls of Congress for gun reform. At one point, Greene revealingly asked Hogg, "How did you get major press coverage?"[75] Democrats also realize the importance of social media, knowing that more "hits" gives them more publicity and greater fundraising power. No longer do age and longevity solely determine power within Congress. Members can become overnight sensations with the right social media posts that are designed to inflame passions but often have little to do with the hard work of passing legislation.

With members of both parties focusing on social media "hits," the motivation to stick with their respective political parties—thanks to a fear of a primary challenge and a desire for approval from their fellow caucus members—has substantially increased. Party unity has become the norm. In 2022, 97 percent of House Democrats and 91 percent of House Republicans cast unified party votes; in the Senate, 95 percent of Democrats and 82 percent of Republicans did the same.[76] Outliers are often scorned by their colleagues and become vulnerable to defeat in intraparty primaries, as Liz Cheney and Adam Kinzinger aptly demonstrate. As gerrymandering becomes commonplace, the number of competitive congressional races has dwindled. Thus, the greatest danger most incumbents face is an intraparty challenge.

Increased partisanship has also come to characterize the presidency despite some oft-repeated pledges to unify the country. In 2000, George W. Bush promised to be "a unifier, not a divider." Barack Obama rose to fame in 2004, telling the Democratic National Convention, "There's not a liberal America and a conservative America—there's the United States of America."[77] In his 2020 victory speech, Joe Biden pledged "to be a president who seeks not to divide but unify, who doesn't see red states and blue states, only sees the United States."[78] Donald Trump was the lone exception, knowing that keeping his base both passionate and engaged would transform the Republican Party into a creature of his own making. The failure to achieve any semblance of national unity has contributed to an overall sense that our presidents have failed to live up to their promises. Bush, Obama, and Biden failed to bring the country together. And Donald Trump did little either to promote the economic well-being of his followers or to prevent the demographic changes taking place that will crest by the middle of this century. Great presidents are rare, as historian James Bryce famously noted, with Abraham Lincoln, George Washington, and Franklin D. Roosevelt the most notable exceptions.[79] Even the so-called near-great presidents like Thomas Jefferson, Theodore Roosevelt, Harry Truman, and Dwight Eisenhower are unique.[80] In his first appearance on the presidential rankings list compiled by the nation's leading historians, Donald Trump placed just above James Buchanan, Andrew Johnson, and Franklin Pierce at the bottom.[81] There is a reason—more than its mere physical limitations—why space is restricted for the carved images on Mount Rushmore.

A partisan presidency has resulted in unilateral actions the constitutional framers hardly envisaged. They designed the presidency to execute laws, not make them. But the vagaries of congressional legislation, combined with the inability of Congress to pass significant reforms, have led presidents to make their own laws by signing executive orders. The result is a roller coaster from one presidency to the next. Donald Trump loved affixing his signature to executive orders, putting his Sharpie on 220 of them.[82] Shortly after being sworn in as president, Joe Biden went straight to the Oval Office and signed 17 executive orders, many reversing Trump's directives.⁸³ After Democrats lost control of Congress in 2010, Barack Obama told his cabinet, "We're not just going to be waiting for legislation. . . . I've got a pen and I've got a phone."⁸⁴ In Obama's case the pen was sometimes mightier than the sword. When Congress failed to pass immigration reform—something that had been a major priority during George W. Bush's second term—Obama signed an executive order that created the DACA program, officially called the Deferred Action for Childhood Arrivals. The 2012 order allowed minors who were brought to the United States illegally to remain free from prosecution if they registered with the federal government and had no criminal or other violations. DACA was a significant accomplishment, with 600,000 applicants, albeit one without any congressional involvement.

Another constitutional failure involving the presidency is the inability of the Twenty-Fifth Amendment to fully work as intended, especially when it comes to the question of presidential disability. When the founders discussed the possibility of an incapacitated president, Delaware delegate John Dickinson asked, "What is the extent of the term 'disability' and who is to be the judge of it?"⁸⁵ Years later, there was no answer, causing Lyndon Johnson to remark upon the amendment's ratification in 1967, "It is hard to believe that until last week our Constitution provided no clear answer."⁸⁶ The search for answers was a decades-long one that intensified after John F. Kennedy's assassination on November 22, 1963. On December 1 of that year, the *New York Times* editorialized that Congress "must face a pressing subject that has baffled the Founding Fathers and at least seven Congresses in the last century and this [one]: the contingencies of presidential disability and succession."⁸⁷ Throughout history, there were well-documented examples of presidents who suffered various disabilities yet continued in office. In 1881, James Garfield lingered for eighty days before succumbing to an assassin's bullet. Twelve years later, Grover Cleveland had secret surgery for oral cancer. In 1919, Woodrow Wilson suffered a crippling stroke and was incapacitated for the last eighteen months of his tenure. Franklin D. Roosevelt's final year was a debilitating one plagued by congestive heart failure and high blood pressure that culminated in a fatal brain aneurysm. Dwight D. Eisenhower had a series of health crises that included a heart attack, stroke, and bouts with Crohn's disease. Recognizing there needed to be an orderly transfer of power, Eisenhower exchanged letters with Vice President Nixon instructing him to act in his stead should he be unable to discharge his duties. John F. Kennedy and Lyndon B. Johnson followed the same practice. While these letters were statements of intent, they had no controlling legal authority.

Recognizing the need for change, Congress approved the Twenty-Fifth Amendment in 1965, and two-thirds of the states ratified it two years later. The amendment dealt with several issues: (1) filling a vice presidential vacancy should the vice president either ascend to the presidency, die, or resign; (2) allowing the president to declare a temporary disability whenever "unable to discharge the duties of his office," with the vice president serving as acting president; and (3) permitting the vice president and a majority of the cabinet to declare a president disabled. If the president disagrees, Congress must resolve the issue with two-thirds of members affirming their decision. The debate surrounding the amendment was a vigorous one. Political scientist James MacGregor Burns argued that giving the vice president any role in declaring a presidential disability could make that person a potential usurper of executive power.[88] Presidential scholar Richard Neustadt believed that any cabinet role would surely complicate the relationship between the president and the department heads.[89]

It is abundantly clear that the Twenty-Fifth Amendment is not working. Buried in Cassidy Hutchinson's bombshell testimony before the January 6 Select Committee was her depiction of Secretary of State Mike Pompeo informing Chief of Staff Mark Meadows that there was a movement afoot inside the cabinet to invoke the Twenty-Fifth Amendment after the January 6 insurrection and declare Donald Trump incapable of discharging his duties. According to Hutchinson, Pompeo told Meadows, "You're technically the boss of all the Cabinet secretaries."[90] Given Vice President Mike Pence's reluctance to initiate a move, two cabinet secretaries, education secretary Betsy DeVos and transportation secretary Elaine Chao, resigned hours after the riot. DeVos told Trump, "There's no mistaking the impact your rhetoric had on the situation, and it is the inflection point for me."[91] Other White House insiders—including the deputy national security adviser, acting chair of the Council of Economic Advisers, the special envoy to Northern Ireland, and Melania Trump's chief of staff—also quickly departed.[92]

Pompeo's decision to refer the matter to the chief of staff, even calling him the "boss," was not without precedent. During his last weeks in office,

Richard Nixon's chief of staff did not invoke the Twenty-Fifth Amendment, and his defense secretary issued a directive not to obey any presidential order without his permission. In 1981, Ronald Reagan's chief of staff made the decision not to invoke the Twenty-Fifth Amendment after the president was shot and severely wounded. From his hospital bed, Reagan asked, "Who's minding the store?"[93] As we have learned, Reagan was in far more serious condition than the public knew at the time.

Leaving any decision to invoke a presidential disability to the chief of staff is completely contrary to the proposals made by the Brownlow Committee, which established the office. In 1936, Franklin Roosevelt named Louis Brownlow, a distinguished student of public administration, to study the operations of the White House. The committee concluded, "The President needs help," and it recommended the creation of the Executive Office of the President, which houses the president's staff.[94] Two years later, Congress passed the Reorganization Act of 1939. But the Brownlow Committee proposed that strict limits be placed on staff members, saying they should have "a passion for anonymity" and were not to interpose themselves between the president and the heads of cabinet departments. Staffers should assist the president, not make policy.[95] The committee would be appalled to learn that a secretary of state thought the chief of staff was his "boss," or that any invocation of a presidential disability rested with that person.

Nonetheless, there was a widespread view within Trump's White House, the military, and Congress that Donald Trump was no longer capable of discharging the duties of the office after January 6, 2021. House Speaker Nancy Pelosi telephoned Joint Chiefs of Staff chairman General Mark Milley and called Trump "unhinged," adding: "Nixon did far less, and the Republicans said to him, 'You have to go.' . . . [There's] nobody around [Trump] with any courage to stop him from storming the Capitol and inflaming, inciting an insurrection. And there he is, the president of the United States in there."[96] The prevailing analogy among those close to Trump was that during the intervening two weeks between the January 6 riot and Joe Biden's inauguration on January 20 they needed to "land the plane."[97] The plane did land, but only after a close encounter with disaster. When the Twenty-Fifth Amendment was ratified, Lyndon Johnson argued that it "further perfected" the Constitution.[98] Nothing could be further from the truth. The vice president, cabinet, and ultimately Congress no longer collectively have either the ability or the will to remove an unhinged president from power.

The Supreme Court is also not working. In Federalist 78, Alexander Hamilton argued that the Court was "the least dangerous" branch, since it had no influence over either "the sword or the purse," provinces reserved to the executive and legislative branches.[99] Today, the Court is roiled by controversy, the latest being the *Dobbs v. Jackson* ruling that overturned *Roe v. Wade*. For decades, Republicans worked to pack the federal courts by nominating judges who agreed with them on cultural issues, especially abortion. The Federalist Society, founded in 1982, became a clearinghouse for Republican judicial appointments, replacing the nonpartisan American Bar Association as an arbiter of justice. When Antonin Scalia died suddenly in February 2016, Senate majority leader Mitch McConnell held up Barack Obama's intended replacement, Merrick Garland, until Donald Trump was installed into the Oval Office. During the 2016 campaign, Trump took the unprecedented step of producing a list of judicial nominees that would assure both congressional Republicans and the Federalist Society (which was instrumental in composing the list). Trump followed suit by naming Neil Gorsuch to the Supreme Court, later followed by Brett Kavanaugh and Amy Coney Barrett, each of whom had received the Federalist Society's stamp of approval. When Ruth Bader Ginsburg died in September 2020, her last wish was that her seat be kept vacant until the election result was clear. Trump and McConnell ignored that deathbed request and rushed through Barrett's nomination in a record thirty days. Today, with a 6–3 conservative supermajority, the Court is poised to overturn several precedents. Dissenting from an opinion keeping a Texas abortion ban in place, Justice Sonia Sotomayor wrote, "The Court thus betrays not only the citizens of Texas, but also our constitutional system of government."[100]

Today, the Court is riddled with partisanship. The *Dobbs* decision, written by Justice Samuel Alito, was prematurely leaked to the press, sowing distrust within the chambers but keeping the 5–4 majority in place, despite pleas from Chief Justice John Roberts not to take *Roe v. Wade* "all the way down to the studs."[101] Amy Coney Barrett has vainly attempted to reassure the public that the Court is not composed of "a bunch of partisan hacks."[102] But polling shows the opposite: 61 percent believe the Court's decisions are motivated by politics; just 32 percent think its judgments are based on dispassionate readings of the law.[103] When the Supreme Court was created, the life expectancy in the United States was just forty-four years; today, it is seventy-nine.[104] A lifetime appointment to the Supreme Court means that the court's composition is subject to infrequent changes, with presidents lucky to make one or two appointments—if that. During the Rehnquist era, the Court went unchanged for eleven years, the longest stretch in its history. Joe Biden has made one appointment, securing the confirmation of Justice Ketanji Brown Jackson, the first African American woman to sit on the Court, but he is unlikely to fill another vacancy.

WHAT CAN BE DONE?

Thomas Jefferson once remarked, "I hold it that a little rebellion every now and then is a good thing, and as necessary in the political world as storms are in the physical."[105] Jefferson did not see the Constitution as an eternal document—and certainly not one that should lay upon the altar of our civil religion—but one that would be altered by amendments and eventually in need of a complete rewrite as conditions changed. Jeremy Bailey maintains that Jefferson even went so far as to "suggest that constitution and other forms of government were less important than the majority will," and that the dead should not govern the living.[106] Abraham Lincoln expressed a similar view:

> Some men look at constitutions with sanctimonious reverence, and deem them like the arc [sic] of the covenant, too sacred to be touched. They ascribe to the men of the preceding age a wisdom more than human and suppose what they did to be beyond amendment. I knew that age well; I belonged to it and labored with it. It deserved well of its country. It was very like the present, but without the experience of the present, and forty years of experience in government is worth a century of book-reading; and this they would say themselves, were they to rise from the dead. I am certainly not an advocate for frequent and untried changes in laws and constitutions. I think moderate imperfections had better be borne with; because, when once known, we accommodate ourselves to them, and find practical means of correcting their ill effects. But I know also that laws and institutions must go hand in hand with the progress of the human mind. As that becomes more developed, more

enlightened, as new discoveries are made, new truths disclosed, and manners and opinions change with the change of circumstances, institutions must advance also, and keep pace with the times.[107]

Whenever there has been a pent-up demand for change, explosions happen. The Revolutionary War occurred because of frustrations with a far-off Britain exercising arbitrary rule over the colonies. The slavery issue led to the Civil War, which resulted in three amendments being added to the Constitution that culminated with legislation nearly a century later to ensure equality for African Americans. The Great Depression made possible Franklin D. Roosevelt's presidency and the New Deal reforms that accompanied it. Today, frustrations with the constitutional processes have led to several proposals for revising the document. Woodrow Wilson once wrote, "It is one thing to advocate reforms; it is quite another to formulate them."[108] The following discussion provides some proposed suggestions—they are by no means exhaustive but are given with the trepidation that if nothing is done, the ongoing stasis will lead to a crisis of untold proportions.

Reform the Electoral College

The Electoral College was designed by Alexander Hamilton to ensure that there would be a separation of the presidency from Congress, state legislatures, and voters. Independent electors would choose presidents not based on policy positions or public promises, but because of their outstanding characters. Hamilton envisioned a civic-minded presidency whose occupants, like George Washington, would place the national interest above sectional ones. By 1796, Hamilton's vision of his idealized president had grown increasingly cloudy, and the Adams-Jefferson contest of 1800 blinded it altogether. The quick development of the two-party system meant that electors would no longer be independent actors but loyal party operatives. In 2020, the Supreme Court unanimously invalidated votes cast by "faithless electors" that were opposed to a state's popular vote winner.[109]

Eliminating the Electoral College requires passage of a constitutional amendment, which is an exceptionally high hurdle. But in 1970 that nearly happened. After the 1968 election that saw third-party candidate George

Wallace nearly pull enough electoral votes to throw the contest into the House of Representatives, Democrats controlled more state delegations that could have installed popular vote loser Hubert Humphrey into the presidency. A Gallup poll conducted after the election found eight out of ten Americans supported an amendment that would scrap the Electoral College.[110] Richard Nixon backed its elimination, and in 1969 a required two-thirds of the House endorsed a constitutional amendment that would do just that.[111] The following year the Senate Judiciary Committee moved the amendment to the floor for debate, but southerners led by Richard Russell and Strom Thurmond rose to conduct a successful filibuster. The South recognized its power in the Electoral College and refused to succumb to an amendment it believed would give northern urban centers even greater political power.[112] James MacGregor Burns predicted that the Electoral College had become "a game of Russian Roulette and one of these days we are going to blow our brains out."[113]

Nonetheless, Electoral College reforms continued. In 1968, Maine and Nebraska altered their state laws to give the winner of a congressional district an electoral vote rather than adhere to the winner-take-all system. In 2020, Donald Trump and Joe Biden won one electoral vote from each of these states they lost.[114] Some believe the idea should be tried elsewhere. However, congressional gerrymandering has become increasingly perfected thanks to sophisticated technologies that would only exaggerate the Electoral College's current imperfections. Another proposed reform is to have the states sign a compact pledging their votes to the popular vote winner, even if that state voted the other way. While this was much discussed after the disputed 2000 election, it has not been brought to fruition because the number of states needed to agree has not reached the magic number of 270 electoral votes required to enforce the interstate compact. As of December 2021, only fifteen states have joined, representing 195 electoral votes.[115] Even in the unlikely event that enough states signed up, there are questions as to the agreement's constitutionality.

The Pew Research Center has found that the Electoral College remains unpopular. Since 2000, decisive majorities, currently standing at 63 percent, support electing presidents by popular vote. Not surprisingly, 80 percent of Democrats favor eliminating the Electoral College, while only 42 percent of Republicans agree.[116] Younger Americans are especially supportive of doing away with the outdated mechanism, with 70 percent calling for its abolition. As mentioned earlier, getting rid of the Electoral College, however, requires a constitutional amendment, which is extremely unlikely to meet the necessary constitutional requirements for adoption. More popular vote misfires result in more political disillusionment, and that increases the possibility for violence.

Critics of eradicating the Electoral College argue it would confine presidential campaigns to television studios. To a large extent, this is already true. Only a handful of states remain competitive, and given the increased polarization of the country into reliably red and blue states, presidential elections are increasingly national contests. In the event of its elimination, presidential candidates would still travel to states to bolster their party's congressional candidates rather than confining themselves to a limited number of battlegrounds. Getting rid of the Electoral College represents a further democratization in the eyes of voters who rebel at taking away voting rights simply to advantage one party in a particular locale. Nationwide voting for president would also limit judicial involvement and reduce the number of federal and state disputes concerning any potential violations of either federal or state law.

Should no one receive a majority of the popular vote, especially if multiple candidates or parties nominated viable candidates, a runoff could occur in mid-December among the top two contenders. This is a practice used in several European countries and is designed to produce centrist candidates with clear mandates. While a multitude of parties is unlikely, given that state laws are written by Republicans and Democrats, eliminating the Electoral College could provide an additional incentive for third parties to form—particularly among conservatives who mourn the loss of what they once knew and seek a restoration, or progressives who long for greater intraparty harmony. Either way, a national majority means claims of a stolen election would be thrown into the dustbin of history.

Institute Some Congressional and State Reforms

The filibuster is not mentioned in the Constitution, nor was it initially employed in the first Congresses. Under the original rules of the Senate, a simple majority was needed to end debate and obtain an up-or-down vote. That changed in 1806 when the Senate, acting on the suggestion of Aaron Burr, ruled any motion to end debate and move to a final vote was an unnecessary duplication, thus creating the conditions under which filibusters could occur. Already indicted for the murder of Alexander Hamilton, Burr praised the Senate as "a sanctuary; a citadel of law, of order, and of liberty."[117] In 1917, the Senate passed Rule XXII, which required a two-thirds majority to end a filibuster. With the Senate expanding to one hundred members thanks to the admission of Alaska and Hawaii, ending a filibuster became even more unlikely. By 1975, reform-minded Democrats amended Rule XXII to reduce the required number to sixty. Since 1917, there have been more than two thousand filibusters, with nearly *half* occurring since 2009.[118]

Today, the filibuster is no longer a marathon talking session. Instead, it is assumed that every bill is subject to a filibuster, meaning sixty votes are required before the Senate will even consider any bill no matter how meritorious. In 2009, Democrats controlled sixty Senate seats, and Obamacare won approval without any Republican votes and was sent to the House. But in 2010, a Republican won a special election to fill the seat held by the late Ted Kennedy. House Speaker Nancy Pelosi had a choice: either amend the bill and send it to the Senate, knowing defeat was certain, or pass the Senate bill and send it to the White House. She chose the latter course, and Obamacare became the singular legislative achievement of the Obama presidency. After 2010, when Republicans secured congressional majorities, Obama's legislative agenda ground to a halt.

Political polarization makes gaining sixty Senate votes a virtual impossibility. Republicans have a solid grasp on small, rural states, which, like the large urban ones, have two senators apiece. Today, the twenty-six least populous states represent just 17 percent of the US population. While the minority vigorously defends the filibuster as a means to prevent "bad things from happening," measures with broad public support have suffered one defeat after another. Meanwhile, frustrated presidents sign executive orders while stymied Senate majorities have increasingly turned to measures designed to circumvent the filibuster. Donald Trump and Mitch McConnell used the budget reconciliation process to pass Trump's tax cuts. Joe Biden and Chuck Schumer used it to pass the American Rescue Act and the Inflation Reduction Act. The reconciliation process, a by-product of the 1970s, was not designed to handle the far-reaching measures that both parties now employ to achieve their legislative priorities.

Senate rules have been amended to bypass the sixty-vote requirement and allow majority votes for cabinet appointees and federal judges, including Supreme Court judges. In 2013, Democrats changed the Senate rules to allow confirmation of executive branch positions—including the cabinet and non–Supreme Court judicial nominees—by majority vote. Four years later, Republicans seized the opportunity to fill a seat vacant by the death of Antonin Scalia and approved a change to require a simple majority to fill Supreme Court vacancies. Neil Gorsuch, Brett Kavanaugh, Amy Coney Barrett, and Ketanji Brown Jackson were confirmed with numbers that fell far short of the previously required sixty votes: Gorsuch received 54 votes; Kavanaugh, 50; Barrett, 52; and Jackson, 53, with few party defections. Between 1969 and 2014, there have been 161 exceptions made to the supermajorities required by Rule XXII.[119] The result has been a record number of tie-breaking votes cast by the last two vice presidents. During his term, Mike Pence broke thirteen ties, and in 2023, Kamala Harris cast thirty-two Senate votes, breaking the record set by Vice President John C. Calhoun, who served from 1829 to 1833.[120]

Adam Jentleson proposes that the Senate set a five-day calendar limit for debate, with each side proposing amendments. Jentleson argues this would allow the minority to have a greater voice in shaping legislation and would restore the Senate to the deliberative body that it once was. After a five-day period, the Senate would invoke cloture using a simple majority.[121] One advantage of Jentleson's proposal would be to repopulate what has become a largely deserted Senate chamber and allow members to truly engage in a fulsome debate. However, eliminating the filibuster altogether is highly unlikely. Besides adopting Jentleson's proposals, the Senate should amend Rule XXII and limit the number of filibusters used during each congressional session. A minimum of six senators (10 percent of the sixty-vote requirement) should be required to conduct a talking filibuster. Under this change, senators must hold the floor and truly debate an issue, not read from Shakespeare, *Green Eggs and Ham*, or *The Godfather*, or other extraneous materials as has been done.[122]

Other prospects for changing the workings of Congress rest with the states. Some states have sought to limit gerrymandering by creating independent commissions to redraw congressional districts. Such commissions are popular with voters but extremely unpopular among those in power. In 2010, 61 percent of California voters approved creating an independent commission to redraw congressional districts after creating a similar commission to do the same for the state legislature. By a 5–4 decision, the Supreme Court ruled that the commission does not have the authority to restrict partisan gerrymandering. Writing for the majority, Chief Justice Roberts concluded that while gerrymandering may be "incompatible with democratic principles," it "does not mean that the solution lies with the federal judiciary."[123] Expressing "deep sadness," Justice Elena Kagan argued that partisan gerrymanders "deprived citizens of the most fundamental of their constitutional rights: the rights to participate equally in the political process, to join with others to advance political beliefs, and to choose their political representatives." In her view, the preordained outcomes "debased and dishonored our democracy, turning upside-down the core American idea that all governmental power derives from the people."[124] Left unchecked, gerrymandering will increase partisan polarization and decrease the ability of our institutions to function effectively and provide broadly acceptable decisions.

Both parties have become quite sophisticated at gerrymandering thanks to computer programs that can redraw district lines with increased accuracy. The result is an ever-greater number of noncompetitive congressional districts. In 2022, just 8.5 percent of seats in the US House were deemed as being truly up for grabs.[125] With each census, the number of competitive seats dwindles. And thanks to these noncompetitive seats, the *real threat* to lawmakers is an intraparty primary challenge. Moreover, the increased number of safe seats distorts any result produced by the House of Representatives should a presidential candidate not receive an Electoral College majority. In 2021, Donald Trump used this as a last resort to retain the presidency, even though he lost the popular vote by seven million.

Another reform is ranked choice voting. Maine began using this system in 2018, and Alaska followed suit in 2022. The result has been a re-creation of what Arthur M. Schlesinger Jr. once called the "vital center."[126] Instead of appealing to base voters, moderate candidates under this system have prevailed to better represent the majority's sentiments. In Maine, Democrat Jared Golden won a seat in Congress in 2018, even though he was not the voters' first choice. Forced to certify the results, Republican governor Paul LePage initialed the document but wrote "stolen election" on it.[127] Golden represents a Trump-supporting congressional district as a Democrat, voting, for example, against Joe Biden's American Rescue

Plan and gun rights legislation. In 2022, Golden won his third term in Congress.

After the death of longtime Alaska Republican congressman Don Young in 2022, a special election was held. Sarah Palin, the vice presidential candidate in 2008, sought the seat but did not win thanks to the ranked choice system that allowed Democrat Mary Peltola to prevail. Endorsing Palin, Donald Trump denounced ranked choice voting as "a total rigged deal."[128] Seeking reelection that fall, Peltola beat Palin again. The ranked choice system also favored moderate, pro-choice Alaska Republican Lisa Murkowski, in her reelection bid. Murkowski, one of the ten Senate Republicans who voted to convict Donald Trump in 2021, was immediately censured by the Alaska state Republican Party. But ranked choice voting put Murkowski over the top, and she defeated a Trump-endorsed candidate in November. Ranked choice voting is also used in numerous municipalities, most notably New York City. In 2021, the ranked choice system allowed a moderate Democrat, Eric Adams, to defeat his more progressive challengers and become the city's new mayor.

Set Term Limits for the Supreme Court

Instituting term limits for the Supreme Court is far easier than amending the Constitution to abolish the Electoral College. The Constitution gives Congress the power to legislate the number of Supreme Court justices. Initially, the number of justices was six, and this was changed six times more before settling on having nine judges in 1869. Given the packing of the Supreme Court during the Trump years, many have called for changes in the number of justices to restore a more evenly divided Court. A more reasonable proposal, one in keeping with the original intent of the Constitution, is to give the justices overlapping and lengthy term limits. Retiring justice Stephen Breyer has endorsed the idea: "I do think that if there were a long term—I don't know, eighteen, twenty years, something like that, and it was fixed—I would say that was fine. In fact, it'd make my life a lot simpler, to tell you the truth."[129] Chief Justice John Roberts supports a similar proposal:

> The Framers adopted life tenure at a time when people simply did not live as long as they do now. A judge insulated from the normal currents of life for

twenty-five or thirty years was a rarity then but is becoming commonplace today. Setting a term of, say, fifteen years would ensure that federal judges would not lose all touch with reality through decades of ivory tower existence. It would provide a more regular and greater degree of turnover among the judges. Both developments would, in my view, be healthy ones.[130]

Today, the average Supreme Court nominee is someone in his or her mid-fifties. Given expanded life expectancies, Supreme Court justices can expect to be on the court for decades. In 2023, Clarence Thomas, who was named by George H. W. Bush in 1991, completed his thirty-second year on the Court. Stephen Breyer served for twenty-eight years before retiring in 2022. Entering the Court at age fifty-one, Ketanji Brown Jackson could potentially remain until the year 2050 given current female life expectancies.

In addition to setting term limits, Congress could strengthen ethics requirements for the justices. Presently, justices remove themselves from cases when they believe they have an ethical conflict. But the decision to do so is solely theirs, unlike for other federal judges who must comply with ethics guidelines set by Congress. When the 2020 election results were challenged in the Supreme Court, Clarence Thomas did not recuse himself, despite his wife's intense lobbying that the electoral votes from contested states be decertified and the Republican-controlled state legislatures have the final say. Congress should institute the same requirements for Supreme Court justices as for other federal judges. Moreover, Congress should bar any justice from accepting speaking fees or having any other outside sources of income. Once retired, the former justices could write books and deliver speeches from which they would derive royalties. Having to adhere to term limits and ethical standards, the Supreme Court would be closer to the people. Changes in membership, which initially can be done by establishing staggered terms, would help reestablish public confidence in the Court and lessen the partisanship that threatens its legitimacy.

Admit the District of Columbia and Puerto Rico to Statehood

For decades, the admission of the District of Columbia and Puerto Rico as states has been under consideration. The US Constitution initially set aside the seat for the federal government as covering an area "not exceeding ten miles square." Over time, modern-day Washington, DC, has expanded to include more than sixty-eight square miles. The District of Columbia with its 701,974 residents contains more people than Vermont or Wyoming, and its population is comparable to that of several other states, including Delaware and Alaska.[131] District residents pay more taxes than the residents of twenty-two other states but have no congressional representation.[132] Leaving office in 1993, Bill Clinton changed the license plate on the presidential limousine to read "Taxation without Representation."[133] Today, the District has one House delegate who can vote in committees but is forbidden from casting a final vote on the floor. In 2009, there was a proposal to grant that delegate full House privileges if Utah received one more House member, thus negating any partisan advantage and bringing the total House membership to 437.[134] But the idea floundered. Twelve years later, the House passed a DC statehood bill for the first time by a vote of 232 to 180.[135] However, the legislation languished in the Senate under its sixty-vote requirement. The House bill would name the new state Douglass Commonwealth, in honor of Frederick Douglass, and would repeal the Twenty-Third Amendment allowing DC residents to vote in presidential elections.[136] Republicans know making DC a state would give Democrats one more House vote and two more senators. Today, African Americans, the most loyal of Democratic constituencies, constitute 47 percent of the District's population, while all minorities constitute 62 percent of the total.[137] Their exclusion from full congressional participation is one more sign of the inequities that have historically confronted minority voters.

In 2016, 86 percent of Washington, DC, voters approved a referendum expressing their support for making the District the nation's fifty-first state. Since then, the efforts to achieve statehood have intensified. On January 6, 2021, DC Metropolitan Police officers were viciously attacked at the Capitol, with several receiving life-altering injuries. The denial of statehood prevented the mayor of Washington, DC, from summoning the National Guard, as this power is reserved for state governors and presidents.[138] The lack of statehood also prevents Washington, DC, from receiving its fair share of federal funds. For example, $755 million from the CARES Act, intended to assist victims of the coronavirus, was withheld from the District.[139] The House-passed proposal would comport with the original intent of the Constitution by setting aside a two-mile radius—including the immediate areas surrounding the White House, Capitol, and National Mall—that would remain under federal control.

As in Washington, DC, there have been many attempts to grant statehood to Puerto Rico. Republican presidents Gerald Ford, Ronald Reagan, and George H. W. Bush favored Puerto Rican statehood, with Ford arguing it would permanently seal "bonds of friendship, tradition, dignity, and individual freedom" between it and the mainland.[140] In 2020, 53 percent of Puerto Ricans supported a statehood referendum. Since 1952, Puerto Rico has been a commonwealth, meaning its residents are US citizens and pay taxes but have no representation in Congress and no vote in presidential elections. A 2019 Gallup poll found 66 percent of Americans supported statehood for the island. But while 83 percent of Democrats backed the idea, only 45 percent of Republicans did.[141] Opposition to Puerto Rican statehood comes largely from Republicans who believe making it a state—like Washington, DC—would enhance Democratic representation in Congress, ensuring one more House seat and two senators. Republicans contend that before Puerto Rico receives statehood, its fiscal affairs should be put in order—an argument they did not make made when the far less prosperous states of North Dakota, South Dakota, Montana, and Washington were added to the union in 1889. Mitch McConnell believes making Puerto Rico and Washington, DC, states is part of the Democrats' "radical agenda."[142] But Florida senator Rick Scott argues that Puerto Rico is not a given for Democratic victories and that Republicans can be competitive there. Scott believes the question is not *if* Puerto Rico becomes a state, but *when*.[143] Adding these two states would address inherent inequities and mitigate some of the polarization that presently characterizes how Congress operates.

Strengthen the Parties

It seems odd to propose strengthening the political parties in an era of extreme polarization. But the weakening of the party establishments has made both vulnerable to unqualified outsiders like Donald Trump who can win nominations without withstanding the judgment of their peers. The late James MacGregor Burns decried this habit of presidential candidates "running alone," a phenomenon that has affected Republicans and

Democrats alike.[144] As noted previously, Dwight Eisenhower began the trend in 1952, and it has only accelerated in the decades since. After the disastrous 1968 Democratic National Convention when Hubert H. Humphrey, who had not competed in a single primary, was nominated, George McGovern led a commission to ensure a greater voice for the rank and file—especially women, minorities, and young voters. McGovern firmly believed that the Democratic Party must either reform or die.[145] The McGovern-Fraser Commission mandated states give women, minorities, and young voters more representation in their state delegations that comported with their electoral composition. To ensure compliance and avoid challenges, many states instituted presidential primaries as the fairest method of choosing candidates whose delegate slates complied with the new mandates. Because primaries are established by state laws, eager Democrats mandated primaries for both parties. In 1960, just seventeen primaries were held. Their sole purpose was to demonstrate the potential strengths of the various candidates. John F. Kennedy won the West Virginia primary against Hubert Humphrey, proving a Catholic could win in an overwhelmingly Protestant state.[146] By 2020, the number of primaries had exploded, with nearly every state giving voters the sole power to award presidential nominations without any input from elected officials who often know the candidates best. Journalist Jonathan Rauch and political scientist Ray LaRaja contend that today's nominating system favors "plutocrats, celebrities, media figures, and activists."[147]

When Democrats conferred their nomination on an outsider, Jimmy Carter, in 1976, they did so without many having any familiarity with Carter, who served only a single term as governor of Georgia. Carter ran alone and governed alone, with most congressional Democrats defying him at will. In 1984, Democrats decided to give the so-called superdelegates seats at their party's convention. Superdelegates included members of Congress, state governors, state party chairs, and members of the Democratic National Committee who, it was believed, would judge which candidate was most likely to win and successfully govern. That year, former vice president Walter Mondale competed against Colorado senator Gary Hart. Hart bested Mondale in the all-important New Hampshire primary and demonstrated strong support among young voters, while Mondale dominated in the South and among older Democrats. The party establishment had little regard for Hart, with few of his Senate colleagues endorsing him. Mondale was nominated and lost forty-nine states to the unbeatable Ronald Reagan, carrying only his home state of Minnesota and the District of Columbia. Undoubtedly, Hart would have done better. But had Hart won, having run alone he, too, would have governed alone.

At the start of 2008, the superdelegates rallied behind Hillary Clinton, but Barack Obama's rise convinced many to withdraw their initial support for Clinton and throw their weight behind Obama. Democrats were mesmerized by the prospect of an African American becoming the first to win a major party presidential nomination and become president. They were aware that Obama's race strengthened the party's prospects of winning more support from minority voters, who were becoming an even greater share of the electorate, and they believed Obama could stimulate a higher turnout among them. That calculus proved accurate: the total African American vote rose from 11 percent of the electorate in 2004 to 13 percent in 2008 and 2012, while the share of white voters declined.[148] In 2016, Hillary Clinton once again sought the Democratic nomination, this time competing against a little-known Vermont senator, Bernie Sanders.[149] The fight was unexpectedly long and hotly contested. But Clinton prevailed thanks to the overwhelming support she received from the superdelegates. To ensure party unity, Clinton pledged to reduce the power of the superdelegates, and the Democratic National Committee followed suit by eliminating any possibility they could buck the choice of their state's primary voters. In effect, the Democratic Party establishment was neutered.[150]

The once powerful Republican establishment has also been eviscerated, as has been thoroughly reviewed earlier in this book, and several long-standing traditions have been abandoned. After the 1952 Eisenhower-Taft battle, Republicans often awarded their presidential nominations to the candidate perceived as next in line. Richard Nixon prevailed in 1960, 1968, and 1972; Gerald Ford was the standard-bearer in 1976; Ronald Reagan seized the helm in 1980 and 1984; George H. W. Bush was the top choice in 1988 and 1992; Bob Dole's long service entitled him to the nomination in 1996; George W. Bush led the ticket in 2000 and 2004; John McCain, won in 2008; and Mitt Romney was nominated in 2012. With the exceptions of Nixon, Ford, and George W. Bush, Republicans frequently resorted to nominating candidates who had been runners-up in their previous presidential contests.

Only Barry Goldwater and Donald Trump were exceptions to this unspoken rule. Goldwater captured the pent-up frustrations of the conservative wing represented by Robert Taft and prevailed in the wake of John F. Kennedy's assassination. In 1964, the country was unprepared to have three presidents in the space of fifteen months, and most Republicans realized they were unlikely to beat Lyndon B. Johnson. In 2016, Donald Trump defied the establishment to win the Republican nomination. During his four years as president, it became well known that many Republican officeholders, and even members of Trump's cabinet, despised him behind closed doors. In March 2016, Lindsey Graham said, "We should have basically kicked [Trump] out of the party."[151] Ted Cruz called Trump a "pathological liar" who was "utterly amoral" and a "sniveling coward."[152] Secretary of State Rex Tillerson privately called him a "fucking moron."[153] But Republicans understood that Trump's rebranding of the party meant that any criticism would result in an instantaneous primary challenge. As much as they disdained Trump, they disdained having the word "former" attached to their names even more.

William "Boss" Tweed, who once ran New York City's infamous Tammany Hall, reportedly once said, "I don't care who does the electing, so long as I do the nominating."[154] Going back to the days of party bosses and eliminating the voices of primary voters is an impossibility. But just as job applicants are subject to peer review, prospective presidents should be exposed to similar scrutiny. One method would be to hold a preprimary meeting that includes elected federal officeholders and members of the party committees. Prospective candidates could argue why they should be nominated and what they would do if elected. After that, the participants would name the top five candidates to be included in party-sponsored debates. This would automatically eliminate several fringe candidates such as those who have been included on prior debate stages in the name of "fairness." In 2016, there initially were seventeen Republican presidential candidates—so many that the debates had to be split in two, with the latter derided as the "kids table."[155] Whether this suggested process would have resulted in Donald Trump being excluded is a great unknown, but he would have faced a significant obstacle to winning the nomination. In 2020, Democrats initially had twenty-six announced candidates, and the crowded debate stages included Marianne Williamson, Tulsi Gabbard, Tom Steyer, and Andrew Yang.[156] Giving elected party leaders and officials the power to decide who will be on the debate stage offers them a greater voice in exercising peer review and helps simplify the choices before voters. The parties would be strengthened, yet voters would still make the final determination as to who their party's nominees would be.[157]

Overruling the 2010 *Citizens United* decision of the Supreme Court would also strengthen the parties. Ever since the turn of the twentieth century, Congress has attempted to regulate the flow of money into political campaigns, with varying degrees of success. But, in 2010, the Supreme Court equated corporate money with speech, arguing that limits on outside spending violated the First Amendment. Chief Justice John Roberts argued the First Amendment "protects more than just the individual on a soapbox and the lonely pamphleteer."[158] The minority decision, written by Justice John Paul Stevens, concluded, "While American democracy is imperfect, few outside the majority of this Court would have thought its flaws included a dearth of corporate money in politics."[159] Barack Obama joined in the criticism, telling Congress and the assembled Supreme Court justices in his 2010 State of the Union address: "With all due deference to separation of powers, last week the Supreme Court reversed a century of law that I believe will open the floodgates for special interests, including foreign corporations, to spend without limit in our elections."[160] Obama was right. Super PACs quickly formed, led by millionaires and billionaires who poured money into presidential campaigns. In 2020, outside spending totaled $1,015,227,123 in the presidential race.[161] These outside groups spend without any limitations, and, unlike the candidates and party committees, they are not subject to federal regulation. This so-called dark money has reached new heights with a *$1.6 billion* contribution from a single individual to a super PAC.[162] Barre Seid, a ninety-year-old electronics executive, donated his company's stock to Marble Freedom Trust, a super PAC controlled by Leonard Leo, cochair of the Federalist Society. *Citizens United* made this large donation possible, and the donation was structured to avoid paying $400 million in federal taxes for the transfer of the stock.[163] Robert Maguire of Citizens for Responsibility and Ethics in Washington (CREW) called the donation "stupefying" and rightly noted that the current campaign finance system gives "wealthy donors, whether they be corporations or individuals, access and influence over the system far greater than any regular American can ever imagine."[164] While the sums involved are unprecedented, both parties welcome the backing from super PACs, knowing that doing otherwise amounts to unilateral disarmament.

Reversing *Citizens United* and allowing Congress to regulate political contributions and strengthen the Federal Election Commission would permit the parties to state their cases without outside influence. This would require congressional regulation of political messages posted on social media. Today, about 48 percent of adults obtain their news from social media, and one-third regularly receive most of their news from Facebook.[165] Unlike television advertising, which is strictly regulated, internet postings are often unverified and designed to incite, not inform. In 2016, social media became vulnerable to foreign actors with malicious intent, especially Russia. Subsequent elections have shown no signs of a truce. While the First Amendment protects free speech, Congress and the courts have previously established limits. Today, our outdated laws regulating political speech need revision. Thus far, Congress has not passed meaningful legislation that would establish strict boundaries as to what can and cannot be posted on social media. Given the inability of both parties to formulate their messages and control their campaigns without interference, it is essential that Congress act to ensure they can deliver unfiltered messages.

TRUTH AND CONSEQUENCES

Advocating adoption of the US Constitution, Alexander Hamilton wrote in Federalist 1, "Of those men who have overturned the liberties of republics, the greatest number have begun their career by paying an obsequious court to the people; commencing demagogues and ending tyrants."[166] Donald Trump has remade the Republican Party in his image, doing so by weaving the strands of its history into a powerful force that threatens our democratic institutions. Instead of the greatest security threat coming from without, as the United States experienced during the forty-year Cold War, today's dangers come from within. Donald Trump remains the leader of the Republican Party. His command is such that he once famously said: "I can stand in the middle of Fifth Avenue and shoot somebody and wouldn't lose any voters, okay? It's like, incredible."[167] Indeed, it is.

The Trump presidency and its chaotic aftermath have thrust the United States into uncharted territory. All institutions of authority are experiencing a crisis of legitimacy, a crisis that is exacerbated by a public long dissatisfied with the government and trusting it less. When the National Election Study asked respondents in 1958 whether they have confidence in government to do the right thing either "almost always" or "most of the time," 73 percent answered in the affirmative; today, only 20 percent do.[168] Unparalleled successes—such as the unconditional victories in World War II or placing the first man on the moon—have faded into the mists of history. Wars in Vietnam, Afghanistan, and Iraq have ended in defeat. At home, successful presidencies are distant memories. Franklin Roosevelt, Harry Truman, and Dwight Eisenhower were part of a long run of productive presidents. But Jimmy Carter's term ended in defeat, as did George H. W. Bush's. Ronald Reagan gave the country greater self-confidence, but his domestic agenda was premised on a distrust of government and a sales pitch that promised, in the words of Daniel Patrick Moynihan, that for "seventy-five cents worth of taxes, you got a dollar's worth of return."[169] Deficits soared. The moral mess of Bill Clinton's presidency led to his impeachment. George W. Bush promised a moral restoration but presided over two unsuccessful wars. Barack Obama enacted Obamacare, but the promise of the first African American president became mired in the prejudices of the past and fears about a changing racial future. Donald Trump increased the extant divisions, never promised unity, and was twice impeached. Joe Biden governs tenuously, with his legitimacy questioned on a scale that only Abraham Lincoln could appreciate.

No nation can sustain such a loss of confidence without political upheaval. In 1980, Moynihan sensed the coming tide, stating, "There is a movement to turn Republicans into Populists, a party of the people arrayed against the Democratic Party of the state."[170] Nearly four decades later, the rampant dissatisfaction that Moynihan forecast would lead to Ronald Reagan's presidency has crested with Donald Trump. But unlike Reagan, who portrayed an eternal sense of optimism, Trump paints a dystopian picture of American carnage, telling his supporters only he can rectify what ails them. But instead of improving their economic lot, Trump preyed on their cultural fears. Losing the 2020 election not only was unacceptable to Trump's outsize ego but also fed his supporters' longstanding belief that the system, once rigged against them, was now rigged against Trump himself. Trump's message both won him scores of admirers and played to a news media whose insatiable craving for audiences in a splintered cable-viewing nation became ever more voracious. During the 2016 campaign, then CBS executive chairman and CEO Les Moonves said of Trump's rise, "It may not be good for America, but it's damn good for CBS."[171]

Liz Cheney believes that "no party, and no people, and no nation can defend and perpetuate a constitutional republic if they accept a leader who has gone to war with the rule of law, the democratic process, or with the peaceful transfer of power, or with the Constitution itself."[172] Given Trump's history, the January 6 insurrection should have come as no surprise. Yet it was shocking to see a two-hundred-year peaceful passage of power be so cavalierly cast aside. When the Marquis de Lafayette encountered a group of Andrew Jackson diehards after John Quincy Adams won the disputed election of 1824, he asked, "How soon do you lay siege to the capital?" Jackson's supporters had no plans to do so, saying, "Now that it is settled all we have to do is obey," adding, "The consequences of a bad election are quickly obviated."[173] That advice was abandoned by Donald Trump's supporters on January 6. Leaving office, Adam Kinzinger said that the siege of the Capitol was "a dishonor to all those who have sacrificed and died in service of our democracy."[174] But whether January 6 represents one sad day, or something even more foreboding, is an open question. The forces that gave rise to Donald Trump have not disappeared. Discontent and calls for violence abound. Today, Cheney maintains, "We stand at the edge of an abyss, and we must pull back."[175]

But pulling back is hardly a foregone conclusion. Joe Biden's presidency is hampered not by legislative losses or internal party divisions but by the overwhelming number of Republicans whose first test of party loyalty is to reject Biden as a legitimately elected president—something Democrats did not do after the previously contested elections of 1876, 2000, and 2004 were settled. Authoritarian regimes embrace violence as a justifiable means to achieve political ends, a phenomenon that an increasing number of Republicans are willing to accept. Today, 40 percent of Republicans believe there are circumstances in which taking arms against the government is justified.[176] The internet is an echo chamber of violent threats against public officials. Trump's lies about the 2020 election are pernicious because they threaten the already rocky foundations of our republic. Decades ago, Robert Welch, leader of the John Birch Society, denounced democracy as "a deceptive phase, a weapon of demagoguery, and a perennial fraud."[177] Donald Trump has transformed the Republican Party into an entity as intolerant of internal dissent and as dismissive of democracy as Welch once was. In a provocative 2021 editorial titled "The Whole Country Is the Reichstag," Adolph Reed Jr. wrote: "It is time to be blunt. The right-wing political alliance anchored by the Republican Party and Trumpism coheres around a single concrete objective—taking absolute power in the U.S. as soon and as definitively as possible. And they're more than ready, even seemingly want, to destroy the social fabric of the country to do so. They smell blood in the water."[178]

The nation's first Republican president, Abraham Lincoln, said, "If destruction be our lot, we must ourselves be its author and finisher. As a nation of freemen, we must live through all time, or die by suicide."[179] As early as 1838, Lincoln sensed "something of an ill-omen among us," citing the "increasing disregard for law which pervades the country; the growing disposition to substitute the wild and furious passions, in lieu of the sober judgment of Courts; and the worse than savage mobs, for the executive ministers of justice."[180] Whether this nation devolves, as Hamilton warned, into a despotism ruled by demagogues, is the question of our time. In 2016, Donald Trump was a candidate whose words were often beyond the bounds of political propriety, but whose language resonated with a dissatisfied public. His lies about the 2020 election, and much else, undermined an essential faith that must exist between the governors and the governed. Whether this nation will continue to live under a constitutional republic, however reformulated, or dies by suicide, is an open question. As Liz Cheney told her colleagues on the January 6th committee, "History has taught us that what begins as words ends as far worse."[181] But reflecting on a day when the dangers so vividly present will have subsided, Cheney reminded her fellow Republicans that when that history is written, its words will say, "There will come a day when Donald Trump is gone, but your dishonor will remain."[182]

Afterword 2023: A Reflection and a Reckoning

Most evenings at 9:00 p.m., a vigil is held outside the Washington, DC, jail protesting the incarceration of "patriots" charged with attacking police officers and interfering with the peaceful transition of power on January 6, 2021. Supporters sing the national anthem while those either awaiting trial or already sentenced turn their cell lights on and off in a form of acknowledgment.[1] These demonstrations are just one indicator, among many others, of the stubborn refusal by Donald Trump's loyalists to acknowledge the desecration and violence that occurred at the US Capitol on that fateful day.

As the 2024 election draws near, the threats to our democracy, and the personal safety of those who defended it, remain under threat. In October 2022, Paul Pelosi, spouse of former House Speaker Nancy Pelosi, was viciously attacked in the early morning hours at his home. His assailant planned to hold Nancy Pelosi hostage and "snap the bones" and break kneecaps if she did not admit that the 2020 election was "stolen."[2] Paul Pelosi was assaulted with a hammer and suffered a fractured skull and injuries to his right arm and hand. The assailant later regretted that he "didn't get more" of his intended targets, which included California governor Gavin Newsom and Hunter Biden.[3] Several Republicans concocted their own fictionalized versions of the assault on Nancy Pelosi's husband, claiming it was a homosexual love affair gone bad. Elon Musk, for example, tweeted that it was "a dispute with a male prostitute," and his false rendition was echoed by Dinesh D'Souza, Donald Trump Jr., and One America News.[4]

Two years after the Capitol insurrection, a commemoration was held for those who were injured or died. The ceremony was attended by all congressional Democrats and one lone Republican, Brian Fitzpatrick, who represented a pro-Biden suburban Philadelphia district.[5] Days later, Solomon Peña, a Republican who lost his New Mexico state legislative race by forty-eight points, fired several bullets into the homes of four Albuquerque Democrats. Peña, an ardent 2020 Trump supporter and election denier who attended the January 6 rally, vowed that Donald Trump's critics "will have to kill us to stop us."[6] While state Republican leaders condemned Peña's actions, they refused to concede that Trump's repeated denunciations of "rigged elections" inspired the violence. Mark Ronchetti, the party's 2022 gubernatorial nominee, pinned the blame on Peña, not Trump, saying, "Blaming Trump—that's not fair to do."[7] Only a single Republican state senator, Mark Moores, admitted that election denialism is "a pox on our house." Unless Republicans came to terms with that reality, he declared, "We cannot be a governing party."[8]

The few Republicans who still believe that elections are honestly conducted and Joe Biden legitimately won in 2020 are lonely voices. Instead of admitting defeat and acknowledging the mayhem that took place on January 6, Republicans immediately began rewriting history. Georgia Republican congressman Andrew Clyde described January 6 as "a normal tourist visit,"[9] while others blamed Antifa, Black Lives Matter, and left-wing Democrats for the violence. Still others saw it as a legitimate protest that simply got out of hand. Today's guided tours of the Capitol are packed with references to its history, *except* for any mention of the insurrection unless a questioner asks.[10] Across the country "Jan. Sixers" have formed prayer chains, instigated letter-writing campaigns, organized vigils, and raised millions of dollars for the legal defenses of those charged.[11] Former Republican congressman Denver Riggleman says the "Jan. Sixers" see themselves as "peaceful patriots" who are "being persecuted as political prisoners," and that such depictions normalize violence and have become "a case study in radicalization and actions based completely on fantasy."[12]

A year after the attempted insurrection, hundreds of those who invaded the Capitol faced the consequences of their actions. During their trials, many of the defendants stated they were there at the invitation of Donald Trump. Gladys Sicknick, mother of deceased Capitol Police officer Brian Sicknick, asked his assailant in court, "How does it feel to be headed to jail for a baldfaced lie?"[13] Others, including members of the Proud Boys and the Oath Keepers, have had their own personal reckonings after receiving guilty verdicts on charges of sedition, violating a statute enacted by Congress in 1861.[14]

In 2023, the Justice Department charged Donald Trump with engaging in a conspiracy whose purpose was "to overturn the legitimate results of the 2020 presidential election by using knowingly false claims of election fraud to obstruct the federal government function by which those results are collected, counted and certified."[15] Trump was also charged with impeding a congressional proceeding and violating "the right to vote and to have one's vote counted."[16] In Georgia, Fulton County district attorney Fanni Willis charged Trump along with a host of his former White House and campaign officials with engaging in a widespread conspiracy to defraud the voters of that state by attempting to invalidate ballots and pressuring Republican state legislators to transmit fraudulent electoral votes to Congress.[17] In addition, the Justice Department charged Trump with retaining classified materials at his Mar-a-Lago residence after leaving the White House and refusing to return them to the government. Reporting to the federal courthouse following his January 6 indictment, Trump posted on Truth Social: "IT IS A GREAT HONOR BECAUSE I AM BEING ARRESTED FOR YOU." Finally, Trump has been charged in New York State on thirty-four counts in connection with the hush money he paid to Stormy Daniels, a pornographic film actress.[18]

Donald Trump's personal freedom will rest with juries of his peers. Those who support charging Trump and allowing the judicial process to proceed maintain there must be one set of laws that apply to all citizens. In 1774, John Adams wrote: "Representative government and trial by jury are the heart and lungs of liberty. Without them we have no other fortification against being ridden like horses, fleeced like sheep, worked like cattle, and fed and clothed like swine and hounds."[19]

Whatever the future has in store for Donald Trump personally, his political longevity will be determined first by Republican voters. The indictments of Trump did not bode well for either his long-term personal future or that of his party. His support among his fellow Republicans, already high prior to his being charged, substantially improved with each count levied against him. The result was to propel Trump as the undisputed front-runner leading into the 2024 Republican presidential contest. Skipping the traditional debates, Trump campaigned as a virtual incumbent whose dominance over the GOP remained unchallenged. Following his indictments, many of Trump's erstwhile opponents leapt to his defense. Florida governor Ron DeSantis posted, "The weaponization of federal law enforcement represents a mortal threat to a free society."[20] Former UN ambassador Nikki Haley said, "This is not how justice should be pursued in our country."[21] Businessman Vivek Ramaswamy, another 2024 Republican aspirant, promised that, should he be elected president, he would immediately pardon Trump on January 20, 2025.[22]

The prospect of another Biden-Trump general election contest in 2024 is likely, with Trump describing his upcoming court trials and the next election as "the final battle."[23] Meanwhile, the ability of the Republican Party to self-correct and chart a new course appears dim. A shocking 80 percent of Republicans believe that even if Trump is convicted of one or more crimes, he should be permitted to serve as president.[24] A party and a nation that remain addicted to what Richard Hofstadter called the "paranoid style" are a party and a nation in trouble.[25] Once more, the virtues and assumptions that political scientists once considered sacred about the utility of political parties, and their vital role in making both our democracy and our Constitution work, have been upended.

REWRITING HISTORY

In many ways, this rewriting of the 2020 election and its aftermath resembles the redefinition of another insurrection mounted against the federal government: the actions of the Confederacy to reject Abraham Lincoln's election as president and secede from the Union. After four bitter years of conflict that culminated with Robert E. Lee's surrender at Appomattox, Southerners recast the Civil War as a "noble cause" that defended states' rights, rather than a fight about slavery. Beginning in the early twentieth century, nearly seven hundred Confederate statutes were erected throughout the South.[26] In *How the South Won the Civil War*, Heather Cox Richardson writes that these monuments were christened as memorials to a southern rebellion against a "consolidated despotism" that "preserved democracy for northerners."[27] According to the National Register for Historic Places, the "Cult of the Lost Cause" was a Southern war waged against a materialistic North that was "grasping for wealth and power," while genteel Southerners emphasized the "veracity and honor in man, chastity, and fidelity in women."[28] But the statutes served another purpose as a constant reminder to African Americans of white supremacy. Only after the 2017 riot in Charlottesville, Virginia, led by white supremacists protesting the removal of Robert E. Lee's statue, was there the beginning of a concerted effort to remove other offending monuments and come to terms with the South's racist past. True to form, Donald Trump called removing Lee's statute "foolish" and compared Lee to George Washington.[29]

Like the post-Civil War period when the South rewrote its history, the House Select Committee's final report on January 6 provides a corrective mechanism that paints a far more accurate picture of that day's events than the one portrayed by Donald Trump and his associates. The committee presented overwhelming evidence placing Trump at the center of a conspiracy to overturn the 2020 election and remain in power. He nearly succeeded. Only the courage demonstrated by Vice President Mike Pence, who defied Trump and accepted the certified results, prevented the Biden presidency from, in the words of Steve Bannon, being "killed in the crib."[30] During his 2020 campaign and as president, Joe Biden has repeatedly described a battle to preserve "the soul of America." At a ceremony awarding a Presidential Citizens Medal to those who defended the Capitol on January 6, Biden cited Capitol Police officer Daniel Hodge's one-word explanation when asked what he was fighting for: "Democracy."[31]

"Defending democracy" has become the byword of the Biden presidency, and his vigorous denunciations of election deniers mitigated Republican gains in the 2022 midterm elections—a defiance of history given that the president's party typically loses many congressional seats. Exit polls found 68 percent of voters believing our democracy remained under threat; only 30 percent called it "secure."[32] An Associated Press VoteCast survey found just 38 percent of independents supported Republican candidates—a dismal showing when inflation, crime, and the southern border crisis should have given Republicans lopsided majorities.[33] Nonetheless, Trump claimed credit for the narrow Republican House majority, saying he "greatly helped."[34] House Speaker Kevin McCarthy, whom Trump once called "my Kevin,"[35] also credited Trump for the win, stating, "I don't think anyone should doubt his influence."[36] The fifteen ballots needed to elect McCarthy as Speaker cemented Trump's dominance, and the Faustian bargains McCarthy made to win elevated Trump's most ardent acolytes—including Jim Jordan, Marjorie Taylor Greene, Matt Gaetz, Andrew Clyde, Scott Perry, and Lauren Boebert—to positions of power. All were given plum assignments, including seats on the Judiciary, Homeland Security, and Appropriations Committees. It is fair to say that today's Republican-controlled House reflects a party that remains subservient to Donald Trump.

In November 2022, Donald Trump officially declared his 2024 presidential candidacy. In his announcement, he criticized "the weaponization of the justice system, the FBI, and the DOJ" and declared himself willing to "face a storm of fire that only a few could understand."[37] While Trump's early declaration failed to forestall any criminal proceedings, it created the unusual circumstance of a leading presidential candidate campaigning among his supporters and in courtrooms. Entering the 2024 presidential campaign, 76 percent of Republicans agreed with Trump that the charges filed against him were politically motivated,[38] instigated by a "deep state" determined to keep Trump from working on behalf of his aggrieved supporters.

The Republican denunciations of government and belief in conspiracy theories threaten the security of the country and its democratic institutions. In yet one more demonstration of his fealty to Trump, Kevin McCarthy announced the creation of the Select Committee on the Weaponization of the Federal Government. Chaired by Jim Jordan, the committee is poised to insert itself into the many federal investigations into Trump with the aim of obstructing any future prosecutions. Massachusetts Democrat Jim McGovern likens McCarthy's committee to the infamous House Un-American Activities Committee, claiming it is "nothing more than a deranged ploy by the MAGA extremists who have hijacked the Republican Party and now want to use taxpayer money to push their far-right conspiracy nonsense."[39]

Republicans' tendency to overreach—best exemplified by their actions during the Monica Lewinsky affair that resulted in Bill Clinton's impeachment—is once again evident in the impeachment inquiry against Joe Biden spearheaded by House Speaker Kevin McCarthy. For many Republicans, impeachment has become just another ordinary political weapon, hardly what the Constitution's framers envisioned. Donald Trump plainly states that House Republicans are seeking Biden's impeachment because "they did it to me."[40] By raising the specter of impeachment, Republicans are emulating their leader by devising a multiact drama replete with heroes who echo Trump's charges and villains, particularly Joe and Hunter Biden, who must be punished.

The threats of violence have surged as the party that once espoused "law and order" has become a party of unremitting grievances. Following Donald Trump's indictment for retaining sensitive classified materials at his Mar a Lago home, Louisiana Republican congressman Clay Higgins tweeted: "This is a perimeter probe from the oppressors. Hold. rPOTUS has this. Buckle up. 1/50K know your bridges. Rock steady calm."⁴¹ Jeff Sharlet, author of *The Undertow: Scenes from a Slow Civil War*,⁴² translates: a "perimeter probe" precedes a bigger attack; "rPOTUS" is a reference to the real president—that is, Trump; "hold" means stand back and stand by; "buckle up" means prepare for war; "1/50K" refers to military scale maps that indicate nearby military installations; and "know your bridges" is a message to militia groups to seize bridges.⁴³

Donald Trump's dominance within the Republican Party did not scare away challengers to his renomination in 2024, but he has issued open threats of reprisal to any candidate who seriously threatens him. Foremost among them was Florida governor Ron DeSantis. When asked about DeSantis's candidacy, Trump replied, "We'll handle that the way I handle things"—a line that could have easily been spoken by Vito Corleone in *The Godfather*.⁴⁴ Whether Trump succeeds in getting himself renominated is an open question as of this writing, but Donald Trump and Trumpism have redefined the Republican Party. The late political analyst Mark Shields once classified partisans as belonging to one of two types: those who seek converts versus crusaders who root out heretics.⁴⁵ Donald Trump was (and is) the ultimate heretic-hunter. After Trump falsely claimed that the 2020 election was stolen, anyone seeking a position of power within his Republican Party was required to pledge an oath of fealty to Trump's Big Lie. Those who believe otherwise are automatically labeled RINOs. Among the excommunicated are Liz Cheney, Adam Kinzinger, nearly all those who voted to impeach Trump, and anyone who testified before the January 6 Select Committee. In 2022, 65 percent of Republicans said their leaders should accept Trump's premise that the 2020 election was stolen,⁴⁶ and an equal percentage believed loyalty to Trump was "important."⁴⁷ These were essential preconditions to Trump's entry into the 2024 presidential contest, and any Republican who was perceived as disloyal stood little chance with primary voters.

Other Republicans have enthusiastically joined Trump in hunting heretics. Ron DeSantis likes to cast himself as a Trump-like Mini-Me and is on the warpath against school superintendents who enforced COVID-19 vaccinations and mask mandates.⁴⁸ He has falsely arrested former convicts who voted legitimately in 2020,⁴⁹ declared a fatwa against the Disney Corporation,⁵⁰ and boasts that he "will never surrender to the woke mob."⁵¹ Ironically, the Trump-DeSantis contest took the idea of heresy to a new level. Mike Lindell, aka the My Pillow Guy and an ardent defender of Trump's Big Lie, claimed DeSantis rigged his own eleven-point reelection victory in Miami–Dade County in 2022, and promised an "investigation."[52] In Arizona, defeated gubernatorial candidate Kari Lake adopted Trump's strategy of calling out heretics, asking at one rally, "We don't have any McCain Republicans in here, do we?" before quickly demanding they "get the hell out."[53] Meghan McCain called Lake's remarks "disgusting" and "hateful."[54] After losing, Lake promoted her own Big Lie and blamed "crooked Democrats and RINOS" for rigging the results.[55] Lake's frivolous lawsuits prompted one judge to order her to pay the attorney's fees incurred by her opponent, Governor Katie Hobbs.[56]

The 2022 midterms are instructive. Arizona's "Trump ticket," so branded by the former president,[57] featured senatorial nominee Blake Masters, the aforementioned Kari Lake, and attorney general candidate Abraham Hamadeh, all of whom lost. In Georgia, the handpicked Trump senatorial candidate, former football star Herschel Walker, was beaten by Raphael Warnock. In Pennsylvania, another Trump-endorsed ticket composed of television doctor Mehmet Oz and election denier Doug Mastriano was soundly defeated. Oz's defeat gave Senate Democrats a one-seat majority, breaking the fifty-fifty deadlock, and Mastriano's loss put Democrat Josh Shapiro into the governor's mansion. At a November rally featuring Joe Biden and Barack Obama, Shapiro cleverly turned the tables on the Republicans by embracing that party's traditional defense of freedom: "It's not freedom to tell a woman what she can and can't do with her body. It's not freedom to tell our kids what books they can and can't read. It sure as hell isn't freedom to say that you can vote, but [the Republican candidate] gets to pick the winner."[58] Shortly after his inauguration, Shapiro named Republican Albert Schmidt as Pennsylvania's new secretary of state. Schmidt, who served as a Philadelphia city commissioner and certified the 2020 election count, was subjected to death threats recounted earlier in this book. For his courage, President Biden awarded Schmidt the Presidential Citizens Medal, citing his "character and commitment" to democracy.[59] At the same ceremony, Biden also awarded medals to Ruby Freeman and Shaye Moss, the Georgia election workers mentioned earlier in this volume who were harassed and threatened by Rudy Giuliani and Donald Trump. Biden noted that both women deserved "the nation's eternal thanks for showing dignity and grace."[60]

A FINAL DENOUEMENT?

Prior to assuming the presidency in 1861, Abraham Lincoln was urged to compromise on the issue of slavery. Lincoln resisted these entreaties, saying, "By no act or complicity of mine shall the Republican Party become a mere sucked egg, all shell and no principle in it."[61] Today's Republican Party resembles that sucked egg, a party still enthralled with Donald Trump's persona and the many contradictions that come with it. More than 150 years after Lincoln spoke those words, Republican Scott Perry took to the House floor to nominate Byron Donalds to become that body's first African American Speaker. In his speech, Perry quoted Frederick Douglass, who "worked with Abraham Lincoln to emancipate the people of color in this country." Perry cited Douglass's loyalty to the Republican Party, saying Douglass would "never be anything but a Republican."[62] When Perry spoke those words, he was met with laughter and jeers. Long ago, the Trump Republican Party forfeited its inheritance.

When parties lose, there comes a necessary period of reflection. As recounted in this book, Republicans underwent a long period of denial following the landslide victories posted by Franklin D. Roosevelt in the 1930s, followed by a period of accommodation symbolized by the nominations of Thomas E. Dewey and Dwight D. Eisenhower, with the latter's promotion of Modern Republicanism. While intraparty divisions lingered, it took Ronald Reagan to bring the Taft and Goldwater wings of the Republican Party together with its more pragmatic elements to forge a governing coalition. Similarly, after landslide losses to Reagan, a period of reflection and reconciliation overcame the Democratic Party. In 1982, Democratic senator Paul Tsongas argued that Democrats must allow "a kind of cleansing realism to work its way in."[63] By the end of the 1980s, Democrats took to heart Tsongas's "cleansing realism" rather than blaming their troubles on flawed candidates. Led by the Democratic Leadership Council, the party supported a strong national defense and middle-class tax cuts and revamped its New Deal–like approach to big government by advocating a "third way" built on public-private partnerships and community alliances.[64] After a decade of losses, the "New Democrats"—whose ranks included Bill Clinton, Al Gore, and Joe Biden—assumed prominent roles.

The metamorphosis of the Republican Party began long before Donald Trump. What an opposition party does (or does not do) matters a great deal in American politics. We often think that great political realignments—such as those led by Andrew Jackson, William McKinley, Franklin D. Roosevelt, and Ronald Reagan—establish a long-term political agenda. They do. But how the opposition party responds also matters. Robert Dahl once observed that "one is inclined to regard the existence of an opposition party as very nearly the most distinctive characteristic of democracy itself and we take the absence of an opposition party as evidence, if not always conclusive proof, for the absence of democracy."[65] Historically, out-of-power parties recognize their weaknesses, adapt, and reform. Losing elections is a powerful elixir for change, while winning parties often adapt the slogan, "If it ain't broke, don't fix it."[66] Losing elections prompts an acceptance by both the victor and the vanquished. For defeated parties, losses have been accepted as conclusive evidence of defeat and a measure that as a party rebrands itself, it is responsive to democratic electorates.

After consecutive losses in 2018, 2020, and 2022, Republicans should be entering a period of reflection and reconciliation. But Donald Trump will not permit either to occur. Instead of redefining conservatism for a twenty-first-century audience composed of multicultural and multiracial voters, Republicans are fixated on stoking their angry base of older white Baby Boomers who once defined the nation's past but not its future. Instead of reckoning with the Trump presidency and the attack on the Capitol on January 6, 2021, Republicans are determined to erase the latter from their collective memories. Rather than rejecting election deniers, Republicans elevated them to positions of power. As this book has observed, there is something within the DNA of the Republican Party that makes it prone to conspiracy theorists, election deniers, and top-down presidential leadership that is fraught with danger.

Rather than rooting out heretics, Republicans should be seeking converts. But Donald Trump and his Trump-like imitators remain focused on expelling heretics, an easy exercise that avoids the hard work of listening to voters who might be open to a libertarian, small government approach to the country's problems. Young voters, in particular, might be receptive to such a message since they are hardly rooted within the Democratic Party despite their overwhelming support for Barack Obama, Hillary Clinton, and Joe Biden. Many are skeptical of a government that, in their lifetimes, has never achieved much success. Joe Biden recognizes this, arguing that one primary mission of his presidency is to demonstrate that government can work. Republicans also have opportunities with Hispanics whose family-oriented values and faith in hard work, self-improvement, and the American Dream create chances for the party to make significant inroads.[67] While there are signs this is occurring in Florida and Texas, there remains the need for a painstaking effort to listen to these voters, learn what makes them tick, and win converts. Instead, Republicans are focused on investigating Joe Biden and creating a series of crises that satisfy the id of the Trump base but do little to expand the party's reach. Only 27 percent of Americans believe the Republican-led House leadership has the right priorities, while 73 percent say it is ignoring the country's most important problems.[68] Today, the faces of the Republican Party are those visages represented by Donald Trump, Kevin McCarthy, Ron DeSantis, Marjorie Taylor Greene, and the fabulist George Santos. Only when Republicans rethink the party's first principles, nominate attractive presidential candidates, and have a successful presidency will they truly have a shot at assembling a governing majority.

In the history books, presidents are often remembered for one line. For George Washington, "George Washington's integrity set a pattern for all other Presidents to follow."[69] For Abraham Lincoln, "Abhorring war, Abraham Lincoln accepted it as the only means to save the Union."[70] For Franklin D. Roosevelt, "Franklin D. Roosevelt led the Nation through its worst depression and greatest war."[71] For Ronald Reagan, "Ronald Reagan envisioned a smaller government, a greater America."[72] For Donald Trump the line is likely to read, "Donald Trump incited an insurrection and was the only president to be twice impeached." Conservative judge J. Michael Luttig writes, "The Republican Party has made its decision that the war against America's Democracy and the Rule of Law it instigated on January 6 will go on, prosecuted to its catastrophic end."[73] Unlike anything envisioned by political scientists, a major political party poses the greatest threat to democracy. The consensus that once existed within academia as to the utility of political parties has been shattered. Until Republicans cease and desist from their war on democracy and reckon with the Trump legacy, they will continue to live in Trump's shadow and be led by a man whose party has gone rogue. How this story ends is unknown, and its final chapters are still being written.

Acknowledgments

I confess that whenever I receive a new book, I open first to the acknowledgments, looking for those who contributed and those scholars whose work I should pay attention to. With that in mind, I have more than the usual list of obligations to acknowledge. The readers of the manuscript, including Stephen Knott, made important contributions to this book. In particular, I am grateful to those political scientists who gave a young man a chance and have shaped my career—especially Gerald Pomper, William Crotty, Norman L. Zucker, and the late Everett C. Ladd, Jerome Mileur, Wilson Carey McWilliams, and James MacGregor Burns.

My colleagues at Catholic University, including Matthew N. Green, Jonathan Askonas, Stephen West, and Diana Rich, read portions of the manuscript and offered useful suggestions. I am grateful to my former graduate students at Catholic University who also read or heard portions of the manuscript and challenged my assumptions, especially David Sollenberger and Samuel Sprunk.

Daniel Allott, an associate editor at *The Hill*, provided me with an opportunity to write a biweekly column that allowed me to develop the theses contained in this book. Allott's interviews with Donald Trump's supporters in his book *On the Road in Trump's America* also provided valuable insights into the appeal of the forty-fifth president.

I am especially grateful to Matthew Kerbel of Villanova University, who, in the forty years we have known each other, has read and commented on my various books, including this one, and been a coauthor with me on several textbooks, the latest being *American Political Parties: Why They Formed, How They Developed, and Where They're Headed*, published by the University Press of Kansas.

David Congdon at the University Press of Kansas has been an indefatigable supporter of this project from its inception. I am especially grateful to him for showing me that I do not have to write *everything* I know about the Republican Party but *enough* about what I know. I am also indebted to Susan Ecklund, who edited this book with care and precision.

Finally, I am grateful to my family members who consistently provided the emotional support I needed to complete this book, including my sister, Janet; my daughter, Jeannette; and my in-laws, Armand and Deborah Prevost. I would not have been able to complete this book without the intellectual and emotional support I received from Samuel Sprunk, mentioned previously, and to whom the book is dedicated.

Notes

PREFACE: THE GATHERING STORM

1. "Watch Donald Trump Endorse Mitt Romney for GOP Presidential Candidate," *PBS NewsHour*, accessed October 23, 2022, YouTube, https://www.youtube.com/watch?v=nmwzGMmGcJw.

2. Rachel Weiner and Philip Rucker, "Donald Trump Endorses Mitt Romney," *Washington Post*, February 2, 2012, YouTube, https://www.youtube.com/watch?v=nmwzGMmGcJw.

3. Mark Leibovich, "Over-the-Top Setting, Run-of-the-Mill Endorsement," *New York Times*, February 2, 2012, https://www.nytimes.com/2012/02/03/us/politics/trump-endorses-romney-in-las-vegas.html.

4. Leibovich.

5. "Late Night Political Jokes of the Week—Romney Grammy, Santorum on Women in the Military, Trump Endorsement," Self-Deprecate Political Humor, February 18, 2012, http://selfdeprecate.com/late-night-political-humor/late-night-political-jokes-week-0218-romney-santorum-women-trump/.

6. Maggie Haberman, *Confidence Man: The Making of Donald Trump and the Breaking of America* (New York: Penguin Press, 2022), 192.

7. Haberman, 190.

8. Haberman, 192.

9. "Transcript of Mitt Romney's Speech on Donald Trump," *New York Times*, March 3, 2016, https://www.cbsnews.com/news/trump-heres-why-im-endorsing-mitt-romney/.

10. Amy Gardner, "A Majority of GOP Nominees Deny or Question the 2020 Election Results," *Washington Post*, October 12, 2022, https://www.washingtonpost.com/nation/2022/10/06/elections-deniers-midterm-elections-2022/.

11. Ronald Reagan, "Remarks at the Annual Convention of the National Association of Evangelicals," Orlando, Florida, March 8, 1983, Ronald Reagan Presidential Foundation and Institute, https://www.reaganfoundation.org/library-museum/permanent-exhibitions/berlin-wall/from-the-archives/remarks-at-the-annual-convention-of-the-national-association-of-evangelicals-in-orlando-florida/.

12. Ralph Waldo Emerson, "Politics," EmersonCentral.com, accessed October 23, 2022, https://emersoncentral.com/texts/essays-second-series/politics/.

13. Paul Krause, "Banishing the Party of Memory?," *Imaginative Conserva-*

tive, July 2, 2020, https://theimaginativeconservative.org/2020/07/banishing-party-memory-paul-krause.html.

14. Emerson, "Politics."

15. Henry R. Luce, "The American Century," *Life*, February 1941, http://www-personal.umich.edu/~mlassite/discussions261/luce.pdf.

16. James Q. Wilson, "A Guide to Reagan Country: The Political Culture of Southern California," *Commentary*, May 1967, 40.

17. See John Kenneth White, *The New Politics of Old Values* (Hanover, NH: University Press of New England, 1990).

18. Ronald Reagan, "Letter Announcing His Alzheimer's Diagnosis," November 5, 1994, Ronald Reagan Presidential Library and Museum, https://www.reaganlibrary.gov/reagans/ronald-reagan/reagans-letter-announcing-his-alzheimers-diagnosis.

19. Emerson, "Politics."

20. Emerson.

21. Ralph Waldo Emerson, "The Conservative" (lecture delivered at the Masonic Temple, Boston, December 9, 1841), American Transcendentalism Web, https://archive.vcu.edu/english/engweb/transcendentalism/authors/emerson/essays/conservative.html.

22. Emerson.

23. John Daniel Davidson, "We Need to Stop Calling Ourselves Conservatives," *The Federalist*, October 20, 2022, https://thefederalist.com/2022/10/20/we-need-to-stop-calling-ourselves-conservatives/.

24. Davidson.

25. Davidson.

26. David Pepper, Twitter, October 19, 2022, 7:54 a.m., https://twitter.com/DavidPepper/status/1582716930510577665.

27. Martin Tolchin, "GOP Memo Tells of Black Vote Cut," *New York Times*, October 25, 1986, https://www.nytimes.com/1986/10/25/us/gop-memo-tells-of-black-vote-cut.html.

28. B. Drummond Ayers Jr., "Feinstein Opponent Hopes to Uncover Ballot Fraud," *New York Times*, November 30, 1994, https://www.nytimes.com/1994/11/30/us/lame-duck-congress-california-feinstein-opponent-hopes-uncover-ballot-fraud.html.

29. Lizette Alvarez, "Senate Election Inquiry Clears Democrats from Louisiana," *New York Times*, October 2, 1997, https://www.nytimes.com/1997/10/02/us/senate-election-inquiry-clears-democrat-from-louisiana.html.

30. Greg Palast, "Florida's 'Disappeared Voters': Disenfranchised by the GOP," *The Nation*, January 18, 2001, https://www.thenation.com/article/archive/floridas-disappeared-voters-disfranchised-gop/.

31. Lawrence Mower, "Police Cameras Show Confusion, Anger over DeSantis' Fraud Arrests," *Tampa Bay Times*, October 18, 2022, https://www.tampabay.com/news/florida-politics/2022/10/18/body-camera-video-police-voter-fraud-desantis-arrests/?utm_source=substack&utm_medium=email.

32. Lori Rozsa, "Man Arrested by DeSantis's Election Police Has His Case Dismissed," *Washington Post*, October 21, 2022, https://www.washingtonpost.com/nation/2022/10/21/florida-desantis-voter-fraud-arrests/.

33. Matthew N. Green and Jeffrey Crouch, *Newt Gingrich: The Rise and Fall of a Party Entrepreneur* (Lawrence: University Press of Kansas, 2022), 85; Steven Levitsky and Daniel Ziblatt, *How Democracies Die* (New York: Crown, 2018), 147.

34. James Salzer, "Gingrich's Language Set New Course," *Atlanta Journal Constitution*, July 5, 2016, https://www.ajc.com/news/local-govt--politics/gingrich-language-set-new-course/O5bgK6lY2wQ3KwEZsYTBlO/.

35. Green and Crouch, *Newt Gingrich*, 23.

36. Dana Milbank, *The Deconstructionists: The Twenty-Five-Year Crack-Up of the Republican Party* (New York: Doubleday, 2022), 273.

37. Steve Eder, David D. Kirkpatrick, and Mike McIntire, "They Legitimized the Myth of a Stolen Election—and Reaped the Rewards," *New York Times*, October 4, 2022, https://www.nytimes.com/2022/10/03/us/politics/republican-election-objectors.html.

38. Mike Rothschild, *The Storm Is Upon Us: How QAnon Became a Movement, Cult, and Conspiracy Theory of Everything* (Brooklyn: Melville House, 2021), 159.

39. Abraham Lincoln, "First Annual Message," December 3, 1861, The American Presidency Project, https://www.presidency.ucsb.edu/documents/first-annual-message-9.

40. Taylor Orth, "Two in Five Americans Say a Civil War Is at Least Somewhat Likely in the Next Decade," YouGov America, August 26, 2022.

41. Andrew Feinberg, "Trump Demands New Election Immediately in Bizarre Post on Truth Social," *Independent*, August 29, 2022, https://www.independent.co.uk/news/world/americas/us-politics/trump-new-election-truth-social-b2155158.html.

42. John Kenneth White, *The Fractured Electorate: Political Parties and Social Change in Southern New England* (Hanover, NH: University Press of New England, 1983).

43. John Kenneth White, *The New Politics of Old Values* (Hanover, NH: University Press of New England, 1990).

44. John Kenneth White, *The Values Divide: American Politics and Culture in Transition* (Washington, DC: Congressional Quarterly Press, 2003).

45. John Kenneth White, *Still Seeing Red: How the Cold War Shapes the New American Politics* (Boulder, CO: Westview Press, 1998).

46. John Kenneth White, *What Happened to the Republican Party? And What It Means for Presidential Politics* (New York: Routledge, 2015).

47. Matthew Dallek, *Birchers: How the John Birch Society Radicalized the American Right* (New York: Basic Books, 2022), 11.

48. Winston S. Churchill, *The Gathering Storm* (Boston: Houghton Mifflin, 1948), 17.

49. Churchill, 17–18.

50. Jamie Raskin, "Representative Raskin's Closing Remarks from January 6th Select Committee Hearing," July 12, 2022, https://raskin.house.gov/2022/7/rep-raskin-s-closing-remarks-from-january-6th-select-committee-hearing.

51. Milbank, *Deconstructionists*, 308.

INTRODUCTION: PASSIONS AND INTERESTS

1. Kate Zernike and William Yardley, "The 2004 Campaign: Complaints; Charges of Dirty Tricks, Fraud, and Voter Suppression Already Flying in Several States," *New York Times*, November 1, 2004, https://www.nytimes.com/2004/11/01/us/the-2004-campaign-complaints-charges-of-dirty-tricks-fraud-and-voter.html.

2. Sheryl Gay Stolberg and James Dao, "Congress Ratifies Bush Victory after Challenge," *New York Times*, January 7, 2005, https://www.nytimes.com/2005/01/07/politics/congress-ratifies-bush-victory-after-challenge.html.

3. Stolberg and Dao.

4. Stolberg and Dao.

5. Stolberg and Dao.

6. *Bush v. Gore*, 531, U.S. 98 (2000), Justia, U.S. Supreme Court, https://supreme.justia.com/cases/federal/us/531/98/.

7. Al Gore, Concession Speech, Washington, DC. ABC News, December 13, 2000, https://abcnews.go.com/Politics/story?id=122220&page=1.

8. Gore.

9. Gore.

10. E. J. Dionne and William Kristol, eds., Bush v. Gore: *The Court Cases and Commentary* (Washington, DC: Brookings Institution Press, 2001), 173.

11. Dionne and Kristol, 173.

12. Dionne and Kristol, 183.

13. Alison Mitchell, "Over Some Objections, Congress Certifies Electoral Vote," *New York Times*, January 7, 2001, https://www.nytimes.com/2001/01/07/us/over-some-objections-congress-certifies-electoral-vote.html.

14. Edward Walsh and Juliet Eilpern, "Gore Presides as Congress Tallies Votes Electing Bush," *Washington Post*, January 7, 2021, https://www.washingtonpost

.com/archive/politics/2001/01/07/gore-presides-as-congress-tallies-votes-electing-bush/0461e40f-3317-4a7e-a1ad-2232aae304db/.

15. Mitchell, "Over Some Objections, Congress Certifies Electoral Vote."

16. Walsh and Eilpern, "Gore Presides as Congress Tallies Votes Electing Bush."

17. Michael F. Holt, *By One Vote: The Disputed Presidential Election of 1876* (Lawrence: University Press of Kansas, 2008), 242.

18. Holt, 242.

19. Holt, 242.

20. Rutherford B. Hayes, "Inaugural Address," March 5, 1877, The American Presidency Project, https://www.presidency.ucsb.edu/documents/inaugural-address-38.

21. Hayes.

22. Hayes.

23. Samuel J. Tilden, Speech to the Manhattan Club, "Samuel Tilden Concedes the 1876 Election to Hayes," *New York Herald*, June 13, 1877, 3, Rutherford B. Hayes, Presidential Library and Museums, https://www.rbhayes.org/hayes/1876-presidential-concession-speech/.

24. Dionne and Kristol, *Bush v. Gore*, 341.

25. E. E. Schattschneider, *Party Government: American Government in Action* (New York: Farrar and Rinehart, 1942), 1.

26. Clinton Rossiter, *Parties and Politics in America* (Ithaca, NY: Cornell University Press, 1960), 1.

27. Rossiter, 11.

28. V. O. Key Jr., *Political Parties and Pressure Groups*, 5th ed. (New York: Thomas Y. Crowell, 1964), 9.

29. Maurice Duverger, *Political Parties* (London: Methuen, 1964), xxiii.

30. Gerald M. Pomper, "The Contribution of Political Parties to American Democracy," in *Party Renewal in America*, ed. Gerald M. Pomper (New York: Praeger, 1980), 5.

31. Gerald M. Pomper, *Passions and Interests: Political Party Concepts of American Democracy* (Lawrence: University Press of Kansas, 1992), 1.

32. Anthony Downs, *An Economic Theory of Democracy* (New York: Harper & Row, 1957).

33. Woodrow Wilson, "Inaugural Address," March 5, 1913, The American Presidency Project, https://www.presidency.ucsb.edu/documents/inaugural-address-48.

34. Martin Van Buren, *The Autobiography of Martin Van Buren*, ed. John C. Fitzpatrick (New York: Augustus M. Kelley Publishers, 1969), 125.

35. Pomper, *Passions and Interests*, 69.

36. James Madison, "Federalist 10," in Alexander Hamilton, John Jay, and James Madison, *The Federalist*, ed. Edward Mead Earle (New York: Modern Library, 1937), 54.

37. Madison, 53.

38. Thomas Jefferson to Francis Hopkinson, March 13, 1789, Founders Online, National Archives, https://founders.archives.gov/documents/Jefferson/01-14-02-0402.

39. Anson D. Morse, "What Is a Party?," *Political Science Quarterly* 11, no. 1 (March 1896): 76.

40. Madison, "Federalist 10," 53.

41. Giovanni Sartori, *Parties and Party Systems: A Framework for Analysis*, vol. 1 (Cambridge: Cambridge University Press, 1976), 3.

42. Sartori, 4.

43. Sartori, 7.

44. Sartori, 4.

45. Pomper, *Passions and Interests*.

46. Sartori, *Parties and Party Systems*, 7.

47. George Washington, Farewell Address, September 19, 1796, United States Senate, https://www.senate.gov/artandhistory/history/resources/pdf/Washingtons_Farewell_Address.pdf.

48. Washington.

49. Washington.

50. Washington.

51. Washington.

52. Sartori, *Parties and Party Systems*, 13.

53. Sartori, 13.

54. Sartori, 23.

55. Sartori, 13.

56. Donald Trump, Speech to 2023 Conservative Political Action Committee Conference, National Harbor, Maryland, March 4, 2023, Rev, https://www.rev.com/blog/transcripts/trump-speaks-at-cpac-2023-transcript.

57. Sidney Tarrow, *Movements and Parties: Critical Connections in American Political Development* (Cambridge: Cambridge University Press, 2021), 4.

58. Tarrow, 5.

59. Samuel Huntington, *Political Order in Changing Societies* (New Haven, CT: Yale University Press, 1968), 91–92.

60. Tarrow, *Movements and Parties*, 5.

61. Deborah Ellis, "The Arc of the Moral Universe Is Long, but It Bends toward Justice," Champions of Change, the White House, Barack Obama, October 21, 2011, https://obamawhitehouse.archives.gov/blog/2011/10/21/arc-moral-un

iverse-long-it-bends-toward-justice#:~:text=Martin%20Luther%20King%2C%20Jr.%2C,time%2C%20but%20it%20does%20happen.

62. Tarrow, *Movements and Parties*, 24.

63. Wilson Carey McWilliams, "Tocqueville and Responsible Parties: Individualism, Partisanship, and Citizenship in America," in *Challenges to Party Government*, ed. John Kenneth White and Jerome Mileur (Carbondale: Southern Illinois University Press, 1992), 196.

64. McWilliams, 196.

65. McWilliams, 196.

66. Elizabeth Kolbert, "Postscript: Mario Cuomo (1932–2015)," *New Yorker*, January 1, 2015, https://www.newyorker.com/news/news-desk/postscript-mario-cuomo.

67. Dominick Mastrangelo, "Trump Jr.: Trump Supporters in D.C. 'Should Send a Message' to GOP 'This Isn't Their Party Anymore,'" *The Hill*, January 6, 2021, https://thehill.com/homenews/532886-donald-trump-jr-gathering-of-trump-supporters-in-dc-should-send-a-message-to-gop/.

68. Brian Naylor, "Read Trump's January 6 Speech, a Key Part of Impeachment Trial," NPR, February 10, 2021, https://www.npr.org/2021/02/10/966396848/read-trumps-jan-6-speech-a-key-part-of-impeachment-trial.

69. David Corn, *American Psychosis: A Historical Investigation of How the Republican Party Went Crazy* (New York: Twelve Hachette Book Group, 2022), 9–10.

70. Michael Kruse, "The One Way History Shows Trump's Personality Cult Will End," *Politico*, April 16, 2022, https://www.politico.com/news/magazine/2022/04/16/history-shows-trump-personality-cult-end-00024941.

71. Kruse.

72. Quoted in Tarrow, *Movement and Parties*, 182.

73. Tarrow, 238.

74. Tarrow, 234.

75. Sartori, *Parties and Party Systems*, 16.

76. Marjorie Taylor Greene, Twitter, February 21, 2023, 10:03 a.m., https://twitter.com/mtgreenee/status/1628062900345602048.

77. Trump, Speech to 2023 Conservative Political Action Committee Conference.

78. Juan J. Linz, *Totalitarian and Authoritarian Regimes* (Boulder, CO: Lynne Rienner, 2000), 159.

79. Linz, 166.

80. Leon Epstein, *Political Parties in the American Mold* (Madison: University of Wisconsin Press, 1986), 9.

81. "Strengthening the Political Parties," a position paper adopted by the

Committee for Party Renewal in 1980 and presented to both national party committees.

82. John H. Aldrich, *Why Parties? The Origin and Transformation of Political Parties in America* (Chicago: University of Chicago Press, 1995), 4.

83. Julius Turner, "Responsible Parties: A Dissent from the Floor," *American Political Science Review* 45, no. 1 (March 1951): 149.

84. Turner, 151.

85. Josh Levy, "'A Republic If You Can Keep It': Elizabeth Willing Powel, Benjamin Franklin, and the James McHenry Journal," Library of Congress, January 6, 2022, https://blogs.loc.gov/manuscripts/2022/01/a-republic-if-you-can-keep-it-elizabeth-willing-powel-benjamin-franklin-and-the-james-mchenry-journal/.

CHAPTER ONE: DEMOCRACY ON TRIAL—AGAIN

1. John Winthrop, "A City on a Hill," 1630, https://www.americanyawp.com/reader/colliding-cultures/john-winthrop-dreams-of-a-city-on-a-hill-1630/.

2. Ronald Reagan, "Farewell Address to the Nation," January 11, 1989, The American Presidency Project, https://www.presidency.ucsb.edu/documents/farewell-address-the-nation.

3. Reagan.

4. David S. Broder, "The Burden and the Power," *Washington Post*, January 20, 1989, https://www.washingtonpost.com/archive/politics/1989/01/20/the-burden-and-the-power/d8d912b0-150a-4106-8f76-d65fe323399e/.

5. Reagan, "Farewell Address to the Nation."

6. Richard B. Wirthlin, Memo to the President, December 16, 1988, reprinted in John Kenneth White, *The New Politics of Old Values* (Hanover, NH: University Press of New England, 1990), 185–189.

7. Joe Biden, "Remarks by President Biden on the Continued Battle for the Soul of the Nation," Philadelphia, Pennsylvania, September 1, 2022, The White House, https://www.whitehouse.gov/briefing-room/speeches-remarks/2022/09/01/remarks-by-president-bidenon-the-continued-battle-for-the-soul-of-the-nation/.

8. Biden.

9. Biden.

10. Biden.

11. Matt Viser, "The Biden-Trump Rematch, in Many Ways, Has Already Begun," *Washington Post*, September 26, 2022, https://www.washingtonpost.com/politics/2022/09/26/biden-trump-rematch/.

12. Joe Biden, "Inaugural Address," January 20, 2021, The American Presidency Project, https://www.presidency.ucsb.edu/documents/inaugural-address-53.

13. Timothy Snyder, *On Tyranny: Twenty Lessons from the Twentieth Century* (New York: Duggan Books, 2017), 112–113.

14. Anne Applebaum, *Twilight of Democracy: The Seductive Lure of Authoritarianism* (New York: Anchor Books, 2021), 158.

15. Donald J. Trump, "Inaugural Address," January 20, 2017, The American Presidency Project, https://www.presidency.ucsb.edu/documents/inaugural-address-14.

16. Yashar Ali, "What George W. Bush Really Thought of Donald Trump's Inauguration," *New York Magazine*, March 29, 2017, https://nymag.com/intelligencer/2017/03/what-george-w-bush-really-thought-of-trumps-inauguration.html.

17. Reagan, "Farewell Address to the Nation."

18. Reagan.

19. Biden, "Remarks by the President on the Continued Battle for the Soul of the Nation."

20. Steven Levitsky and Daniel Ziblatt, *How Democracies Die* (New York: Crown, 2018), 230.

21. Gerald Ford, "Remarks on Taking the Oath of Office," August 9, 1974, The American Presidency Project, https://www.presidency.ucsb.edu/documents/remarks-taking-the-oath-office.

22. Arthur M. Schlesinger Jr., *The Vital Center: The Politics of Freedom* (Boston: Houghton Mifflin, 1949), 1.

23. Harry S. Truman, "Address in Oklahoma City," September 28, 1948, The American Presidency Project, https://www.presidency.ucsb.edu/documents/address-oklahoma-city.

24. Jean Bethke Elshtain, *Democracy on Trial* (New York: Basic Books, 1995), xi.

25. Elshtain, 61.

26. Elshtain, xii.

27. Elshtain, 44.

28. Alan Wolfe, *One Nation after All* (New York: Viking, 1998), 275–322.

29. Stephanie Kramer, Conrad Hackett, and Kelsey Beveridge, "Modeling the Future of Religion in America," Pew Research Center, September 2022, file:///C:/Users/Owner/Downloads/US-Religious-Projections_FOR-PRODUCTION-9.13.22.pdf.

30. Elshtain, *Democracy on Trial*, 119–121.

31. Elshtain, 36.

32. Robert Putnam, "Bowling Alone: America's Declining Social Capital," *Journal of Democracy* 6, no. 1 (January 1995): 65–78.

33. Harry F. Rosenthal, "Voter Turnout Lowest since 1924," Associated Press, November 6, 1996, https://apnews.com/article/92ec2885c0e0492a79a016fe9849 1477.

34. Elshtain, *Democracy on Trial*, 20.

35. See John Kenneth White, *The Values Divide: American Politics and Culture in Transition* (New York: Chatham House, 2003), 131–142.

36. Snyder, *On Tyranny*, 9.

37. Bob Woodward, *Rage* (New York: Simon & Schuster, 2020), 369.

38. Yasmeen Abutaleb, "Apocalypse Now: Democrats Embrace a Dark Midterm Message," *Washington Post*, October 2, 2022, https://www.washingtonpost.com/politics/2022/10/02/democrats-dark-apocalyptic-message-midterms/.

39. Levitsky and Ziblatt, *How Democracies Die*, 23–24.

40. Jon Greenberg, "Most Republicans Still Falsely Believe Trump's Stolen Election Claims," *Poynter*, June 26, 2022, https://www.poynter.org/fact-checking/2022/70-percent-republicans-falsely-believe-stolen-election-trump/.

41. Trump, "Inaugural Address."

42. Snyder, *On Tyranny*, 123.

43. Amy B. Wang, "Trump Wanted 'Totally Loyal' Generals like Hitler's, New Book Says," *Washington Post*, August 8, 2022, https://www.washingtonpost.com/politics/2022/08/08/trump-book-hitler-milley-kelly/.

44. "Full Document: Trump's Call with the Ukrainian President," *New York Times*, October 30, 2019, https://www.nytimes.com/interactive/2019/09/25/us/politics/trump-ukraine-transcript.html.

45. "Full Transcript: Mitt Romney's Speech Announcing Vote to Convict Trump," *New York Times*, February 5, 2020, https://www.nytimes.com/2020/02/05/us/politics/mitt-romney-impeachment-speech-transcript.html.

46. Levitsky and Ziblatt, *How Democracies Die*, 64.

47. Benjamin Weiser, "Trump Pushed Officials to Prosecute His Critics, Ex-U.S. Attorney Says," *New York Times*, September 8, 2022, https://www.nytimes.com/2022/09/08/nyregion/geoffrey-berman-trump-book.html?partner=IFTTT.

48. Dana Milbank, *The Destructionists: The Twenty-Five-Year Crack-Up of the Republican Party* (New York: Doubleday, 2022), 214.

49. Daniel Patrick Moynihan, "More Than Social Security Was at Stake," *Washington Post*, January 18, 1983, A-17.

50. Kellyanne Conway, *Meet the Press*, January 22, 2017, YouTube, https://www.youtube.com/watch?v=MA1vD_L8Mjs.

51. Elle Hunt, "Trump's Inauguration Crowd: Sean Spicer's Claims versus the Evidence," *The Guardian*, January 22, 2017, https://www.theguardian.com/us

-news/2017/jan/22/trump-inauguration-crowd-sean-spicers-claims-versus-the-evidence.

52. Samuel L. Popkin, *Crackup: The Republican Implosion and the Future of Presidential Politics* (New York: Oxford University Press, 2021), 156.

53. Milbank, *Destructionists*, 214.

54. Milbank, 214.

55. David Foster Wallace, *A Supposedly Fun Thing I'll Never Do Again* (Boston: Little, Brown, 1997), 22.

56. Maggie Haberman, *Confidence Man: The Making of Donald Trump and the Breaking of America* (New York: Penguin Press, 2022), 158.

57. Heather Cox Richardson, "Letters from an American," Substack, August 3, 2022, https://heathercoxrichardson.substack.com/p/august-3-2022.

58. Jonathan Askonas, "Reality Is Just a Game Now," *The New Atlantis*, Spring 2022, https://www.thenewatlantis.com/publications/reality-is-just-a-game-now.

59. Applebaum, *Twilight of Democracy*, 16.

60. Askonas, "Reality Is Just a Game Now."

61. Askonas.

62. Elizabeth Dwoskin and Jeremy B. Merrill, "Trump's 'Big Lie' Fueled a New Generation of Social Media Influencers," *Washington Post*, September 20, 2022, https://www.washingtonpost.com/technology/2022/09/20/social-media-influencers-election-fraud/.

63. Barack Obama, *The Audacity of Hope: Thoughts on Reclaiming the American Dream* (New York: Crown, 2006), 31.

64. Applebaum, *Twilight of Democracy*, 108.

65. White, *New Politics of Old Values*, 12.

66. White, 8.

67. "Rockne Premiere," The History Museum, accessed October 3, 2022, https://www.historymuseumsb.org/rockne-premiere/.

68. Applebaum, *Twilight of Democracy*, 74.

69. Applebaum, 75.

70. Ruth Ben-Ghait, "Opinion: Businesses Strike Back as DeSantis Criticizes Corporate America," CNN, August 25, 2022, https://www.cnn.com/2022/08/25/opinions/florida-businesses-desantis-political-fight-ben-ghiat/index.html.

71. Ben-Ghait.

72. Fareed Zakaria, "Fareed Zakaria: GPS," CNN, September 18, 2022, https://transcripts.cnn.com/show/fzgps/date/2022-09-18/segment/01.

73. Eric Hoffer, *The True Believer* (New York: Harper & Row, 1951), xi.

74. Heather Cox Richardson, "Letters from an American," Substack, Octo-

ber 2, 2022, https://heathercoxrichardson.substack.com/p/october-2-2022?utm_source=email.

75. Richardson.

76. Applebaum, *Twilight of Democracy*, 110.

77. Elshtain, *Democracy on Trial*, 112.

78. Baron de Montesquieu, *The Spirit of Laws*, vol. 1 (London: George Bell and Sons, 1897), 21.

79. Montesquieu, 1:vii.

80. Department of Justice News, "Attorney General Merrick B. Garland Administers the Oath of Allegiance and Delivers Congratulatory Remarks at Ellis Island Ceremony in Celebration of Constitution Week and Citizenship Day," New York City, September 17, 2022, Office of Public Affairs, US Department of Justice, https://www.justice.gov/opa/speech/attorney-general-merrick-b-garland-administers-oath-allegiance-and-delivers?utm_source=substack&utm_medium=email.

81. Department of Justice News, "Attorney General Merrick B. Garland Administers the Oath of Allegiance."

82. Montesquieu, *Spirit of Laws*, 1:22.

83. Montesquieu, 1:26.

84. Glenn Kessler, Salvador Rizzo, and Meg Kelly, "Trump's False or Misleading Claims Total 30,573 over Four Years," *Washington Post*, January 24, 2021, https://www.washingtonpost.com/politics/2021/01/24/trumps-false-or-misleading-claims-total-30573-over-four-years/.

85. Jonathan Lemire, *The Big Lie: Election Chaos, Political Opportunism, and the State of American Politics after 2020* (New York: Flatiron Books, 2022), 10.

86. Lemire, 11.

87. Lemire, 2.

88. Eric Holder, *Our Unfinished March: The Violent Past and Imperiled Future of the Vote—A History, a Crisis, a Plan* (New York: One World, 2022), 128.

89. Lemire, *Big Lie*, 17.

90. Holder, *Our Unfinished March*, 128.

91. "Transcript of Mitt Romney's Speech on Donald Trump," *New York Times*, March 3, 2016, https://www.nytimes.com/2016/03/04/us/politics/mitt-romney-speech.html.

92. Milbank, *Deconstructionists*, 254.

93. Rebecca Shabad, "Biden Blasts MAGA Philosophy as 'Semi-Fascism,'" NBC News, August 26, 2022, https://www.nbcnews.com/politics/2022-election/biden-blasts-maga-philosophy-semi-fascism-rcna44953.

94. Heather Cox Richardson, *To Make Men Free: A History of the Republican Party* (New York: Basic Books, 2014), 280–281.

95. Franklin D. Roosevelt, "Radio Campaign Address," Hyde Park, New York, November 4, 1940, Franklin D. Roosevelt Presidential Library and Museum, http://docs.fdrlibrary.marist.edu/php11440.html.

96. Levitsky and Ziblatt, *How Democracies Die*, 77.

97. "Roosevelt Wins!," British Pathé film, YouTube, accessed October 4, 2022, https://www.youtube.com/watch?v=JFGLSUmmshs.

98. Dwight D. Eisenhower, "Radio and Television Remarks Following the Victory," November 7, 1956, The American Presidency Project, https://www.presidency.ucsb.edu/documents/radio-and-television-remarks-following-the-election-victory.

99. Popkin, *Crackup*, 177.

100. Jeremy W. Peters, *Insurgency: How Republicans Lost Their Party and Got Everything They Ever Wanted* (New York: Crown Books, 2022), 298.

101. Kyle Cheney, "'Afraid of Losing Their Power': Judge Decries GOP Leaders Who Back Trump Election Claims," *Politico*, September 27, 2022, https://www.politico.com/news/2022/09/27/oath-keeper-trial-trump-jan-6-00059091.

102. Cheney.

103. David Leonhardt, "'A Crisis Is Coming': The Twin Threats to American Democracy," *New York Times*, September 17, 2022, https://www.nytimes.com/2022/09/17/us/american-democracy-threats.html.

104. Joe Biden, "Remarks by President Biden at the United We Stand Summit," September 15, 2022, The White House, https://www.whitehouse.gov/briefing-room/speeches-remarks/2022/09/15/remarks-by-president-biden-at-the-united-we-stand-summit/.

CHAPTER TWO: A BROKEN PARTY, 1932–1952

1. Karl Rove, *The Triumph of William McKinley; Why the Election of 1896 Still Matters* (New York: Simon & Schuster, 2015), 363.

2. Rove, 378.

3. Rove, 378.

4. James MacGregor Burns, *The Lion and the Fox* (New York: Harcourt Brace and World, 1956), 76.

5. Herbert Hoover, Acceptance Speech, Palo Alto, California, August 11, 1928. For excerpts from the speech, see Spencer Howard, "Kicking Off a Presidential Campaign—Herbert Hoover's 1928 Acceptance Speech," Hoover Heads, National Archives, August 11, 2020, https://hoover.blogs.archives.gov/2020/08/11/kicking-off-a-presidential-campaign-herbert-hoovers-1928-acceptance-speech.

6. Herbert Hoover, "Inaugural Address," March 4, 1929, The American Presidency Project, https://www.presidency.ucsb.edu/documents/inaugural-address-9.

7. Stefan Lorant, *The Presidency* (New York: Macmillan, 1951), 580–581.

8. Heather Cox Richardson, *To Make Men Free: A History of the Republican Party* (New York: Basic Books, 2021), 273–274. The *New York Times* suggested that if this were true, the only proper course for the administration was to shut up.

9. Lorant, *The Presidency*, 587.

10. Ted Morgan, *FDR: A Biography* (New York: Simon & Schuster, 1985), 349.

11. Morgan, 339.

12. Franklin D. Roosevelt, "Address Accepting the Democratic Presidential Nomination at the Democratic National Convention in Chicago," July 2, 1932, The American Presidency Project, https://www.presidency.ucsb.edu/documents/address-accepting-the-presidential-nomination-the-democratic-national-convention-chicago-1.

13. Lorant, *The Presidency*, 592; Andrew E. Busch, *Truman's Triumphs: The 1948 Election and the Making of Postwar America* (Lawrence: University Press of Kansas, 2012), 6.

14. Richardson, *To Make Men Free*, 271–272.

15. Busch, *Truman's Triumphs*, 6.

16. Richardson, *To Make Men Free*, 278.

17. Everett C. Ladd with Charles D. Hadley, *Transformations of the American Party System: Political Coalitions from the New Deal to the 1970s* (New York: W. W. Norton, 1975), 58–59.

18. Herbert Hoover, "Address Accepting the Republican Presidential Nomination," August 11, 1932, The American Presidency Project, https://www.presidency.ucsb.edu/documents/address-accepting-the-republican-presidential-nomination.

19. Lorant, *The Presidency*, 593.

20. Morgan, *FDR*, 362.

21. Morgan, 363.

22. Burns, *The Lion and the Fox*, 143.

23. Burns, 143.

24. Richardson, *To Make Men Free*, 275.

25. Burns, *The Lion and the Fox*, 142.

26. James MacGregor Burns, *Roosevelt: The Soldier of Freedom, 1940–1945* (New York: Harcourt Brace and Jovanovich, 1970), 3.

27. William D. Hassett, *Off the Record with FDR, 1942–1945* (New York: Enigma Books, 2016), 261.

28. Arthur M. Schlesinger Jr., *The Politics of Upheaval: The Age of Roosevelt* (Boston: Houghton Mifflin, 1960), 544–545.

29. Kirk H. Porter and Donald Bruce Johnson, *National Party Platforms, 1840–1968* (Urbana: University of Illinois Press, 1970), 365.

30. Michael A. Davis, *Politics as Usual: Thomas Dewey, Franklin Roosevelt, and the Wartime Campaign of 1944* (De Kalb: Northern Illinois University Press, 2014), 24.

31. Porter and Johnson, *National Party Platforms*, 365.

32. Cited in George F. Will, "Democrats, Temper Your Enthusiasm," *Washington Post*, November 25, 2021, A-27. Nationwide, only 45 percent of Americans said yes; 55 percent said no (Gallup poll, June 22–27, 1936). Text of question: "Do you believe the acts and policies of the Roosevelt administration may lead to a dictatorship?"

33. Lorant, *The Presidency*, 612.

34. Franklin D. Roosevelt, "Address at the Democratic State Convention, Syracuse, N.Y.," September 29, 1936, The American Presidency Project, https://www.presidency.ucsb.edu/documents/address-the-democratic-state-convention-syracuse-ny.

35. Burns, *The Lion and the Fox*, 151.

36. Franklin D. Roosevelt, "Inaugural Address," March 4, 1933, The American Presidency Project, https://www.presidency.ucsb.edu/documents/inaugural-address-8.

37. Morgan, *FDR*, 440.

38. Franklin D. Roosevelt, "October 31, 1936: Speech at Madison Square Garden," Miller Center, University of Virginia, https://millercenter.org/the-presidency/presidential-speeches/october-31-1936-speech-madison-square-garden.

39. Burns, *The Lion and the Fox*, 283.

40. Schlesinger, *Politics of Upheaval*, 642.

41. Busch, *Truman's Triumphs*, 18.

42. John W. Jeffries, *A Third Term for FDR* (Lawrence: University Press of Kansas, 2017), 42.

43. Morgan, *FDR*, 441.

44. "Editorial Comment of Representative Newspapers on Vote Outcome," *New York Times*, November 5, 1936, 4.

45. In 2008, Obama received 69,499,428 votes, whereas in 2004 John Kerry received 59,027,115 votes.

46. Ladd with Hadley, *Transformations of the American Party System*, 60.

47. Schlesinger, *Politics of Upheaval*, 524.

48. Jeffries, *Third Term for FDR*, 56.

49. Willkie voted for Alf Landon in 1936 but supported Democrat Herbert Lehman for reelection as New York's governor in 1938 against Thomas E. Dewey. He changed his party registration to Republican in 1939.

50. Jeffries, *Third Term for FDR*, 434.

51. John Robert Greene, *I Like Ike: The Presidential Election of 1952* (Lawrence: University Press of Kansas, 2017), 104.

52. Davis, *Politics as Usual*, 78. Thomas E. Dewey said of Willkie, "Gosh, you like to have a fellow who identifies himself with the party if he expects to be its spokesman, its leader." Davis, 84.

53. Kirk and Porter, *National Party Platforms*, 391.

54. Lorant, *The Presidency*, 642.

55. "Text of President Roosevelt's Speeches in Philadelphia and Wilmington," *New York Times*, October 24, 1940, 14.

56. Burns, *The Lion and the Fox*, 443.

57. Morgan, *FDR*, 535; Jeffries, *Third Term for FDR*, 138.

58. Lorant, *The Presidency*, 641.

59. Burns, *The Lion and the Fox*, 446.

60. "Text of President Roosevelt's Speeches in Philadelphia and Wilmington."

61. "Text of President Roosevelt's Speeches in Philadelphia and Wilmington."

62. "Text of President Roosevelt's Speeches in Philadelphia and Wilmington."

63. Jeffries, *Third Term for FDR*, 145.

64. Burns, *The Lion and the Fox*, 454. Willkie later defended his performance, citing his wins in Michigan and Indiana, while Republican governors in those states lost. Davis, *Politics as Usual*, 26.

65. Davis, *Politics as Usual*, 26.

66. Jim Bishop, *FDR's Last Year: April 1944–April 1945* (New York: William Morrow, 1974), 88.

67. Franklin D. Roosevelt, "Address to the Democratic National Convention in Chicago," July 20, 1944, The American Presidency Project, https://www.presidency.ucsb.edu/documents/address-the-democratic-national-convention-chicago.

68. Herbert Brownell with John P. Burke, *Advising Ike: The Memoirs of Attorney General Herbert Brownell* (Lawrence: University Press of Kansas, 1993), 55.

69. Bishop, *FDR's Last Year*, 69.

70. "Lehman Plurality Officially 64,004," *New York Times*, December 8, 1938, https://www.nytimes.com/1938/12/08/archives/lehman-plurality-officially-64004-state-board-puts-his-vote-finally.html.

71. "Dewey's Plurality Officially 647,628," *New York Times*, December 15, 1942, https://www.nytimes.com/1942/12/15/archives/deweys-plurality-officially-647628-state-board-of-canvassers.html.

72. Davis, *Politics as Usual*, 8.

73. Davis, 9.

74. Davis, 69.

75. Morgan, *FDR*, 738.

76. Bishop, *FDR's Last Year*, 147.

77. Davis, *Politics as Usual*, 167.

78. David M. Jordan, *FDR, Dewey, and the Election of 1944* (Bloomington: Indiana University Press, 2011), 221.

79. Davis, *Politics as Usual*, 161.

80. Bishop, *FDR's Last Year*, 158.

81. Burns, *The Lion and the Fox*, 284.

82. Bishop, *FDR's Last Year*, 149.

83. Bishop, 150.

84. Bishop, 151.

85. Davis, *Politics as Usual*, 164.

86. Bishop, *FDR's Last Year*, 196.

87. Davis, *Politics as Usual*, 41.

88. Lorant, *The Presidency*, 669.

89. Richard Norton Smith, *Thomas E. Dewey and His Times* (New York: Simon & Schuster, 1982), 438.

90. Michael Bowen, *The Roots of Modern Conservatism: Dewey, Taft, and the Battle for the Soul of the Republican Party* (Chapel Hill: University of North Carolina Press, 2011), 43.

91. Gallup poll, June 1–5, 1945. Text of question: "Do you approve or disapprove of the way Harry Truman is handling his job as President?" Approve, 87 percent; disapprove, 3 percent; no opinion, 10 percent.

92. Gallup poll, November 15–20, 1946. Text of question: "Do you approve or disapprove of the way Truman is handling his job as President?" Approve, 34 percent; disapprove, 53 percent; no opinion, 13 percent.

93. A. J. Baime, *Dewey Defeats Truman: The 1948 Election and the Battle for America's Soul* (Boston: Houghton Mifflin Harcourt, 2020), 135–136.

94. Porter and Johnson, *National Party Platforms*, 451.

95. Busch, *Truman's Triumphs*, 79, 104. An exasperated Truman confronted James Roosevelt, saying, "If your father knew what you were doing to me, he would turn over in his grave. But get this straight: Whether you like it or not, I'm going to be the next President of the United States. That will be all. Good day." Quoted in Baime, *Dewey Defeats Truman*, 127. Also endorsing Eisenhower were Senator Claude Pepper, former Interior secretary Harold Ickes, and Chicago boss Jacob Arvey.

96. Lorant, *The Presidency*, 689.

97. Lorant, 689.

98. Smith, *Thomas E. Dewey and His Times*, 504.

99. Smith, 503.

100. Smith, 503.

101. Busch, *Truman's Triumphs*, 103.

102. Gallup poll, October 15–25, 1948. Text of question: "If the presidential election were being held today, how would you vote—for Harry Truman, for Thomas Dewey, for Henry Wallace, or for J. Strom Thurmond?" Truman, 45 percent; Dewey, 50 percent; Wallace, 4 percent; Thurmond, 2 percent.
103. Smith, *Thomas E. Dewey and His Times*, 503.
104. Baime, *Dewey Defeats Truman*, 44.
105. Brownell with Burke, *Advising Ike*, 66.
106. Bowen, *Roots of Modern Conservatism*, 28.
107. Harry S. Truman, "Address in Philadelphia upon Accepting the Nomination of the Democratic National Convention," July 15, 1948, The American Presidency Project, https://www.presidency.ucsb.edu/documents/address-philadelphia-upon-accepting-the-nomination-the-democratic-national-convention.
108. David McCullough, *Truman* (New York: Simon & Schuster, 1992), 658–659.
109. Busch, *Truman's Triumphs*, 110.
110. McCullough, *Truman*, 703.
111. Baime, *Dewey Defeats Truman*, 349.
112. Baime, 333.
113. Lorant, *The Presidency*, 718.
114. Baime, *Dewey Defeats Truman*, 344.
115. Bowen, *Roots of Modern Conservatism*, 76.
116. McCullough, *Truman*, 712.
117. Baime, *Dewey Defeats Truman*, 345.
118. Bowen, *Roots of Modern Conservatism*, 77.
119. Baime, *Dewey Defeats Truman*, 345.
120. Smith, *Thomas E. Dewey and His Times*, 547. This was not a new position on Dewey's part. In 1943, Dewey said that "anybody who thinks that an attack on the fundamental idea of security and welfare is appealing to people generally is living in the Middle Ages." See Greene, *I Like Ike*, 18.
121. Thomas E. Dewey, *Thomas E. Dewey on the Two-Party System*, ed. John A. Wells (Garden City, NY: Doubleday, 1966), 20.
122. Smith, *Thomas E. Dewey and His Times*, 548; Dewey, *Thomas E. Dewey on the Two-Party System*, 21.
123. Smith, *Thomas E. Dewey and His Times*, 547.
124. Bowen, *Roots of Modern Conservatism*, 7.

CHAPTER THREE: THE PRICE OF VICTORY

1. Gallup poll, February 8–14, 1952. Text of question: "Do you approve or disapprove of the way Truman is handling his job as President?" Approve, 22 percent; disapprove, 65 percent; no opinion, 13 percent.

2. Heather Cox Richardson, *To Make Men Free: A History of the Republican Party* (New York: Basic Books, 2021), 276.

3. Richardson, 282.

4. Michael A. Davis, *Politics as Usual: Thomas Dewey, Franklin Roosevelt, and the Wartime Presidential Campaign of 1944* (De Kalb: Northern Illinois University Press, 2014), 10.

5. W. H. Lawrence, "Taft Fights to Stop Eisenhower with Coalition in Ballot Today: Platform Wins without Clash," *New York Times*, July 11, 1952.

6. Dwight D. Eisenhower, *The Eisenhower Diaries*, ed. Robert H. Ferrell (New York: W. W. Norton, 1981), 214.

7. The first mention of Eisenhower as a presidential candidate came in 1943 when the *Washington Post* ran a headline that read, "Eisenhower Urged for President." Eisenhower responded tartly: "Why can't a simple soldier be left alone to carry out his orders? And I furiously object to the word 'candidate'—I ain't and won't." Quoted in Susan Eisenhower, *How Ike Led: The Principles behind Eisenhower's Biggest Decisions* (New York: Thomas Dunne Books, 2020), 102 (in subsequent short notes, this author is cited as S. Eisenhower; all short cites to works by Dwight Eisenhower use his last name, with no initial).

8. David Halberstam, *The Fifties* (New York: Villard Books, 1993), 209.

9. S. Eisenhower, *How Ike Led*, 102.

10. Dwight D. Eisenhower, *Mandate for Change, The White House Years, 1953–1956* (New York: Signet Books, 1963), 44.

11. Eisenhower, 44.

12. Eisenhower, 45.

13. Eisenhower, 43.

14. S. Eisenhower, *How Ike Led*, 107.

15. Richardson, *To Make Men Free*, 311.

16. Michael Bowen, *The Roots of Modern Conservatism: Dewey, Taft, and the Battle for the Soul of the Republican Party* (Chapel Hill: University of North Carolina Press, 2011), 122.

17. A. J. Baime, *Dewey Defeats Truman: The 1948 Election and the Battle for America's Soul* (Boston: Houghton Mifflin Harcourt, 2020), 81.

18. Richard Nixon, *RN: The Memoirs of Richard Nixon* (New York: Grosset & Dunlap, 1978), 83.

19. Joe Scarborough, *The Right Path: From Ike to Reagan, How Republicans Once Mastered Politics—and Can Again* (New York: Random House, 2013), 5.

20. John Robert Greene, *I Like Ike: The Presidential Election of 1952* (Lawrence: University Press of Kansas, 2017), 74.

21. Dwight D. Eisenhower, *At Ease: Stories I Tell My Friends* (Garden City, NY: Doubleday, 1967), 371.

22. Eisenhower, 372.
23. Davis, *Politics as Usual*, 10.
24. S. Eisenhower, *How Ike Led*, 113.
25. Bowen, *Roots of Modern Conservatism*, 132.
26. Cited in Greene, *I Like Ike*, 8. The only time Article 5 has ever been invoked by NATO was after the September 11, 2001, terrorist attacks against the United States.
27. Greene, 34.
28. Halberstam, *The Fifties*, 209.
29. Gallup poll, June 1952. Others and no opinion responses totaled 8 percent.
30. Richard Norton Smith, *Thomas E. Dewey and His Times* (New York: Simon & Schuster, 1982), 586.
31. Bowen, *Roots of Modern Conservatism*, 84.
32. Greene, *I Like Ike*, 102.
33. Greene, 95.
34. Smith, *Thomas E. Dewey and His Times*, 594.
35. Greene, *I Like Ike*, 22.
36. Bowen, *Roots of Modern Conservatism*, 123.
37. S. Eisenhower, *How Ike Led*, 113.
38. Greene, *I Like Ike*, 92.
39. Nixon, *RN*, 89.
40. Roper Organization poll, July 1952. Text of question: "Both Conventions this time, you know, were pretty hot contests. Do you feel that Eisenhower will be able to really unite the various factions within the Republican Party such as the Taft and MacArthur groups, or do you feel that underneath there will actually be a lot of disagreement and dissatisfaction among the Republicans?" Will be able to unite, 44 percent; lots of disagreement and dissatisfaction, 37 precent; don't know, 19 percent.
41. Adlai Stevenson, "Speech Accepting the Democratic Presidential Nomination," Chicago, July 26, 1952, American Rhetoric, https://www.americanrhetoric.com/speeches/adlaistevenson1952dnc.html.
42. Gallup poll, March 14–19, 1952.
43. Malcolm Moos, *The Republicans: A History of Their Party* (New York: Random House, 1956), 476.
44. Greene, *I Like Ike*, 110.
45. John W. Jeffries, *A Third Term for FDR: The Election of 1940* (Lawrence: University Press of Kansas, 2017), 49.
46. Nixon, *RN*, 82.
47. Gallup poll, June 15–20, 1952. Text of question: "Leaving aside any feelings you may have about these men [Robert A. Taft, Harry S. Truman, Douglas

MacArthur, Dwight D. Eisenhower, Estes Kefauver], which one do you think makes the most impressive showing on T.V.?" Taft, 8 percent; Truman, 13 percent; MacArthur, 30 percent; Eisenhower, 29 percent; Kefauver, 19 percent.

48. Gallup poll, June 15–20, 1952. Text of question: "Here is a list of men who have been mentioned as possible presidential candidates this year [1952] for the Republican Party. Which one would you like to see nominated as the Republican candidate for President?" Eisenhower, 52 percent; Taft, 21 percent; Warren, 11 percent; MacArthur, 10 percent; Stassen, 4 percent; none of these (volunteered), 1 percent; don't know/no answer, 2 percent.

49. Greene, *I Like Ike*, 49.

50. Among the Democratic officeholders who endorsed Eisenhower were former secretary of state and South Carolina governor Jimmy Byrnes and Texas governor Allan Shivers. Powerful Virginia senator Harry Byrd said he could not "in good conscience, endorse the national Democratic platform or the Stevenson-Sparkman ticket." Greene, *I Like Ike*, 144, 145.

51. The Eisenhower forces filed charges against delegates from Texas, Louisiana, Florida, Mississippi, Georgia, Puerto Rico, Kansas, and Missouri. If Taft had won that fight, he would have undoubtedly been the Republican nominee. Greene, 93.

52. Eisenhower noted in his memoirs that upon his return from Europe, "I found myself constantly seeking information, both as to the practices and methods . . . [of] the specific charges and countercharges made about unfairness in Texas, Georgia, and Louisiana." Eisenhower, *Mandate for Change*, 68. In a letter to the GOP convention delegates, Eisenhower wrote, "*No* Republican Candidate whose nomination rests on corrupt methods can attack effectively the corruption of the Democratic administration. . . . Remember November! Vote for the Fair Play Amendment. You can't fight corruption with corruption!" Greene, *I Like Ike*, 97.

53. Richard Hofstadter, "The Pseudo Conservative Revolt (1955)," in *The Radical Right*, 3rd ed., ed. Daniel Bell (New York: Routledge, 2017), 77.

54. Bowen, *Roots of Modern Conservatism*, 165.

55. Greene, *I Like Ike*, 129.

56. Eisenhower, *Mandate for Change*, 107.

57. David McCullough, *Truman* (New York: Simon & Schuster, 1992), 910–911.

58. Greene, *I Like Ike*, 20.

59. McCullough, *Truman*, 911–912.

60. "Text of Stevenson Speech of Welcome to Convention, *New York Times*, July 22, 1952, https://timesmachine.nytimes.com/timesmachine/1952/07/22/84335536.pdf?pdf_redirect=true&ip=0.

61. Only one of the Stevenson states, West Virginia, was outside the South.

62. Eisenhower also came close to winning Kentucky and South Carolina.

63. Like Taft, Stevenson was a flawed presidential candidate. On one occasion, unlike Eisenhower, Stevenson dodged the routine task of kissing a baby, telling the parent that he had not had time to wash and that his germs could harm the child. See Greene, *I Like Ike*, 142.

64. Dean Acheson, *Present at the Creation: My Years in the State Department* (New York: W. W. Norton, 1969), 485.

65. Acheson, 693. Truman himself later admitted: "The cards were stacked against us. I don't think [any Democrat] could have won this election." Greene, *I Like Ike*, 173.

66. Smith, *Thomas E. Dewey and His Times*, 604.

67. CBS News, Election Night, November 4, 1952, YouTube, https://www.youtube.com/watch?v=5vjDod8D9Ec.

68. Republican control of the Senate was brief. In 1954, Oregon senator Wayne Morse left the Republican Party and allied himself with the Democrats.

69. Greene, *I Like Ike*, 171.

70. S. Eisenhower, *How Ike Led*, 126.

71. The 1952 margins in the House were smaller than the thirty-seat additions the Republicans won in 1950. The Senate would soon become 48–48 once Oregon senator Wayne Morse defected to the Democratic Party, leaving Vice President Nixon to break the tie.

72. Gallup poll, October 17–22, 1952. Text of question: "Looking ahead for the next few years, which political party—the Republican or Democratic—do you think will be best for people like yourself? If no difference or no opinion, ask: Well, if you had to make up your mind today on which party has your best interests at heart, which party would you choose—the Democratic or Republican Party?" Democratic, 51 percent; Republican, 30 percent; would choose Democratic Party if had to choose 4 percent; would choose Republican party if had to choose, 7 percent; no difference or no opinion, 8 percent.

73. Moos, *Republicans*, 493.

74. Bowen, *Roots of Modern Conservatism*, 161.

75. Greene, *I Like Ike*, 31; S. Eisenhower, *How Ike Led*, 112.

76. Eisenhower, *Mandate for Change*, 47; S. Eisenhower, *How Ike Led*, 112.

77. Theodore J. Lowi, *The Personal President: Power Invested, Promise Unfulfilled* (Ithaca, NY: Cornell University Press, 1985), 74.

78. Dwight D. Eisenhower, "Remarks at the Headquarters of the Republican National Committee," November 5, 1956, The American Presidency Project, https://www.presidency.ucsb.edu/documents/remarks-the-headquarters-the-republican-national-committee.

79. Eisenhower.

80. Herbert Brownell with John P. Burke, *Advising Ike: The Memoirs of Attorney General Herbert Brownell* (Lawrence: University Press of Kansas, 1993), 70.

81. Greene, *I Like Ike*, 178.

82. Greene, 177.

83. S. Eisenhower, *How Ike Led*, 134.

84. Greene, *I Like Ike*, 177.

85. Dwight D. Eisenhower, "The President's News Conference," November 14, 1956, The American Presidency Project, https://www.presidency.ucsb.edu/documents/the-presidents-news-conference-318.

86. Richardson, *To Make Men Free*, 316.

87. Adlai Stevenson, "Address Accepting the Presidential Nomination at the Democratic National Convention in Chicago," August 17, 1956, The American Presidency Project, https://www.presidency.ucsb.edu/documents/address-accepting-the-presidential-nomination-the-democratic-national-convention-chicago.

88. John F. Kennedy, *The Strategy of Peace* (New York: Harper & Brothers, 1960), 178.

89. S. Eisenhower, *How Ike Led*, 136.

90. Dwight D. Eisenhower, "Address at the Cow Palace on Accepting the Nomination of the Republican National Convention," August 23, 1956, The American Presidency Project, https://www.presidency.ucsb.edu/documents/address-the-cow-palace-accepting-the-nomination-the-republican-national-convention.

91. Arthur Larson, *A Republican Looks at His Party* (New York: Harper & Brothers, 1956).

92. Nixon, *RN*, 119.

93. S. Eisenhower, *How Ike Led*, 119.

94. Bowen, *Roots of Modern Conservatism*, 195.

95. Steven Wagner, *Eisenhower Republicanism: Pursuing the Middle Way* (De Kalb: Northern Illinois University Press, 2006), 122.

96. Cited in Democratic National Committee, press release, May 17, 1957, Theodore Sorensen Papers, 1953–1960, Box 10, John F. Kennedy Presidential Library and Museum, Boston, MA.

97. Democratic National Committee, 1957 press release.

98. Wagner, *Eisenhower Republicanism*, 115.

99. Greene, *I Like Ike*, 177.

100. Dwight D. Eisenhower, letter to Edgar Eisenhower, November 8, 1954; Greene, *I Like Ike*, 177; S. Eisenhower, *How Ike Led*, 134.

101. Wagner, *Eisenhower Republicanism*, 114.

102. Bowen, *Roots of Modern Conservatism*, 184–185.

103. Wagner, *Eisenhower Republicanism*, 114.

104. James Reston, "Eisenhower in a Landslide," *New York Times*, November 7, 1956, 3.

105. CBS News, Election Night, November 6, 1956, YouTube, https://www.youtube.com/watch?v=J7wdcYh7oIg&t=18s.

106. Nixon, *RN*, 180.

107. Dwight D. Eisenhower, "Radio and Television Remarks Following the Election Victory," November 7, 1956, The American Presidency Project, https://www.presidency.ucsb.edu/documents/radio-and-television-remarks-following-the-election-victory.

108. Wagner, *Eisenhower Republicanism*, 122.

109. Wagner, 122.

110. Wagner, 122.

111. Smith, *Thomas E. Dewey and His Times*, 608.

112. Sidney M. Milkis, *The President and the Parties: The Transformation of the American Party System since the New Deal* (New York: Oxford University Press, 1993), 228.

113. Greene, *I Like Ike*, 179.

114. Stevenson, "Address Accepting the Presidential Nomination at the Democratic National Convention in Chicago."

115. Joe McGinniss, *The Selling of the President 1968* (New York: Trident Press, 1969), 27.

116. Lowi, *Personal President*, 113.

117. Lowi, xi.

118. McGinniss, *Selling of the President 1968*, 26.

119. McGinniss, 195.

120. McGinniss, 27.

121. H. R. Haldeman, *The Haldeman Diaries: Inside the Nixon White House* (New York: G. P. Putnam's Sons, 1974), 476.

122. According to the Pew Research poll, 42 percent of Republicans and Republican-leaning independents viewed Ronald Reagan as the best president of the past forty years; 37 percent named Donald Trump. Pew Research Center poll, September 13–19, 2021; "Republicans View Reagan, Trump as Best Recent Presidents," Pew Research Center, press release, December 20, 2011.

123. Lowi, *Personal President*, xi.

124. Committee on Political Parties, *Toward a More Responsible Two-Party System* (New York: Rinehart, 1950), 94 (emphasis in original).

125. Lowi, *Personal President*, xi.

126. Jeremy D. Bailey, *The Idea of Presidential Representation: An Intellectual and Political History* (Lawrence: University Press of Kansas, 2019), 83.

127. Bailey, 83.

128. James MacGregor Burns, *Running Alone: Presidential Leadership from JFK to Bush II* (New York: Basic Books, 2006), 168.

129. Burns, 93.

130. Nixon, *RN*, 769.

131. Richard Nixon, "Remarks on Accepting the Presidential Nomination of the Republican National Convention," August 23, 1972, The American Presidency Project, https://www.presidency.ucsb.edu/documents/farewell-radio-and-television-address-the-american-people. After resigning the presidency in 1974, Nixon lamented that before "the Watergate bullshit came along, I was going to build a new Republican Party and a new majority." Quoted in Burns, *Running Alone*, 105.

132. President Ford Committee, "Ford Campaign Strategy Plan," August 1976, 70, courtesy of the Gerald R. Ford Presidential Library and Museum, Ann Arbor, MI.

133. Arthur M. Schlesinger Jr., *The Imperial Presidency* (Boston: Houghton Mifflin, 1973).

134. George E. Reedy, *The Twilight of the Presidency: From Johnson to Reagan* (New York: New American Library, 1987), 26.

135. Michael Duffy, "That Sinking Feeling," *Time*, June 7, 1993.

136. Harold Seidman, *Politics, Position, and Power: The Dynamics of Federal Organization* (New York: Oxford University Press, 1998), 87.

137. "Ronald Reagan and David Brinkley: A Farewell Interview," ABC News broadcast, December 22, 1988.

138. Associated Press, "Donald Trump: 'I'm Going to Be So Presidential You People Will Be Bored,'" April 22, 2016.

139. "Lindsey Graham Speech Transcript January 6: Says Biden Is 'Lawfully' Elected," Rev, January 26, 2021, https://www.rev.com/blog/transcripts/lindsey-graham-speech-transcript-january-6-says-biden-is-lawfully-elected.

140. "Kevin McCarthy Speech Transcript as House Debates 2nd Trump Impeachment," Rev, January 13, 2021, https://www.rev.com/blog/transcripts/kevin-mccarthy-speech-transcript-as-house-debates-2nd-trump-impeachment.

141. "Mitch McConnell Speech Transcript after Vote to Acquit Trump in 2nd Impeachment Trial," Rev, February 13, 2021, https://www.rev.com/blog/transcripts/mitch-mcconnell-speech-transcript-after-vote-to-acquit-trump-in-2nd-impeachment-trial.

142. Tom Porter, "There Is No Way the Republican Party Can Win without Trump," *Business Insider*, May 9, 2021, https://www.businessinsider.in/politics/world/news/there-is-no-way-the-republican-party-can-win-without-trump-says-sen-lindsey-graham/articleshow/82497396.cms.

143. Jeremy W. Peters, "'But the People Like Me the Best, by Far,'" *New York Times*, January 5, 2022.

144. Paul Kane, Mariana Sotomayor, and Jacqueline Alemany, "In Congress, January 6 Left Legacy of Fear and Anger," *Washington Post*, January 4, 2022, A-1.

145. Theodore H. White, *The Making of the President, 1960* (New York: Atheneum House, 1961), 415.

146. Quinnipiac University Polling Institute, March 3–5, 2018. Text of question: "Thinking about the United States presidents we have had since World War Two: Harry Truman, Dwight Eisenhower, John Kennedy, Lyndon Johnson, Richard Nixon, Gerald Ford, Jimmy Carter, Ronald Reagan, George Bush Senior, Bill Clinton, George W. Bush, Barack Obama, and Donald Trump, which one would you consider the best president?" Harry Truman, 3 percent; Dwight Eisenhower, 4 percent; John Kennedy, 10 percent; Lyndon Johnson, 2 percent; Richard Nixon, 1 percent; Jimmy Carter, 3 percent; Ronald Reagan, 28 percent; George Bush Senior, 1 percent; Bill Clinton, 10 percent; George W. Bush, 1 percent; Barack Obama, 24 percent; Donald Trump, 7 percent; don't know/no answer, 6 percent.

147. Donald Trump, "Address Accepting the Presidential Nomination at the Republican National Convention in Cleveland, Ohio," July 21, 2016, The American Presidency Project, https://www.presidency.ucsb.edu/documents/address-accepting-the-presidential-nomination-the-republican-national-convention-cleveland.

148. James Thomas Flexner, *Washington: The Indispensable Man* (New York: New American Library, 1974), 227.

149. Stephen F. Knott, *The Lost Soul of the American Presidency: The Decline into Demagoguery and the Prospects for Renewal* (Lawrence: University Press of Kansas, 2019), 18.

150. George Washington, letter to James Madison, November 30, 1785, Founders Online, https://founders.archives.gov/GEWN-04-03-02-0357.

151. Knott, *Lost Soul of the American Presidency*, 7.

152. Knott, 31.

153. Bailey, *Idea of Presidential Representation*, 52–53.

154. Thomas Jefferson, "Inaugural Address," March 4, 1805, The American Presidency Project, https://www.presidency.ucsb.edu/documents/inaugural-address-20.

155. Bailey, *Idea of Presidential Representation*, 16.

156. Bailey, 17.

157. Knott, *Lost Soul of the American Presidency*, 32.

158. Clinton Rossiter, *The American Presidency* (New York: New American Library, 1962), 29.

159. Rossiter, 29.

160. Rossiter, 30.

CHAPTER FOUR: OF CONSPIRACY THEORIES, LIES, AND STOLEN ELECTIONS

1. Maureen Dowd, "New Races (Their Own) for 2 Bush Sons," *New York Times*, November 30, 1993, 1.

2. George Bush, *All the Best: My Life in Letters and Other Writings* (New York: Scribner, 1999), 87.

3. Jon Meacham, *Destiny and Power: The American Odyssey of George Herbert Walker Bush* (New York: Random House, 2015), 124. In 1988, Bush expressed similar sentiments, this time about religious extremists within the Republican Party. In his diary, Bush wrote: "There's something terrible about those who carry it to extremes. They're scary. They're there for spooky, extraordinary right-winged reasons. They don't care about the Party. They don't care about anything. They're the excesses. . . . They will destroy this party if they're permitted to take over." David Corn, *American Psychosis: A Historical Investigation of How the Republican Party Went Crazy* (New York: Twelve Hachette Book Group, 2022), 168–169.

4. Dowd, "New Races (Their Own) for 2 Bush Sons." Notably, when Bush ran for the presidency in 1980, he resigned from the Council on Foreign Relations. See James Mann, "The Birchers and the Trumpers," *New York Review of Books*, June 23, 2022, 36.

5. Malcolm Moos, *The Republicans: A History of Their Party* (New York: Random House, 1956), 375.

6. Greg Mitchell, *The Campaign of the Century: Upton Sinclair's Race for Governor of California* (New York: Random House, 1992), 32.

7. "1951 Speech Kit," Republican Congressional Campaign Committee, Gerald R. Ford Congressional Papers, Box G-1, Gerald R. Ford Library, Ann Arbor, MI.

8. "1951 Speech Kit." In an open letter to Soviet leader Nikita Khruschev in 1958, Robert Welch, founder of the John Birch Society, claimed that Roosevelt's action had saved the communist regime from financial collapse. Alan F. Westin, "The John Birch Society (1962)," in *The Radical Right*, 3rd ed., ed. Daniel Bell (New York: Routledge, 2017), 243.

9. "1951 Speech Kit."

10. Franklin D. Roosevelt, "Address at the Democratic State Convention, Syracuse, N.Y.," September 29, 1936, The American Presidency Project, https://www

.presidency.ucsb.edu/documents/address-the-democratic-state-convention-syracuse-ny.

11. Roosevelt.
12. Roosevelt.
13. Roosevelt.
14. "Editorial Comment of Representative Newspapers on Vote Outcome," *New York Times*, November 5, 1936, 4.
15. Michael A. Davis, *Politics as Usual: Thomas Dewey, Franklin Roosevelt, and the Wartime Presidential Campaign of 1944* (De Kalb: Northern Illinois University Press, 2014), 187.
16. Davis, 188.
17. Davis, 187–188.
18. Heather Cox Richardson, *To Make Men Free: A History of the Republican Party* (New York: Basic Books, 2021), 286.
19. Davis, *Politics as Usual*, 169.
20. Davis, 170.
21. Richard Norton Smith, *Thomas E. Dewey and His Times* (New York: Simon & Schuster, 1982), 434.
22. Robert Welch, *The Blue Book of the John Birch Society* (Boston: Western Islands Publishers, 1961), 84.
23. Welch, 84.
24. "The Issue in 1950: Communism vs. Democracy," *New Republic*, election supplement, October 9, 1950, 10.
25. Herbert Parmet, *Richard Nixon and His America* (Boston: Little, Brown, 1990), 107.
26. David Halberstam, *The Fifties* (New York: Villard Books, 1993), 57.
27. Tom Wicker, *One of Us: Richard Nixon and the American Dream* (New York: Random House, 1991), 39.
28. Robert D. Ubriaco Jr., "Bread and Butter Politics or Foreign Policy Concerns? Class versus Ethnicity in the Midwestern Polish American Community during the 1946 Congressional Elections," *Polish American Studies* 51, no. 2 (Autumn 1994): 16.
29. Eric Goldman, *The Crucial Decade—And After: America, 1945–1960* (New York: Alfred A. Knopf, 1966), 34.
30. "Earl Browder, Ex-Communist Leader, Dies at 82," *New York Times*, June 28, 1973, 50, https://www.nytimes.com/1973/06/28/archives/earl-browder-excommunist-leader-dies-at-82-doctrine-invalidated.html.
31. Otto Friedrich, "I Have Never Been a Quitter," *Time*, May 2, 1994, 45, https://content.time.com/time/subscriber/article/0,33009,980616,00.html.

32. Stephen Ambrose, *Nixon: The Education of a Politician, 1913–1962* (New York: Simon & Schuster, 1987), 136.

33. Roger Morris, *Richard Milhous Nixon: The Rise of an American Politician* (New York: Henry Holt, 1990), 332.

34. Morris, 333.

35. Ubriaco, "Bread and Butter Politics at the Factory Gate."

36. A. J. Baime, *Dewey Defeats Truman: The 1948 Election and the Battle for America's Soul* (Boston: Houghton Mifflin Harcourt, 2020), 83.

37. Baime, 83.

38. Baime, 84.

39. Baime, 84.

40. "Joseph McCarthy, Wheeling Speech, West Virginia, February 9, 1950," Ellen Herman, Department of History, University of Oregon, https://pages.uoregon.edu/eherman/teaching/texts/McCarthy_Wheeling_Speech.pdf.

41. All eighty-one names had been cleared by the Loyalty Review Board established by President Truman.

42. "Joseph McCarthy, Wheeling Speech."

43. Parmet, *Richard Nixon and His America*, 199.

44. Parmet, 199.

45. Bruce L. Felknor, *Political Mischief: Smear, Sabotage, and Reform in U.S. Elections* (New York: Praeger, 1992), 35.

46. Fred I. Greenstein, *The Hidden-Hand Presidency: Eisenhower as Leader* (New York: Basic Books, 1982), 160.

47. John Kenneth White, *Still Seeing Red: How the Cold War Shapes the New American Politics* (Boulder, CO: Westview Press, 1997), 156.

48. Carl Solberg, *Hubert Humphrey: A Biography* (New York: W. W. Norton, 1984), 158.

49. Solberg, 158.

50. Richard Gid Powers, *Not without Honor: The History of American Anticommunism* (New York: Free Press, 1995), 244.

51. Seymour Martin Lipset, *Political Man: The Social Bases of Politics* (Garden City, NY: Anchor Books, 1963), 171.

52. Halberstam, *The Fifties*, 250.

53. Michael Lind, "The Myth of Barry Goldwater," *New York Review of Books*, November 30, 1995, 24.

54. Dean Acheson, *Present at the Creation: My Years in the State Department* (New York: W. W. Norton, 1969), 364.

55. National Opinion Research Center poll, December 1–21, 1952. Text of first question: "As you know, there has been a lot of talk about communists or disloyal

people in the State Department in Washington. Do you think there is any truth to these charges, or not?" Yes, 81 percent; no, 19 percent. Text of second question: "Do you think such people have done any serious harm to our country's interests, or not?" Have, 58 percent; have not, 28 percent; don't know, 14 percent.

56. Parmet, *Richard Nixon and His America*, 237.

57. Kirk H. Porter and Donald Bruce Johnson, *National Party Platforms, 1840–1968* (Urbana: University of Illinois Press, 1970), 500.

58. Susan Eisenhower, *How Ike Led: The Principles behind Eisenhower's Biggest Decisions* (New York: Thomas Dunne Books, 2020), 192 (in subsequent short notes, this author is cited as S. Eisenhower; all short cites to works by Dwight Eisenhower use his last name, with no initial).

59. Robert A. Divine, *Foreign Policy and U.S. Presidential Elections, 1952–1960* (New York: New Viewpoints, 1974), 35.

60. Stephen Ambrose, *Eisenhower: Soldier and President* (New York: Simon & Schuster, 1990), 269, 276, 282.

61. Ambrose, 283.

62. Ambrose, 284.

63. Divine, *Foreign Policy and U.S. Presidential Elections*, 60.

64. S. Eisenhower, *How Ike Led*, 183.

65. S. Eisenhower, 184.

66. S. Eisenhower, 191.

67. Greenstein, *Hidden-Hand Presidency*, 169.

68. Greenstein, 170.

69. S. Eisenhower, *How Ike Led*, 192.

70. S. Eisenhower, 189.

71. Greenstein, *Hidden-Hand Presidency*, 218.

72. Greenstein, 218.

73. See W. H. Lawrence, "Truman Condemns Brownell Charges," *New York Times*, November 17, 1953, 1. In a November 6, 1953, speech, Attorney General Herbert Brownell said of Truman's assistant Treasury secretary, Harry Dexter White: "Harry Dexter White was known to be a Communist spy by the very people who appointed him to the most sensitive and important position he ever held in Government service." In 1948, White was called to testify before the House Committee on Un-American Activities; he died later that year.

74. "Text of Address by Truman Explaining to Nation His Actions in the White Case," *New York Times*, November 17, 1953, 26.

75. Greenstein, *Hidden-Hand Presidency*, 194.

76. Dwight D. Eisenhower, *Mandate for Change: The White House Years, 1953–1956* (New York: Signet Books, 1963), 383. Brownell told Eisenhower that Harry Dexter White was a Russian spy whose activities were "reported in detail by the

FBI." Eisenhower told Brownell that "as a responsible official of the government" he had to make the decision whether to report this, adding: "If he felt that it was his duty to review this case in public, he should do so on a purely factual basis." Eisenhower, 383.

77. Years later, long after Cohn had died, Trump often wondered aloud, "Where's my Roy Cohn?" Michael S. Schmidt, "Obstruction Inquiry Shows Trump's Struggle to Keep Grip on Russia Investigation," *New York Times*, January 4, 2018, https://www.nytimes.com/2018/01/04/us/politics/trump-sessions-russia-mcgahn.html.

78. White, *Still Seeing Red*, 312.

79. White, 117.

80. Nancy Beck Young, *Two Suns of the Southwest: Lyndon Johnson, Barry Goldwater, and the 1964 Battle between Liberalism and Conservatism* (Lawrence: University Press of Kansas, 2019), 67.

81. Greenstein, *Hidden-Hand Presidency*, 189.

82. Greenstein, 195.

83. Greenstein, 200.

84. Greenstein, 186.

85. Corn, *American Psychosis*, 48.

86. Celine Castronuovo, "Cheney on Trump: 'I Will Do Everything I Can' to Keep Him away from the White House," *The Hill*, May 12, 2021, https://thehill.com/homenews/house/553063-cheney-on-trump-i-will-do-everything-i-can-to-make-sure-he-gets-nowhere-near/.

87. Corn, *American Psychosis*, 48.

88. Corn, 48.

89. Corn, 49.

90. S. Eisenhower, *How Ike Led*, 200.

91. The eleven participants at the meeting were William J. Grede, a former National Association of Manufacturers president and former chair of the Wisconsin Republican Party; Laurence E. Bunker, a former aide to Douglas MacArthur; T. Coleman Andrews, a former IRS commissioner in the Eisenhower administration; Ernest G. Swigert, a former president of the National Association of Manufacturers; W. B. McMillan, president of the Hussmann Refrigerator Company of St. Louis; Fred Koch, president of the Rock Island Oil and Refinery Company, which later became Koch Industries; Revilo P. Oliver, professor at the University of Illinois; Louis Ruthenbury, board chair of the Servel Corporation; William R. Kent, a Milwaukee businessman; Fitzhugh Scott, president of a Milwaukee architectural firm; and Robert Stoddard, chair of the *Worcester Telegram and Gazette*. Edward H. Miller, *A Conspiratorial Life: Robert Welch, the John Birch Society, and the Revolution of American Conservatism* (Chicago: University of Chicago Press,

2021), 193; Matthew Dallek, *Birchers: How the John Birch Society Radicalized the American Right* (New York: Basic Books, 2022), 21. Roger Stone once told an interviewer that Donald Trump's father, Fred Trump, contributed to the John Birch Society and was a friend of Robert Welch. Mann, "The Birchers and the Trumpers," 36.

92. Welch, *Blue Book of the John Birch Society*, 19.
93. Dallek, *Birchers*, 35.
94. Welch, *Blue Book of the John Birch Society*, xv, 12.
95. Dallek, *Birchers*, 63, 77.
96. Welch, *Blue Book of the John Birch Society*, 112.
97. Robert Welch, *The Politician* (Belmont, MA: Belmont Publishers, privately printed for Robert Welch, 1963), 132. Russell Kirk famously refuted Welch's charge, saying, "Eisenhower is not a communist; he's a golfer." Alvin Feltzenberg, "The Inside Story of William F. Buckley's Crusade against the John Birch Society," *National Review*, June 20, 2017, https://www.nationalreview.com/2017/06/william-f-buckley-john-birch-society-history-conflict-robert-welch/.
98. Welch, *Blue Book of the John Birch* Society, 111. Welch went on to say about Nixon: "But for the dirtiest deal in American political history, participated in if not actually engineered by Richard Nixon in order to make himself vice president (and to put Warren on the Supreme Court as part of that deal), Taft would have been nominated in Chicago in 1952. It is almost certain that Taft would then have been elected president by a far greater plurality than was Eisenhower, that a grand rout of the Communists in our government and in our midst would have been started, that McCarthy would be alive today, and that we wouldn't even be in this mess that we are supposed to look to Nixon to lead us out of" (112).
99. Mann, "The Birchers and the Trumpers," 36; John S. Huntington, *Far-Right Vanguard: The Radical Roots of Modern Conservatism* (Philadelphia: University of Pennsylvania Press, 2021), 168; Westin, "The John Birch Society (1962)," 240. Some estimates place the actual membership at fifty to sixty thousand. The John Birch Society was particularly strong in the Sun Belt, especially California and Texas.
100. Dallek, *Birchers*, 51, 41. Eventually, the chapters became open to women, who became ardent supporters of Welch and the organization.
101. Stanley Mosk and Howard H. Jewell, "The Birch Phenomenon Analyzed: A Report by the California Attorney General Examines the Methods and Speculates on the Motives of the Controversial John Birch Society," *New York Times*, August 20, 1961, https://timesmachine.nytimes.com/timesmachine/1961/08/20/118049087.html?pageNumber=240; Huntington, *Far-Right Vanguard*, 160.
102. David R. Jones, "H. L. Hunt: Magnate with Mission; One of Richest Men in Nation, Oilman Aids Right Wing," *New York Times*, August 17, 1964, 1.

103. Jones.

104. John Savage, "The John Birch Society Is Back," *Politico*, July 16, 2017.

105. Savage; Huntington, *Far-Right Vanguard*, 162. Walker had labeled Harry Truman, Eleanor Roosevelt, and Dean Acheson as "definitely pink." Corn, *American Psychosis*, 64.

106. Dallek, *Birchers*, 73, 78. The military report concluded that Walker had made "derogatory remarks of a serious nature about certain prominent Americans, the American Press, and TV industry and commentators, which linked the persons and institutions with Communism and Communist influence" (73). After leaving the military, Walker toured the country and gave speeches endorsing Welch and the John Birch Society. Mann, "The Birchers and the Trumpers," 36.

107. Theo Zenou, "A 1955 Book on Right Wing Extremists Predicted the January 6 Attack," *Washington Post*, June 11, 2022, https://www.washingtonpost.com/history/2022/06/11/radical-right-extremism-bell-hofstadter/.

108. Corn, *American Psychosis*, 65.

109. Dallek, *Birchers*, 101.

110. Eric Trickey, "Long before QAnon, Ronald Reagan and the GOP Purged John Birch Extremists from the Party," *Washington Post*, January 15, 2021, https://www.washingtonpost.com/history/2021/01/15/john-birch-society-qanon-reagan-republicans-goldwater/; Mann, "The Birchers and the Trumpers," 37. Robert Welch donated $2,000 to Goldwater's 1958 Senate campaign and once said of him, "I'd love to see him president of the United States." Huntington, *Far-Right Vanguard*, 147.

111. Young, *Two Suns of the Southwest*, 71.

112. Trickey, "Long before QAnon." Goldwater also blamed the "radical press, the radical left" for labeling the Birchers as "conservative." Young, *Two Suns of the Southwest*, 67.

113. Lou Cannon, *Governor Reagan* (New York: Public Affairs, 2003), 153. Reagan was aware of the animus the Birchers had toward Richard Nixon's unsuccessful 1962 gubernatorial campaign and did not want to alienate members of the organization. Reagan also labeled Welch's accusations against Eisenhower "utterly reprehensible" and stated he would not seek assistance from "any blocs or groups." The *Des Moines Register* noted, "The record now is sufficiently confused so that it is probably difficult to know just what the relationship between Reagan and the Birch Society leaders really is." Corn, *American Psychosis*, 81.

114. Welch, *Blue Book of the John Birch Society*, xiv.

115. Welch, 19–20.

116. Welch, 23.

117. Welch, 28.

118. Welch, 49.

119. Welch, 127.

120. Welch, 127.

121. Welch, 115. The *Literary Gazette of Moscow* cited this virulent anticommunism as a sign that Lenin's prophecy was coming to pass: "Lenin said that the most ardent foes of communism will eventually become frightened and suspicious of anybody who does not agree with them." The *Gazette* called Welch an "unexpectedly new supporter." Mosk and Jewell, "The Birch Phenomenon Analyzed."

122. Welch, *Blue Book of the John Birch Society*, 130.

123. Savage, "The John Birch Society Is Back."

124. Savage.

125. Savage.

126. WABC News, "Danger on the Right? The John Birch Society," October 1964, YouTube, https://www.youtube.com/watch?v=nWuELwU5UIo&t=1638s.

127. Dallek, *Birchers*, 280.

128. Welch, *Blue Book of the John Birch Society*, 95.

129. Welch, 96.

130. Welch, 146, 147.

131. Joseph E. Persico, *The Imperial Rockefeller: A Biography of Nelson A. Rockefeller* (New York: Simon & Schuster, 1982), 201.

132. Theodore H. White, *The Making of the President, 1960* (New York: New American Library, 1961), 229.

133. Barry M. Goldwater, *Conscience of a Conservative* (New York: Victor Publishing, 1960), 9.

134. Barry Goldwater, "1960 Republican Convention Address," July 25, 1960, C-SPAN, https://www.c-span.org/video/?4009-1/1960-republican-convention-address.

135. Young, *Two Suns of the Southwest*, 66.

136. Huntington, *Far-Right Vanguard*, 150.

137. Theodore H. White, *The Making of the President, 1964* (New York: Atheneum, 1965), 93. Goldwater supported Nixon, warning against a Kennedy-led "Armageddon." Huntington, *Far-Right Vanguard*, 151.

138. Nixon, in part, blamed his 1962 loss on the John Birch Society. Nixon defeated a member of the John Birch Society in the Republican primary and called upon Republicans to "repudiate once and for all Robert Welch and those who accept his viewpoints." California's Birchers refused to vote for Nixon. Mann, "The Birchers and the Trumpers," 37.

139. White, *Making of the President, 1964*, 208.

140. Dallek, *Birchers*, 127.

141. Dallek, 127.

142. White, *Making of the President, 1964*, 213.

143. Barry Goldwater, acceptance speech, Republican National Convention, San Francisco, July 17, 1964. Nelson Rockefeller called Goldwater's speech "dangerous, irresponsible, and frightening." Huntington, *Far-Right Vanguard*, 172. James Mann writes that Goldwater's famous declaration "can be read as an apologia for the Birch Society." Mann, "The Birchers and the Trumpers," 37.

144. Matthew Dallek, "The Conservative Sixties," *The Atlantic*, December 1995.

145. White, *Making of the President, 1964*, 228.

146. Aaron B. Wildavsky, "The Goldwater Phenomenon: Purists, Politicians, and the Two-Party System," in *The American Party Process: Readings and Comments*, ed. Norman L. Zucker (New York: Dodd Mead, 1968), 446.

147. Wildavsky, 445.

148. White, *Making of the President, 1964*, 210.

149. White, 210.

150. Richard Hofstadter, "The Paranoid Style in American Politics," *Harper's*, November 1964.

151. Hofstadter.

152. Dallek, *Birchers*, 189.

153. For more on this point, see Ken Hughes, "A Rough Guide to Richard Nixon's Conspiracy Theories," Miller Center, accessed April 17, 2002, https://millercenter.org/the-presidency/educational-resources/a-rough-guide-to-richard-nixon-s-conspiracy-theories. In 1962, Nixon told speechwriter Stephen Hess that he "could not look myself in the mirror" if he endorsed the Birchers. Dallek, *Birchers*, 92.

154. "Nixon's the One Still Preoccupied with Enemies," *New York Times*, December 3, 2008, https://www.nytimes.com/2008/12/03/world/americas/03iht-nixon.1.18356903.html.

155. Irving Kristol, "New Left, New Right," *Public Interest*, Fall 1966, 5.

156. Daniel Patrick Moynihan, "The Paranoid Style in American Politics Revisited," *Public Interest*, Fall 1985, 117.

157. Moynihan, 126.

158. Hofstadter, "The Paranoid Style in American Politics."

159. Publius Decius Mus, "The Flight 93 Election," *Claremont Review of Books*, September 5, 2016, https://claremontreviewofbooks.com/digital/the-flight-93-election/. Publius Decius Mus is the pseudonym used by Richard Anton.

160. Donald Trump, "Inaugural Address," January 20, 2017, The American

Presidency Project, https://www.presidency.ucsb.edu/documents/inaugural-address-14.

161. *The Economist*/YouGov poll, March 26–29, 2022. Text of question: "Do you think the following statements are true or not true? Regardless of who is officially in charge of the government and other organizations, there is a single group of people who secretly control events and rule the world together." 2020 Trump voters: Definitely true, 16 percent; probably true, 41 percent; probably false, 18 percent; definitely false, 10 percent; not sure, 15 percent.

162. Aaron Blake, "The Final Clinton-Trump Debate Transcript Annotated," *Washington Post*, October 19, 2016.

163. Blake.

164. Donald Trump, "Election Night Remarks, 2020," November 4, 2020, YouTube, https://www.youtube.com/watch?v=zbgk8fdAWdQ.

165. *USA Today* Staff, "Read the Full Transcript from the First Presidential Debate between Joe Biden and Donald Trump," *USA Today*, September 30, 2020, https://www.usatoday.com/story/news/politics/elections/2020/09/30/presidential-debate-read-full-transcript-first-debate/3587462001/.

166. Claes Ryn, "Memorandum: How the 2020 Election Could Have Been Stolen," *American Conservative*, January 5, 2021, https://www.theamericanconservative.com/the-2020-election-what-happened-a-political-scientists-memorandum/.

167. David Frum, "Dinesh D'Souza and the Decline of Conservatism," *The Atlantic*, August 12, 2018, https://www.theatlantic.com/ideas/archive/2018/08/dinesh-dsouza-is-making-a-comeback/567233/.

168. Ryan Nobles, Annie Grayer, Zachary Cohen, and Jamie Gangel, "First on CNN: January 6 Committee Has Text Messages between Ginni Thomas and Mark Meadows," March 25, 2022, https://www.cnn.com/2022/03/24/politics/ginni-thomas-mark-meadows-text-messages/index.html.

169. Nobles et al.

170. Nobles et al.

171. Mann, "The Birchers and the Trumpers," 36.

172. Dallek, *Birchers*, 55.

173. Trickey, "Long before QAnon."

174. Alan Felzenberg, "The Inside Story of William F. Buckley's Crusade against the John Birch Society," *National Review*, June 20, 2017, https://www.nationalreview.com/2017/06/william-f-buckley-john-birch-society-history-conflict-robert-welch/.

175. Trickey, "Long before QAnon." See also William F. Buckley, "Goldwater, the John Birch Society, and Me," *Commentary*, March 2008, https://www.commentary.org/articles/william-buckley-jr/goldwater-the-john-birch-society-and

-me/#. Matthew Dallek writes that Buckley was worried about maintaining subscriptions and support for *National Review*, prompting him to single out Robert Welch for criticism and attempting to separate him from his supporters. Dallek, *Birchers*, 13.

176. Daniel Allott, *On the Road in Trump's America: A Journey into the Heart of a Divided Nation* (Alexandria, VA: Republic Book Publishers, 2020), 20.

177. Allott, 10.

178. Mike Rothschild, *The Storm Is Upon Us: How QAnon Became a Movement, Cult, and Conspiracy Theory of Everything* (Brooklyn: Melville House, 2021), xv.

179. Rothschild, 3.

180. Rothschild, 15–16.

181. Rothschild, 45.

182. Rothschild, xiv.

183. Rothschild, 10.

184. Rothschild, 30; Isaac Arnsdorf, "How a QAnon Splinter Group Became a Feature of Trump Rallies," *Washington Post*, September 26, 2022, https://www.washingtonpost.com/politics/2022/09/26/trump-qanon-rallies-negative48/.

185. Rothschild, *Storm Is Upon Us*, xiv.

186. Arnsdorf, "How a QAnon Splinter Group Became a Feature of Trump Rallies."

187. Robert Tracinski, "Did the John Birch Society Win in the End?," *The Bulwark*, April 13, 2022.

188. John Aloysius Farrell, "Christie, Nixon and the Case for Revenge Politics," *Politico*, January 10, 2014, https://www.politico.com/magazine/story/2014/01/chris-christie-was-right-102045/.

189. Roderick P. Hart, "Donald Trump and the Return of the Paranoid Style," *Presidential Studies Quarterly* 50, no. 2 (June 2020): 348.

190. Chris Moody and Kristen Holmes, "Donald Trump's History of Suggesting Obama Is a Muslim," CNN, September 18, 2015, https://www.cnn.com/2015/09/18/politics/trump-obama-muslim-birther/index.html.

191. Gregory Krieg, "Fourteen of Trump's Most Outrageous 'Birther' Claims—Half from 2011," CNN, September 16, 2016. https://www.cnn.com/2016/09/09/politics/donald-trump-birther. Accessed October 5, 2022. In 2011, Jerome R. Corsi, echoing Trump, published a book titled *Where's the Birth Certificate? The Case That Barack Obama Is Not Eligible to Be President* (Washington, DC: WND Books, 2011).

192. Corn, *American Psychosis*, 276.

193. Maggie Haberman, *Confidence Man: The Making of Donald Trump and the Breaking of America* (New York: Penguin Press, 2022), 188.

194. Moody and Holmes, "Donald Trump's History of Suggesting Obama Is a Muslim."

195. David Maraniss points out that the nurses who helped deliver Obama remembered it well, since Obama's mother was named Stanley Ann Dunham, prompting them to exclaim, "Stanley had a baby!" David Maraniss, *Barack Obama: The Story* (New York: Simon & Schuster, 2012), 166.

196. Josh Clinton and Carrie Roush, "Poll: Persistent Partisan Divide over 'Birther' Question," NBC News, August 10, 2016.

197. Sophie Tatum and Jim Acosta, "Report: Trump Continues to Question Obama's Birth Certificate," CNN, November 29, 2017.

198. Haberman, *Confidence Man*, 185.

199. Moody and Holmes, "Donald Trump's History of Suggesting Obama Is a Muslim."

200. CNN/ORC International poll, September 4–8, 2015. Text of question: "Do you happen to know what religion Barack Obama is? Is he Protestant, Catholic, Jewish, Mormon, Muslim, something else, or not religious?" Republicans: Protestant/Christian, 28 percent; Catholic, 2 percent; Jewish, less than 1 percent; Mormon/LDS, less than 1 percent; Muslim/Islam/Islamic, 43 percent; something else, 1 percent; not religious, 15 percent; no opinion, 10 percent.

201. Moody and Holmes, "Donald Trump's History of Suggesting Obama Is a Muslim."

202. Moody and Holmes.

203. Donald Trump, "Former President Trump Announces 2024 Presidential Bid," Mar-a-Lago, Palm Beach, Florida, November 15, 2022, YouTube, https://www.youtube.com/watch?v=8tSYwJ1_htE.

204. Hart, "Donald Trump and the Return of the Paranoid Style," 362.

205. Hart, 362.

206. Hart, 363.

207. *The Economist*/YouGov poll, March 26–29, 2022, https://docs.cdn.yougov.com/3ixnq9227y/econTabReport.pdf. Text of question: "Do you think the following statements are true or not true? Top Democrats are involved in elite child sex-trafficking rings." Trump voters: Definitely true, 26 percent; probably true, 27 percent; probably false, 5 percent; definitely false, 3 percent; not sure, 39 percent.

208. Colby Itkowitz, "Grooming Claims Part of Anti-LGBTQ Push in GOP," *Washington Post*, April 15, 2022, A-1.

209. Itkowitz.

210. John Wagner and Mariana Alfaro, "The Latest: Stefanik, Number 3 House Republican, Appears to Allude to Conspiracy Theory," *Washington Post*, May 13, 2022, https://www.washingtonpost.com/politics/2022/05/13/trump-pence-kemp-georgia-biden/#link-E6A4KLTRRFFIVGTJQHKCNEBJAM; see also

Elise Stefanik, Twitter, May 13, 2022, 1:52 p.m., https://twitter.com/elisestefanik/status/1525187193702055940?lang=en.

211. "Immigration Attitudes and Conspiratorial Thinkers: A Study Issued on the 10th Anniversary of the Associated Press–NORC Center for Public Affairs Research," May 2022, The Associated Press–NORC Center for Public Affairs Research, https://apnorc.org/wp-content/uploads/2022/05/Immigration-Report_V15.pdf.

212. Barack Obama, "Disinformation Is a Threat to Our Democracy," *Medium*, April 21, 2022, https://barackobama.medium.com/my-remarks-on-disinformation-at-stanford-7d7af7ba28af.

213. University of Massachusetts Amherst poll, December 14–20, 2021. Text of question: "Do you believe that Joe Biden's election in 2020 was legitimate or not legitimate?" Republicans: Definitely legitimate, 6 percent; probably legitimate, 15 percent; probably not legitimate, 25 percent; definitely not legitimate, 46 percent; not sure, 6 percent. "Toplines and Crosstabs December 2021 National Poll: Presidential Election & Jan 6th Insurrection at the US Capitol," December 28, 2021, Department of Political Science, University of Massachusetts Amherst, https://polsci.umass.edu/toplines-and-crosstabs-december-2021-national-poll-presidential-election-jan-6th-insurrection-us.

214. Obama, "Disinformation Is a Threat to Our Democracy."

215. Obama.

216. Jonathan Haidt, "After Babel: How Social Media Dissolved the Mortar of Society and Made America Stupid," *The Atlantic*, May 2022, 62.

217. Committee on Political Parties, *Toward a More Responsible Two-Party System* (New York: Rinehart, 1950).

218. Politico: Congress Minutes, "Nancy Pelosi Offered Perhaps Some Surprising Advice to Republicans," April 19, 2022, https://www.politico.com/minutes/congress/04-19-2022/pelosis-words-to-gop/.

219. Haidt, "After Babel," 59.

220. Obama, "Disinformation Is a Threat to Our Democracy."

221. Miller, *Conspiratorial Life*, 1.

CHAPTER FIVE: A PARTY TRANSFORMED

1. Heather Cox Richardson, *How the South Won the Civil War: Oligarchy, Democracy, and the Continuing Fight for the Soul of America* (New York: Oxford University Press, 2022), 201. When Jackson referred to "property," he clearly meant the slaves.

2. Heather Cox Richardson, *To Make Men Free: A History of the Republican Party* (New York: Basic Books, 2014).

3. Heather Cox Richardson, "Letters from an American," Substack, May 15, 2022, https://heathercoxrichardson.substack.com/p/may-15-2022.

4. Everett Carll Ladd with Charles D. Hadley, *Transformations of the American Party System: Political Coalitions from the New Deal to the 1970s* (New York: W. W. Norton, 1975), 57.

5. Richardson, "Letters from an American," May 15, 2022.

6. Theodore G. Bilbo, *Separation or Mongrelization: Take Your Choice* (Poplarville, MS: Dream House Publishing, 1947), 74.

7. *Dred Scott v. Sandford*, 60 U.S. 393 (1856), Justia, U.S. Supreme Court, https://supreme.justia.com/cases/federal/us/60/393/#tab-opinion-1964281.

8. Cited in William Rehnquist, "My Life in Law," Speech at Duke University Law School, April 13, 2002, Supreme Court of the United States, https://www.supremecourt.gov/publicinfo/speeches/viewspeech/sp_04-13-02.

9. Kirk H. Porter and Donald Bruce Johnson, *National Party Platforms, 1840–1968* (Urbana: University of Illinois Press, 1970), 39.

10. From 1875 to 1881, Democrats held majorities in the House of Representatives, and they held the Senate from 1879 to 1881. Republicans had the presidency from 1868 to 1884 until Grover Cleveland was elected that year.

11. Richardson, "Letters from an American," May 15, 2022.

12. Richardson.

13. Andrew Glass, "Grant Signs KKK Act into Law, April 20, 1871," *Politico*, April 19, 2019, https://www.politico.com/story/2019/04/20/this-day-in-politics-april-20-1279376.

14. "The Enforcement Acts of 1870 and 1871," US Senate, accessed June 20, 2022, https://www.senate.gov/artandhistory/history/common/generic/EnforcementActs.htm#:~:text=In%20response%2C%20Congress%20passed%20a,force%20to%20protect%20African%20Americans. Grant and the Republican Party had been slower to support African American suffrage in the North. The 1868 Republican platform read, "The guaranty by Congress of equal suffrage to all loyal men at the South was demanded by every consideration of public safety, of gratitude, and of justice, and must be maintained; while the question of suffrage in all the loyal States properly belongs to the people of those states." Porter and Johnson, *National Party Platforms*, 39.

15. Bilbo, *Separation or Mongrelization*, 28.

16. Joshua Miller, "The Politics of Race and the Development of the Law-and-Order President, 1790–1974" (PhD diss., Catholic University of America, 2019), 97.

17. Eric Foner, *A Short History of Reconstruction, 1863–1871* (New York: Harper & Row, 1990), 184.

18. Richardson, "Letters from an American," May 15, 2022. Richardson adds

that southerners feared Black men would "butcher white folks and take all their possessions for themselves." Richardson, *How the South Won the Civil War*, xix.

19. Eric Holder with Sam Koppelman, *Our Unfinished March: The Violent Past and Imperiled Future of the Vote—A History, A Crisis, A Plan* (New York: Our World, 2022), 60.

20. It took nearly a century to ratify the Twenty-Fourth Amendment, which repealed the poll tax.

21. Holder with Koppelman, *Our Unfinished March*, 60.

22. Stefan Lorant, *The Presidency* (New York: Macmillan, 1951), 333. After the election, Tilden said, "I prefer four years of Hayes' administration to four years of civil war" (336).

23. Richardson, "Letters from an American," May 15, 2022.

24. Richardson.

25. Richardson.

26. Milton Viorst, *Fall from Grace* (New York: Simon & Schuster, 1968), 64.

27. Richardson, *To Make Men Free*, 175.

28. Porter and Johnson, *National Party Platforms*, 80.

29. Porter and Johnson, 80.

30. Porter and Johnson, 80.

31. Benjamin Harrison, "Letter Accepting the Presidential Nomination," September 11, 1888, The American Presidency Project, https://www.presidency.ucsb.edu/documents/letter-accepting-the-presidential-nomination-0.

32. Benjamin Harrison, "Inaugural Address," March 4, 1889, https://www.presidency.ucsb.edu/documents/inaugural-address-41.

33. Benjamin Harrison, "First Annual Message," December 3, 1889, https://www.presidency.ucsb.edu/documents/first-annual-message-14.

34. Harrison.

35. Benjamin Harrison, "Second Annual Message," December 1, 1890, https://www.presidency.ucsb.edu/documents/second-annual-message-14.

36. Harrison.

37. Richardson, *To Make Men Free*, 177.

38. Heather Cox Richardson also notes that western Republicans joined southern Democrats to keep nonwhites from voting. Richardson, *How the South Won the Civil War*, 101.

39. Malcolm Moos, *The Republicans: A History of Their Party* (New York: Random House, 1956), 176.

40. Richardson, *To Make Men Free*, 174.

41. Richardson, 174. Richardson notes that Republicans were in such a hurry to bring Idaho into the union that they bypassed the usual procedures and called

for volunteers to write a state constitution. Opponents noted that New Mexico and Arizona had far more people than Wyoming and Idaho, and that the admission of these states was an attempt by the GOP to manipulate election outcomes. Richardson, *How the South Won the Civil War*, 101.

42. Richardson, *To Make Men Free*, 176. Another metric shows that the nine new Pacific and Rocky Mountain states had fewer than three million people but eighteen senators, while the six New England states with five million people had only twelve. Richardson, *How the South Won the Civil War*, 101.

43. Richardson, *How the South Won the Civil War*, 100.

44. George F. Hoar, "Are the Republicans In to Stay?," *North American Review* 149, no. 396 (November 1889): 621.

45. Porter and Johnson, *National Party Platforms*, 106.

46. Michael Kazin, *The Populist Persuasion: An American History* (Ithaca, NY: Cornell University Press, 2017), 40.

47. Kazin, xii.

48. A. James Reichley, *The Life of the Parties: A History of American Political Parties* (New York: Free Press, 1992), 230.

49. "President to See Movies," *Washington Star*, February 18, 1915, https://www.newspapers.com/image/332036937/?clipping_id=30174748&fcfToken=eyJhbGciOiJIUzI1NiIsInR5cCI6IkpXVCJ9.eyJmcmVlLXZpZXctaWQiOjMzMjAzNjkzNywiaWFoIjoxNjY2OTY1NTY5LCJleHAiOjE2NjcwNTE5Njl9.myF4Tac9fCs_lUANaho5M3xrru6HASt_SSatYK_pWVo.

50. Bilbo, *Separation or Mongrelization*, 3, 4.

51. Bilbo, 4.

52. Martha M. Hamilton and Aaron Wiener, "The Roots of the 'Great Replacement Theory' Believed to Fuel Buffalo Suspect," *Washington Post*, May 15, 2022, https://www.washingtonpost.com/history/2022/05/15/great-replacement-theory-buffalo-bilbo/.

53. Bilbo, *Separation or Mongrelization*, 40.

54. Bilbo, 103.

55. Hamilton and Wiener, "The Roots of the 'Great Replacement Theory' Believed to Fuel Buffalo Suspect."

56. Ladd with Hadley, *Transformations of the American Party System*, 58.

57. African Americans were becoming an important Democratic constituency, and in 1934 Arthur Mitchell of Chicago became the first African American Democrat to win a seat in Congress.

58. Hubert H. Humphrey, "1948 Democratic National Convention Address," Philadelphia, Pennsylvania, July 14, 1948, American Rhetoric, https://www.americanrhetoric.com/speeches/huberthumphey1948dnc.html.

59. They were Alabama, Louisiana, Mississippi, and South Carolina.

60. Jon Meacham, *His Truth Is Marching On: John Lewis and the Power of Hope* (New York: Random House, 2020), 154.

61. Meacham, 169.

62. Richardson, *How the South Won the Civil War*, xiii–xiv.

63. James Mann, "The Birchers and the Trumpers," *New York Review of Books*, June 23, 2022, 36.

64. Michael W. Combs and Gwendolyn M. Combs, "Revisiting *Brown v. Board of Education*: A Cultural, Historical-Legal, and Political Perspective," Management Department Faculty Publications 48, University of Nebraska–Lincoln, 653, accessed June 21, 2022, https://digitalcommons.unl.edu/cgi/viewcontent.cgi?article=1047&context=managementfacpub.

65. Dwight D. Eisenhower, *Waging Peace, 1956–1961* (Garden City, NY: Doubleday, 1965), 173.

66. Eisenhower, 173.

67. Richardson, *How the South Won the Civil War*, 161.

68. John F. Kennedy, "Radio and Television Report to the American People on Civil Rights," June 11, 1963, The American Presidency Project, https://www.presidency.ucsb.edu/documents/radio-and-television-report-the-american-people-civil-rights.

69. Lyndon B. Johnson, "Special Message to the Congress: The American Promise," March 15, 1965, The American Presidency Project, https://www.presidency.ucsb.edu/documents/special-message-the-congress-the-american-promise. The full title of the 1965 law was "An Act to enforce the fifteenth amendment to the Constitution, and for other purposes." Heather Cox Richardson, "Letters from an American," Substack, August 6, 2022, https://heathercoxrichardson.substack.com/p/august-6-2022.

70. The nineteen Senate no votes were Harry Byrd (D-VA), James Eastland (D-MS), Allen Ellender (D-LA), Sam Ervin (D-NC), Joseph Hill (D-AL), Spessard Holland (D-FL), Benjamin Jordan (D-NC), Russell Long (D-LA), John McClellan (D-AR), Willis Robertson (D-VA), Donald Russell (D-SC), Richard Russell (D-LA), George Smathers (D-FL), John Sparkman (D-AL), John Stennis (D-MS), Herman Talmadge (D-GA), Strom Thurmond (R-SC), John Tower (R-TX), and J. William Fulbright (D-AR).

71. Lyndon B. Johnson, "Remarks in the Capitol Rotunda at the Signing of the Voting Rights Act," August 6, 1965, The American Presidency Project, https://www.presidency.ucsb.edu/documents/remarks-the-capitol-rotunda-the-signing-the-voting-rights-act. Like the 1890 Lodge Bill, the Voting Rights Act authorized the court appointment of federal "examiners" to oversee elections.

72. Colbert I. King, "The House Debates Voting Rights, Sounding Like the Days of Jim Crow," *Washington Post*, August 28, 2021, A-19.

73. King.

74. "Text of Governor Rockefeller's Statement Criticizing 'Radical Right' of the Republican Party," *New York Times*, July 15, 1963, https://www.nytimes.com/1963/07/15/archives/text-of-rockefellers-statement-criticizing-radical-right-of-the.html.

75. Combs and Combs, "Revisiting *Brown v. Board of Education*," 653.

76. "Jackie Robinson Explains Why He Cannot Support Nixon in 1968," September 17, 1968, Seth Kaller Inc., https://www.sethkaller.com/item/2134-25679-Jackie-Robinson-Explains-Why-He-Cannot-Support-Nixon-in-1968. In 1964, Robinson left the Republican convention and refused to back Barry Goldwater, saying: "A new breed of Republicans has taken over the GOP. It is a new breed which is seeking to sell to Americans a doctrine which is as old as mankind—the doctrine of racial division, the doctrine of racial prejudice, the doctrine of white supremacy." Robinson added that he now knew "how it felt to be a Jew in Hitler's Germany." Richardson, *How the South Won the Civil War*, 165.

77. The only exception to Republican presidential majorities occurred in 1976, when Jimmy Carter won every state in the Old Confederacy except Virginia.

78. "Ronald Reagan's 1980 Neshoba County Fair Speech," *Neshoba Democrat*, April 8, 2021, https://neshobademocrat.com/stories/ronald-reagans-1980-neshoba-county-fair-speech,49123; Richardson, *How the South Won the Civil War*, 178. Reagan's pollster, Richard Wirthlin, advised Reagan not to give the speech, saying he would be labeled an "insensitive racist." Richard Wirthlin with Wynton C. Hall, *The Greatest Communicator: What Ronald Reagan Taught Me about Politics, Leadership, and Life* (Hoboken, NJ: John Wiley, 2004), 68.

79. The states supporting Abraham Lincoln in 1860 and Barack Obama in 2008 were California, Connecticut, Illinois, Indiana, Iowa, Maine, Massachusetts, Minnesota, New Hampshire, New York, Ohio, Oregon, Pennsylvania, Rhode Island, Vermont, and Wisconsin.

80. Roper Center for Public Opinion Research, 1980 exit polls, accessed June 21, 2022, https://ropercenter.cornell.edu/how-groups-voted-1980.

81. Roper Center for Public Opinion Research, 1980 exit polls.

82. Exit polls, 2020, CNN Politics, accessed June 21, 2022, https://www.cnn.com/election/2020/exit-polls/president/national-results. Biden's support from African Americans totaled 87 percent; Hispanics, 65 percent; Asians, 61 percent.

83. Ben J. Wattenberg, *The Birth Dearth: What Happens When People in Free Countries Don't Have Enough Babies?* (New York: Pharos Books, 1988); William H. Frey, "The U.S. Will Become 'Minority White' in 2045, Census Projects, Brookings, March 14, 2018, https://www.brookings.edu/blog/the-avenue/2018/03/14/the-us-will-become-minority-white-in-2045-census-projects/.

84. Mark Silva, "GOP Chairman: 'Message Received,'" *Washington Post*, No-

vember 9, 2006, A-1; Edward Gillespie, "Populists Beware: The GOP Must Not Become an Anti-immigrant Party," *Wall Street Journal*, April 2, 2006, A-6.

85. Republican National Committee, "Growth and Opportunity Project," 2013, 15, accessed June 21, 2022, https://s3.documentcloud.org/documents/624293/republican-national-committees-growth-and.pdf.

86. Christopher S. Parker and Matt A. Barreto, *Change They Can't Believe In: The Tea Party and Reactionary Politics in America* (Princeton, NJ: Princeton University Press, 2013), 37.

87. Rachel M. Blum, *How the Tea Party Captured the GOP: Insurgent Factions in American Politics* (Chicago: University of Chicago Press, 2020), 101.

88. Parker and Barreto, *Change They Can't Believe In*, 21.

89. Parker and Barreto, 37.

90. Parker and Barreto, 34.

91. Theda Skocpol and Vanessa Williamson, *The Tea Party and the Remaking of Republican Conservatism* (New York: Oxford University Press, 2016), 199.

92. Skocpol and Williamson, 199.

93. Aaron Blake, "Origins of Right's Rising Embrace of 'Replacement Theory,'" *Washington Post*, May 17, 2022, A-10.

94. Porter and Johnson, *National Party Platforms*, 33.

95. "What Charlottesville Changed," *Politico*, August 12, 2018, https://www.politico.com/magazine/story/2018/08/12/charlottesville-anniversary-supremacists-protests-dc-virginia-219353/.

96. Joe Biden, "'We Are Living Through a Battle for the Soul of This Nation,'" *The Atlantic*, August 27, 2017, https://www.theatlantic.com/politics/archive/2017/08/joe-biden-after-charlottesville/538128/.

97. Biden.

98. Joe Biden, "Remarks by President Biden and First Lady Biden Honoring the Lives Lost in Buffalo, New York and Calling on All Americans to Condemn White Supremacy," May 17, 2022, The White House, https://www.whitehouse.gov/briefing-room/speeches-remarks/2022/05/17/remarks-by-president-biden-and-first-lady-biden-honoring-the-lives-lost-in-buffalo-new-york-and-calling-on-all-americans-to-condemn-white-supremacy/.

99. Biden.

100. "President Donald Trump on Charlottesville: You Had Very Fine People on Both Sides," YouTube, accessed June 20, 2022, https://www.youtube.com/watch?v=JmaZR8E12bs.

101. Rosie Gray, "'Really Proud of Him': Alt-Right Leaders Praise Trump's Comments," *The Atlantic*, August 15, 2017, https://www.theatlantic.com/politics/archive/2017/08/really-proud-of-him-richard-spencer-and-alt-right-leaders-praise-trumps-comments/537039/.

102. Biden, "'We Are Living Through a Battle for the Soul of This Nation.'"
103. Biden.
104. Kazin, *Populist Persuasion*, xiii.
105. Kazin, xiii–xiv.
106. Daniel A. Cox, "After the Ballots Are Counted: Conspiracies, Political Violence, and American Exceptionalism," American Enterprise Institute, February 11, 2021, https://www.americansurveycenter.org/research/after-the-ballots-are-counted-conspiracies-political-violence-and-american-exceptionalism/.
107. Mariana Sotomayor, "Stefanik Echoed Racist Theory Allegedly Espoused by Buffalo Suspect," *Washington Post*, May 15, 2022, https://www.washingtonpost.com/politics/2022/05/15/stefanik-buffalo-replacement/.
108. "Editorial: How Low, Ms. Stefanik?," *Albany Times Union*, September 17, 2021, https://www.timesunion.com/opinion/article/Editorial-How-low-Ms-Stefanik-16465746.php.
109. Peter Wehner, "What in the World Happened to Elise Stefanik?," *New York Times*, July 26, 2022, https://www.nytimes.com/2022/07/26/opinion/elise-stefanik-trump.html.
110. Blake, "Origins of Right's Rising Embrace of 'Replacement Theory.'"
111. Rosalind S. Helderman, "Texas GOP Endorses Far-Right Rhetoric," *Washington Post*, June 21, 2022, A-2.
112. Vaughn Hillyard, NBC reporter, Twitter, October 9, 2022, 4:14 p.m., https://twitter.com/VaughnHillyard/status/1579218776767500288.
113. Richardson, "Letters from an American," May 15, 2022.
114. "Tucker Carlson Feigned Ignorance over 'Great Replacement Theory' Despite Talking about It Often," *Politifact*, May 19, 2022, https://www.politifact.com/article/2022/may/19/tucker-carlson-feigned-ignorance-over-great-replac/.
115. Paul Farhi, "Fox, Others Have Long Embraced Racist Theory, *Washington Post*, May 16, 2022, C-1.
116. Steve Peoples, "Republican Senate Candidates Promote 'Replacement' Theory," *Associated Press*, May 17, 2022, https://apnews.com/article/2022-midterm-elections-republicans-replacement-theory-00800c89953aa58e746988ed591e7ed9.
117. Peoples.
118. Blake, "Origins of Right's Rising Embrace of 'Replacement Theory.'"
119. Yahoo News/YouGov, survey, May 19–22, 2022. Text of question: "Do you agree or disagree with the following statement: A group of people in this country are trying to replace native-born Americans with immigrants and people of color who share their political views." Trump voters: Agree, 61 percent; disagree, 22 percent; not sure, 17 percent. Biden voters: Agree, 16 percent; disagree, 71 percent; not sure, 13 percent.

120. Daniel A. Cox, "After the Ballots Are Counted: Conspiracies, Political Violence, and American Exceptionalism," American Enterprise Institute, February 11, 2021.

121. Ronald Ingelhart and Pippa Norris, "Trump and the Populist Authoritarian Parties: The Silent Revolution in Reverse," *Perspectives on Politics* 15, no. 2 (June 2017): 452.

122. Wilson Carey McWilliams, "The Old Populism vs. the New," *Commonweal*, June 2, 1995, 24.

123. Michael Lind, "Trumpism and Clintonism Are the Future," *New York Times*, April 16, 2016, https://www.nytimes.com/2016/04/17/opinion/campaign-stops/trumpism-and-clintonismare-the-future.html.

124. "Transcript: Hillary Clinton's Full Remarks in Reno, Nevada," *Politico*, August 25, 2016, https://www.politico.com/story/2016/08/transcript-hillary-clinton-alt-right-reno-227419.

125. Issac Stanley-Becker and Drew Harwell, "Suspect Was Allegedly Inspired by Racist Theory Fueling Global Carnage," *Washington Post*, May 16, 2022, A-1.

126. Stanley-Becker and Harwell.

127. Matt Zapotosky, "Charleston Church Shooter: 'I Would Like to Make It Crystal Clear, I Do Not Regret What I Did,'" *Washington Post*, January 4, 2017, https://www.washingtonpost.com/world/national-security/charleston-church-shooter-i-would-like-to-make-it-crystal-clear-i-do-not-regret-what-i-did/2017/01/04/05b0061e-d1da-11e6-a783-cd3fa950f2fd_story.html.

128. Zapotosky.

129. John Eligon, "The El Paso Screed, and the Racist Doctrine Behind It," *New York Times*, August 7, 2019; Tara Law and Josiah Bates, "El Paso Shooter Told Police He Was Targeting Mexicans," *Time*, August 9, 2019, https://time.com/5643110/el-paso-texas-mall-shooting/.

130. Michael Feola, "How 'Great Replacement' Theory Led to the Buffalo Mass Shooting," *Washington Post*, May 25, 2022.

131. Maki Becker, Ben Tsujimoto, and Jerry Zremski, "Vice President Kamala Harris Says, 'Enough Is Enough' as Buffalo Buries Last of Ten Tops Massacre Victims," *Buffalo News*, June 2, 2022, https://buffalonews.com/news/local/crime-and-courts/vp-kamala-harris-says-enough-is-enough-as-buffalo-buries-last-of-10-tops-massacre/article_8935d666-de91-11ec-b582-0b8a9ce3d90a.html.

132. Al Gore won 547,398 more votes than George W. Bush in 2000, and Hillary Clinton won an even greater majority of 2,868,524 votes over Donald Trump in 2016. Dave Leip's Atlas of U.S. Elections, accessed June 20, 2022, https://uselectionatlas.org/RESULTS/.

133. Pew Research Center poll, January 8–12, 2021. Text of question: "Thinking about the way presidents are elected in this country, would you prefer to

change the current system so that the candidate who receives the most votes wins or keep the current system so the candidate who wins the Electoral College wins?" Total: Change the current system, 55 percent; keep the current system, 43 percent. Republicans: Change the current system, 37 percent; keep the current system, 61 percent. Democrats: Change the current system, 71 percent; keep the current system, 28 percent.

134. Claes Ryn, *The New Jacobinism: Can Democracy Survive?* (Washington, DC: National Humanities Institute, 1991), 33, 35.

135. Statement of J. Michael Luttig before the United States House Select Committee on the January 6, 2021, Attack on the United States Capitol, Washington, DC, June 16, 2022, https://s3.documentcloud.org/documents/22061497/jml-final.pdf.

136. Joe Biden, "Remarks by President Biden on Protecting the Sacred Constitutional Right to Vote," Philadelphia, July 13, 2021, https://www.whitehouse.gov/briefing-room/speeches-remarks/2021/07/13/remarks-by-president-biden-on-protecting-the-sacred-constitutional-right-to-vote/.

137. Ryan Goodman, "Timeline: False Alternate Slate of Electors Scheme, Donald Trump and His Close Associates," Just Security, June 18, 2022, https://www.justsecurity.org/81939/timeline-false-alternate-slate-of-electors-scheme-donald-trump-and-his-close-associates/.

138. Aaron Blake, "The Significance of Trump's Fake Electors, Explained," *Washington Post*, June 7, 2022. If Pence had not counted the disputed electoral votes, neither Trump nor Biden would have the necessary 270 electoral votes to claim the presidency, and the alternate method of choosing a president established by the Constitution would have each of the fifty state delegations in the House cast one vote. Because Republicans controlled more state delegations, Trump would have been installed for a second term.

139. Goodman, "Timeline."

140. Goodman.

141. Goodman.

142. Goodman.

143. Goodman.

144. US District Court Central District of California Southern Division, John C. Eastman vs. Bennie G. Thompson, Select Committee to Investigate the January 6 Attack on the US Capitol, and Chapman University, Opinion issued by Judge David O. Carter, Just Security, June 7, 2022, https://www.justsecurity.org/wp-content/uploads/2022/06/january-6-clearinghouse-judge-carter-eastman-documents-order-june-7-2002.pdf.

145. United States District Court Central District of California Southern Divi-

sion, John C. Eastman vs. Bennie G. Thompson, Select Committee to Investigate the January 6 Attack on the US Capitol, and Chapman University, Opinion issued by Judge David O. Carter, March 28, 2022, 5, Courthouse News Service, https://www.courthousenews.com/wp-content/uploads/2022/03/eastman-select-committee-order.pdf.

146. United States District Court Central District of California Southern Division, March 28, 2022, 7–8.

147. United States District Court Central District of California Southern Division, March 28, 2022, 8.

148. United States District Court Central District of California Southern Division, March 28, 2022, 10.

149. United States District Court Central District of California Southern Division, March 28, 2022, 32.

150. United States District Court Central District of California Southern Division, March 28, 2022, 44.

151. James MacGregor Burns, *Cobblestone Leadership: Majority Rule, Minority Power* (Norman: University of Oklahoma Press, 1990), 29.

152. Biden, "Remarks by President Biden on Protecting the Sacred Constitutional Right to Vote."

153. Holder with Koppelman, *Our Unfinished March*, 21.

154. Nick Corasanti and Reid J. Epstein, "What Georgia's Voting Law Really Does," *New York Times*, April 2, 2021, updated August 18, 2021, https://www.nytimes.com/2021/04/02/us/politics/georgia-voting-law-annotated.html; Elise Viebeck, "A Growing Disparity in State Rules for Voting," *Washington Post*, September 7, 2021, A-1.

155. "Donald Trump: 'I Just Want to Find 11,780 Votes,'" BBC News, January 3, 2021, https://www.bbc.com/news/av/world-us-canada-55524676.

156. Dartunorro Clark, "Georgia Legislator Arrested, Pulled Out of State Capitol as Governor Signs Voting Law," NBC News, March 25, 2021, https://www.nbcnews.com/politics/politics-news/georgia-legislator-arrested-pulled-out-state-capitol-governor-signs-new-n1262120.

157. Viebeck, "A Growing Disparity in State Rules for Voting."

158. Viebeck.

159. Ben Giles, "Arizona Republicans Strip Some Power from Democratic Secretary of State," NPR, June 30, 2021, https://www.npr.org/2021/06/30/1011154122/arizona-republicans-strip-some-election-power-from-democratic-secretary-of-state. In 2022, Arizonans elected Katie Hobbs as governor and Kris Mayes as attorney general. Both are Democrats.

160. Giles.

161. Elise Viebeck, "A Growing Disparity in State Rules for Voting," *Washington Post*, September 7, 2021, A-1; Eva Ruth Moravec and Elise Viebeck, "Texas Voting Bill Heads to Governor," *Washington Post*, September 1, 2021, A-1.

162. Moravec and Viebeck, "Texas Voting Bill Heads to Governor."

163. Moravec and Viebeck,

164. Associated Press, "Right in the Trash: Texas Ballot Rejections Soar, AP Finds," *Politico*, March 16, 2022, https://www.politico.com/news/2022/03/16/texas-mail-ballots-votes-trash-00017844.

165. Biden, "Remarks by President Biden on Protecting the Sacred Constitutional Right to Vote."

166. Holder with Koppelman, *Our Unfinished March*, 12.

167. King, "The House Debates Voting Rights." The John Lewis Voting Rights Advancement Act of 2021 set forth the following criteria for states to obtain preclearance to any changes in their voting laws if "(1) 15 or more voting rights violations occurred in the state during the previous 25 years; (2) 10 or more violations occurred during the previous 25 years, at least one of which was committed by the state itself; or (3) three or more violations occurred during the previous 25 years and the state administers the elections." H.R. 4, "John R. Lewis Voting Rights Advancement Act of 2021," https://www.congress.gov/bill/117th-congress/house-bill/4/text?q=%7B%22search%22%3A%5B%22john+lewis+voting%22%2C%22john%22%2C%22lewis%22%2C%22voting%22%5D%7D&r=2&s=2.

168. King, "The House Debates Voting Rights."

169. King.

170. Viebeck, "A Growing Disparity in State Rules for Voting."

171. Caitlin O'Kane, "Dozens of Armed 'Stop the Steal' Protestors Threaten Michigan Secretary of State Outside Her Home," CBS News, December 7, 2020, https://www.cbsnews.com/news/michigan-protest-jocelyn-benson-secretary-of-state/.

172. Matt Smith, "Election Officials Still Face Violent Threats in Wake of 2020 Election, Ask FBI to Do More," WISN, November 11, 2021, https://www.wisn.com/article/election-officials-face-violent-threats-in-wake-of-2020-election/38223928.

173. "Election Officials under Attack: How to Protect Administrators and Safeguard Democracy," Brennan Center for Justice and Bipartisan Policy Center, June 16, 2021, 6, file:///C:/Users/Owner/Downloads/BCJ-129%20ElectionOfficials_v7%20(1).pdf.file:///C:/Users/jkwhi/Downloads/BCJ-129%20ElectionOfficials_v7.pdf.

174. Testimony of Brad Raffensberger before the House Select Committee to

Investigate the January 6th Attack on the United States Capitol, NPR, June 21, 2022, https://www.npr.org/2022/06/21/1105848096/jan-6-committee-hearing-transcript.

175. Testimony of Rusty Bowers before the House Select Committee to Investigate the January 6th Attack on the United States Capitol, NPR, June 21, 2022, https://www.npr.org/2022/06/21/1105848096/jan-6-committee-hearing-transcript. Bowers's daughter died on January 28, 2021.

176. Brennan Center for Justice and Bipartisan Policy Center, "Election Officials under Attack."

177. In 2023, newly elected governor Josh Shapiro appointed Schmidt to be Pennsylvania's secretary of state. Gillian McGoldrick and Jonathan Lai, "Al Schmidt, a Republican Former Philly Elections Official, Is Named John Shapiro's Pa. Secretary of State," *Philadelphia Inquirer*, January 5, 2023, https://www.inquirer.com/politics/election/al-schmidt-pennsylvania-secretary-of-state-20230105.html.

178. Evan Osnos, "What It Means to Be Targeted by the President," *New Yorker*, June 22, 2022, https://www.newyorker.com/news/daily-comment/what-it-means-to-be-targeted-by-the-president.

179. Heather Cox Richardson, "Letters from an American," Substack, November 10, 2022, https://heathercoxrichardson.substack.com/p/november-10-2022.

180. Testimony of Wandrea "Shaye" Moss before the House Select Committee to Investigate the January 6th Attack on the United States Capitol, NPR, June 21, 2022, https://www.npr.org/2022/06/21/1105848096/jan-6-committee-hearing-transcript.

181. Hearing of the House Select Committee to Investigate the January 6th Attack on the United States Capitol, NPR, June 21, 2022, https://www.npr.org/2022/06/21/1105848096/jan-6-committee-hearing-transcript. In fact, Freeman handed Moss a ginger mint.

182. Hearing of the House Select Committee to Investigate the January 6th Attack on the United States Capitol.

183. Paul Waldman and Greg Sargent, "Emotional January 6 Hearing Shows Election Workers Were the Real Heroes," *Washington Post*, June 21, 2022, https://www.washingtonpost.com/opinions/2022/06/21/january-6-election-workers-real-heroes/.

184. Testimony of Wandrea "Shaye" Moss before the House Select Committee.

185. Hearing of the House Select Committee to Investigate the January 6th Attack on the United States Capitol.

186. Testimony of Wandrea "Shaye" Moss before the House Select Committee.

187. Testimony of Wandrea "Shaye" Moss before the House Select Committee.

188. Hearing of the House Select Committee to Investigate the January 6th Attack on the United States Capitol.

189. Testimony of Wandrea "Shaye" Moss before the House Select Committee.

190. Benjamin Ginsberg and Martin Shefter, *Politics by Other Means: Politicians, Prosecutors, and the Press from Watergate to Whitewater* (New York: W. W. Norton, 2002), 1. The book was first published in 1990.

191. Andrew Romano, "Poll: Half of Americans Now Predict U.S. May 'Cease to Be a Democracy' Someday," *Yahoo News*, June 15, 2022, https://news.yahoo.com/poll-half-of-americans-now-predict-us-may-cease-to-be-a-democracy-someday-090028564.html?guccounter=1&guce_referrer=aHR0cHM6Ly93d3cuZ29vZ2xlLmNvbS8&guce_referrer_sig=AQAAAFoyyDgCjRIcuYgmLsbrBh_P6CJcY3wP6zmOm7cyNdosXqDMrIOvIsrDv5X74v_Q96ejFERNCnEDY7Pp9WVjnDNBU1AQYYn5UG8SeO9wR6kOFfowW_EqHpOIxCpV76GUKkgpaZmDKEnuO8uPF3Ij5A797BKq9ctCZ4xqYVdLR9zS.

192. Jamie Raskin, *Unthinkable: Trauma, Truth, and the Trials of American Democracy* (New York: HarperCollins, 2022), 413.

193. Raskin, 413.

194. J. Michael Luttig, Testimony before the House Select Committee to Investigate the January 6th Attack on the United States Capitol, June 16, 2022, author's personal recording.

195. Jan-Werner Müller, *What Is Populism?* (Philadelphia: University of Pennsylvania Press, 2016), 75–76.

CHAPTER SIX: A CLEAR AND PRESENT DANGER

1. Thomas E. Dewey, *Thomas E. Dewey on the Two-Party System* (Garden City, NY: Doubleday and Company, 1966), 30.

2. Dewey, 30.

3. Dewey, 3.

4. Dewey, 30.

5. Dewey, 30.

6. Dewey, 9 (emphasis added).

7. Liz Cheney, "A Time for Choosing," Ronald Reagan Presidential Library Address, Simi Valley, California, June 29, 2022, Ronald Reagan Presidential Foundation and Institute, https://www.reaganfoundation.org/programs-events/events-calendar/a-time-for-choosing-with-congresswoman-liz-cheney/.

8. Nelson Rockefeller, "Text of Rockefeller's Statement Criticizing 'Radical Right' of the Republican Party," *New York Times*, July 15, 1963, 23.

9. Rockefeller.

10. Rockefeller.

11. Rockefeller.

12. Lyndon B. Johnson, "Annual Message to the Congress on the State of the Union," January 10, 1967, The American Presidency Project, https://www.presidency.ucsb.edu/documents/annual-message-the-congress-the-state-the-union-28.

13. Jamie Raskin, *Unthinkable: Trauma, Truth, and the Trials of American Democracy* (New York: HarperCollins, 2022), 412.

14. Peter Wehner, "A Withering Indictment of the Entire GOP," *The Atlantic*, June 29, 2022, https://www.theatlantic.com/ideas/archive/2022/06/hutchinson-testimony-deranged-seditious-president/661424/.

15. Aaron Blake, "More Republicans Now Call January 6 a 'Legitimate Protest' Than a Riot," *Washington Post*, July 7, 2022, https://www.washingtonpost.com/politics/2022/07/07/many-republicans-no-longer-call-jan-6-an-insurrection-or-even-riot/.

16. Blake.

17. Susan Page and Chelsey Cox, "Exclusive: The January 6 Hearings Sparked Many Headlines but Haven't Changed Many Minds, Poll Shows," *USA Today*, July 26, 2022, https://www.usatoday.com/story/news/politics/2022/07/26/jan-6-hearings-reinforced-voters/10144853002/.

18. Page and Cox.

19. Phil Helsel, "January 6 Rioter Who Talked of Shooting Nancy Pelosi Is Sentenced to 60 Days," NBC News, July 21, 2022, https://www.nbcnews.com/news/us-news/jan-6-rioter-talked-shooting-nancy-pelosi-was-sentenced-60-days-rcna39484.

20. Kevin Liptak, "Biden Castigates Trump for Failing to Act during January 6 Insurrection," CNN.com, July 25, 2022, https://www.cnn.com/2022/07/25/politics/january-6-joe-biden-donald-trump/index.html#:~:text=President%20Joe%20Biden%20castigated%20his,law%20enforcement%20to%20save%20olives.

21. The ten Republicans are Tom Rice (defeated), Jaime Herrera Beutler (defeated), Liz Cheney (defeated), Peter Meijer (defeated), Dan Newhouse (survived primary), David Valadao (survived primary), John Katko (retired), Fred Upton (retired), Anthony Gonzalez (retired), and Adam Kinzinger (retired). Both Newhouse and Valadao were reelected in 2022.

22. Matthew Green, "Gauging Trump's Electoral Influence," *Mischiefs of Faction* (blog), May 18, 2022, https://www.mischiefsoffaction.com/post/gauging-trump-s-electoral-influence.

23. "Remarks by President Biden at a Reception for the Democratic National Committee," Beverly Hills, California, June 10, 2022, White House, https://www.whitehouse.gov/briefing-room/speeches-remarks/2022/06/11/remarks-by-president-biden-at-a-reception-for-the-democratic-national-committee-2/.

24. Kamala Harris, Brian Taylor Cohen podcast, July 24, 2022, YouTube, https://www.youtube.com/watch?v=RpwEQtYS_0o.

25. E. E. Schattschneider, *Party Government* (New York: Rinehart, 1942), 85.

26. Schattschneider, 85.

27. Gerald Ford, "Your Washington Review," January 27, 1965, Gerald R. Ford Presidential Library, https://www.fordlibrarymuseum.gov/library/document/0054/4525467.pdf#pagemode=bookmarks.

28. Bruce Bartlett, "'Trump Is What Happens When a Political Party Abandons Ideas,'" *Politico*, June 24, 2017, https://www.politico.com/magazine/story/2017/06/24/intellectual-conservatives-lost-republican-trump-215259/.

29. Arthur Larson, *A Republican Looks at His Party* (New York: Harper & Brothers, 1956), 167.

30. Daniel Bell, "The Dispossessed (1962)," in *The Radical Right*, ed. Daniel Bell (New York: Routledge, 2017), 8.

31. Richard Hofstadter, "The Pseudo-conservative Revolt (1955)," in Bell, *Radical Right*, 77.

32. Hofstadter, 78.

33. Hofstadter, 89–90.

34. Hofstadter, 90.

35. Clinton Rossiter, *Conservatism in America* (1955; Cambridge, MA: Harvard University Press, 1982), 213.

36. Rossiter, 213.

37. Hofstadter, "The Pseudo-conservative Revolt," 95.

38. Kevin D. Williamson, "Trumpism Expanded the GOP Tent. Don't Expect Republicans to Abandon It Now," *Washington Post*, November 9, 2020, https://www.washingtonpost.com/outlook/2020/11/09/trump-trumpism-gop-republicans-election-outreach/.

39. "Trump Tells Crowd to 'Knock the Crap' Out of Tomato Throwers," NBC News, February 1, 2016, https://www.nbcnews.com/video/trump-tells-crowd-to-knock-the-crap-out-of-tomato-throwers-613684291706.

40. Williamson, "Trumpism Expanded the GOP Tent."

41. Roxanne Roberts, "Hillary Clinton's 'Deplorables' Speech Shocked Voters Five Years Ago—But Some Feel It Was Prescient," *Washington Post*, August 31, 2021, https://www.washingtonpost.com/lifestyle/2021/08/31/deplorables-basket-hillary-clinton/.

42. Williamson, "Trumpism Expanded the GOP Tent."

43. Stephen F. Knott, *The Lost Soul of the American Presidency: The Decline into Demagoguery and the Prospects for Renewal* (Lawrence: University Press of Kansas, 2019), 210.

44. Mark Leibovich, *Thank You for Your Servitude* (New York: Penguin Press, 2022), 145.

45. Daniel Allott, *On the Road in Trump's America: A Journey into the Heart of a Divided Nation* (Alexandria, VA: Republic Book Publishers, 2020), 186.

46. Allott, 197–198.

47. Tim Alberta, *American Carnage: On the Front Lines of the Republican Civil War and the Rise of President Trump* (New York: HarperCollins, 2019), 259.

48. Allott, *On the Road in Trump's America*, 2.

49. Allott, 220.

50. Donald Trump remarks at Agenda First Policy Summit, Washington, DC, July 26, 2022, YouTube, https://www.youtube.com/watch?v=qBC3eJToRAU.

51. Jessica Chasmar, "Donald Trump Changed Political Parties at Least Five Times: Report," *Washington Times*, June 16, 2015, https://www.washingtontimes.com/news/2015/jun/16/donald-trump-changed-political-parties-at-least-fi/.

52. Michael Kruse and Noah Weiland, "Donald Trump's Greatest Self-Contradictions," *Politico*, May 5, 2016, https://www.politico.com/magazine/story/2016/05/donald-trump-2016-contradictions-213869/.

53. Kruse and Weiland.

54. Kruse and Weiland.

55. Kruse and Weiland, "Donald Trump's Greatest Self-Contradictions."

56. Kruse and Weiland.

57. Bell, "The Dispossessed," 20.

58. Alexander Hamilton, "Federalist 70," in *The Federalist*, ed. Edward Mead Earle (New York: Modern Library, 1960), 454.

59. Woodrow Wilson, *Constitutional Government in the United States* (New Brunswick, NJ: Transaction Publishers, 2002), 23–24.

60. Wilson, 25–26.

61. Jeffrey M. Jones, "Confidence in U.S. Institutions Down; Average at New Low," Gallup, July 5, 2022, https://news.gallup.com/poll/394283/confidence-institutions-down-average-new-low.aspx.

62. Dale Vinyard, *The Presidency* (New York: Scribner's, 1971), 107.

63. Louis Hartz, *The Liberal Tradition in America* (New York: Harcourt Brace Jovanovich, 1955), 9.

64. Bill Bishop, *The Big Sort: Why the Clustering of Like-Minded America Is Tearing Us Apart* (Boston: Mariner Books, 2009).

65. "36 Facts about the 2020 Election," The Cook Political Report, December 22, 2020, https://www.cookpolitical.com/analysis/national/national-politics/36-facts-about-2020-elections.

66. Herbert Agar, *The United States, the Presidents, the Parties, and the Constitution* (London: Eyre and Spottiswoode, 1950), 689–690.

67. Thomas E. Mann and Norman J. Ornstein, *The Broken Branch: How Congress Is Failing America and How to Get It Back on Track* (New York: Oxford University Press, 2006), xi–xii.

68. Frances E. Lee, *Insecure Majorities: Congress and the Perpetual Campaign* (Chicago: University of Chicago Press, 2016), 1.

69. Woodrow Wilson, *Congressional Government: A Study in American Politics* (Boston: Houghton Mifflin, 1885), 26.

70. George Goodwin Jr., *The Little Legislatures: Committees of Congress* (Amherst: University of Massachusetts Press, 1970).

71. Barbara Sinclair, *Party Wars: Polarization and the Politics of National Policy Making* (Norman: University of Oklahoma Press, 2006), 346.

72. Lee, *Insecure Majorities*, 54.

73. Matthew N. Green and Jeffrey Crouch, *Newt Gingrich: The Rise and Fall of a Party Entrepreneur* (Lawrence: University Press of Kansas, 2022), 124.

74. Dana Farrington, "Watch: Sen. McCain Calls for Compromise in Return to Senate Floor," NPR, July 25, 2017, https://www.npr.org/2017/07/25/539323689/watch-sen-mccain-calls-for-compromise-in-return-to-senate-floor.

75. Jack Holmes, "Madison Cawthorn Laid Out the Present and Future of Republican Politics," *Esquire*, January 29, 2021, https://www.esquire.com/news-politics/politics/a35364914/madison-cawthorn-future-republican-politics-staff-legislating/.

76. Niels Lesniewski and Ryan Kelly, "2022 Vote Studies: Division Hit New High in Senate, Fell in House," *Roll Call*, March 24, 2023, https://rollcall.com/2023/03/24/2022-vote-studies-division-hit-new-high-in-senate-fell-in-house/.

77. "Transcript of Obama's Keynote Address at the 2004 Democratic National Convention," *PBS NewsHour*, July 27, 2004, https://www.pbs.org/newshour/show/barack-obamas-keynote-address-at-the-2004-democratic-national-convention.

78. Amber Phillips, "Joe Biden's Victory Speech, Annotated," *Washington Post*, November 7, 2020, https://www.washingtonpost.com/politics/2020/11/07/annotated-biden-victory-speech//.

79. In *The American Commonwealth*, Bryce wrote, "Who now knows or cares to know anything about the personality of James K. Polk or Franklin Pierce? The remarkable thing is that being so commonplace they reached so high." James Bryce, *The American Commonwealth*, vol. 1 (New York: Macmillan, 1941), 77.

80. "Presidential Historians Survey," C-SPAN, June 30, 2021, https://www.c-span.org/presidentsurvey2021/?page=overall.

81. "Presidential Historians Survey."

82. See "Executive Orders," last updated August 22, 2023, The American Presidency Project, https://www.presidency.ucsb.edu/statistics/data/executive-orders.

83. Alice Ollstein, Arjun Kakkar, and Beatrice Jin, "The 17 Things Joe Biden Did on Day One," *Politico*, January 21, 2021, https://www.politico.com/interactives/2021/interactive_biden-first-day-executive-orders/.

84. "Obama Cabinet Mtg—I've Got a Pen and a Phone," YouTube, accessed August 5, 2022, https://www.youtube.com/watch?v=EnmDqIvQDos.

85. Lyndon B. Johnson, "Remarks at Ceremony Marking Ratification of the Presidential Inability (25th) Amendment to the Constitution," February 23, 1967, The American Presidency Project, https://www.presidency.ucsb.edu/documents/remarks-ceremony-marking-the-ratification-the-presidential-inability-25th-amendment-the.

86. Johnson.

87. "If the President . . . ," *New York Times*, editorial, December 1, 1963, https://timesmachine.nytimes.com/timesmachine/1963/12/01/105228942.pdf?pdf_redirect=true&ip=0.

88. James M. Ronan, *Living Dangerously: The Uncertainties of Presidential Disability and Succession* (Lanham, MD: Lexington Books, 2015), 61.

89. Ronan, 61.

90. House Select Committee to Investigate the January 6 Attack on the Capitol, transcript, NPR, June 28, 2022, https://www.npr.org/2022/06/28/1108396692/jan-6-committee-hearing-transcript.

91. House Select Committee to Investigate the January 6 Attack on the Capitol.

92. "The Trump Administration Officials Who Resigned over Capitol Violence," *New York Times*, January 17, 2021, https://www.nytimes.com/article/trump-resignations.html.

93. Ronan, *Living Dangerously*, 93.

94. Brownlow Committee, "Report of the President's Committee on Administrative Management (The Brownlow Committee Report)," 1937, Teaching American History, accessed August 8, 2022, https://teachingamericanhistory.org/document/report-of-the-presidents-committee-on-administrative-management-the-brownlow-committee-report/.

95. Brownlow Committee.

96. Bob Woodward and Robert Costa, *Peril* (New York: Simon & Schuster, 2021), xix, xxii–xxiii.

97. Susan B. Glasser and Peter Baker, "Inside the War between Trump and His Generals," *New Yorker*, August 8, 2022, https://www.newyorker.com/magazine/2022/08/15/inside-the-war-between-trump-and-his-generals.

98. Johnson, "Remarks at Ceremony Marking Ratification of the Presidential Inability (25th) Amendment to the Constitution."

99. Alexander Hamilton, "Federalist 78," in Earle, *The Federalist*, 502–511.

100. *Whole Woman's Health et al. v. Jackson*, December 10, 2021, Supreme Court of the United States, https://www.supremecourt.gov/opinions/21pdf/21-463_3ebh.pdf.

101. *Dobbs, State Health Office of the Mississippi Department of Health v. Jackson Women's Health Organization*, June 24, 2022, Supreme Court of the United States, https://www.supremecourt.gov/opinions/21pdf/19-1392_6j37.pdf.

102. Chandelis Duster, "Justice Amy Coney Barrett Says Supreme Court Is 'Not a Bunch of Partisan Hacks,'" CNN, September 13, 2021, https://www.cnn.com/2021/09/13/politics/amy-coney-barrett-supreme-court-not-partisan/index.html.

103. "Majority Say Supreme Court Motivated by Politics, Not the Law," Quinnipiac University press release, November 19, 2021, https://poll.qu.edu/poll-release?releaseid=3828.

104. "Life Expectancy in the United States, 1790 to 2014," Our World in Data, https://ourworldindata.org/grapher/life-expectation-at-birth-by-sex?country=~USA; "U.S. Life Expectancy, 1950–2023," United Nations, World Population Prospects, https://www.macrotrends.net/countries/USA/united-states/life-expectancy#:~:text=The%20current%20life%20expectancy%20for,a%200.08%25%20increase%20from%202019.

105. Thomas Jefferson to James Madison, letter, January 30, 1787, Thomas Jefferson Encyclopedia, https://www.monticello.org/research-education/thomas-jefferson-encyclopedia/a-little-rebellionquotation/.

106. Jeremy D. Bailey, *Thomas Jefferson and Executive Power* (Cambridge: Cambridge University Press, 2007), 10.

107. Knott, *Lost Soul of the American Presidency*, 34.

108. Wilson, *Constitutional Government*, 39.

109. *Chiafalo v. Washington*, decided July 6, 2020, Supreme Court of the United States, https://www.supremecourt.gov/opinions/19pdf/19-465_i425.pdf. In 2016, ten electors bolted from their party's ticket and cast votes that were opposed to their state's tallies.

110. Gallup poll, November 8–14, 1968. Text of question: "Would you approve or disapprove of an amendment to the Constitution which would do away with the Electoral College and base the election of a President on the total vote cast throughout the nation?" Approve, 80 percent; disapprove, 12 percent; no opinion, 8 percent.

111. Adam Jentleson, *Kill Switch: The Rise of the Modern Senate and the Crippling of American Democracy* (New York: Liveright, 2021), 241. The vote in the House was 339 in favor to 70 opposed.

112. Jentleson, 241–242.

113. Dick Polman, "Confessions of an Electoral College Dropout," *Philadelphia Inquirer*, December 8, 2008, https://www.inquirer.com/philly/blogs/americandebate/Confessions_of_an_Electoral_College_dropout.html.

114. Donald Trump won Nebraska but lost the congressional district contain-

ing Omaha. Joe Biden won Maine but lost that state's northern congressional district filled with rural Trump supporters.

115. "National Popular Vote Interstate Compact," *Ballotpedia*, accessed August 9, 2022, https://ballotpedia.org/National_Popular_Vote_Interstate_Compact.

116. Rebecca Salzer and Jocelyn Kiley, "Majority of Americans Continue to Favor Moving Away from Electoral College," Pew Research Center, press release, August 5, 2022, https://www.pewresearch.org/fact-tank/2022/08/05/majority-of-americans-continue-to-favor-moving-away-from-electoral-college/.

117. Jentleson, *Kill Switch*, 47.

118. Tim Lau, "The Filibuster, Explained," Brennan Center for Justice, April 26, 2001, https://www.brennancenter.org/our-work/research-reports/filibuster-explained.

119. Lau.

120. "Votes to Break Ties in the Senate," accessed September 20, 2023, https://www.senate.gov/legislative/TieVotes.htm.

121. Jentleson, *Kill Switch*, 246–247.

122. Katie Yee, "Five Texts That Have Been Read during Filibusters," *Literary Hub*, September 24, 2020, https://lithub.com/5-texts-that-have-been-read-during-filibusters/.

123. *Rucho v. Common Cause*, 588 U.S. (2019), Supreme Court of the United States, https://www.supremecourt.gov/opinions/18pdf/18-422_9ol1.pdf.

124. *Rucho v. Common Cause*.

125. "US House Battlegrounds, 2022," *Ballotpedia*, https://ballotpedia.org/U.S._House_battlegrounds,_2022.

126. Arthur M. Schlesinger Jr., *The Vital Center: The Politics of Freedom* (Boston: Houghton Mifflin, 1949).

127. Scott Thistle, "LePage Takes Parting Shot at 'Stolen Election' That Cost Fellow Republican His Seat in Congress," *Portland Press Herald*, December 28, 2018, https://www.pressherald.com/2018/12/28/lepage-leaves-note-of-protest-on-golden-election-certificate/.

128. Liz Ruskin, "Trump Bashed Alaska's Ranked Choice Voting, but Republicans Likely Need Those Second Votes to Win," Alaska Public Media, July 14, 2022, https://alaskapublic.org/2022/07/14/trump-bashed-ranked-choice-voting-in-alaska-but-republicans-likely-need-those-2nd-votes-to-win/.

129. Center for American Progress, "The Need for Supreme Court Term Limits," August 3, 2020, https://www.americanprogress.org/article/need-supreme-court-term-limits/.

130. Center for American Progress.

131. "Washington, District of Columbia Population 2022," World Population Review, accessed September 20, 2023, https://worldpopulationreview.com/us

-cities/washington-dc-population; Muriel Bowser, "Why Statehood for D.C.," Mayor's Office, District of Columbia, accessed August 22, 2022, https://statehood.dc.gov/page/why-statehood-dc#:~:text=Washington%2C%20DC%20is%20large%20enough,%2C%20Alaska%2C%20and%20several%20others.

132. Bowser, "Why Statehood for D.C."

133. Rosa Cartagena, "Biden's Limo Has 'Taxation without Representation' on the License Plate," *Washingtonian*, January 20, 2021. Barack Obama and Joe Biden had similar license plates installed in their limousines after George W. Bush and Donald Trump had the offending plates removed.

134. "Effort to Allocate House Seats to D.C., Utah Clears Major Hurdle in Senate," *PBS NewsHour*, February 24, 2009, https://www.pbs.org/newshour/politics/politics-jan-june09-dcvote_02-24.

135. Bowser, "Why Statehood for D.C."

136. John Hudak, "The Politics and History of the D.C. Statehood Vote," Brookings, June 25, 2020, https://www.brookings.edu/blog/fixgov/2020/06/25/the-politics-and-history-of-the-d-c-statehood-vote/.

137. Bowser, "Why Statehood for D.C."

138. Washington, DC's National Guard is the only one in the United States that must be summoned into action by the president.

139. Bowser, "Why Statehood for D.C."

140. "Former Presidents Support Statehood for Puerto Rico," *Puerto Rico Report*, December 5, 2018, https://www.puertoricoreport.com/former-presidents-support-statehood-for-puerto-rico/; "Gerald Ford to Ask Congress to Make Puerto Rico the Nation's 51st State in 1977," *New York Daily News*, January 1, 1977, https://www.nydailynews.com/news/politics/president-ford-asks-congress-puerto-rico-state-1977-article-1.2921381.

141. Justin McCarthy, "Americans Continue to Support Puerto Rico Statehood," Gallup, July 18, 2019, https://news.gallup.com/poll/260744/americans-continue-support-puerto-rico-statehood.aspx.

142. Darragh Roche, "McConnell Warns D.C. and Puerto Rico Statehood Part of Democrats' Radical Agenda," *Newsweek*, September 1, 2020, https://www.newsweek.com/mcconnell-washington-dc-puerto-rico-statehood-democrats-1528873.

143. "Senator Rick Scott: Puerto Rico Destined for Statehood," *Puerto Rico Report*, February 26, 2022, https://www.puertoricoreport.com/sen-rick-scott-puerto-rico-destined-for-statehood/.

144. James MacGregor Burns, *Running Alone: Presidential Leadership—JFK to Bush II* (New York: Basic Books, 2006).

145. George McGovern, *Grassroots: The Autobiography of George McGovern* (New York: Random House, 1977), 137.

146. William B. Dickson Jr., "Presidential Primaries, 1960," *CQ Researcher*, January 6, 1960, file:///C:/Users/jkwhi/Downloads/presidential-primaries-1960-january-6-1960.pdf.

147. Jonathan Rauch and Ray La Raja, "Too Much Democracy Is Bad for Democracy," *The Atlantic*, December 2019, https://www.theatlantic.com/magazine/archive/2019/12/too-much-democracy-is-bad-for-democracy/600766//.

148. CNN, 2004 exit poll, accessed August 12, 2022, https://www.cnn.com/ELECTION/2004/pages/results/states/US/P/00/epolls.0.html; "Election Results, 2008," *New York Times*, November 5, 2008, https://www.nytimes.com/elections/2008/results/president/national-exit-polls.html; "How Groups Voted in 2012," Roper Center for Public Opinion Research, accessed August 12, 2022, https://ropercenter.cornell.edu/how-groups-voted-2012.

149. Also running for the Democratic nomination were former Maryland governor Martin O'Malley and former Rhode Island governor Lincoln Chafee.

150. Some may argue that the Democratic establishment reasserted its power in 2020 with Joe Biden's nomination. But Biden won the nod because voters determined that in the midst of a pandemic, he was the best choice to beat Donald Trump, which was their top priority.

151. Nolan D. McCaskill, "Graham: We Should Have Kicked Trump Out of the Party," *Politico*, March 3, 2016, https://www.politico.com/blogs/2016-gop-primary-live-updates-and-results/2016/03/lindsey-graham-donald-trump-kicked-out-220402.

152. Mike DeBonis, "Ted Cruz Once Called Trump 'Utterly Amoral' and a 'Sniveling Coward.' Then He Worked to Save His Presidency," *Washington Post*, February 15, 2020, https://www.washingtonpost.com/powerpost/ted-cruz-once-called-trump-utterly-amoral-and-a-sniveling-coward-then-he-worked-to-save-his-presidency/2020/02/15/db635480-4e70-11ea-bf44-f5043eb3918a_story.html.

153. Woodward and Costa, *Peril*, 127.

154. Greenblatt, "Presidential Primaries," 5.

155. The 2016 GOP field included former Florida governor Jeb Bush; neurosurgeon Ben Carson; Texas senator Ted Cruz; Ohio governor John Kasich; former Virginia governor Jim Gilmore; Florida senator Marco Rubio; real estate entrepreneur Donald Trump; former Texas governor Rick Perry; Wisconsin governor Scott Walker; Louisiana governor Bobby Jindal; South Carolina senator Lindsey Graham; former New York governor George Pataki; former Arkansas governor Mike Huckabee; former Pennsylvania senator Rick Santorum; Kentucky senator Rand Paul; former Hewlett Packard CEO Carly Fiorina; and New Jersey governor Chris Christie.

156. The 2020 Democratic candidates were former vice president Joe Biden; Vermont senator Bernie Sanders; Hawaii congresswoman Tulsi Gabbard; Massachusetts senator Elizabeth Warren; former New York City mayor Michael Bloomberg; Minnesota senator Amy Klobuchar; former South Bend, Indiana, mayor Pete Buttigieg; hedge fund manager and activist Tom Steyer; former Massachusetts governor Deval Patrick; businessman and attorney Andrew Yang; Colorado senator Michael Bennet; Maryland congressman John Delaney; New Jersey senator Cory Booker; author Marianne Williamson; former Pennsylvania congressman Joe Sestak; Miramar, Florida, mayor Wayne Messam; former Texas congressman Beto O'Rourke; Ohio congressman Tim Ryan; New York City mayor Bill de Blasio; New York senator Kirsten Gillibrand; Massachusetts congressman Seth Moulton, Washington State governor Jay Inslee; former Colorado governor John Hickenlooper; California congressman Eric Swalwell; and former West Virginia state senator Richard Ojeda.

157. In 2020, Democrats tried to limit access to the debate stage by requiring candidates to raise money from a minimum of two hundred thousand donors and reach the 4 percent mark in at least four qualifying polls, or 6 percent in two early-state polls. Greenblatt, "Presidential Primaries."

158. *Citizens United v. Federal Elections Commission*, 558 U.S. (2010), Supreme Court of the United States, https://www.supremecourt.gov/opinions/09pdf/08-205.pdf.

159. *Citizens United v. Federal Elections Commission*.

160. Barack Obama, "Address before a Joint Session of Congress on the State of the Union," January 27, 2010, The American Presidency Project, https://www.presidency.ucsb.edu/documents/address-before-joint-session-the-congress-the-state-the-union-17.

161. "Outside Spending by Race," *Open Secrets*, accessed August 12, 2022, https://www.opensecrets.org/outsidespending/summ.php?cycle=2020&disp=R&pty=A&type=G.

162. Kenneth P. Vogel and Shane Goldmacher, "An Unusual $1.6 Billion Donation Bolsters Conservatives," *New York Times*, August 22, 2022, https://www.nytimes.com/2022/08/22/us/politics/republican-dark-money.html?utm_source=substack&utm_medium=email.

163. Andrew Perez, The Lever, Andy Kroll, and Justin Elliott, "How a Secretive Billionaire Handed His Fortune to the Architect of the Right-Wing Takeover of the Courts," *ProPublica*, August 22, 2022, https://www.propublica.org/article/dark-money-leonard-leo-barre-seid.

164. Casey Tolan, Curt Devine, and Drew Griffin, "Massive Dark Money Windfall: New Conservative Group Got $1.6 Billion from Single Donor," CNN, August 22, 2022, https://www.cnn.com/2022/08/22/politics/dark-money-donati

on-conservative-group-invs/index.html?utm_source=substack&utm_medium= email.

165. Mason Walker and Katerina Eva Matsa, "News Consumption across Social Media in 2021," Pew Research Center, September 20, 2021, https://www.pewresearch.org/journalism/2021/09/20/news-consumption-across-social-media-in-2021/.

166. Alexander Hamilton, "Federalist 1," in Earle, *The Federalist*, 6.

167. Alberta, *American Carnage*, 274.

168. "Public Trust in Government: 1959–2022," Pew Research Center, June 6, 2022, https://www.pewresearch.org/politics/2022/06/06/public-trust-in-government-1958-2022/.

169. Daniel Patrick Moynihan, *Came the Revolution: Argument in the Reagan Era* (New York: Harcourt Brace Jovanovich, 1988), 151.

170. Everett Carll Ladd, *Where Have All the Voters Gone?* (New York: W. W. Norton, 1982), 111.

171. Alberta, *American Carnage*, 280.

172. Cheney, "A Time for Choosing."

173. Adam Gopnik, "Why Don't the French Celebrate LaFayette?," *New Yorker*, August 23, 2021, https://www.newyorker.com/magazine/2021/08/23/why-dont-the-french-celebrate-lafayette.

174. Adam Kinzinger, Closing Statement, Hearings of the House Select Committee to Investigate the January 6th Attack on the United States Capitol, July 21, 2022, https://www.npr.org/2022/07/22/1112138665/jan-6-committee-hearing-transcript.

175. Cheney, "A Time for Choosing."

176. *Washington Post*/University of Maryland poll, December 17–19, 2021, https://docs.google.com/spreadsheets/d/1CyE_aWwBrcvS44t9k-Ra4eK2sF218GEkMdTaFvjIwTU/edit#gid=0.

177. Robert Welch, *The Blue Book of the John Birch Society* (Boston: Western Islands Publishers, 1961), 96.

178. Adolph Reed Jr., "The Whole Country Is the Reichstag," Nonsite.org, August 23, 2021, https://nonsite.org/the-whole-country-is-the-reichstag/.

179. Abraham Lincoln, "Lyceum Address," January 27, 1838, Abraham Lincoln Online, http://abrahamlincolnonline.org/lincoln/speeches/lyceum.htm.

180. Lincoln.

181. Cheney, "A Time for Choosing."

182. Rachel Treisman, "Liz Cheney Offers a Stark Message to the GOP Members Who Continue to Support Trump," NPR, June 9, 2022, https://www.npr.org/2022/06/09/1104083111/liz-cheney-stark-message-gop-trump-supporters.

AFTERWORD 2023: A REFLECTION AND A RECKONING

1. Annie Gowen, "Supporters Raise Millions to Rebrand January 6 Rioters as 'Patriots,'" *Washington Post*, January 6, 2023, https://www.washingtonpost.com/nation/2023/01/06/jan-6-prisoners-supporters/.

2. Zach Schonfeld, "Prosecutors: Alleged Paul Pelosi Attacker Threatened to Break Speaker's Kneecaps," *The Hill*, October 31, 2022, https://thehill.com/homenews/house/3712992-prosecutors-alleged-paul-pelosi-attacker-threatened-to-break-speakers-kneecaps/.

3. Maham Javid, Adela Suliman, and Ben Brasch, "Pelosi Attacker Wanted to Hurt More People, According to Jailhouse Call," *Washington Post*, January 29, 2023, https://www.washingtonpost.com/politics/2023/01/29/paul-pelosi-attack-david-depape-interview/. Pelosi's attacker is facing state and federal felony charges, including the attempted kidnapping of a federal officer and assault on a family member of a federal official. If convicted, he could face life in prison. Eduardo Medina, "Paul Pelosi Attack Suspect Tells TV Station He Has No Remorse," *New York Times*, January 28, 2023, https://www.nytimes.com/2023/01/28/us/politics/pelosi-attacker-interview.html.

4. Aaron Blake, "A Retrospective on the Right's Paul Pelosi Conspiracy Theories," *Washington Post*, January 27, 2023, https://www.washingtonpost.com/politics/2023/01/27/pelosi-footage-debunked-claims/. Donald Trump claimed the attacker was trying to escape from Paul Pelosi. See Blake. Once the videotape of the assault was released, there was no apology offered by those promoting various conspiracy theories.

5. Rebecca Beitsch, "House Democrats, One GOP Lawmaker Mark January 6 Attack," *The Hill*, January 6, 2023, https://thehill.com/homenews/3802324-house-democrats-one-gop-lawmaker-mark-jan-6-attack/.

6. Amy Gardner and Dan Rosenzweig, "Even after New Mexico Shootings, Little GOP Reckoning over Election Denialism," *Washington Post*, January 23, 2023, https://www.washingtonpost.com/politics/2023/01/23/solomon-pena-new-mexico-election-denialism/.

7. Gardner and Rosenzweig.

8. Gardner and Rosenzweig.

9. Mychael Schnell, "GOP Representative Clyde Defends 'Normal Tourist Visit' Comparison for January 6," *The Hill*, July 28, 2021, https://thehill.com/homenews/house/565223-gop-rep-defends-description-of-normal-tourist-visit-on-jan-6/.

10. Joe Heim, "Official U.S. Capitol Tour Guides Told to Only Mention January 6 If Asked," *Washington Post*, January 5, 2023, https://www.washingtonpost.com/dc-md-va/2023/01/04/january-6-attack-capitol-tour/.

11. Gowen, "Supporters Raise Millions to Rebrand January 6 Rioters as 'Patriots.'"

12. Gowen.

13. Rachel Weiner and Spencer S. Hsu, "Man Sentenced to Nearly Seven Years in January 6 Assault of Officer Brian Sicknick," *Washington Post*, January 27, 2023, https://www.washingtonpost.com/dc-md-va/2023/01/27/sicknick-attack-jan-6-sentencing/.

14. Rachel Weiner, "Four Other Oath Keepers Found Guilty of January 6 Seditious Conspiracy," *Washington Post*, January 23, 2023, https://www.washingtonpost.com/dc-md-va/2023/01/23/oathkeepers-verdict-seditious-conspiracy-jan6-guilty/. The statute makes seditious conspiracy a crime if two or more persons conspired together "to overthrow, or put down, or to destroy by force, the Government of the United States, or to oppose by force the authority of the Government of the United States; or by force to prevent, hinder, or delay the execution of any law of the United States." Stephen A. Douglas, the 1860 Democratic presidential nominee, supported an earlier version of the statute, saying it was necessary to fulfill the Constitution's command "to provide for the domestic tranquility." See Catherine M. Tarrant, "To 'Insure Domestic Tranquility': Congress and the Law of Seditious Conspiracy, 1859–1861," *American Journal of Legal History* 15, no. 2 (April 1971): 107–123. In 1954, four seditious conspiracy convictions were obtained when four pro-independence Puerto Rican nationalists stormed the Capitol and opened fire on the House floor. Another conviction came in 1995, when Egyptian cleric Sheikh Omar Abdel-Rahman and nine followers were convicted in a seditious conspiracy trial in which the accused were charged with a plot to blow up the United Nations, an FBI building, and two tunnels and a bridge linking New York and New Jersey. They were convicted. In 1988 jurors acquitted white supremacists charged in Arkansas with seditious conspiracy. Another acquittal came in 2010 when a Michigan militia group plotted to incite an uprising against the government. Alanna Durkin Richer and Lindsay Whitehurst, "Explainer: Rare Sedition Charge at Center of January 6 Trial," *Associated Press*, September 28, 2022, https://apnews.com/article/what-does-sedition-charge-mean-3aa820dda5f501dd874c4dd6d60ca1ce.

15. *United States of America v. Donald J. Trump*, https://www.jan-6.com/_files/ugd/2cf5f9_e0790657e2dc4bc2bd8675069a6e7911.pdf.

16. *United States of America v. Donald J. Trump*.

17. *The State of Georgia v. Donald John Trump, Rudolph William Louis Giuliani, John Charles Eastman, Mark Randall Meadows, Kenneth John Chesebro, Jeffrey Robert Clark, Jenna Lynn Ellis, Ray Stallings Smith III, Robert David Cheeley, Michael A. Roman, David James Shafer, Shawn Micah, Tresher Still, Stephen Cliffgard Lee, Harrison William Prescott Floyd, Trevian C. Kuth, Sidney Kathleen Powell,*

Cathleen Alston Latham, Scott Graham Hall, Misty Hampton AKA Emily Misty Hayes, https://d3i6fh83elv35t.cloudfront.net/static/2023/08/CRIMINAL-INDICTMENT-Trump-Fulton-County-GA.pdf. Altogether, ninety-one charges have been levied against Donald Trump in federal and state courts. Janie Boschma, Curt Merrill, and Abby Turner, "Former President Donald Trump's Fourth Indictment, Annotated," CNN Politics, August 15, 2023, https://www.cnn.com/interactive/2023/08/politics/annotated-trump-indictment-georgia-election-dg/#:~:text=The%2041%2Dcount%20indictment%20was,federal%20and%20two%20state%20cases.

18. *The People of the State of New York against Donald J. Trump*, https://manhattanda.org/wp-content/uploads/2023/04/Donald-J.-Trump-Indictment.pdf.

19. "A Forgotten History: Trial by Jury and the American Revolution," West Virginia Association of Justice," https://www.wvaj.org/?pg=TrialbyJuryAmericanRevolution.

20. Ron DeSantis, X, June 8, 2023, 9:53 p.m., https://twitter.com/rondesantis/status/1666986884604522499?s=46&t=KsD1ya8eYKXtlDdaMJf-Aw.

21. Nikki Haley, X, June 9, 2023, 11:27 a.m., https://twitter.com/NikkiHaley/status/1667191774391984130.

22. Allan Smith and Henry J. Gomez, "Few of Trump's Rivals Challenge Him after the Federal Indictment," NBC News First Read, June 9, 2023, https://www.nbcnews.com/politics/2024-election/trumps-rivals-challenge-federal-indictment-rcna88254?cid=eml_firstread_20230609&%243p=e_sailthru&_branch_match_id=1104022503629244034&utm_medium=Email%20Sailthru&_branch_referrer=H4sIAAAAAAAAAzWMwQrCMBBEvybeopakShVEBOlvlJhu7eJ2GzZb%2B%2FvGgzCHmQfzZtWUL3XNz8iw5yqkVBHyu%2FbpZlzroxWGHJBolu1QwCr4Qg4obELX%2BXc2%2Fm5cX7Lve%2FXXxHUpJK2EijGX6hrXWiCIiiuXrbItKVvBT6Bs4xyIgF9gJxhBAlnkEaMuwGolcug6d2yN7yOOxj9goWFCySoQxqGofXNqzl%2F7vQf1ywAAAA%3D%3D.

23. "President Trump: 'This Is the Final Battle,'" YouTube, accessed June 12, 2023, https://www.youtube.com/watch?v=fwcX6_ktTpM.

24. Anthony Salvanto, Kabir Khanna, Fred Backus, and Jennifer De Pinto, "CBS News Poll: After Trump Indictment, Most See Security Risk, but Republicans See Politics," CBS News, June 11, 2023, https://www.cbsnews.com/news/cbs-news-poll-most-see-security-risk-after-trump-indictment/.

25. Richard Hofstadter, "The Paranoid Style in American Politics," *Harper's*, November 1964, https://harpers.org/archive/1964/11/the-paranoid-style-in-american-politics/.

26. Mitch Landrieu, *In the Shadow of Statutes: A White Southerner Confronts History* (New York: Viking, 2018), 168.

27. Heather Cox Richardson, *How the South Won the Civil War* (New York: Oxford University Press, 2020), 131.

28. Landrieu, *In the Shadow of Statutes*, 166–167.

29. Jeremy Diamond, "Trump Calls Removal of Confederate Monuments 'So Foolish,'" CNN, August 17, 2017, https://www.cnn.com/2017/08/17/politics/trump-tweet-confederate-statues/index.html.

30. Ryan Bort, "Steve Bannon Admits He Talked with Trump about 'Killing' Biden Presidency Ahead of January 6th," *Rolling Stone*, September 22, 2021, https://www.rollingstone.com/politics/politics-news/steve-bannon-january-6-kill-biden-presidency-1230904/.

31. Joe Biden, "Remarks by President Biden at Presentation of the Presidential Citizens Medal," January 6, 2023, The White House, https://www.whitehouse.gov/briefing-room/speeches-remarks/2023/01/06/remarks-by-president-biden-at-presentation-of-the-presidential-citizens-medal/.

32. National Election Pool, exit poll, November 8, 2022, https://www.cnn.com/election/2022/exit-polls/national-results/house/0.

33. "GOP Midterm Messaging Fell Short with Independent Voters," *PBS NewsHour*, December 26, 2022, https://www.pbs.org/newshour/politics/gop-midterm-messaging-fell-short-with-independent-voters.

34. Donald J. Trump, TruthSocial, January 7, 2023, https://truthsocial.com/@realDonaldTrump/posts/109650001658211763.

35. Mike DeBonis, "'There's My Kevin': McCarthy Emerges as Trump's Trusted Link to Capitol Hill," *Washington Post*, February 5, 2017, https://www.washingtonpost.com/powerpost/theres-my-kevin-mccarthy-emerges-as-trumps-trusted-link-to-capitol-hill/2017/02/05/1aa9960e-eb41-11e6-bf6f-301b6b443624_story.html.

36. Kevin McCarthy, Twitter, January 7, 2023, 7:27 a.m., https://twitter.com/RonFilipkowski/status/1611716233992216580?s=20&t=RaP9zzze1_2wna52kijCmjQ.

37. Donald J. Trump, "Former President Trump Announces 2024 Presidential Bid Transcript," November 16, 2022, Rev, https://www.rev.com/blog/transcripts/former-president-trump-announces-2024-presidential-bid-transcript.

38. Salvanto et al., "CBS News Poll."

39. Luke Broadwater and Catie Edmondson, "Divided House Approves GOP Inquiry into 'Weaponization' of Government," *New York Times*, January 10, 2023, https://www.nytimes.com/2023/01/10/us/politics/house-republican-committee-weaponization-government.html.

40. Kelly Garrity, "'They Did It to Me': Trump Says Biden Impeachment Inquiry Might Be Motivated by Revenge," *Politico*, September 14, 2023, https://www.politico.com/news/2023/09/14/trump-biden-impeachment-revenge-00116027.

41. Mark Ballard, "Clay Higgins Calls for War over Trump Indictments, Author Says," Nola.com, June 9, 2023, https://www.nola.com/news/politics/clay-higgins-urges-war-over-trump-indictments-author-says/article_db78acde-0701-11ee-af01-73c2414fd4d7.html.

42. Jeff Sharlet, *The Undertow: Scenes from a Slow Civil War* (New York: W. W. Norton, 2023).

43. Ballard, "Clay Higgins Calls for War over Trump Indictments."

44. Bess Levin, "All the Ways Donald Trump Will Probably 'Handle' Ron DeSantis in 2024," *Vanity Fair*, January 17, 2023, https://www.vanityfair.com/news/2023/01/donald-trump-ron-desantis-2024-threats.

45. Mark Shields, "Heretics or Converts—Democrats Better Decide," *Noozhawk*, April 17, 2010, https://www.noozhawk.com/041710_mark_shields/.

46. Jennifer Agiesta and Ariel Edwards-Levy, "CNN Poll: Americans Are Split over Confidence in Incoming House GOP Majority or Biden," *CNN Politics*, December 12, 2022, https://www.cnn.com/2022/12/12/politics/cnn-poll-elections-political-parties/index.html.

47. Salvanto et al., "CBS News Poll."

48. Andrew Atterbury, "DeSantis-Backed School Boards Begin Ousting Florida Educators," *Politico*, November 30, 2022, https://www.politico.com/news/2022/11/30/desantis-school-board-covid-00071305.

49. Romy Ellenbogen and Bianca Padro Ocasio, "DeSantis Touted Their Arrest. But Ex-Felons Say They Weren't Told They Couldn't Vote," *Tampa Bay Times*, August 19, 2022, https://www.tampabay.com/news/florida-politics/2022/08/19/desantis-touted-their-arrest-but-ex-felons-say-they-werent-told-they-couldnt-vote/.

50. Michael Kranish, "How DeSantis Used Disney's Missteps to Wage War on Corporate America," *Washington Post*, October 19, 2022, https://www.washingtonpost.com/politics/2022/10/19/desantis-disney-corporate-america-war/.

51. Tim Craig and Lori Rozsa, "DeSantis Takes Aim at Federal Government as He Is Sworn in to Second Term," *Washington Post*, January 3, 2023, https://www.washingtonpost.com/nation/2023/01/03/florida-desantis-inauguration/.

52. Caroline Vakil, "Mike Lindell Questions DeSantis 2022 Election Win: 'I Don't Believe It,'" *The Hill*, December 23, 2022, https://thehill.com/homenews/campaign/3786368-mike-lindell-questions-desantis-2022-election-win-i-dont-believe-it/.

53. Virginia Chamlee, "Kari Lake Called John McCain a 'Hero' When He Died—Now She's Calling Him a 'Loser,'" *People*, November 7, 2022, https://people.com/politics/kari-lake-calls-john-mccain-loser-campaign-trail/.

54. Chamlee.

55. Nick Reynolds, "Kari Lake Accuses Republicans of Rigging Election," *Newsweek*, January 20, 2023, https://www.newsweek.com/kari-lake-accuses-republicans-rigging-election-arizona-governors-race-1775468.

56. Arizona Republicans also rejected a resolution that called on the party to accept Joe Biden's 2020 win in the state and "not belabor or try to overturn

old resolutions." The measure did not muster enough support to be considered by the state party. See Yvonne Wingett Sanchez, "Election Losses Only Deepen Arizona Republicans' Insistence on Fraud," *Washington Post*, January 27, 2023, https://www.washingtonpost.com/politics/2023/01/27/arizona-republicans-division/?utm_source=rss&utm_medium=referral&utm_campaign=wp_politics. Arizona's Republican Party has elected an election denier, Jeff DeWitt, to be its new state chair. Yvonne Wingett Sanchez and Isaac Arnsdorf, "New Arizona GOP Chair Wooed Election Deniers to Secure Spot, *Washington Post*, January 28, 2023, https://www.washingtonpost.com/politics/2023/01/28/arizona-republicans-dewit/.

57. Stacey Barchenger, "Trump Coming to Arizona for Rally in Support of Kari Lake, Blake Masters, and Other GOP Candidates," *Arizona Republic*, July 15, 2022, https://www.azcentral.com/story/news/politics/elections/2022/07/11/donald-trump-hold-arizona-rally-support-kari-lake-blake-masters/10032481002/.

58. Peter Hall and John L. Micek, "Shapiro Rallies with Biden, Obama; Tours Philly with Wolf in Final Weekend of Governor's Race," *Pennsylvania Capital Star*, November 5, 2022, https://www.penncapital-star.com/campaigns-elections/shapiro-rallies-with-biden-obama-tours-philly-with-wolf-in-final-weekend-of-governors-race/.

59. Biden, "Remarks by President Biden at Presentation of the Presidential Citizens Medal."

60. Biden.

61. Jon Meacham, *And There Was Light: Abraham Lincoln and the American Struggle* (New York: Random House, 2022), 209.

62. "Rep. Scott Perry (R-PA) Nominates Rep. Byron Donalds (R-FL) for Speaker of the House," YouTube, January 4, 2023, https://www.youtube.com/watch?v=LuoqhwH_Bc4&t=5s.

63. Paul Tsongas, speech, National Press Club, Washington, DC, October 5, 1982, quoted in John Kenneth White, *The New Politics of Old Values* (Hanover, NH: University Press of New England, 1990), 134.

64. Anthony Giddens, *The Third Way: The Renewal of Social Democracy* (Malden, MA: Polity Press, 1998).

65. Robert Dahl, ed., *Political Oppositions in Western Democracies* (New Haven, CT: Yale University Press, 1966), xiii.

66. See Philip A. Klinkner, *The Losing Parties: Out Party National Committees, 1956–1993* (New Haven, CT: Yale University Press, 1994), 1.

67. Sandra L. Hanson and John Kenneth White, eds., *The Latino/a American Dream* (College Station: Texas A&M University Press, 2016).

68. CNN/SSRS poll, January 19–22, 2023. Text of question: "So far, would you say that the Republican leaders in the House have had the right priorities, or that

they haven't paid enough attention to the country's most important problem?" Have the right priorities, 27 percent; haven't paid enough attention to the country's most important problem, 73 percent. "CNN Poll Conducted by SSRS," press release, January 26, 2023, https://www.documentcloud.org/documents/23587463-cnn-pollcnn-poll-conducted-by-ssrs.

69. Frank Freidel, *The Presidents of the United States of America* (Washington, DC: White House Historical Association, 1975), 8.

70. Freidel, 38.

71. Freidel, 69.

72. "Ronald Reagan: Fortieth President 1981–1989," National Archives, accessed January 30, 2023, https://clintonwhitehouse3.archives.gov/WH/glimpse/presidents/html/rr40.html.

73. Charlie Sykes, "Judge Luttig Has a Warning for America," *The Bulwark*, March 29, 2023, https://morningshots.thebulwark.com/p/judge-luttig-has-a-warning-foramerica?utm_source=direct&utm_campaign=post&utm_medium=web.

Index

13th Amendment, 110
14th Amendment, 110, 111, 117
15th Amendment, 111
25th Amendment, 149, 150, 151
9/11/2001 terrorist attacks, 11, 18, 20, 22, 30, 73, 100, 106
1/6/2021 insurrection, x, xv, 7, 8, 10, 12, 15, 17, 23, 26, 71, 72, 74, 75, 103, 104, 123, 124,127, 128, 132, 134, 137, 138, 150, 151, 170, 172, 173, 175, 176, 181, 182

Acheson, Dean, 59
Adams, Eric, 160
Adams, John, 128, 154, 174
Adams, John Quincy, 170
Adorno, Theodor W., 140
age of anxiety, 20, 22
Aldrich, John, 13
Alito, Samuel, 152
Allott, Daniel, 103, 141, 142, 183
alternative facts, 10, 11, 24, 25, 26, 27, 28, 31, 45, 65, 75, 86, 88, 95, 106, 108, 127, 168, 175
Amarasigam, Amarnath, 125
American Dream, 17, 115, 124, 182
American Political Science Association, 68
Antifa, 122, 173
Anti-Mason Party, 107
antisemitism, 123
Anton, Richard, 100
Applebaum, Anne, 18, 25, 27
Arendt, Hannah, 28
artificially based realities, 24, 25, 26, 27, 28, 30, 31, 79
Askonas, Jonathan, 25, 26, 183
authoritarianism, 4, 11, 12, 19, 21, 23, 25, 68, 95, 130, 137, 170

Babbitt, Ashli, xvi
Baker, Howard, 136
Baker, James, 69
Bannon, Steve, 30, 108, 176
Barreto, Matt, 120, 121
Bartlett, Bruce, 139
Bell, Daniel, 139, 140, 143
Ben-Ghiat, Ruth, 11
Berlin, Isaiah, 28
Berman, Geoffrey, 23
Bezos, Jeff, 23
Biden, Hunter, 172
Biden, Joseph R., xi, 10, 16, 17, 18, 19, 22, 23. 24. 30, 32, 71, 72, 73, 24, 30, 32, 71, 72, 73, 104, 121, 122, 123, 127, 129, 130, 138, 159, 175, 176, 179, 182; 2020 election and, 9, 102, 120, 122, 128, 129, 131, 141, 145, 148, 151, 155, 176; legitimacy questioned, 108, 169, 170, 173, 177
Biggs, Andy, 127
Bilbo, Theodore G., 110, 116
Birchers, 77, 90, 92, 93, 103, 104, 117, 121
Bishop, Bill, 145
Bishop, Dan, 131
Boebert, Lauren, 141, 176
Boehner, John, 32, 146
Bohlen, Chip, 86, 89
Bositis, David, xiii
Bowers, Rusty, 132
Boxer, Barbara, 1
Bozell, Brent, 57
Breyer, Stephen, 160, 161
Bricker, John, 56, 62, 66, 80, 81, 85
Brooke, Edward, 136
Brownell, Herbert, 48, 61, 87
Brownlow Commission, 69, 151
Bryce, James, 8, 148

Buchanan, James, 148
Buchanan, Patrick J., 32
Buckley, William F., 103
Burke, Edmund, 7
Burns, James MacGregor, 39, 46, 69, 70, 128, 150, 163, 183
Burr, Aaron, 156, 157
Bush, George H. W., 77, 103, 119, 138, 161, 163, 165, 169
Bush, George W., 18, 22, 25, 33, 69, 71, 73, 134, 149, 169; 2000 election and, 2–3, 148, 165; 2004 election and, xvii, 1, 165
Bush, Jeb, 77
Bush, Prescott, 44
Butler, Hugh, 81
Byran, William Jennings, 114, 115

Cameron, Donald, 114
Carlson, Tucker, 123
Carter, David O., 127, 128
Carter, Jimmy, 14, 16, 62, 73, 136, 164, 169
Carville, James, 35, 142
Chao, Elaine, 150
Cheney, Dick, 16
Cheney, Liz, 72, 89, 123, 135, 136, 138, 147, 170, 171, 178
Chodorov, Frank, 57
Churchill, Winston, xvii
Civil Rights Act of 1964, 40, 118, 119
Civil War, xvi, 33, 35, 64, 110, 120, 154, 175, 176, 178
Clay, Lucius, 60
Cleveland, Grover, 33, 113, 129, 149
Clifford, Clark, 47
Clinton, Bill, 22, 70, 71, 73, 162, 169, 180; 1996 election and, 21; impeachment of, 22, 177
Clinton, Hillary, 104, 165, 181; 2016 election and, x, 11, 73, 100, 101, 103, 125, 141, 165
Clyde, Andrew, 173, 176
Cobb, Danielle, 138

Cohn, Roy, 88
Cold War, xi, xvii, 20, 28, 168
Collins, Susan, 146
Comey, James, 141
Committee for Party Renewal, 13
Constant, Benjamin, 8
Coolidge, Calvin, 21, 48, 51, 53
Corn, David, 10
Coxe, Tench, 75
Criswell, W. A., 92
Cruz, Ted, 106, 141, 166
Cuomo, Mario, 10
Cutler, Bryan, 132

Daley, William, 2
Dallek, Matthew, xvii
Davidson, John Daniel, xii
Davis, John W., 21
Davis, Rodney, 131
Declaration of Independence, 2, 18
deep state, 13, 91, 99, 101, 105, 177
DeLay, Tom, 1
democracy, 19, 20, 27, 29; crisis of, 14, 32, 107, 154, 169; threats to, x, xiii, xv, xvii, 2, 13, 17, 19, 22, 24, 31, 32, 37, 108, 115, 122, 124, 126, 127, 134, 136, 137, 168, 169, 170, 172, 182
Democratic National Committee (DNC), ix, 44, 164, 165
Democratic Party, 5, 6, 9, 10, 43, 48, 49, 60, 69, 92, 95, 112, 115, 122, 123, 137, 144, 164, 165, 169, 180, 181; Civil Rights and, 40, 116–177, 120, 136, 165; conservative Democrats, 70, 71; control of Congress and, 66, 89, 91; despair of, 47, 59, 114; losses by, 82, 149; moderation of, 71; New Deal and, 36, 80, 84; party unity and, 147, 165; populism espoused by, 115; South and, 58, 61, 111, 116, 117, 129, 144
DeSantis, Ron, xiv, 27, 28, 107, 174, 178, 179, 182
DeVos, Betsy, 150

Dewey, Thomas E., xv, 32, 36, 37, 50, 51, 52, 53, 55, 59, 66, 135, 180; 1944 election and, 31, 43, 44, 45, 46, 80; 1948 election and, 47, 48, 83
Dickinson, John, 149
Dirksen, Everett, 55, 99, 136
Dixiecrats, 117, 125, 131
Dolan, John, 100
Dole, Bob, 21
Donalds, Byron, 180
doubt in government, 17, 20, 42, 144, 169
Douglas, Stephen, 2
Douglass, Frederick, 162, 180
D'Souza, Dinesh, 172
Duke, David, 122
Dulles, John Foster, 57
Duverger, Maurice, 5

Eastman, John, 127, 128
Ehrlichman, John, 71
Eisenhower, Dwight D., xi, xv, 32, 47, 50, 67, 69, 82, 88, 89, 90, 91, 95, 98, 117, 118, 138, 145, 148, 149, 164, 165, 169, 180; 1952 election and, 14, 52–60, 67, 85–86, 87; 1956 election and, 63–66; Citizens for Eisenhower and, 60, 61; Modern Republicanism and, 15, 61, 62, 64, 66, 94, 96, 139
Eisenhower, Edgar, 64
Eisenhower, Mamie, 52
Eisenhower, Milton, 87
Eisenhower, Susan, 85, 87
Electoral College, 3, 30, 36, 46, 49, 65, 126, 127, 154, 155, 156, 159, 160; ballots cast by, 36, 46; reform of, 154, 155, 156
Ellsberg, Daniel, 99
Elshtain, Jean Bethke, 20, 21
Emerson, Ralph Waldo, xi, xii
Epstein, Leon, 12

Fair Deal, 14, 55, 58, 64
fake news, 25, 86

Farley, James, 36
Feinstein, Diane, xiii
Fess, Simeon D., 34
filibuster reform, 156, 157
Flanders, Ralph, 89
Flynn, Michael, 104
Ford, Gerald R., 16, 20, 41, 70, 73, 99, 103, 136, 139, 163, 165
freedom, xii, xvii, 4, 5, 16, 19, 37, 38, 78, 86, 88, 89, 92, 93, 94, 96, 99, 110, 115, 118, 120, 145, 163, 168, 171, 174, 179
Freeman, Ruby, 132, 133
Frum, David, 102

Gabbard, Tulsi, 166
Gaetz, Matt, 141, 176
Gallup Organization, 38, 46, 47, 51, 60, 155, 163
Garfield, James, 149
Garland, Merrick, 29, 152
gerrymandering, 158, 159
Gerson, Michael, 141
Gillespie, Ed, 120
Gingrich, Newt, ix, xiii, xiv, 22, 147
Ginsberg, Benjamin, 133
Ginsberg, Ruth Bader, 152
Gipp, George, 27
Giuliani, Rudy, 24, 132, 133, 179
Golden, Jared, 159, 160
Goldwater, Barry M., xiv, xv, 44, 57, 64, 85, 88, 92, 93, 96, 97, 98, 99, 103, 117, 119, 135, 136, 166, 180
Gore, Al, xiii, 1, 2, 3, 180
Gorsuch, Neil, 152, 158
Gosar, Paul, 141
Graham, Lindsey, 71, 72, 166
Grant, Ulysses S., 33, 111
Great Depression, 34, 35, 37, 45, 48, 53, 58, 79, 154, 182
Great Replacement Theory, 122, 123, 124, 125, 126
Greene, John Robert, 67

Greene, Marjorie Taylor, 12, 107, 123, 141, 147, 176, 182
Griffith, D. W., 115

Haberman, Maggie, x, 25
Hagerty, James, 87
Hague, Frank, 47
Haidt, Jonathan, 109
Haley, Nikki, 174
Hall, Leonard, 67, 88
Hamadeh, Abraham, 179
Hamilton, Alexander, 74, 143, 152, 154, 157, 168, 171
Hancock, Winfield Scott, 112
Harding, Warren, 48, 51, 65
Harris, Kamala, 138, 158
Harris, Katherine, xiii
Harrison, Benjamin, 110, 113, 114, 118, 128
Harrison, Russell, 114
Hart, Gary, 164, 165
Hart, Roderick P., 167
Hartz, Louis, 145
Hassett, Bill, 46
Hatfield, Mark, 136
Hayes, Rutherford B., 3, 112
Higgins, Clay, 177
Hill, Lister, 119
Hiss, Alger, 81
Hitler, Adolf, 39, 42, 45, 118
Hoar, George, 114
Hobby, Oveta Culp, 60
Hodge, Daniel, 176
Hoffman, Paul, 60
Hofstadter, Richard, 98, 100, 140, 175
Hogg, David, 147
Holder, Eric, 130
Hoover, Herbert, xv, 33, 34, 35, 36, 37, 40, 48, 51, 58, 78, 79, 140
Hope, Bob, 27
Huffington, Michael, xiii
Hume, David, 7
Humphrey, Hubert H., 49, 84, 117, 164
Hunt, H. L., 91

Huntington, Samuel, 9
Hutchinson, Cassidy, 150

Ingalls, David S., 52
Ingelhart, Ronald, 124
Ingraham, Laura, 123

Jackson, Amy Berman, 24, 32
Jackson, Andrew, 170, 181
Jackson, Henry "Scoop," 60
Jackson, James, 110
Jackson, Ketanji Brown, 153, 158, 161
Jefferson, Thomas, xvi, 6, 74, 75, 128, 148, 153, 154
Jenkins, Woody, xiii
Jenner, William E., 81
Jentleson, Adam, 158
John Birch Society, xiv, 77, 81, 90, 91, 92, 93, 94, 95, 96, 97, 99, 103, 104, 108, 109, 117, 118, 120, 121, 136, 171
Johnson, Andrew, 111, 148
Johnson, Eddie Bernice, 2
Johnson, Lyndon B., xv, 16, 40, 49, 114, 150, 166
Johnson, Ron, 124
Jordan, Jim, 131, 141, 176, 177

Kagan, Elena, 159
Kavanaugh, Brett, 152, 158
Kazin, Michael, 122
Kelly, John, 23
Kelly, Megyn, 11
Kemp, Brian, 129
Kennedy, John F., 58, 60, 73, 84, 106, 118, 144, 149, 150, 164, 166; assassination of, 58, 118, 149
Kennedy, Joseph P., 84
Kennedy, Robert F., 92
Kerry, John, 1, 23
Key, V. O., 5
King, Desmond, 11
King, Martin Luther, xv, 9
Kinzinger, Adam, 147, 170, 178

Kissinger, Henry, 69, 99
Knott, Stephen, 75, 183
Know-Nothing Party, 8, 107
Kristol, Irving, 99
Ku Klux Klan, 111, 114, 116, 119, 120, 121, 122, 126, 147

Lafayette, Marquis de, 170
Lake, Kari, 179
Landon, Alf, 36, 37, 38, 39, 40, 52, 66, 99, 140
Landrieu, Mary, xiii
La Raja, Ray, 164
Larson, Arthur, 63, 86, 94, 139
Lee, Frances E., 146
Lee, J. Bracken, 89
Lee, Robert E., 175
Leibovich, Mark, ix
Lemire, Jonathan, 29
Leo, Leonard, 167
LePage, Paul, 159
Letterman, David, x
Levitsky, Steven, 22, 31
Lewis, John, 118, 131
Lincoln, Abraham, xvi, xvii, 2, 35, 73, 74, 110, 118, 120, 148, 153, 169, 171, 175, 180, 182
Lind, Michael, 124–125
Lindell, Mike, 179
Linton, Ralph S., 116
Linz, Juan J., 12
Lippmann, Walter, 34, 49
Lipset, Seymour Martin, 85
Lodge, Henry Cabot, 49, 52, 53, 55, 60, 65
Longworth, Alice Roosevelt, 49
Lord, Mary Pillsbury, 60
Lovett, Jon, ix
Lowi, Theodore J., 61, 67, 68
Lubell, Samuel, 59, 66
Luccock, Halford E., 30
Luce, Claire Booth, 47, 80
Luce, Henry, xii, 54
Luttig, J. Michael, 126, 134, 182

MacArthur, Douglas, 51
Machiavelli, Niccolo, 105
Macron, Emmanuel, 32
Maguire, Robert, 167
Make America Great Again (MAGA), x, 17, 177
Manafort, Paul, 24
Mann, Thomas, 146
Mansfield, Harvey, 4
Mansfield, Mike, 60
Marshall, George C., 81, 84, 86
Martin, Joseph, 60
Mastriano, Doug, 179
McCain, John, 71, 106, 147, 165
McCain, Meghan, 179
McCarthy, Joseph R., 20, 58, 61, 83, 87, 90, 91, 130
McCarthy, Kevin, 72, 177, 182
McConnell, Mitch, 72, 152, 157, 163
McCormick, Anne O'Hare, 43
McDonell, Scott, 131
McGovern, George, 164
McGovern, Jim, 177
McGovern-Fraser Commission, 164

McKinney, Pam, 142
McKinley, William, 33, 71, 181
McWilliams, Wilson Carey, 9, 10, 124, 183
Meadows, Mark, 24, 102, 127, 150
media, 11, 13, 25, 55, 75, 103, 105, 108, 109, 121, 132, 144, 164
Mehlman, Ken, 120
Mencken, H. L., 34
Mercieca, Jessica, 11
Milbank, Dana, xiv
Milkis, Sidney, 11, 66
Miller, Edward H., 109
Miller, Jason, 127
militia group, 22, 178
Modern Republicanism, 15, 61, 62, 63, 64, 65, 66, 94, 139, 180
Monroe, James, 74
Montesquieu, Baron de, 29

Moonves, Les, 170
Moore, C. F., 52
Moores, Mark, 173
Morris, Roger, 82
Morton, Oliver P., 112
Moss, Wandrea "Shaye," 132, 133
Mounk, Yascha, 32
Mount, Robert T., 64
Moynihan, Daniel Patrick, 24, 100, 169
Müller, Jan-Werner, 115, 134
Murrow, Edward R., 59
Musk, Elon, 172
Mussolini, Benito, 39

New Deal, xi, xiv, 11, 34, 36, 37, 38, 40, 41, 43, 44, 45, 50, 52, 55, 58, 62, 64, 67, 78, 79, 81, 82, 83, 84, 94, 140, 154, 180
Nixon, Richard M., x, xi, 16, 41, 54, 56, 63, 65, 66, 68, 71, 73, 82, 84, 89, 91, 97, 105, 145, 149, 151, 155; 1960 election and, 95, 96, 97, 119, 165; 1968 election and, xiv, 23, 67, 103, 119, 136, 165; 1972 election and, 69, 70, 165; resignation of, 19, 20; Watergate and, 14, 99
Norris, Pippa, 124
North Atlantic Treaty Organization (NATO), 54, 142

Oath Keepers, 23, 173
Obama, Barack, x, xvi, 11, 22, 24, 26, 29, 73, 103, 106, 108, 109, 146, 148, 149, 152, 157, 167, 179, 181; 2008 election and, 40, 120,121, 165; 2012 election and, 120; birth certificate of, 105–106
Obamacare, 121, 157, 169
O'Konski, Alvin, 81
O'Neill, Thomas P., "Tip," 71
Ornstein, Norman, 146
Oz, Mehmet, 138, 179

Palin, Sarah, 160
Parker, Christopher S., 120, 121
Pearl Harbor, 49, 80, 81

Pelosi, Nancy, 109, 138, 147, 151, 157, 172
Pelosi, Paul, 172
Peltola, Mary, 160
Peña, Solomon, 172
Pence, Mike, 127, 128, 138, 150, 158, 176
Percy, Charles, 136
Perry, Rick, 129
Perry, Scott, 124, 176, 180
polarization, 29, 40, 156, 157, 159, 163
political parties, 7, 10, 32, 74, 75, 85, 137, 139, 182; disputed elections and, 1–4; embody memory and hope, xi–xii; as essential instruments of democracy, 4–14; 175; need to strengthen, 163–168
political violence, xvi, 6, 17, 23, 125, 128, 130, 131, 135, 156, 170, 172, 173
politics of fear, xii, xiii, xvi, xvii, 6, 20, 21, 22, 42, 82, 83, 84, 88, 100, 105, 109, 112, 122, 140, 145, 147, 169
Pompeo, Mike, 150
Pomper, Gerald M., 5, 6, 7, 183
populism, 8, 10, 98, 107, 115, 122, 124, 169
Populist Party, 107, 115
presidential elections, 1800, 74, 128, 154; 1820, 39; 1860, 120, 121, 180; 1876, 3, 4, 170; 1884, 164; 1888, 113; 1912, 5, 51; 1924, 21, 40; 1928; 33, 34, 36, 39, 51; 1932, 34, 40, 78; 1936, 36, 37, 39, 40, 66, 82; 1940, 37, 40, 41, 46, 56; 1944, 43, 44; 1948, 46, 49, 52, 58, 83, 117; 1952, 44, 50, 51, 54, 56, 58, 60, 66, 86, 91, 139, 164, 165; 1956, 61, 62, 63, 65; 1960, 66, 73, 95, 96, 164, 165; 1964, 44, 92, 93, 117, 136, 1968, 23, 103, 136, 154, 164, 165 1972, 70, 165 1976, 164, 165; 1980, 26, 165; 1988, 165; 1992, 165; 2000, 1, 2, 4, 148, 155, 165, 170; 2004, 1, 4, 32, 148, 165, 170; 2008, 40, 119, 120, 165; 2012, 120; 2016, 23, 24, 41, 73, 100, 121, 125, 141, 152, 166, 168, 170, 171; 2020, xv, xvi, 9, 22, 24, 26, 32, 38, 68, 72, 74, 101, 102, 120, 122, 124, 128, 129, 132, 134, 138, 143, 148, 155, 164, 170, 171, 172, 173, 176, 178, 179, 181; 2024, x, 32, 107, 134, 172,

174, 176, 177, 178; stolen elections and, x, xiii, xvi, 13, 24, 26, 50, 72, 102, 101, 112, 131, 173, 178
Price, Raymond, 67
Priebus, Reince, 24, 120
Proud Boys, 23, 103, 173
Pulliam, Eugene, 86
Putin, Vladimir, 30, 104, 108, 109
Putnam, Robert, 21

QAnon, xvi, 103, 104
Quay, Matthew, 114

Raffensberger, Brad, 132
Ramaswamy, Vivek, 174
ranked choice voting, 159
Raskin, Jamie, 134, 137
Rauch, Jonathan, 164
Reagan, Ronald, xi, xii, 14, 26, 27, 57, 68, 71, 73, 93, 97, 100, 103, 136, 138, 145, 163, 165, 169, 180, 181, 182; 1980 election and, x, 119, 120; 1984 election and, 36, 165; assassination attempt upon, 151; Farewell Address of, 16–19
Reed, Adolph, Jr., 171
Reedy, George, 70
Rehnquist, William, 153
Republican National Committee (RNC), xiii, 34, 44, 60, 61, 64, 67, 80, 81, 120
Republican Party, xiv, xv, 14, 15, 70, 109, 175, 180–182; African Americans and, 35, 110–120, 125–126, antidemocratic thinking of, xv, 13, 17–20, 32, 134, 135–171; conspiracy theories entertained by, 32, 41–45, 77–85, 89–99, 107–108; desperation of, 21, 31, 40, 42, 47–50, 71, 75, 79, 81, 100, 114, 121, 127; divisions within, 51–56, 64, 88, 96–99; Eisenhower and, 60–66, 85–86; fear of future, 100, 105, 106, 121; Great Replacement Theory and, 39, 40, 122–126, 132; as majority party, 33–34; paranoia of, 98, 99, 100, 103, 107, 174;

Pseudo-Conservatives and, 140, 141, 144; Radical Right and, xvii, 17, 92, 99, 121, 122, 125, 136, 139, 140; Tea Party and, 120–121; weakened by FDR, 35–41, 45–50, 52
Reston, James, 65
Rice, Kathleen, 73
Richardson, Heather Cox, 110, 175
Roberts, Cliff, 60
Roberts, John, 152, 159, 160, 167
Robinson, Claude, 48
Robinson, Jackie, 119
Rockefeller, Nelson A., 96, 97, 119, 136
Rockne, Knute, 27
Romney, Ann, ix
Romney, Mitt, ix, x, 23, 30, 71, 120, 165
Ronchetti, Mark, 173
Roosevelt, Elliot, 47
Roosevelt, Franklin D., xi, xv, 11, 19, 32, 54, 55, 58, 59, 63, 64, 68, 69, 72, 73, 84, 91, 94, 105, 145, 148, 149, 151, 154, 169, 180, 181, 182; 1932 election and, 33–37; 1936 election and, 36–40, 66, 82; 1940 election and, 37, 40–43; 1944 election and, 37, 43–46, 47, 58; accusations of conspiracy against, 78–82
Roosevelt, Franklin D., Jr., 27, 47
Roosevelt, James, 47
Roosevelt, Theodore, 33, 51, 148
Rossiter, Clinton, 1, 4, 75, 140
Rove, Karl, 33
Rumbough, Stanley M., 60
Russell, Richard, 118, 155
Ryan, Paul, 141
Ryn, Claes, 102, 126

Santorum, Rick, 1
Santos, George, 182
Sartori, Giovanni, 7, 8, 12
Scalia, Antonin, 106, 152, 158
Schattschneider, E. E., 4, 138, 139
Schiff, Adam, 30, 141
Schlesinger, Arthur M., Jr., 20, 70, 159

Schmidt, Al, 132, 179
Schumer, Chuck, 157
Scott, Rick, 72, 163
Scranton, William, 97
Seid, Barre, 167
Shapiro, Josh, 179
Sharlet, Jeff, 178
Sharpton, Al, 126
Shefter, Martin, 133
Shultz, George, 69
Sicknick, Brian, 173
Sicknick, Gladys, 173
Skocpol, Theda, 121
Smith, Al, 33
Smith, Richard Norton, 66
Snyder, Timothy, xvii, 18
socialism, 53, 54, 57, 78, 95, 112
social media, 25, 103, 107, 108, 109, 125, 141, 147, 168
Sotomayor, Sonia, 152
Spangler, Harold, 48
Spencer, Richard, 122
Spicer, Sean, 24
Stalin, Josef, 79, 81
Stassen, Harold, 66
Stefanik, Elise, 107, 123
Stevens, John Paul, 167
Stevenson, Adlai, 57, 58, 62, 65, 67, 88
Stone, Roger, 30, 106
Sulzberger, Arthur Hays, 86
Suskind, Ron, 25
Symington, Stuart, 60

Taft, Robert, 14, 44, 47, 49, 50, 51, 52, 53, 54, 55, 56, 57, 58, 61, 64, 65, 80, 85, 91, 116, 139, 140, 165, 166, 180
Tarrow, Sidney, 9, 11
Taylor, Zachary, 66
Tea Party, 120–121
Thomas, Clarence, 102, 161
Thomas, Ginni, 102
Thurmond, Strom, 48, 117, 118, 119, 147, 155
Tilden, Samuel J., 3, 112

Tillerson, Rex, 166
Tocqueville, Alexis de, 20, 85
Tower, John, 118
Truman, Harry S., 20, 52, 55, 64, 77, 88, 91, 105, 117, 148, 169; 1944 election and, 46, 58, 80; 1948 election and, 36, 46–49, 52, 58; 1952 election and, 51, 54, 56–58; Joseph McCarthy and, 84, 87, 90
Trump, Donald J., xiv, 13, 14, 15, 22, 23, 78, 87, 88, 105, 115, 121, 137, 142, 144, 148, 160, 163, 166, 168; 2012 campaign and, ix–x; 2016 campaign and, x, 22, 30, 73, 100–101, 106, 125, 141, 170, 171; 2020 campaign and, x, xi, xvi, 22, 26, 32, 101, 108, 120, 124, 127, 129, 132, 145, 155, 169–170; 2024 campaign and, x, 12; as victim, 101, 102, 107, 124; character of, 75, 142, 143; Charlottesville, Virginia and, 121–122; conspiracies promoted by, 102–107, 112, 131, 133; demagoguery of, 25; impeachments of, 23, 68; indictment of, 18, 68, 173, 174; insurrection promoted by, x, xv, xvi, 10, 11, 12, 71–74, 127–128, 170; lies told by, 29, 32, 50, 76, 105, 106, 170; movement led by, 8, 9, 11, 28, 41, 71; presidency of, xvii, 11, 17–18, 22–24, 67–69, 73–74, 101, 148, 150–152, 157–159, 169; racism of, 122, 124, 126; threat to democracy by, 17, 30, 89, 128–129, 134, 138, 141, 170, 171
Trump, Donald, Jr., 10, 127, 172
Trump, Melania, 150
Trumpism, 122, 124, 125, 139, 141, 171, 178
Tsongas, Paul, 180
Tweed, William "Boss," 166

US Constitution, 2, 3, 6, 14, 18, 20, 32, 36, 40, 75, 76, 78, 92, 106, 111, 113, 118, 126, 128, 129, 143, 144, 150, 153, 154, 156, 160, 161, 163, 168, 170, 175, 177

Vallee, Rudy, 27
Van Buren, Martin, 6

Vance, J. D., 124, 138
Vann, Robert L., 35
Vinehout, Kathy, 103
Voltaire, M. de, 7
Voorhis, Jerry, 82, 83
voting rights, suffrage and, xvi, 5, 35, 113, 114, 115, 116, 117, 118; suppression of, xiii, 113
Voting Rights Act of 1965, 40, 118, 123, 130, 132

Walker, Edwin, 92
Walker, Hershel, 138
Wallace, David Foster, 24
Wallace, Henry, 81
Wallace, George C., 118, 119, 154–155
Warnock, Raphael, 179
Warren, Earl, 47, 81, 117
Washington, George, 7, 10, 73, 74, 148, 154, 175, 182
Wayne, John, 56
Wehner, Peter, 137
Weinberg, Sidney, 60
Weinberger, Caspar, 69
Welch, Robert, 81, 90, 92, 96, 97, 103, 108, 109, 117, 171

Weyrich, Paul, xiii
White, E. B., 19, 20
White, Theodore H., 73, 97
Williams, Walter, 60
Williamson, Kevin, 141
Williamson, Marianne, 166
Williamson, Vanessa, 121
Willis, Charles F., 60
Willis, Fanni, 174
Willkie, Wendell, 36, 40, 41, 42, 43, 51, 52, 54, 135
Wilson, James Q., xii
Wilson, Woodrow, xv, 5, 33, 115, 143, 146, 149, 154
Winthrop, John, 16, 30
Wirthlin, Richard B., 17
Wolfe, Alan, 21
World War II, xii, xvii, 4, 19, 23, 26, 30, 41, 43, 52, 60, 73, 80, 86, 90, 92, 169

Yang, Andrew, 166
Young, Don, 160

Zelensky, Volodymyr, 23
Ziblatt, Daniel, 22, 31

www.ingramcontent.com/pod-product-compliance
Lightning Source LLC
Chambersburg PA
CBHW030531230426
43665CB00010B/840